Communicative Constructions and the Refiguration of Spaces

Through a variety of empirical studies, this volume offers fresh insights into the manner in which different forms of communicative action transform urban space. With attention to the methodological questions that arise from the attempt to study such changes empirically, it offers new theoretical foundations for understanding the social construction and reconstruction of spaces through communicative action. Seeing communicative action as the basic element in the social construction of reality and conceptualizing communication not only in terms of the use of language and texts, but as involving any kind of objectification, such as technologies, bodies and nonverbal signs, it considers the roles of both direct and mediatized (or digitized) communication. An examination of the conceptualization of the communicative (re-)construction of spaces and the means by which this change might be empirically investigated, this book demonstrates the fruitfulness of the notion of refiguration as a means by which to understand the transformation of contemporary societies. As such, it will appeal to sociologists, social theorists, and geographers with interests in social construction and urban space.

Gabriela B. Christmann is Associate Professor in the Department of Sociology at the Technische Universität Berlin and Head of the Research Department 'Dynamics of Communication, Knowledge and Spatial Development' at the Leibniz Institute for Research on Society and Space, Germany.

Hubert Knoblauch is Professor of Sociology at the Technische Universität Berlin, Germany. He is the author of *PowerPoint, Communication, and the Knowledge Society*, the co-author of *Videography: Introduction to Interpretive Videoanalysis of Social Situations*, and the co-editor of *Social Constructivism as Paradigm?* and the author of the monograph *The Communicative Construction of Reality*.

Martina Löw is Professor of Sociology at the Technische Universität Berlin, Germany. She is the author of *The Sociology of Space* and co-editor of *Spatial Sociology: Relational Space after the Turn*.

The Refiguration of Space

Based on the premise that what is social always takes on a spatial form, this series explores the changes wrought in the relations of human-beings to spaces and their spatial practices by current social transformations, conflicts, crises and uncertainties. Welcoming studies from disciplines across the social sciences, such as sociology, geography and urban studies, books in the series consider the ways in which people (re-)negotiate and (re-)construct spatial orders according to a common pattern of 'refiguration', a process that often involves conflict and is frequently shaped by phenomena such as mediatization, translocalisation and polycontexturalisation.

Series Editors

Hubert Knoblauch is *Professor of Sociology at Technische Universität Berlin, Germany.*

Martina Löw is *Professor of the Sociology of Planning and Architecture at the Technische Universität Berlin, Germany.*

Titles in the series

Spatial Transformations
Kaleidoscopic Perspectives on the Refiguration of Spaces
Edited by Angela Million, Christian Haid, Ignacio Castillo Ulloa, Nina Baur

Communicative Constructions and the Refiguration of Spaces
Theoretical Approaches and Empirical Studies
Edited by Gabriela B. Christmann, Hubert Knoblauch and Martina Löw

For more information about this series, please visit:
https://www.routledge.com/The-Refiguration-of-Space/book-series/ROS

Communicative Constructions and the Refiguration of Spaces

Theoretical Approaches and Empirical Studies

Edited by
Gabriela B. Christmann,
Hubert Knoblauch and Martina Löw

First published 2022
by Routledge
2 Park Square, Milton Park, Abingdon, Oxon OX14 4RN

and by Routledge
605 Third Avenue, New York, NY 10158

Routledge is an imprint of the Taylor & Francis Group, an informa business

© 2022 selection and editorial matter, Gabriela Christmann, Hubert Knoblauch and Martina Löw; individual chapters, the contributors

The right of Gabriela Christmann, Hubert Knoblauch and Martina Löw to be identified as the authors of the editorial material, and of the authors for their individual chapters, has been asserted in accordance with sections 77 and 78 of the Copyright, Designs and Patents Act 1988.

The Open Access version of this book, available at www.taylorfrancis.com, has been made available under a Creative Commons Attribution-Non Commercial-No Derivatives 4.0 license.

Trademark notice: Product or corporate names may be trademarks or registered trademarks, and are used only for identification and explanation without intent to infringe.

British Library Cataloguing-in-Publication Data
A catalogue record for this book is available from the British Library

Library of Congress Cataloging-in-Publication Data
Names: Christmann, Gabriela B., editor. | Knoblauch, Hubert, editor. | Löw, Martina, editor.
Title: Communicative constructions and the refiguration of spaces : theoretical approaches and empirical studies / Gabriela Christmann, Hubert Knoblauch and Martina Löw.
Description: Abingdon, Oxon; New York, NY: Routledge, 2022. | Series: The refiguration of space |
Includes bibliographical references and index.
Identifiers: LCCN 2021034022 (print) | LCCN 2021034023 (ebook) | ISBN 9780367419974 (hardback) | ISBN 9781032163345 (paperback) | ISBN 9780367817183 (ebook)
Subjects: LCSH: Public spaces. | Communication in human geography. | Spatial behavior. | Space perception. | Urbanization–Social aspects. | Communication–Social aspects.
Classification: LCC HT185 .C655 2022 (print) | LCC HT185 (ebook) | DDC 307.76–dc23
LC record available at https://lccn.loc.gov/2021034022
LC ebook record available at https://lccn.loc.gov/2021034023

ISBN: 978-0-367-41997-4 (hbk)
ISBN: 978-1-03-216334-5 (pbk)
ISBN: 978-0-367-81718-3 (ebk)

DOI: 10.4324/9780367817183

Typeset in Bembo
by Newgen Publishing UK

Contents

List of contributors vii

PART I
Introduction 1

1 Introduction: Communicative constructions and the refiguration of spaces 3
GABRIELA B. CHRISTMANN, HUBERT KNOBLAUCH, AND MARTINA LÖW

PART II
Theoretical and methodological approaches 17

2 From the constitution to the communicative construction of space 19
HUBERT KNOBLAUCH AND SILKE STEETS

3 The symbolic construction of spaces: Perspectives from a sociology of knowledge approach to discourse 36
REINER KELLER

4 Digital media, data infrastructures, and space: The refiguration of society in times of deep mediatization 57
ANDREAS HEPP

5 Cities, regions, and landscapes as augmented realities: Refiguration of space(s) through digital information technologies 76
GERTRAUD KOCH

6 The theoretical concept of the communicative (re)construction of spaces 89
GABRIELA B. CHRISTMANN

7 Eliciting space: Methodological considerations in analyzing communicatively constructed spaces 113
MARTINA LÖW AND SÉVERINE MARGUIN

PART III
Empirical studies 137

8 Digital urban planning and urban planners' mediatized construction of spaces 139
GABRIELA B. CHRISTMANN AND MARTIN SCHINAGL

9 Centers of coordination refigured? Control of synthetic space 154
RENÉ TUMA AND ARNE JANZ

10 Architectures of asylum: Negotiating home-making through concrete spatial strategies 174
PHILIPP MISSELWITZ AND ANNA STEIGEMANN

11 Over the counter: Configuration and refiguration of ticket-sales conversation through institutional architectures for interaction 194
HEIKO HAUSENDORF

12 Innovation and communication: Spatial pioneers and the negotiation of new ideas 225
ANIKA NOACK AND TOBIAS SCHMIDT

13 Talking about hip places: Imaginaries and power among East German reinventions of urban culture 246
HANS-JOACHIM BÜRKNER

14 A systemic model of communication in spatial planning 273
URSULA STEIN

Index 286

Contributors

Hans-Joachim Bürkner, emeritus Professor Dr, is a geographer. He was a researcher at the Leibniz Institute for Research on Society and Space, Erkner (near Berlin), Germany, and at the same time a professor of geography at the University of Potsdam, Germany.

Gabriela B. Christmann, Professor Dr, is a sociologist. She is head of the research department Dynamics of Communication, Knowledge and Spatial Development at the Leibniz Institute for Research on Society and Space, Erkner (near Berlin), Germany. She is also adjunct professor at the Technische Universität Berlin.

Heiko Hausendorf, Professor Dr, is a linguist with a special interest in spoken and written discourse (conversation analysis, text linguistics). He holds a chair in Linguistics of German at the German Department of the University of Zurich and is co-chair of the Zurich University Research Priority Program "Language and Space".

Andreas Hepp, Professor Dr, holds a chair in Media and Communications and is head of the Centre for Media, Communication and Information Research at the University of Bremen, Germany. He has been visiting researcher and professor at leading institutions such as the London School of Economics and Political Science, Université Paris II Panthéon, Stanford University, and others.

Arne Janz, MA, is a sociologist. He is a doctoral researcher in the context of the Collaborative Research Centre "Refiguration of Spaces" at the Technische Universität Berlin, Germany.

Reiner Keller, Professor Dr, holds a chair in Sociology at the University of Augsburg, Germany.

Hubert Knoblauch, Professor Dr, is a sociologist and holds a chair in General Sociology at the Technische Universität Berlin, Germany. He is co-chair of the Collaborative Research Centre "Refiguration of Spaces" at the Technische Universität Berlin.

Gertraud Koch, Professor Dr, is a social and cultural anthropologist at the University of Hamburg, Germany. Her research areas are diversity in urban spaces, working cultures, digital cultures, and qualitative and digital methods.

Martina Löw, Professor Dr, is a sociologist. She holds a chair in Sociology of Architecture and Planning and is also head of the Collaborative Research Centre "Refiguration of Spaces" at the Technische Universität Berlin, Germany.

Séverine Marguin, Dr, is a sociologist. She is head of the Methods-Lab within the Collaborative Research Centre "Refiguration of Spaces" at the Technische Universität Berlin, Germany. Her research interests are architectures of knowledge as well as experimental, visual, and mapping methods.

Philipp Misselwitz, Professor Dr, is an architect and urban planner. He directs the Habitat Unit in the Department of Urban Planning at the Institute of Architecture, Technische Universität Berlin, Germany. He is also visiting professor at the University of Witwatersrand, Johannesburg, South Africa.

Anika Noack, Dr, is a sociologist. She is Head of the Unit "Transformation" in the Federal Institute for Building, Urban and Spatial Research, Cottbus, Germany. Before she was a research fellow at the Brandenburg University of Technology Cottbus-Senftenberg and the Leibniz Institute for Research on Society and Space, Germany.

Martin Schinagl, MA, is a sociologist and urban anthropologist. He is a researcher at the Leibniz Institute for Research on Society and Space, Erkner, Germany, and a fellow of the Collaborative Research Centre "Refiguration of Spaces" at the Technische Universität Berlin. Recently, he completed a dissertation project on the digitalization of urban planning practices.

Tobias Schmidt, Dr, is a sociologist. He is a postdoctoral researcher at the Centre for Research on Digitalization and Care at the University of Applied Sciences, Kempten, Germany. Previously he was a research fellow at the Leibniz Institute for Research on Society and Space, Erkner, Germany.

Silke Steets, Professor Dr, is a professor of sociology at the Friedrich Alexander University Erlangen-Nuremberg, Germany. Her research interests include social theory and qualitative research methods. She has worked empirically on topics related to space, popular culture, religion, contemporary art, materiality, and the city.

Anna Steigemann, Professor Dr, is an urban researcher and sociologist. She is a senior researcher at the Habitat Unit in the Department of Urban Planning at the Institute of Architecture, Technische Universität Berlin, Germany, and the Chair for International Urbanism and Design, at the Technische

Universität Berlin. She is also professor of Sociological Dimensions of Space at the Universität Regensburg, Germany.

Ursula Stein, Professor Dr Ing, is trained in urban and regional planning and in systemic organizational development. She runs her studio Stein Stadt- und Regionalplanung in Frankfurt am Main, Germany, and teaches Communication in Planning at the University of Kassel as a honorary professor.

René Tuma, Dr, is a sociologist and postdoctoral researcher at the Technische Universität Berlin, Germany. His fields of work are sociology of knowledge, sociology of technology, sociology of violence, and videographic studies of interaction.

I
Introduction

1 Introduction

Communicative constructions and the refiguration of spaces

Gabriela B. Christmann, Hubert Knoblauch, and Martina Löw

Introduction

It has long been a guiding assumption that spaces become social reality only against the background of human attributions of meaning and that they must be understood as *social* constructions. What is comparably new is the idea of systematically considering the *communicative* construction of spaces. This is astonishing given that in both the past and the present, spaces have always been conceived, planned, and shaped on the basis of communicative processes. Already in premodern societies, communicative action among their members was essential for developing socially shared conceptions of, and practical routines for, the spatial environment – and thus for the social construction of a spatial reality. Particularly in modern, functionally differentiated, and highly complex societies, however, we can observe that ideas of space, either about the value of historical building complexes or about specific urban designs for the future, typically are intensively negotiated, often even among the broad public. The practical importance of communication is proven not least by the fact that in the context of urban policy and urban planning, terms such as governance with stakeholders, communicative planning, network building, and citizen participation – all of which refer to communicative processes – have become a matter of course.

However, although it has been recognized that communicative action plays an important role in the construction of spaces (see, e.g., Paasi 1989; Hastings 1999; Lees 2004), this idea has *barely received theoretical treatment*. This applies even for spatial theories following the linguistic and, particularly, the cultural turn that served as a catalyst for the spatial sciences in the course of the 1990s. The latter, rather, had the effect of stimulating intensive – and sometimes polemic – debate on the question of what had happened to physical space and how the relation of the physical and the cultural or social were to be considered. It was Latour (2005) who, by contributing to actor-network theory, developed a countermovement to the massive neglect of physical and material aspects of sociality. Besides this, insufficient attention has been paid to the fact that spaces are in a process of constant transformation and that, therefore,

DOI: 10.4324/9780367817183-2

the social or communicative construction of spaces already created should, strictly speaking, be conceptualized as a permanent process of *re*construction. The reconstruction of space means that by way of communicative actions between social actors, some dimensions of existing spatial constructions may be modified or even newly developed, while others may be consolidated. It is, however, in these small steps of communicative *re*construction that digital mediatization along with accelerated globalization and its countertendencies particularly contribute to the refiguration of spaces, in which spatialities (and the ways in which human actors perceive, experience, and create them) considerably alter their character.

Against this background, until now, there has also been *little empirical research* on the communicative construction of spaces. This holds true for sociology, social geography, and the planning sciences. There is a lack of systematic insight into the mechanisms of how space is communicatively constructed. Only a little is known about space-related communicative processes among groups of actors, networks, and institutions and in the context of public discourse. In particular, we know little about the consequences of comprehensive mediatization and digitalization processes on the construction of spaces. Although Castells (1996, 1997, 1998), in his trilogy on the information age, had in the 1990s already pointed to the significance of information technologies and communication, he only looked at the structural changes to the global economy, and he mainly described transformations in work and employment.

What we can observe is that for a long time, individuals in all societal fields have been increasingly exposed to media and technology in both analogue and digital form (Hepp, Hjarvard, and Lundby 2015; Hepp 2020). It can consequently be assumed that the increased usage and experience of these novel tools may have catalyzed changes in human action, particularly the way in which individuals, communities, professions, and organizations communicate and work. Such changes may have also influenced the organization of our social world, our living environment, and even spatial arrangements. This is why Knoblauch and Löw (2017, 3) argue that mediatization and digitalization processes have led to a "refiguration of spaces". There is increasing evidence that mediatized and especially digitalized communication may result in different experiences, forms of knowledge, ways of acting, social processes, and possibly also different constructions of spaces. The fact that social actors can be (virtually) present in several places simultaneously and that, depending on the media they use, they are able to act in various forms of translocality, illustrates this argument. Spatial constructs may be arranged in entirely new ways. In this context, Knoblauch and Löw (2020, 282 f.) see indications that since the 1960s – processually – a big refiguration of spaces has taken place. They state that the territorially based, centralized, and hierarchically structured figuration of spaces typical of modernism have not yet disappeared entirely, but that it has in the meantime been confronted and reshaped considerably by other ordering principles, such as deterritorialized, decentralized, and level structures.

There is, thus, a need both for theoretical concepts and empirical analyses of communicative construction and the refiguration of spaces. The present volume takes this as its starting point. It intends, on the one hand, to provide a foundation for the theoretical framing of communicative action in the construction and refiguration of spaces, doing so most of all on the basis of communicative constructivism,[1] a development from social constructivism (see Part II); on the other hand, the volume aims to provide insights into communication-oriented empirical research on spaces (see Part III).

This introductory chapter will first provide an overview of the theoretical milestones of social-science-based spatial research. In the next section, it will be shown in what ways, to date, the social construction of spaces has been theoretically understood. It will become clear that aspects of communicative action, when they feature at all, play a minor and at best only marginal role. In the last section, the chapter will introduce the concept of the volume as a whole as well as the individual contributions.

From the objectively given to (communicatively) constructed space: Milestones of spatial theory

The history of spatial theory shows that although spaces were initially conceived of as invariant, objectively given entities (such as by Aristotle 1995 [4th century BCE]), from early on there have been attempts to grasp them as relational or social constructs: Important examples from spatial philosophy are Theophrastus (in antiquity), John Scotus Eriugena (in the Middle Ages), and Einstein (in modern times). Aristotle's disciple *Theophrastus* (2000 [4th century BCE]) already assumed that spaces as such have no reality and that they are, instead, created by the specific relations obtained by bodies to each other. This is an idea that would later be called the relational concept of space. In the Middle Ages, *Eriugena* (1984 [9th century CE]) contributed the idea that space only exists dependent on the viewer's perspective and must therefore be considered "relative". Eriugena thus anticipated a mode of thought that would later be developed in the sociology of knowledge, whose starting point is the assumption that objects are structured by human experiences that may differ according to viewers' perspectives. *Einstein* (1960) added another important element to spatial theory, emphasizing a person's physicality and their capability to act and to actively design spaces. In his thinking, the shaping power of human *action* becomes the focus of attention. In the early sociology of space (Simmel, Park), we can also identify conceptions that assume the spatial is shaped by the social. In his reflections on the border, which can be considered a specific spatial manifestation, *Simmel* (1903) came to the conclusion that the boundary "is *not a spatial fact* with *sociological consequences,* but a *sociological fact* that forms itself *spatially*" (Simmel 1903, 36). Boundaries must therefore be understood as a result of social processes. However, Simmel did not go into detail about how such social processes can be conceptualized. In a quite different field, that of urban research, it was *Park* who, as the most prominent representative of the Chicago School, pointed to the fact that citizens' ways of perceiving a city is a crucial factor in that city's constitution. Instead of merely comprising a collection of physical objects, infrastructures, and individuals, the city can be understood as existing in and through the city-related knowledge of its subjects. For this reason, it is most of all a cultural phenomenon: "The city is, rather, a state of mind, a body of customs and traditions" (Park 1968, 1). Interestingly, Park considered the local press and its narratives an important element in the creation of a city and its specific local culture. It is in these narratives that a city is constituted and established in its specific way (Park 1972, 101 f.). What Park was suggesting here is, in a sense, a communicative construction of the city by media narratives.

Today, it is the work of contemporary thinkers such as Henri Lefebvre, Pierre Bourdieu, Anthony Giddens, Martina Löw, Doreen Massey, and Nigel Thrift that can be considered milestones on the path toward explaining social constructions of space. These authors count among the most prominent and most-cited thinkers when it comes to conceptualizing the social construction of spaces.[2] When elaborating on the idea that it is social *subjects* who — ideally and physically — make spaces a reality, these theoreticians mainly place the concepts of knowledge and/or acting at the focus of the construction of space. But in their work, too, it is only rarely that the concept of communicative action, or of communication, shines through.

Lefebvre's (1991/1974) Marxist approach to the production of space is guided by the assumption that each society, according to its specific characteristics, produces its respectively specific space. Space is described as a social product produced at the micro-social level in the course of everyday perceptions and appropriations. Three dimensions are significant for the production of space: The first is the way in which space is perceived — in a comparably non-reflective way — in the everyday practices of members of society and how it is thereby (re) produced (*espace perçu*). The second is the way in which space is conceptualized in specific societal fields in a much more reflective way (*espace conçu*); according to Lefebvre, it is typically experts from academia, urban planning, administration, and the visual arts who create the conceptualized space at the level of language, discourse, maps, plans, and images. Here, he points out in passing the role of communication in the production of space. Last but not least is the way in which citizens, by way of complex symbolizations, give expression to space as lived (*espace vécu*) while imagining and envisioning it and while undermining and reshaping existing spatial structures. On the whole, however, the emphasis of Lefebvre's concept is placed rather more on the space-producing power of knowledge than on that of action.

For *Bourdieu*, who is influenced by Marxist thought as well as by the structuralist Lévi-Strauss, it is the concept of action — or, more precisely, of habitus-led action — that is at the fore. Indeed, Bourdieu is not a theoretician of space in the strict sense, but rather conceptualizes social spaces as spaces of social relationships in order to discuss the effects that social spaces have on physical ones. Similar to Lefebvre, who assumes that the specific constitution of a society finds expression through its own production of space, for Bourdieu (1991) it is a fact that by way of habitus, the social structure is impressed into the physical – and by this means into the spatial. Schroer (2006, 88) expresses this as follows: "Similar to the way in which social structures are inscribed into the body, they are also inscribed into the physical space. Thus, in Bourdieu body and space are, in a way, the visible part of the social world".

Giddens (1984), too, understands space to be the result of human action. The core of his approach is structuration theory. Employing a more dynamic concept of structure, this says that action and structure are mutually related to one other. Structures are produced by way of human action, but to be lasting, they must always also be reproduced by action. Giddens admits that structures themselves provide orienting framework conditions for acting without, however, having any determining effect as such. Against this background, he understands spaces to be settings within which social practices occur, the practices themselves constituting the spatial setting and reproducing it in a repetitive way. Accordingly, spaces are not geographic but social places, providing a horizon of meaning for interactions between actors.

The sociologist *Löw* looks back to Giddens, taking inspiration most of all from his theory of structuration. In her concept of relational space, she attempts to answer the question of the extent to which spaces can be explained both as achievements of human synthesizing operations (*Syntheseleistungen*) *and* as materialities (Löw 2016, 139). According to her theoretical approach, in the process of creating space, two closely interwoven components need be distinguished from one another. The first component, spacing, describes the creation of space as the placing or positioning of living beings and social goods. Spacing can be considered an activity of arrangement or of building sociomaterial fabrics. Since space is created by active placing, it loses its alleged naturalness. The second component focuses on achievements of human synthesizing operations – in the sense of processes of perception, imagination, and remembering – by which socio-material structures are created cognitively (Löw 2016, 159). However, once spaces have been created or arranged as ordering structures, they can influence human action.

Like Löw, *Massey* (2003) also endorses a dynamic and relational concept of space. Speaking, first of all, of places more than of spaces, she emphasizes the processuality, the infiniteness, and the variety of spaces she considers to be created by way of constant, fluid interactions between subjects and objects. Places exist at first in the form of imaginaries and are, as senses of places, part of our memories. Specific spatial imaginaries have their own characteristics and are based on specific local traditions, cultures, and ways of using language. However, in the course of globalization processes, faced with worldwide flows of communication and migration, local imaginaries are subject to change. This is due to the fact that spaces of interaction, as well as the action spaces of subjects, are now clearly extended beyond the bounds of concrete places. Action spaces can thereby vary considerably from one social group to the next. Notably, communication also makes an incidental entrance into Massey's work. Communicative action and different communicative forms, including mediatized (or digitalized) forms of communication, are the means by which experiences of other places are communicated; in this way it has become possible for the subject to extend their experiences of their own place, as well as of many other places in the world.

Whereas Massey considers the space-constituting potential of communication, the geographer *Thrift* (2007), in his study on nonrepresentational theory, counteracts such ideas. He breaks with assumptions that – as a consequence of the cultural turn or, more precisely, the linguistic turn – presume the structuring power of symbolic representation, be it in the form of discourses, texts, or language. Following Latour's (2005) actor-network theory, Thrift instead considers embodied subjects and their practices. He understands space-constituting actors to be embedded into networks in which embodied knowledge and power relations have effect. Like Massey, Thrift also emphasizes the processual nature and fluidity of spaces. Warf (2004, 298) correctly describes Thrift's theoretical approach as follows: "Thrift has worked assiduously to portray geographies as embodied, embedded, contingent, and ever changing, harnessing the fluidity of spatial relations to demonstrate how they are imbricated in changing human relations of power". It is useful that Thrift grants actors, body practices, materialities, and power relations high significance for the construction of spaces. However, this does not per se reduce the significance of systems of symbolic representation, which is why, in his criticism of Thrift, Lorimer (2005, 83) argues that spatial research may not be about the "non-representational" but about the "more-than-representational". Consideration of systems of symbolic representation is therefore not put into question, but rather supplemented. The focus is on developing approaches through which forms of communicative action – embodied acting, materiality, discourse, and knowledge – can be related to each other.

Modern work on spatial theory has thus developed quite different approaches to explain the social construction of space. Nevertheless, it has also revealed common ground, with some authors emphasizing the significance of action and practices (e.g. Bourdieu, Giddens, Thrift) and others, that of knowledge (e.g. Lefebvre), while yet others conceptualize both as forming an inseparable interrelationship (e.g. Löw, Massey). Theoretical approaches variously conceptualize spatial structures that are fixed (e.g. Bourdieu) or dynamic (e.g. Löw or Massey). That communicative action, discourses, and language may be significant for the process of the social construction of space has become obvious only as a result of some approaches (Park, Lefebvre, Massey), even if these aspects have not usually been developed further there.

It should be mentioned, in addition, that some other approaches deal with the issue, taking inspiration either from Luhmann's (1987) theory of autopoietic systems (see Pott 2007; Kuhm 2000) or from Foucault's (1972, 1994) poststructuralist discourse analysis (see Mattissek 2007; Glasze and Mattissek 2009). As is known, however, these approaches struggle to cope with the dimensions of the subject and of human action. Communications are only considered in a highly abstract manner as processes within systems or structures that create knowledge. Systems theory, in particular, faces a double problem – not only because it has lost the subject's action, but also because in its further development by Luhmann, it has lost space. Luhmann's systems approach is thus a spaceless theory, laying emphasis on a world society in which places do not really matter anymore.

What is promising, therefore, is the theoretical development, beginning with social constructivism, that has been occurring in sociology. The approach taken by communicative constructivism (Knoblauch 2018) has begun to further develop Berger and Luckmann's (1966) social construction of reality by systematically elaborating on the important role of communicative action. This approach takes the physicality of actors and the materiality of their actions into consideration. Furthermore, discourses are not mere distillations of knowledge orders from an ensemble of verbal expressions and texts, but are conceptualized as belonging to the context of constellations of actors and *dispositifs*. Here, *dispositifs* are those institutional regulations and material objects by way of which discourses become socially effective and can be translated into material orders and even spatial arrangements.

The concept of this volume

This volume is divided into three parts. It comprises an introduction (Part I), a section concerning theoretical approaches (Part II), and a section presenting empirical studies (Part III). The first part of the volume (by Christmann, Knoblauch, and Löw) highlights the milestones and gaps in spatial theory. In Part II (through contributions by Knoblauch and Steets; Keller; Hepp; Koch; Christmann; and Löw and Marguin), against the background of theories coming from sociology and the communication sciences, this volume aims to provide new theoretical foundations to the dimension of space-related communicative action as a crucial part in the social construction and *re*construction of spaces, as the core of spatial transformations, and thus as the nucleus of the refiguration of spaces.[3] In addition, some of these contributions (Keller; Christmann; Löw and Marguin) consider methodological questions implied in their respective theoretical concepts. In Part III, the volume takes on a more empirical nature. Here, by way of specific examples from the urban context and by addressing a broad range of empirical subjects, authors coming from sociology, anthropology, linguistics, geography, and urban planning show how subjects shape and reshape spaces and open up new spaces by way of communicative action – be it through predominantly mediatized or digitalized communicative forms (Christmann and Schinagl; Tuma and Janz) or mainly through direct, face-to-face interaction (Misselwitz and Steigemann; Hausendorf; Noack and Schmidt; Bürkner). In the context of spatial planning practice, the ways that planners and stakeholders organize a communicative construction of spaces on the basis of strategically initiated communication processes are examined (Stein). The volume thus aims to provide copious empirical insight into different forms of communicative action and processes of (re)constructing urban spaces, and to present some basic transformations occurring in contemporary society that are accounted for by the notion of refiguration. The following summary of each contribution elucidates the overarching dramaturgy of the volume.

In the first of the theoretical chapters, Knoblauch and Steets provide a general theoretical foundation to a new approach termed "communicative constructivism". The authors reflect on how spaces are created through communicative processes that go beyond language and include objectivations of all kinds, such as artefacts, objects, technologies, symbols, and bodies, as well as their relations to each other. At the same time, they emphasize that we must not disregard the importance of subjective meaning in such processes; that is, that bodily-physical performances of acting subjects are always meaningful and directed toward another subject.

Keller argues that the potential of discourse-analytical approaches for investigating spacing processes and phenomena is far from exhausted. He draws attention to the fact that spaces, locations, and cities are often an expression of relations and politics of knowledge. Both natural and built spaces, for example, are shaped in multiple ways by the various knowledge of experts and citizens. Such politics of knowledge include *dispositifs* that allow one to establish legitimate statements as well as regimes of justification. By making the concept of the *dispositif* essential, Keller also brings into view the institutional and material apparatus through which discourses not only create knowledge orders but even structure material worlds. He emphasizes that discourse analysis is not purely an analysis of language and texts, but also of material worlds.

Hepp explores what happens to social worlds in the era of datafication. He starts from the assumption that humans are today living in an era not simply of mediatization and digitalization, but of *deep* mediatization in which almost all elements of our social world are intricately related to digital media. Hepp develops a figurational approach to media and communication to explain how we can imagine a refiguration of society (including spaces) as part of deep mediatization, and he provides an understanding of how profound today's media-related changes are for the individual as well for our institutions, organizations, and communities.

Koch investigates how actors, by way of information and communications technologies, are able to open up new spaces and how spatial augmented realities are created. She gives a concise overview of the state of research on augmented realities and discusses the implications for the theoretical conceptualization of spaces. Koch argues that augmented realities, which need be understood as a welding together of factual and virtual environments, provide the means for the refiguration of spatiotemporal possibilities of experiencing and acting. It must therefore be asked how these information and communications technologies will influence the future appropriation and use of the urban – for instance, whether parking meters will begin to disappear from the cityscape to be replaced by digital reading devices – but also to what extent there will be a reorganization of the public and the private.

With the concept of the communicative (re)construction of spaces, Christmann suggests an approach which brings together social constructivism, communicative constructivism, and a relational theory of space. First, Christmann explains how, by way of communicative action by subjects in a social context, commonly shared spatial knowledge and shared action routines develop. However, the guiding assumption is that constructions of space are not static, but may be changed by way of communicative negotiation processes. Therefore, second, the communicative reconstruction of space is theoretically conceptualized. In this context, the significance of discourses and *dispositifs* is highlighted.

Löw and Marguin discuss the methodological consequences deducible from theoretical considerations about the communicative construction and analysis of the refiguration of spaces. One of the conclusions is that the construction of spaces, as it occurs among actors, cannot be reconstructed by means only of interviews, but also requires observation of concrete instances of communicative action; that is, of speech acts, bodily acts, and the different practices of spacing. Methodologies that can visually record and analyze situations and processes of communicative action are therefore needed. Furthermore, complex forms of mapping are also required as instruments both to reconstruct physical arrangements and to integrate heterogeneous data.

The empirical section of the volume begins with an example of digital urban planning. Christmann and Schinagl report on a research project that investigates transformations in the communicative action of planners resulting from mediatization processes, particularly from the increasing use of digital tools such as geographical information systems and computer-aided design. The authors ask how the process of digitalization in urban planning can be described and systematized, how this digitalization affects planning practices, and, on this basis, the extent to which the refiguration of spaces can be described.

Tuma and Janz address the changing role of centers of coordination and their current role in the control of spaces. Centers of coordination are equipped with technical information and communication systems and infrastructures to monitor, record, and regulate specific processes within a controlled area. Since these centers are an emblem of the mediatization of spaces, the aim is not only to observe and explain particular changes to the centers themselves, but also to interpret this information as an indication of the refiguration of the spaces controlled. The term "polycontexturalization" highlights the integration of multiple dimensions and functions into newly designed operations centers that rely on algorithmic control (such as integrated traffic control, environmental control, and law enforcement in smart cities).

Misselwitz and Steigemann focus on the agency of refugees in the process of creating appropriate shelters and emergency accommodation, taking the example of Tempohomes in Berlin. Refugees are considered as (urban) actors who – by physically adapting their built environment according to their needs – reconstruct the outcomes of paternalistic planning and techno-managerial approaches and co-produce the spatial reality of refugee accommodations.

Hausendorf focuses on architectural appearances as forms of communication that provide a rich and powerful set of usability cues for participants. He begins from the assumption that within institutionalized communication, the social construction of space cannot be grasped without taking into account the architectural affordances of buildings, settings, furnishings, and technologies. This point is supported by empirical evidence from an ongoing study on communication at railway station counters, and the way that the counter's "architecture for interaction" has recently undergone significant refiguration is shown. The chapter also aims to theoretically develop the social construction of space within an ethnomethodological framework, emphasizing the concept of situational anchoring – under the condition of the co-presence of actors – where space becomes interactively achieved not only by anchoring the interaction in resources such as language, but also in bodies and architectural factors.

Noack and Schmidt analyze how actors in the socially disadvantaged district of Moabit in Berlin, Germany, see their own urban neighborhoods and how, through various forms of direct forms of communication, they try to shape them in new ways. The authors are particularly interested in urban pioneers committed to initiating new solutions for social problems in their neighborhoods. They show the degree to which the actors must adapt to the given historical, political, economic, and social framework and how they are, at the same time, capable of negotiating, modifying, and reinventing this framework. In terms of theory and concepts, the authors draw on Knoblauch's concept of communicative action and Christmann's approach of the communicative (re)construction of spaces to combine these considerations with concepts from innovation theory.

Using the example of the Schiffbauergasse, a creative quarter in the city of Potsdam, Germany, Bürkner aims to investigate contradictions between the top-down and the spontaneously grassroots constructions of urban places. He presents the ideas developed by the actors involved, especially ideas about the qualities and the appropriate usage of the location. Furthermore, he discusses the ways in which these actors have launched their ideas in public discourse. The conceptual starting point for his analysis is the imaginaries approach, the conceptual goal of which is to define in more detail the conditions; that is, the social contexts, fields of action, resources, and communicative strategies by which different (sometimes disputed) imaginaries are brought together to form communicative projects.

In the context of spatial planning, Stein reflects on how planners and stakeholders jointly shape spaces. In her chapter, she first suggests a systematic model of communication based on radical constructivism, adapted for the purpose of planning practices. The model is based on the assumption that by means of encounter, communication, and common experiences, different perceptions of reality by different groups of actors may be brought together. Stein then presents four examples from planning practice (three from Germany and one from Luxembourg) in the context of which planners created local encounters and organized communication processes between the various local stakeholders: Part of the planners' communicative strategy was to organize walks and hikes in order to raise stakeholders' awareness of the specific materiality of places. The volume as a whole thus leads from theory, via empirical research, to implications for practice.

Notes

1 The most systematic considerations of communicative constructivism are found in Knoblauch (2020), Knoblauch and Steets (2022), Keller, Knoblauch, and Reichertz (2013), Keller (2022), and Christmann (2010, 2016, 2022).
2 These thinkers are regularly discussed in the secondary literature of a variety of space-related disciplines. On this see, above all, Hubbard, Kitchin, and Valentine (2004).
3 The chapter presents findings of the Collaborative Research Center 1265, Re-Figuration of Spaces, at the Technische Universität Berlin, Germany. It is funded by the German Research Foundation under project no. 290045248.

References

Aristotle. 1995. *Physik. Vorlesung über die Natur. Philosophische Schriften in sechs Bänden. Bd. 6* [Physics. Lecture on nature. Philosophical writings in six volumes. Vol. 6]. Hamburg: Felix Meiner Verlag.
Berger, Peter L., and Thomas Luckmann. 1966. *The Social Construction of Reality: A Treatise in the Sociology of Knowledge*. Garden City, NY: Anchor.
Bourdieu, Pierre. 1991. "Physischer, sozialer und angeeigneter physischer Raum" [Physical, social, and appropriated physical space]. In *Stadt-Räume* [Urban spaces], edited by Martin Wentz, 25–34. Frankfurt am Main and New York: Campus.
Castells, Manuel. 1996. *The Information Age: Economy, Society and Culture. Volume I: The Rise of the Network Society*. Oxford: Blackwell.
Castells, Manuel. 1997. *The Information Age: Economy, Society and Culture. Volume II: The Power of Identity*. Oxford: Blackwell.
Castells, Manuel. 1998. *The Information Age: Economy, Society and Culture. Volume III: End of Millennium*. Oxford: Blackwell.
Christmann, Gabriela B. 2010. "Kommunikative Raumkonstruktionen als (Proto-)Governance" [Communicative constructions of space as (proto-)governance]. In *Governance und Raum* [Governance and space], edited by Heiderose Kilper, 27–48. Baden-Baden: Nomos.
Christmann, Gabriela B., ed. 2016. *Zur kommunikativen Konstruktion von Räumen: Theoretische Konzepte und empirische Analysen* [On the communicative construction of spaces: Theoretical concepts and empirical analyses]. Wiesbaden: Springer VS.
Christmann, Gabriela B. 2022. "The Theoretical Concept of the Communicative (Re)Construction of Spaces". In *Communicative Constructions and the Refiguration of Spaces*, edited by Gabriela Christmann, Hubert Knoblauch, and Martina Löw, 89–112. Abingdon: Routledge.
Einstein, Albert. 1960. "Vorwort" [Foreword]. In *Das Problem des Raumes: Die Entwicklung der Raumtheorien* [The problem of space: The development of spatial theories], edited by Max Jammer, xii–xvii. Darmstadt: Wissenschaftliche Buchgesellschaft.
Eriugena, Johannes Scotus. 1984. *Über die Einteilung der Natur* [On the classifiaction of nature]. Hamburg: Felix Meiner Verlag.
Foucault, Michel. 1972. *The Archaeology of Knowledge*. New York: Pantheon Books.

Foucault, Michel. 1994. *The Order of Things*. New York: Vintage Books.
Giddens, Anthony. 1984. *The Constitution of Society: Outline of the Theory of Structuration*. Cambridge: Polity Press.
Glasze, Georg, and Annika Mattissek, eds. 2009. *Handbuch Diskurs und Raum* [Handbook on discourse and space]. Bielefeld: transcript.
Hastings, Annette. 1999. "Discourse and Urban Change: Introduction to the Special Issue". *Urban Studies* 36 (1): 7–12.
Hepp, Andreas. 2020. *Deep Mediatization*. London and New York: Routledge.
Hepp, Andreas, Stig Hjarvard, and Knut Lundby. 2015. "Mediatization: Theorizing the Interplay between Media, Culture and Society". *Media, Culture & Society*, 37 (2): 314–324.
Hubbard, Phil, Rob Kitchin, and Gill Valentine, eds. 2004. *Key Thinkers on Space and Place*. Los Angeles: Sage.
Keller, Reiner. 2022. "The Symbolic Construction of Spaces: Perspectives from a Sociology-of-Knowledge Approach to Discourse". In *Communicative Constructions and the Refiguration of Spaces*, edited by Gabriela Christmann, Hubert Knoblauch, and Martina Löw, 36–56. Abingdon: Routledge.
Keller, Reiner, Hubert Knoblauch, and Jo Reichertz, eds. 2013. *Kommunikativer Konstruktivismus. Theoretische und empirische Arbeiten zu einem neuen wissenssoziologischen Ansatz* [Communicative constructivism: Theoretical and empirical work on a new sociological approach]. Wiesbaden: Springer VS.
Knoblauch, Hubert. 2018. "From the Social to the Communicative Construction of Reality". In *Social Constructivism as Paradigm? The Legacy of the Social Construction of Reality*, edited by Michaela Pfadenhauer and Hubert Knoblauch, 275–291. London: Routledge.
Knoblauch, Hubert. 2020. *The Communicative Construction of Reality*. London and New York: Routledge.
Knoblauch, Hubert, and Martina Löw. 2017. "On the Spatial Re-Figuration of the Social World". *Sociologica* 11 (2): 1–27.
Knoblauch, Hubert, and Martina Löw. 2020. "The Re-Figuration of Spaces and Refigured Modernity – Concept and Diagnosis". *Historical Social Research* 45 (2): 263–292.
Knoblauch, Hubert, and Silke Steets. 2022. "From the Constitution to the Communicative Construction of Space". In *Communicative Constructions and the Refiguration of Spaces*, edited by Gabriela Christmann, Hubert Knoblauch, and Martina Löw, 19–35. Abingdon: Routledge.
Kuhm, Klaus. 2000. *Raum als Medium gesellschaftlicher Kommunikation. Eine systemtheoretische Neubeschreibung lokaler und regionaler Differenzen in der Weltgesellschaft* [Space as a medium of social communication. A system-theoretical redescription of local and regional differences in world society]. Working Paper 39. Bremen: Universität Bremen, ZWE Arbeit und Region.
Latour, Bruno. 2005. *Reassembling the Social: An Introduction into Actor-Network Theory*. Oxford: Oxford University Press.
Lees, Loretta. 2004. "Urban Geography: Discourse Analysis and Urban Research". *Progress in Human Geography* 28 (1): 101–107.
Lefebvre, Henri. 1991/1974. *The Production of Space*. Cambridge and Oxford: Basil Blackwell.
Lorimer, Hayden. 2005. "Cultural Geography: The Business of Being 'More-than-Representational'". *Progress in Human Geography* 29 (1): 83–94.

Löw, Martina. 2016. *The Sociology of Space. Materiality, Social Structures and Action*. New York: Palgrave Macmillan.
Luhmann, Niklas. 1987. *Soziale Systeme. Grundriß einer allgemeinen Theorie* [Social systems. Outline of a general theory]. Frankfurt am Main: Suhrkamp.
Massey, Doreen. 2003. "The Conceptualization of Place". In *A Place in the World? Places, Cultures and Globalization*, edited by Doreen Massey and Pat Jess, 45–85. Oxford: Oxford University Press.
Mattissek, Annika. 2007. "Diskursive Konstitution städtischer Identität – Das Beispiel Frankfurt am Main" [Discursive constitution of urban identity – the example of Frankfurt am Main]. In *Kulturelle Geographien. Zur Beschäftigung mit Raum und Ort nach dem Cultural Turn* [Cultural geographies. On the preoccupation with space and place after the cultural turn], edited by Christian Berndt and Robert Pütz, 83–111. Bielefeld: transcript.
Paasi, Ansi. 1989. "The Media as Creator of Local and Regional Culture". In *The Long-Term Future of Regional Policy – A Nordic View*. Report on a Joint NordREFO/OECD seminar in Reykjavik, 151–165. Helsinki: NordREFO/OECD.
Park, Robert E. 1968. "The City: Suggestions for the Investigation of Human Behavior in the Urban Environment". In *The City*, edited by Robert E. Park, Ernest W. Burgess, and Roderick D. McKenzie, 1–46. Chicago: University of Chicago Press.
Park, Robert E. 1972. "Reflections on Communication and Culture". In *The Crowd and the Public and Other Essays*, 98–116. Chicago: University of Chicago Press.
Pott, Andreas. 2007. "Sprachliche Kommunikation durch Raum – das Angebot der Systemtheorie" [Linguistic communication through space – the offer of systems theory]. *Geographische Zeitschrift* 95 (1/2): 56–71.
Schroer, Markus. 2006. *Räume, Orte, Grenzen. Auf dem Weg zu einer Soziologie des Raums* [Spaces, places, borders. On the way to a sociology of space]. Frankfurt am Main: Suhrkamp.
Simmel, Georg. 1903. "Soziologie des Raumes" [Sociology of space]. *Jahrbuch für Gesetzgebung, Verwaltung und Volkswirtschaft im Deutschen Reich* [Yearbook for legislation, administration and national economy in the German Reich] 27 (1): 27–71.
Theophrastus (from Eresos). 2000. *Die Metaphysik Theophrasts. Beiträge zur Altertumskunde, Band 139* [The metaphysics of Theophrast. Contributions to the study of antiquity, Vol. 139]. München: Saur.
Thrift, Nigel. 2007. *Non-Representational Theory. Space, Politics, Affect*. London: Routledge.
Warf, Barney. 2004. "Nigel Thrift". In *Key Thinkers on Space and Place*, edited by Phil Hubbard, Rob Kitchin, and Gill Valentine, 294–300. Los Angeles: Sage.

II
Theoretical and methodological approaches

2 From the constitution to the communicative construction of space

Hubert Knoblauch and Silke Steets

Introduction

For centuries, the assumption that space preceded social reality, or indeed all human existence and action, was widespread in Western thought. Only in recent decades have there been increasing calls to understand space as part of the social world and thus as something that is socially produced. As these voices have become more numerous, powerful, and concerted across many disciplines, one can certainly now speak of a "spatial turn" (Soja 1989). As a result, space is today a legitimate object of research in social and cultural sciences far beyond geography. At the same time, numerous attempts have been made to re-conceptualize the notion of space as constituted by human actions or formed by social superstructures (such as capitalism).

The aim of this chapter is to show how space can indeed be understood as a *social* phenomenon. In order to do so, we start by briefly sketching the core arguments of the sociology of space debate as it has occurred in the past decades. Since we consider Martina Löw's *Raumsoziologie* (2001; here referred to in its English translation as *The Sociology of Space*, Löw 2016) a significant contribution to this debate, there is a focus on its origin in German-speaking discourse (see the section headed "Space and sociology"). This provides us with the specific discursive background against which Löw developed her approach. We then (in "From dualism to duality of space") reconstruct her core arguments and focus on some of the critical problems they entail. In order to remedy these problems, we propose to connect Löw's model with the theory of communicative constructivism (Knoblauch 2020). This allows us to anchor space in a triadic relationship unfolding between subjects and "objectivations" (Berger and Luckmann 1966) and formed by processes of subjectivation and objectivation ("From constitution to communicative construction"). It thus becomes clear that the (always fleeting) *spatiality* of the social is first realized in the physical performance of "communicative actions". However, in order to constitute a (more stable) *space*, spatiality must be consolidated and "hardened", which can be described as a twofold process: Spatiality turns into space, on the one hand, through material objectivations (Steets 2016) and the way they mediate bodies with one another and, on the other hand, through processes of subjectivation,

DOI: 10.4324/9780367817183-4

by which we mean an (always perspectival) internalization of spatiality as knowledge (see "Subjectivation, knowledge, and mediatization"). The last part of the paper deals with digital mediatization, a fundamental transformation in the way (the now digitized) objectivations mediate social relationships. We consider this particularly important for understanding our present society. Since it allows for new forms of space synthesis and, thus, synthetic social situations ("Digitalization and synthetic situation"), we argue that it points to a refiguration of space ("The refiguration of space").[1]

Space and sociology

Although within sociology there is no coherent body of work that acknowledges space as a fundamental category of the social, the topic was raised quite early on by classic sociologist Georg Simmel (1992/1903). Other important impulses came from France, starting with the Durkheim school (Halbwachs 1960; Mauss 1979) and followed by contributions from Foucault (1986/1967), Bourdieu (1996), and particularly Lefebvre (1991/1974). It was the English translation of Lefebvre's *La production de l'espace* (1974) in 1991 that catalyzed the English-speaking debate on space, for which it has since formed a central point of reference. Researchers mainly in geography and urban studies, such as Harvey (1989) and Soja (1996), took it up and developed it further. Others formulated their own theory of space, combining critical spatial analysis with postcolonial thinking (Massey 1999). Not least, the booming branch of globalization theories (Sassen 1991; Castells 1996) led to the insight that in an ever more globally connected world, we are unable to understand social transformation without understanding its spatial dimension.

Although these conceptual developments certainly formed the background to German-language discourse, it was to unfold in a very specific way. Center stage was the fundamental question of whether there could or should at all be a *sociological* concept of space, since space always seemed to involve materialities. Consequently, economist and urban researcher Läpple (1991, 163) attested a general "blindness to space" to the social sciences in Germany and strongly urged a conceptual debate. Eventually, it was Martina Löw's book *Raumsoziologie* (2001) that became the focus of this debate.

Following Läpple, Löw's intention was to overcome what she called the "absolutist notion of space" (Löw 2016, 9) and to replace it with a sociologically founded "relational" concept. In the "absolutist" understanding adopted from classical physics, space appears as a naturally given and immovable physical background foil on which social processes unfold. Consequently, for example, the experience of an ever faster overcoming of spatial distances (through more effective transport technologies and, since the early 1990s, the instantaneous transmission of digitized information on the Internet) appears simply as a dissolution of space that would make it a "lost dimension" (Virilio 1991). Since, however, this diagnosis largely exhausts the socio-analytical (and obviously misleading) potential of such an approach to space, voices (including Löw's) calling for a conceptual reorientation of spatial thinking, along with the analysis of new spatial phenomena, became more prominent.

At the same time, Löw's suggestion for rethinking space met with harsh critique by well-known representatives of urban and regional sociology (Häußermann and Siebel 1978). Their main point of contention was whether it was sociologically legitimate to introduce space as an explanatory variable for social processes and, thus, to conceive of it as something that actively influences people's actions. The reason for this skepticism surrounding space goes back to the very beginnings of urban sociology at the University of Chicago. Its main figure, Robert E. Park (1967/1925), had indeed developed a problematic research perspective based on two rather unrelated strands of theory: human ecology and pragmatism. Whereas he used human ecology (based on the assumption of a *natural* competition between human beings over scarce resources) to account for the spatial order of a city (as a segregated mosaic of little worlds), he applied pragmatist concepts to understand the *social* as symbolic interaction processes (within those little worlds). Although the Chicago School brought to light groundbreaking insights into the little worlds of urban scenes and vocational classes, Park failed to theoretically connect human ecology (explaining space) with pragmatism (explaining the social). Rather, it seemed that a "natural" order of space formed the preconditions for the little worlds to develop and, thus, that space determined the social.

With this in mind, Hartmut Häußermann and Walter Siebel strongly opposed any naturalistic conception of space within sociology, justifying their criticism with a historical Marxist argument: Since the categories "town and country" in developed industrial capitalism no longer referred to different "forms of production, reproduction, and rule", and since the former class opposition described by this differentiation had shifted to another level, namely that of capital and labor (i.e. a seemingly non-spatial antagonism), "town and country are no longer categories" (Häußermann and Siebel 1978, 486, own translation). The very concepts of "town" or "city" had therefore become, they argued, useless for a critical sociology – and with it any attempt at sociological reflection on space (for a similar position, cf. Saunders 1981). In return, Löw (2016, 32 ff.) argued that, here, something is generally rejected as "space" that was previously introduced as reified territory – that is, as a naturalized segment of the earth's surface – only to then be declared (most plausibly) as irrelevant to sociology. Be this as it may, what interests us here are the consequences of these opposing positions, for in this discursive constellation Löw was confronted with the task of formulating a sociologically adequate concept of space as one that overcomes the dualism of space and sociality.

Looking at this debate from today's perspective, two problems come to the fore: (1) Although the arguments refer to the relevance of *social* theories, "the social" is regarded as something given as a matter of fact or, at best, implicitly defined. The fact that sociology has to deal with "sociality" was apparently so unanimously agreed upon that the question of what constitutes the social did not arise in the first place or else appeared unambiguous or uncontested.

(2) The goal of overcoming the dualism between space and the social manifests in various, opposing constructions: Starting from the question of how one can understand space as something belonging not to nature, but socially shaped and as such also socially effective, the dualism to be overcome emerges, first, as an *antithesis of nature and society*. Going further, one is often confronted with a second contrast, between the *material world of things* and the *social world of human existence*, which is not the same. Then, the dualism also emerges in a temporal form – for instance when space is understood as something that precedes action; that is, as an *opposition of space and action*. We elaborate on ways these oppositions can be combined in theoretically coherent and consistent ways in more detail below. In order to do so, it is necessary first of all to reconstruct Martina Löw's sociology of space, which provides the basis for such an elaboration.

From dualism to duality of space

In 2001, Martina Löw presented what is still probably the most far-reaching theoretical proposal for overcoming the dualism of space and sociality. Inspired by the results of her empirical dissertation on the space-making practices of women living alone (Löw 1993) and the incipient debate about space and sociality sketched above, she started searching for a sociological argument suitable for overcoming dualistic ways of thinking. She found it in the theory of structuration by Anthony Giddens (1984). Giddens' goal was to formulate a social theory that conceptualized subjective action and objective structures not as opposites, but as a duality. Using the basic notion of a "duality of structure" (Giddens 1984, 25–28), he argues that through the repetition of everyday actions (i.e. through the formation of routines), people generate structural elements that solidify into social structures mediated through institutions. Institutions are simply understood by Giddens as structures permanently reproduced in routines. He illustrates this with the example of language (Giddens 1984, 24): All members of a language community share the same rules and linguistic practices, save for a number of insignificant deviations. In the act of speaking (acting), they reproduce these rules (structural elements), which enable them to speak (act) in the first place, but at the same time limit their speech to the framework of the rules. Through the constant reproduction of linguistic practices (everyday routine actions), rules and structural motifs are institutionalized recursively, but can always be changed; for instance, through deviant (linguistic) practices.

It is this basic idea that Löw transfers to the realm of spatial thinking, enabling her to elaborate on what she calls a "duality of space" (Löw 2016, xiv). This key concept indeed overcomes dualistic spatial thinking. It claims that through repeated, recursive spatial action by humans, spatial structures are formed, which in turn constitute the conditions for the human actions affected by them. Thus, space is not something that is unconnected to sociality but is, instead, constituted by it. It is on these grounds that Löw understands space as "a relational arrangement of living beings and social goods" (Löw 2016, ix). The term "arrangement" (German: *(An)ordnung*) means both "to arrange something" and "to be in an arranged order" and emphasizes the double character that hides behind the duality of space: Space arises in human actions – that is, in the arrangement of things – and is, at the same time, a spatial order prior to action. Imagine, for example, a supermarket. The arrangement of the shelves (fruit and vegetables first, refrigerated goods in the middle, confectionery at the end), the origin of the offered products (from all over the world), the placement of the goods on the shelves (expensive brands at eye level), the routes taken by people around the shelves (mostly counterclockwise), the layout of the tills (parallel to each other) – all this is highly institutionalized despite existing exceptions. Thus, for the supermarket staff as well as for shoppers, it is an order given prior to their actions (stocking up, clearing out). Nevertheless, this order is constantly re-established by the daily placement of the goods. Deviating arrangements are possible, but usually cause confusion in everyday life (since they irritate routines and conventionalized ideas of space).

According to Löw, spatial structures are formed analogously to Giddens' social structures above all through the development and institutional consolidation of routines. With regard to the aspect of agency, she analytically distinguishes two different aspects of space formation that are, however, empirically mutually dependent: "Spacing and the operation of synthesis" (Löw 2016, 135). *Spacing* means erecting, deploying, or positioning social goods and living beings (including oneself) in places. Social goods are the result of material and symbolic action. They can be distinguished into primarily symbolic goods (such as songs, values, prescriptions, etc.) and primarily material goods (such as houses, tables, chairs, etc.), although in almost all cases both components are combined. However, an arrangement created through acts of spacing, Löw argues, only becomes effective as space if human beings actively amalgamate the arranged elements to spaces through processes of perception, imagination, or memory. Löw calls this the operation of *synthesis*.

As much as the duality of space helps us to think of space in connection with sociality, we see two problems in Löw's theory: First, Löw seems to overemphasize the quite *cognitive* and always *subjective* operation of synthesis, which for her is central to all spatial formations. Put differently, the amalgamation of spatial elements into a spatial wholeness appears to be performed mainly by the consciousness of a perceiving, imagining, and remembering subject. Löw's operation of synthesis as a building block of her spatial theory does indeed give her the very useful idea that several spaces can overlap in concrete places; for example, a public square with stairs and railings may simultaneously be a place for "strolling and standing" and a "skater parkour". Yet spaces seem strangely immaterial, existing predominantly in people's subjective minds. This raises the question of how materiality can be better taken into account in the relational spatial constitution.

The second theoretical element we want to take up and develop further is that of the relationality of spaces. In contrast to the absolutist concept of space, which is arguably limited for socio-analytical purposes and which only makes empirical spaces recognizable when they present themselves as territory, Löw argues for a relational concept of space. Interestingly, however, she thinks of this relationality only in terms of spaces and not in terms of the social, which, according to her, shapes spaces but remains indeterminate as such. This is associated with a problem that has crept into Löw's theory via Giddens. Even though Giddens succeeded in linking action, practice, and structure, his understanding of (human) action remains strikingly pre-social. And even if his contribution was decisive in coining the concept of "social theory", through him, Löw conveys a relationship at the beginning of every "spatial constitution" between individual human beings and the (spatial) world (on Löw's understanding of the concept of "constitution", cf. Löw 2016, 129 ff., 2018, 22 ff.). Although this "single-digit" relationship can be analyzed anthropologically, phenomenologically, or pragmatically, it is not a social phenomenon in itself. Yet, if we regard space as a characteristic of individual consciousness, action, or experience, it is just as pre-social as natural space. How, we must therefore ask, can we consistently think of space as a *social* phenomenon?

From constitution to communicative construction

Communicative constructivism[2] is directed precisely against such a single-digit relationship. Instead of starting from a static relation between ego and world, it aims to develop a processual concept of communicative action in order to view wo/man's (spatial) being in the world as based on social relations. As human beings, we have always been interconnected with others – and, thanks to our bodies and their sensuality and performance in action, these relations can make sense even beyond the use of signs or language. Moreover, these relations are not ontological objects, but are constructed processually through communicative action. That is, we refer to communicative action as the temporally and spatially performed process by which social reality is constructed. The relationality of communicative action is due to what we call "reciprocity", which, in turn, is inherent in the bodily performance, affectivity, and sensual experience pertaining between at least two subjects. By virtue of bodily performance, the relation of communicative action between two subjects is, in fact, triadic and can be represented schematically as follows (see Figure 2.1).

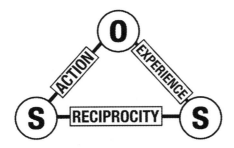

Figure 2.1 The triadic relation of communicative action.
Source: Own representation.

By a triadic relation, we mean that the reciprocity between the two subjects (S) always implies the mutual reference to a (mediating) third (O) – be it the spoken and heard word, the joint execution of the mutual gaze, or a material object onto which a shared interest is directed. This third – which we identify with what Berger and Luckmann (1966) call "objectivation" – is integrated into the relation by virtue of its reciprocal orientation, attention, and bodily performativity. Due to the body's materiality and its sensuality, it constitutes the basis for the materiality of communicative action. The ways objectivations affect subjects' bodies may be unspecific, unclear, or implicit, but still make sense in a very sensual way (Christmann 2016, 2022; Christmann, Knoblauch, and Löw 2022).

The spatial dimension of communicative action can be explained using finger-pointing as an example. Finger-pointing plays a fundamental, even "revolutionary" role in the ontogenetic development of human beings in early childhood. While they first might seem to only coordinate their actions on the basis of ego-driven, one-sided motives, their competence to point with a finger (evolving around the age of 9 months) clearly shows that they acquire a specifically human form of sociality characterized by reciprocity (Tomasello 2008). Interesting for us here is the fact that this reciprocity unquestionably entails a *spatial* dimension.

For, in a very practical sense, finger-pointing is determined by bodies' positions or standpoints. First of all, it is the "here" of my position that is constitutive of the reciprocity needed in pointing. Alfred Schutz (1962) already underlines the locational character of any subjectivity when he takes the subject to be the spatial "point zero of a coordinate system". However, Schutz remains within a subjectivistic frame of argument, since he assumes that this "zero point" is the sole reference point of action, of communicative action, or, in our example, of pointing. This subjectivist understanding is shared in Bühler's (2011) well-known theory of pointing or "deixis". What Schutz calls "here" is somewhat more abstract than what Bühler calls "*haecceitas*". For Bühler, the standpoint is explained in subjectivistic terms by the fact that it starts from this "here". This "*origo*", as Bühler calls it, is the identical point to which all that is shown is related, and this *origo* is for him the physical subject from which the deixis starts out.[3]

This subjectivist model has already been criticized by Hanks (1996), who developed a relational concept of pointing. He emphasizes that finger-pointing cannot be considered a solitary act for the simple reason that it only makes sense *if we point to someone else*. In doing so, it is by no means guided solely by the subjective reference from which the finger points. Rather, the "art" of pointing consists in the characteristic that it is spatially oriented *to someone else*. That is, in pointing, we position and align our body in a way that the other can see our finger, and we choose our finger and body orientation in a way that both our orientation to the reference as well as the other's bodily standpoint are considered. The one who points anticipates the position of the other and makes his/her own position visible to that other. The space in which the pointing occurs therefore by no means pertains only to the subjective consciousness of the one who points; neither can it be reduced to a mere physical feature and its cognitive equivalent in the brain. Rather, pointing only makes sense when we take into account the standpoint of the other subject, to whom something is shown. This relational reference is explained by the fundamental reciprocity of communicative action that Schutz (1962, 316) calls the "interchangeability of the standpoints". This means that actors in communicative action are automatically able to reversely anticipate the visual and kinesthetic perception in the bodily executions they perform. This is why pointing does not simply mean pointing to something; it also incorporates showing it to someone else; that is, anticipating the perspective of the other – such as by making something visible for others to see (and not hiding my pointing finger behind my back).

As a primordial example of communicative action, pointing implies still another relation. It is the embodied finger that we grasp as objectivation. Objectivations are in a certain sense pre-forms of objectifications, they are (still) fleeting phenomena bound to the body, such as gestures. Starting from the reciprocal relation of the subjects, objectivation (here the pointing finger) is not only a third element that symbolically expands the relation to one of a surface, since at the same time the pointing finger refers to something beyond this relation – and thus creates a space between subjects and objectification which is performed and perceived as something in the common environment. So, by virtue of the objectification, the triad expands into space in a way resembling what Löw calls "spacing".

With regard to the triadic relation, we are thus dealing with a performative linking of elements to yield a space that is not – as Löw's operation of synthesis suggests – primarily anchored in consciousness. Rather, this connection is to be located in between communicative action and interaction. There is, however, an additional aspect to pointing we need to consider: The fact that the finger refers to something else has a spatial meaning too, for the practice of pointing not only establishes the space between the subjects and an objectivation; as something relating to something else, it also relates to *somewhere* else. Pointing, therefore, implies a form of appresentation (Schutz 1962): The bodily Gestalt of an extended hand and finger must be extended in the minds of both subjects in order to be understood as pointing. This extension establishes the reference as the basic "meaning" of pointing, and this meaning is also spatial. Its spatiality is not restricted to what happens in the common environment perceived reciprocally, but may rather go beyond it. Pointing as a basic form of signification (i.e. as indication) may simply direct one's attention somewhere else, or to a place that is not present and that transcends the "here" of the actors, their bodily perception, and their material environment. In the performance of pointing, "close" and "distant" spaces are already separated, as is "back" from "front" or "top" from "bottom". Such differentiations receive their meaning in the bodily relation of communicative action. This meaning, however, by no means consists only in the intentionality of the gesture. Rather, the performative act of pointing is the sensual phenomenon that creates space by way of the reciprocity of visual perception and bodily performance, so action does not remain representational-performative, referring only to somewhere, but also includes a real body performance that is to be perceived in the common environment. Action may thus be performative in a very material way, as it may change this reality so as to "mediate" between bodies, objectivations, and objects, as when one prods someone else in order to attract attention, cracks the branch of a tree in order to indicate direction, or constructs an object, such as a pointing stick.

Subjectivation, knowledge, and mediatization

Up to this point, we have still been dealing with very fleeting indexical forms of spatiality that are directly linked to the *situational* performance of actions, such as finger-pointing. Insofar as spatial arrangements occur in this context – for example, by placing bodies in relation to each other in a way that the shared view of a third thing arises – they remain situational in a sense described by ethnomethodology as situated action.[4] Spatial orientation arises from the very act of handling the resources that are available in that situation. That is, as soon as, for instance, the act of pointing ends in time, the arrangement of the bodies and their respective orientation to one another dissolves too. Face formations, which shape space through the arrangement of bodies in interactions (such as the circle that forms between three subjects talking to one another), are situational in a very similar way (Kendon 2004).

Certainly, the body (understood here as both objectified by virtue of other subjects and subjectified as one's own body with its distinct positionality) is already an element that gives the transience of communicative action a duration that goes beyond the performativity of the situation. For Giddens (and Löw), the body is therefore also a resource for permanence, since it allows for the repetition of actions and thus routines. However, routines not only serve as essential mechanisms for the formation of practices. If we understand them as reciprocally typified sequences of action (Berger and Luckmann 1966), they can also be recognized as parts of the embodied and habitualized subjective stock of knowledge. Just as for any subjective knowledge, spatial knowledge can be seen as a result of processes of *subjectivation* of communicative action: In performing actions, both the sensual experience of these actions (i.e. the way in which something like finger-pointing *feels*) and their relational location within the spatiality of the social (i.e. from where something is shown for whom) are internalized. The experience of spatiality thus always has a decidedly subjective accent ("positionality"), which is responsible for the formation of one's own perspective as well as for one's own sensuality and affectivity. In short: It is not only the practical handling of things and spaces (through which, for example, routines and body techniques are formed) that is subjectified, but also the social relation that shapes precisely *this* experience of space – of course from the perspective defined by the respective positionality of a body. Thus, women usually experience visiting a football match in a stadium differently from men, because this space in our society carries a masculine connotation. Insofar as spatial knowledge is subjectified and becomes part of a thus shaped consciousness and bodily habitus, it can remain available as knowledge beyond the respective situation.[5]

The subjectivation of spatial actions as spatial knowledge is only one side of the process in which spatiality is stabilized by body, knowledge, and imagination. This stabilization can be put on a continual footing by permanent social roles (e.g. a bouncer) or long-term (and long-term narrated) biographies (e.g. of an architect) and thus find determined biographical articulations (Schutz and Luckmann 1984). Spatial knowledge becomes even more powerful if it is objectified in signs and symbols (images, models, animations, maps, etc.) and, above all, in language. However, objectivations are already crucial at the level of situational performance. More precisely, material objectifications, when detached from the body, play a central role in the "hardening" of spaces (Steets 2016). These can be – to continue with the example of pointing – twisted branches, the sun rising in the east or, already clearly symbolic, the arrow pointing the way. Thus, material objectifications *mediate* between subjects[6] and thereby create order and stabilize or rearrange it: The staff that we pass on in a relay creates a different kind of order between subjects than, for example, the barrier that we lower in front of another, the revolving door creates a different kind of order than the swinging door, the room in which we meet creates a different kind of order than the wall that is built between us. Objectifications play a mediating role in communicative action, because they order the relationships to and between the bodies in a spatial way. We therefore call this operation "mediation". It is important to note that mediation does not necessarily mean establishing a connection, as do doors, paths, or bridges. It can also mean to separate, as the examples of walls or border fences show.

While the temporality of communicative action is given a social form through sequencing, the situational spatiality of communicative action yields spaces through mediation between bodies, objectivations, and objectifications. Mediation points our attention to the arrangements that emerge from, solidify, or change the placement and/or movement of objectifications. It also reminds us that spacing is, of course, always related to communicative actions that can enter into their own syntheses with them. Examples would be configurations of humans at dining tables (Linke 2018) or tactical formations in football. Just as the temporality of the social can become completely situational in the borderline case, so can mediation be stabilized and "hardened" far beyond the situation: Buildings carved in stone with their hardened spaces conveying light and darkness, large and small, inside and outside, form their own communicative form that precedes any situational appropriation. As soon as institutionalized uses emerge, this form can take on correspondingly fixed meanings, as in the examples of the monastery cell, the apartment block, or the coworking space. Taken together, sequencing and mediation allow the description of movements, circulation, and mobility. Since the socially consolidated forms of temporality and spatiality of the social vary culturally, sequencing and mediation are theoretical instruments that can be used for the empirical analysis of social change.

Although communicative action can already make sense spatially as an embodied and objectified relation, we should not obscure the fact that this sense takes on a new character when objectifications become signs and sign systems. For example, the conventionalization of gesture language, topographic mapping, or even the linguistic word fields of "space" in different languages are examples of signs that presuppose a comprehensive knowledge of their conventionalized meaning. This in turn demands that signs can also refer to signs, such as the arrow or the deictic word "there", both of which can be empractically introduced by pointing a finger. This means that signs allow us to talk about objectifications, bodies, and things, and thus also about spaces, and, again subjectified, they can guide spatial action. If mediation is associated with signs (i.e. conventionalized objectifications), we are dealing with a special form of mediation, which we call "mediatization". By means of linguistic, visual, and other signs, a (for instance, linguistic, visual, or audiovisual) *discourse* about space becomes possible that produces, maintains, and transforms its own lexicon or a special sign language, such as in city views or CAD (computer-aided design). These discourses form the basis for the reconstructions of spaces and their legitimation (Christmann 2016).

Digitalization and synthetic situation

Mediatization refers to the structural change in the mediation of communicative action through the use of signs. It is thus very closely linked to the history, rise, and change of media, which is why, among others, Krotz (2001) describes the historical dimension of mediatization as a metaprocess. Following Innis (2007/1950), he assumes that the transformation of communication media (with their very ability to mediate communication spatially) has a great influence on the size, density, and power of political units – from the limitations of communication with clay tablets in early ancient Egyptian civilization to the flexibility that parchment gave the Roman administration in classical antiquity, to the possibilities of book printing and mass media in early modernity. While the central social, cultural, and economic significance of mass media was discovered quite late on by Innis, Deutsch, or Habermas, we stress here that the more recently developed forms of digital communication lead to a completely new significance for communications technologies. Digitalization has an impact on society as a whole, similar to the changes affected by modern mass communication. Because of the breadth of the changes it causes across various spheres of society, we see a new form of society evolving, which we call "communication society". What makes it new is the fact that digital mediatization affects and transforms the very structure of communicative action; that is, what we have delineated above as the fundamental process of social construction.

In a nutshell, the transformation consists of an extension of a principle of communication based on signs to the realm of material production, as well as to technical and physical mediation that previously worked without signs. This extension mainly comes about by the connection of electrotechnical circuits with the switching algebra and its binary sign system that, like the circuits, only allow for two distinct states: 0/1 (equivalent to off/on). The binary sign system makes possible not only programming and data storage, but also the ("cybernetic") control of different technologies, objects, and now also organic bodies. This becomes particularly clear in the tendencies toward the intra-activity of technical systems interacting with one another based on digitalized sign systems; for example, in autonomous cars, robots, or what has been dubbed Industry 4.0. In this way, technologies not only move as vehicles in space, but are also connected to feedback loops fed by big data in such a way that they can act and communicate without a human subject.

Even though this change from *communicative action* to subjectless *communication* based on and controlled by intra-active sign systems certainly requires a more in-depth analysis, we focus here on the associated changes in space. We can capture an important aspect of these changes with the concept of the "synthetic situation" as suggested by Knorr-Cetina (2014). This implies a notion of synthesis that is by no means performed solely or even primarily in the conscious mind. Following Goffman (1963), it can, rather, be understood as resulting from the interaction of the actors who, through their communicative action, create a social situation even when they do not orient themselves toward each other in a recognizable way or share a common focus.[7] However, while Goffman still limits a "situation" to the social ecology of a (contained) physical space, digital mediatization, by means of scopic media, fundamentally extends the "situation" translocally into what can be described as a "synthetic situation". Knorr-Cetina illustrates this extension with the case of globally acting financial brokers who, with the help of screens of simultaneously linked financial information systems, interact translocally with one another in such a way that they carry out actions by means of symbolic, audiovisual representations (monetary values, stock market levels, etc.). Thus, translocality is achieved by technologically mediated means of communication, such as keyboards, computer mice, and voice control, depending on transnational infrastructures and affecting the circulation of money, products, and entire national economies (in indeed material ways).

The synthetic situation defines a novel form of social situation which translocally synthesizes spatially distributed communicative actions by means of mediation and mediatization. Although during the Cold War one could have launched a nuclear missile at the push of a button, unleashing devastating effects on the other side of the world in just a few hours, the synthetic situation is characterized by the fact that its translocal effects can be monitored and manipulated (by hand!) *simultaneously* in different places. We could have described this peculiar feature as "response presence" (Goodwin 1994), but this phrase overlooks the fact that the coordination is not performed by words (which would need to be understood by humans) and through the "communication power" (Reichertz 2009) of its speakers. Rather, the presence does not depend on language (and fleeting hearing, as with the telephone), but on the interactive coordination of bodily material effects that are mediated through digital visualizations that represent translocal spaces, actors, and things.

A less complex example for such a translocal space is telemedical surgery. Here a physical intervention into a body can be performed at one location on the basis of audiovisual transmission of the "translocal body" from another location. In fact, one might suspect that different forms of synthesis need to be distinguished in order to account for the specific interplay between mediatized representations by various signs systems (words, visual icons, maps, etc.), the digitalized activities effected by digital software and hardware on objects, nondigital technologies and infrastructures (water, electricity, etc.), and, of course, human actors, their knowledge, and the role of subjective forms of synthesis (do actors need to know about the spatial distribution of action, and do they depend on its cognitive representation?). In general, the notion of the synthetic situation clearly illustrates that digital mediation can bring about fundamental changes for the way spaces are formed and conceived.[8]

The refiguration of space

Digital mediatization doesn't just overcome the physical notion of the situation. As Knorr-Cetina's study on money transactions vividly demonstrates, it also bridges what has been considered as separate spheres of microsocial action and macrosocial structures. Digital mediatization thus creates spaces that Löw's notion of the operation of synthesis can no longer capture. In order to characterize the relational order that emerges across conventional scales, we have proposed the concept of "refiguration" (Knoblauch and Löw 2017). Digital mediatization is certainly one of the factors fostering it. Epistemologically, we use the notion of refiguration as a sensitizing concept that leaves the qualities and extensions of the suspected transformations to qualitative empirical analysis. Despite its sensitivity, it implies a number of hypotheses that give focus to the empirical studies guided by this notion: Based on the role of mediatization in communicative action and society in general, refiguration first assumes that any social order depends on and consists in spatial orders; second, digital mediatization is characterized by two antagonistic spatial logics, which can be best characterized as figurations of (a) flat horizontal networks and (b) vertical hierarchies. The material and institutional dissemination of these spatial logics parallels and enforces models of social order that confront what has existed before with new developments. The conflictual nature of this antagonism thus comes to the fore, especially in terms of spatial figurations (think of locals vs. nomads, international metropolises vs. hinterlands, or transnational networks vs.

bounded nation states). The assumption is that (among other processes) digital mediatization plays a central role here, as it affects communicative action in such a fundamental way that it turns objectivations and bodies via digitalization into signs. On an institutional level, refiguration means that the principle of centrally institutionalized communication is superseded, but not substituted, by networked forms of communication. At a spatial level, refiguration results from the conflict between two spatial logics intertwined with these transformations in communicative action that manifests them as the opposing trends of de- and re-territorialization, of de- and re-centralization, and of homogenization and heterogenization. In suggesting an epochal change of figurations beyond modernity, and late and postmodernity, the notion of refiguration is designed to explain the conflictual dynamics of these processes (with digital mediatization as one of its more recent spatial causes) and to analyze how the spatiality of contemporary society is changing. Since it allows us to analyze different types of society, the above-sketched notion of communicative action and the sociological understanding of space derived from it forms the social theory basis for grasping the core aspects of this refiguration.

Notes

1 The chapter presents findings of the Collaborative Research Center 1265 "Re-Figuration of Spaces" at the Technische Universität Berlin, Germany. It is funded by the German Research Foundation under project no. 290045248.
2 By communicative constructivism we refer to a movement that builds on and develops further the approach formulated in *The Social Construction of Reality* by Berger and Luckmann (1966). Its position, relation to social constructivism, and the range of arguments referred to in the following sections is elaborated in much more detail in Knoblauch (2020).
3 This is true, in a transcendent sense, of linguistic deixis and of what Husserl (1982) called indexicality: words like "I", "here", and "now" are part of a conventionalized language system as well as their opposites, "you", "there", or "earlier", but they can only be understood on the basis of the relation, the situation, and the position.
4 Suchman (1987) illustrates situated action on the basis of the navigation of ships in Micronesia, which is based on different situational features, such as wind direction or water currents, and does not use maps.
5 This internalization is the prerequisite for the constitution of subjective imaginations of space, which of course can be massively transformed by language, and symbolic and medial representations (the imaginary). These cultural patterns of the imaginary also shape the affective aspects of space (the oppressive, the sublime) and its atmosphere (on the internalization of built spaces, cf. Steets 2016).
6 Material objectifications do not necessarily have to be human products or cultural objects. As Schutz (1962) argues, for instance, birds can become the common object of action. Objectifications must not be defined as "nature" in order to represent reciprocally perceptible, recognizable, and comprehensible products of reciprocal action.
7 We may therefore assume that this social synthesis can be subjectified in ways which fuse with other aspects of spatial knowledge, imagination, and affectivity.

8 These newly mediatized syntheses will be also subjectified in a way that will affect subjective knowledge, imagination, and cognitive representation. We may suspect that they will also affect subjective spatial knowledge, imagination, and affectivity.

References

Berger, Peter L., and Thomas Luckmann. 1966. *The Social Construction of Reality: A Treatise in the Sociology of Knowledge*. New York: Penguin Books.
Bourdieu, Pierre. 1996. "Physical Space, Social Space and Habitus". *Rapport* 10 (3): 7–22.
Bühler, Karl. 2011. *Theory of Language: The Representational Function of Language*. Amsterdam: John Benjamins.
Castells, Manuel. 1996. *The Information Age: Economy, Society and Culture. Volume I: The Rise of the Network Society*. Malden: Blackwell Publishers.
Christmann, Gabriela B. 2016. "Das theoretische Konzept der kommunikativen Raum(re)konstruktion" [The theoretical concept of the communicative (re)construction of spaces]. In *Zur kommunikativen Konstruktion von Räumen: Theoretische Konzepte und empirische Analysen* [On the communicative construction of spaces: Theoretical concepts and empirical analyses], edited by Gabriela B. Christmann, 89–111. Wiesbaden: Springer VS.
Christmann, Gabriela B. 2022. "The Theoretical Concept of the Communicative (Re)construction of Spaces". In *Communicative Constructions and the Refiguration of Spaces*, edited by Gabriela Christmann, Hubert Knoblauch, and Martina Löw, 89–112. Abingdon: Routledge.
Christmann, Gabriela B., Hubert Knoblauch, and Martina Löw. 2022. "Introduction: Communicative Constructions and the Refiguration of Spaces". In *Communicative Constructions and the Refiguration of Spaces*, edited by Gabriela Christmann, Hubert Knoblauch, and Martina Löw, 3–15. Abingdon: Routledge.
Foucault, Michel. 1986/1967. "Of Other Spaces". *Diacritics* 16 (1): 22–27.
Giddens, Anthony. 1984. *The Constitution of Society: Outline of the Theory of Structuration*. Cambridge: Polity Press.
Goffman, Erving. 1963. *Behavior in Public Places: Notes on the Social Organization of Gatherings*. New York: The Free Press.
Goodwin, Charles. 1994. "Professional vision". *American Anthropologist* 96 (3): 606–633.
Halbwachs, Maurice. 1960. *Population and Society: Introduction to Social Morphology*. Glencoe: The Free Press.
Hanks, William F. 1996. *Language and Communicative Practices*. Boulder, CO: Westview Press.
Harvey, David. 1989. *The Condition of Postmodernity*. Oxford: Blackwell.
Häußermann, Hartmut, and Walter Siebel. 1978. "Thesen zur Soziologie der Stadt" [Theses on the sociology of the city]. *Leviathan* 6 (4): 484–500.
Husserl, Edmund. 1982. *Ideas Pertaining to a Pure Phenomenology and to a Phenomenological Philosophy – First Book: General Introduction to a Pure Phenomenology*. The Hague: Nijhoff.
Innis, Harold A. 2007/1950. *Empire and Communications*. Toronto: Dundurn.
Kendon, Adam. 2004. *Gesture: Visible Action as Utterance*. Cambridge: Cambridge University Press.
Knoblauch, Hubert. 2020. *The Communicative Construction of Reality*. London: Routledge.

Knoblauch, Hubert, and Martina Löw. 2017. "On the Spatial Re-Figuration of the Social World". *Sociologica* 11 (2): 1–27.
Knorr-Cetina, Karin. 2014. "Scopic Media and Global Coordination: The Mediatization of Face-to-Face Encounters". In *Mediatization of Communication*, edited by Knut Lundby, 39–62. Berlin: De Gruyter.
Krotz, Friedrich. 2001. *Die Mediatisierung sozialen Handelns* [The mediatization of social action]. Wiesbaden: VS Verlag für Sozialwissenschaften.
Läpple, Dieter. 1991. "Essay über den Raum: Für ein gesellschaftswissenschaftliches Raumkonzept" [Essay about space: Toward a sociological concept of space]. In *Stadt und Raum: Soziologische Analysen* [City and space: Sociological analyses], edited by Hartmut Häußermann, Detlev Ipsen, Thomas Krämer-Badoni, Dieter Läpple, Marianna Rodenstein, and Walter Siebel, 157–207. Pfaffenweiler: Centaurus.
Lefebvre, Henri. 1991/1974. *The Production of Space*. Oxford: Blackwell.
Linke, Angelika. 2018. "Der Esstisch. Eine historische Skizze zur raumsemiotischen Nutzung eines Möbelstücks" [The dining table. A historical sketch on the space-semiotic use of a piece of furniture]. *Historische Anthropologie* [Historical anthropology] 26 (3): 350–378.
Löw, Martina. 1993. *Raum ergreifen: Alleinwohnende Frauen zwischen Arbeit, sozialen Beziehungen und der Kultur des Selbst* [Seizing space: Women living alone between work, social relationships, and the culture of the self]. Bielefeld: Kleine.
Löw, Martina. 2001. *Raumsoziologie* [Sociology of space]. Frankfurt am Main: Suhrkamp.
Löw, Martina. 2016. *The Sociology of Space: Materiality, Social Structures, and Action*. New York: Palgrave Macmillan.
Löw, Martina. 2018. *Vom Raum aus die Stadt denken – Grundlagen einer raumtheoretischen Stadtsoziologie* [Thinking the city from space – basics of a theoretically oriented sociology of the city]. Bielefeld: Transcript.
Massey, Doreen B. 1999. "Spaces of Politics". In *Human Geography Today*, edited by Doreen Massey, John Allen, and Philip Sarre, 279–294. Cambridge: Blackwell.
Mauss, Marcel. 1979. *Seasonal Variations of the Eskimo*. London: Routledge & Kegan Paul.
Park, Robert E. 1967/1925. "The City: Suggestions for the Investigation of Human Behavior in the Urban Environment". In *The City*, edited by Robert E. Park, Ernest W. Burgess, and Roderick D. McKenzie, 1–46. Chicago: University of Chicago Press.
Reichertz, Jo. 2009. *Kommunikationsmacht* [Communication power]. Wiesbaden: VS Verlag für Sozialwissenschaften.
Sassen, Saskia. 1991. *The Global City: New York, London, Tokyo*. Princeton, NJ: Princeton University Press.
Saunders, Peter. 1981. *Social Theory and the Urban Question*. New York: Holmes & Meier.
Schutz, Alfred. 1962. "Symbol, Reality and Society". In *Alfred Schutz Collected Papers I: The Problem of Social Reality*, 287–356. The Hague: Nijhoff.
Schutz, Alfred, and Thomas Luckmann. 1984. *The Structures of the Lifeworld*. Vol. 1. Evanston, IL: Northwestern University Press.
Simmel, Georg. 1992/1903. "Soziologie des Raumes" [Sociology of space]. In *Schriften zur Soziologie* [Writings on sociology], edited by Otthein Rammstedt, 221–242. Frankfurt am Main: Suhrkamp.
Soja, Edward W. 1989. *Postmodern Geographies: The Reassertion of Space in Critical Social Theory*. London: Verso.
Soja, Edward W. 1996. *Thirdspace: Journeys to Los Angeles and Other Real and Imagined Places*. Malden: Blackwell.

Steets, Silke. 2016. "Taking Berger and Luckmann to the Realm of Materiality: Architecture as a Social Construction". *Cultural Sociology* 10 (1): 93–108.
Suchman, Lucy. 1987. *Plans and Situated Actions: The Problem of Human Machine Communication*. Cambridge: Cambridge University Press.
Tomasello, Michael. 2008. *Origins of Human Communication*. Cambridge, MA: The MIT Press.
Virilio, Paul. 1991. *The Lost Dimension*. New York: Semiotext(e).

3 The symbolic construction of spaces
Perspectives from a sociology of knowledge approach to discourse

Reiner Keller

Introduction

Spatial and urban research have for some time now been using the concept of discourse, in the sense of contemporary discourse research. A keyword investigation of the specialist journal *Urban Studies* shows that, in older numbers, the term "discourse" was indeed being used, but more in the context of book discussions, or to characterize a speech, a position, or a single thematic discussion. In 1993, however, a rather different focus emerged. In a text on urban marketing there is mention of discourses, and the increasing understanding that cities must, and do, also live from their symbolic construction and their image. Then, in 1999, *Urban Studies* devoted an entire special issue to the significance of discourses for urban and spatial research. Since then, very many studies have appeared that deal with discourses on the city in general or on individual cities in particular, or which also focus on particular urban districts.

The fact that "natural" and "human" spaces are *also* always symbolic constructions and orders has, of course, long been known to social science spatial and urban research. Here it has no need of the visions of urban planners or architects, or of political projects concerned with spatial ordering. In sociology this was most emphatically stated by the Chicago School in the first third of the 20th century: "The city is a state of mind" was an early dictum of Robert E. Park, the principal advocate of this position. This is not only reminiscent of Georg Simmel's article on "Die Großstadt und das Geistesleben" (The metropolis and mental life), in which Simmel analyses how the increase in the density and speed of human encounters in the everyday life of cities leads to a particularly "blasé" state of mind; it also suggests that the city, its neighborhoods, buildings, streets, and squares, are always involved in relations of meaning. In the 1960s, for example, Anselm Strauss, a member of the second generation of Chicago sociologists, made a number of attempts to put the imaginary of cities and the urban environment on the sociological agenda. "The city, then", he writes in 1961, "sets problems of meaning. The streets, the people, the buildings, and the changing scenes do not come already labelled. They require explanation and interpretation" (Strauss 1961, 12). And some pages later he says: "The city, I am suggesting, can be viewed as a complex related set of symbolized areas"

DOI: 10.4324/9780367817183-5

(Strauss 1961, 59). In *Images of the American City* (Strauss 1961) and *The American City: A Sourcebook of Urban Imagery* (Strauss 1968), he discusses and illustrates the meaning of the symbolic orders in the urban setting, in the pictures, myths, and imagination that link people with places.

The reference to the symbolic orders of spaces in no way means that we dispense with analyzing interests and their role in the construction of spaces. For instance, the variety of urban research with a Marxist provenance following the ideas of Henri Lefebvre has emphasized this repeatedly. Nor does this reference imply that we forget the analysis of the materialities that we encounter in the form of "natural" or "artificial" spaces. To see this, we have no need of the more recent actor-network theory. Indeed, it is rather the case that Michel Foucault, with his concept of *dispositif*, already made available for us the appropriate conceptual tools for dealing with the symbolic and the material in spatial analysis; for example, where he investigates the panoptic organization and rationale of prison buildings or hospitals. The fact that spaces are symbolic locations is perhaps nowhere made clearer than in his references to "other spaces", social heterotopias and the anxieties, hopes, and desires that arise there (Foucault 1984/1982, 1986; Keller 2018).

In this chapter, however, I wish to make a plea for the use of the term "discourse" for the investigation of the symbolic order of space (and thereby also of the urban setting). To my mind, the essential advantages of this are in treating symbolic order not just as a pure (hyper)textual practice of sign usage, but in providing an analytical vocabulary that is able to make use of the concept of *dispositif* (often translated as "apparatus") and thereby to address and examine the concrete materiality of symbolic orders as well. Of course it must also be made clear what application of the term "discourse" is being used. Indeed, today it is less possible than ever before to assume that with the terms "discourse" and "discourse research", we are dealing with an unambiguous object and a clear research perspective. If we leave aside Habermas' normative discourse ethics or "discourse analysis" as a type of conversation analysis that concentrates on the sequence and the coordination of linguistic interaction, then both internationally and in the German social science context, there are still several very differently focused perspectives in the form of *Kritische Diskursanalyse/critical discourse analysis*, discourse analysis based on hegemony theory, discursive institutionalism, and the approaches that derive, to a greater or lesser extent, from Foucault. And here we are not including the very complex situation that prevails in discourse linguistics. In the present context, we shall not consider any of these approaches. This chapter represents, rather, a genuine sociology of knowledge perspective on discourse research (a sociology of knowledge approach to discourse, SKAD), developed by the author in the German-speaking sphere at the end of the 1990s and since adopted in sociology as well as many related disciplines (Keller 2010; Keller and Truschkat 2012; Keller 2011; Keller, Hornidge, and Schünemann 2018).

The research program of SKAD embeds the discourse perspective in the social constructivism founded in the 1960s by Peter L. Berger and Thomas

Luckmann (Berger and Luckmann 1966). This facilitates the avoidance of a variety of bottlenecks and problems that are found in the other perspectives mentioned above: *Kritische Diskursanalyse* and critical discourse analysis have both developed ideologically critical projects that focus predominantly on language use. They pursue a gesture of exposure, which draws attention, from the position of observer that they adopt, to places where a concealed interest in domination (e.g. by capitalism, fascism, racism) lurks in the spoken word. Perspectives from hegemony theory in discourse research employ a relatively narrow conceptual repertoire to reconstruct the genesis and structuring of symbolic orders with a claim to hegemony; that is, with a claim to represent the general good. This very severely limits the perspective of discourse research to the analysis of antagonistic constellations, where all parties claim to represent the whole. Discursive institutionalism, in turn, is inclined to overemphasize the significance and role of individual actors in the discourse process, or else to restrict the question of change in political processes to the discursive power of individuals. And research based on Foucault remains, as a rule, very vague and opaque in respect of its actual empirical procedure.

The sociology of knowledge approach presented below hopefully avoids these limitations. It introduces a theoretical and conceptual framework for social science discourse research that does not imply any strongly discourse-theoretical determination, but rather offers a heuristic of analysis that remains receptive to the empirically very different mechanisms, dynamics, and sequencing of discourse processes. The embedding we shall undertake of the discourse perspective into social constructivism brings discourse research back to Foucault's questions about the social functioning of power/knowledge regimes, or alternatively it places the analyses of knowledge processes in a central position. It allows one, in addition, to relate to the methodological developments of interpretive and qualitative social research, which on the one hand reflect the position of the investigator and on the other hand maintain transparency in the processing of empirical databases. There now follows a brief clarification of the starting point in social constructivism, and this in turn is followed by a short discussion of Foucault's understanding of discourse and the main concepts and procedures of SKAD. Finally, there is a brief consideration of how the suggested perspective might be used to investigate the discursive order of the spatial dimension.

Social constructivism

The classic sociological study *The Social Construction of Reality*, authored by Peter L. Berger and Thomas Luckmann in 1966, brought together several sociological and philosophical traditions (elements of sociology of knowledge in Durkheim, Mannheim, Marx, and Weber, the philosophical anthropology of Plessner and Gehlen, Alfred Schutz's social phenomenology, and arguments from symbolic interactionism) in a fundamental theory of the sociology of knowledge, which views society from two perspectives: as objective reality and as subjective reality. It stresses the interactive production and establishment of knowledge and symbolic orders and their typification, stabilization, routinization, habitualization, and institutionalization. At the same time, institutional orders are symbolic orders accompanied by the most varied kinds of legitimization theory that explain why reality is the way it is. Every social order, every institutional order, every symbolic order of materialities is the result of complex historical production processes where, in particular, communicative elements of action and interaction play a central role. They may be understood as a complex socio-historically consolidated and changeable structure of collective knowledge that is always more or less stabilized, contested, and undergoing change. The high significance of the communicative elements – and recently there has also been reference to "communicative constructivism" (Keller, Knoblauch, and Reichertz 2013) – is essentially derived from the meaning of the sign-based appresentation of knowledge and symbolic orders. Signs, which we use for orientation in realities and to exchange with others, are socially crystallized and typified carriers of meaning. They are viewed here as typified forms that we again use to relate to or access the reality of the world. They come from complex social interaction processes and are temporarily stabilized in social universes of discourse so that human actors can use them to transform their personal lived experience (*Erleben*) into reflexively accessible experience (*Erfahrung*), to forge action plans, to interpret situations in which they find themselves, and to produce interactive integration of actions. The concept of knowledge, in turn, relates to everything that is accepted as "existing". This includes beliefs as much as natural laws or the orientation patterns that we use in our everyday lives. "Knowledge", therefore, refers to what humans use for orientation in the world, and in no sense to what has established itself in complex social processes as tested, "true", or "proven". Knowledge also includes routinized physical skills, social institutions such as marriage, ideas such as freedom, political ideologies, or large-scale (especially social-science-based) theoretical constructions to explain the world. It materializes in the form of texts, rituals, objects: a law, a funeral service, a ring, an underground network, and so on. The social construction of reality is a lasting and ongoing process of constant performative production; it is not at all a question of the intentional result of individual efforts, but much more of a byproduct of collective life.

We may beat our heads against symbolic orders just as much as against the materiality of a wall. For "newcomers", the socially produced institutions and reality orders seem to be something that confronts them with claims to validity and conformity – although, from a historical point of view, it is a question of constructs produced by humans. With objects, this is probably clearer in the first instance. The pot that someone has designed, and someone else has made, can be used by me as long as I orient myself to what the pot provides me with in terms of its form, size, and material properties – although these do not "force" me to use it in a particular way (I can, for example, misuse it as a musical instrument, or I can warm up milk, peas, or socks in it). But if I want to cook with it, I have to include its properties in my orientation and action plans (Keller

2019). What is true of objects and artefacts is equally true of institutions and the knowledge that they manifest:

> This acquired objectivity of man's cultural products pertains both to the material and the non-material ones. It can readily be understood in the case of the former. Man manufactures a tool and by that action enriches the totality of physical objects present in the world. Once produced, the tool has a being of its own that cannot be readily changed by those who employ it. Indeed, the tool (say, an agricultural implement) may even enforce the logic of its being upon its users, sometimes in a way that may not be particularly agreeable to them. For instance, a plow, though obviously a human product, is an external object not only in the sense that its users may fall over it and hurt themselves as a result, just as they may be falling over a rock or a stump or any natural object. More interestingly, the plow may compel its users to arrange their agricultural activity, and perhaps also other aspects of their lives, in a way that conforms to *its* own logic and that may have been neither intended nor foreseen by those who originally devised it. The same objectivity, however, characterizes the non-material elements of culture as well.
>
> (Berger 1967, 9)

Via socialization processes and permanent communication, societies or social collectives provide their members – especially newcomers – with the "correct" knowledge of the world; that is to say, with the main elements of a reality order that is then acquired as existing in one (and only one!) particular way rather than any other. This world knowledge also incorporates the relevant self-perception of having a particular "self", of belonging here or somewhere else, of being able and obliged to act in this or that way, of being able to justify something in one way or another, of being able to desire one person or another, and so on. Of course, the elements and levels of this world of knowledge, or social stock of knowledge, differ according to their degree of freedom, and much is admitted or hindered by the quality of the world that we characterize today as physical. You cannot fly without assistance. You rarely doubt that trains or roads exist. You see that in politics, totally different and conflicting claims are made about the state of our society. Your neighbor believes in UFOs, whereas you only believe the earth is flat. But all of these are specifications within a more or less common "universe of discourse" – a term from pragmatic sociology and philosophy – a meaning horizon of shared and differentiated significances, within which there may well be irreconcilable niches but all depend on the same world of signs.

One essential advantage of the co-constitutional position developed by Berger and Luckmann is that they do not simply divide the origin and effect of processes of social structuring into action and emergent effects but, rather, against the accepted dualisms of the Durkheim tradition on the one hand and the Weber tradition on the other, and in agreement with Karl Marx, they emphasize active human behavior in social production. And they do not deny emergent effects that have to be consolidated in institutions and role relationships, embodied in action and "carried out", in order to be effective in reality. In addition, one invaluable advantage of this foundation for the sociology of knowledge is that it orients sociology of knowledge research according to the methodology and methods of qualitative or interpretative social research. Where the world appears to us to be a meaningful order which must be interpreted and which can be changed by interpretation, a social science hermeneutics (Hitzler and Honer 1997) is needed to underpin the foundations of its own interpretive procedures.

Berger and Luckmann, however, in their basic work, proposed an unnecessary and far-reaching strategy when they required that sociology of knowledge should address first and foremost the paramount everyday reality of humans; that is, the ways in which social reality is experienced, lived, produced, and changed in their everyday lives. This had far-reaching consequences, because the ensuing research (with the exception of Berger and Luckmann themselves and sociological neo-institutionalism) was indeed interested primarily in knowledge phenomena at the micro level (e.g. in interactions, small groups, life-world arrangements). This positioning was unnecessary because it seriously restricted the investigative horizon that had been opened up by these authors, even though, at the same time, the importance of meso- and macrostructural levels of knowledge production (for instance, in the shape of scientific or religious knowledge) could not and cannot be denied for actors in everyday life (see Christmann 2016, 2022; Christmann, Knoblauch, and Löw 2022).

Discourses

The work of Michel Foucault is, without doubt, the primary source of inspiration for present-day social science discourse research. For example, his history of science study *Les Mots et les Choses* (*The Order of Things*) published in 1966 (Foucault 1991/1966), together with *L'Archéologie du savoir* (*The Archaeology of Knowledge*) from 1969 (Foucault 2010/1969), provide the governing idea for a type of discourse research that analyses the historical rules of knowledge production, with the support of archives or textual materials or corpora. Foucault's essential achievement here is to define discourses as practices that produce the things about which they speak. With this a further variety of social constructivism is launched that establishes the construction of the world in the practice of making statements about the world. In his *Archaeology* (Foucault 2010/ 1969), a number of conceptual suggestions are developed for this purpose (e.g. discursive formation, statement) that Foucault himself does not in fact subsequently use. Where he does use the term "discourse" again, this is on the one hand to emphasize more strongly the connection between knowledge and power in the structuring of what can be said (*L'ordre du discours* [the order of discourse]; this book has been translated as *The Discourse on Language*, Foucault 2010/1972) and on the other hand to treat discourses as contributions to social conflicts of meaning-making. It is just this latter perspective, present in *I, Pierre*

Rivière (Foucault 1982/1973), that is often omitted in discussions of Foucault's work. Here, together with a group of collaborators, Foucault analyses a spectacular murder case from the early 19th century. In this collection of historical documents, the murderer's own account and confession is contrasted with various police, psychiatric, and court reports, and these come to very different assessments of the mental capabilities of the accused. It is therefore a matter of competing definitions of the situation and a conflict of interpretations, the outcome of which has many consequences. This characterization of discourses as fighting parties in "games of truth" (Michel Foucault) is important in that it brings the term close to sociological interest in social conflicts and problem definitions, thereby giving the participating actors and their statements a higher value than it seemed likely to be the case with *The Archaeology of Knowledge* a few years earlier.

However, the immensely rich work of Foucault does lack a number of elements that are important for an empirical approach to discourse analysis. It does not develop any theory of the sign or the use of signs, even though statements, which he defines as the core elements of discourses – all take the form of signs. In addition there is no methodology for data assessment – that is, for the reconstruction of statements and discourses; in this case more recent social science hermeneutics and the ideas formulated there on the theory of interpretation can give helpful pointers. Finally, the role of social actors in the processes of problematization that interested him is not really discussed to any depth.

The sociology of knowledge approach to discourse

Integrating a discourse perspective derived from Foucault into social-constructivist sociology of knowledge allows one, on the one hand, to overcome the above-mentioned gaps in Foucault's program and, on the other hand, to make a contribution to compensating for the social-constructivist neglect of knowledge processes at the social meso and macro levels. SKAD refers to a social science research program for the analysis of social relations of knowledge and all kinds of politics of knowledge and meaning-making (Keller 2010/2005, 2011; Keller, Hornidge, and Schünemann 2018). In and by means of discourses, the sociocultural meaning and facticity of physical and social realities are constituted by social actors through the use of language or symbols. In SKAD, the main focus is on the investigation of these processes of the social construction of interpretive and action structures (knowledge regimes, knowledge policies) at the level of institutions, organizations, or collective actors, and on investigating the social effects of these processes (e.g. Keller 1998). Discourses may be understood as structured and structuring attempts to create and stabilize meanings, or in general terms as more or less far-reaching symbolic orders, that thereby attempt to institutionalize a fixed meaning relation, an order of knowledge, for specific fields of practice in social collectives. The discursive construction of reality constitutes an (eminently important) extract from what Peter Berger and Thomas Luckmann (1966) called the "social construction of reality". SKAD's location of discourse analysis in Berger and Luckmann's sociology of knowledge aims to analyze discourses not in isolation as a semiotic processing system, but as social practice. Competing definitions of reality and the derivative institutional orders or social infrastructures (such as *dispositifs*, speaker positions, practices, subject positions, and objects) may count as social "engagement" of discourses or as an example of discursive combats around meaning-making and world-making. The speaker positions that occur and perform discursive events and practices in such conflicts and the corresponding discourse arenas are not "masters of the universe of discourse", but are (co-)constituted by the existing structures of discursive orders or formations. And yet in no sense do they behave as discourse marionettes, but rather as intelligently interested bearers of statements, as articulators with more or less strong potential in terms of resources and creativity. The symbolic orders that are thereby produced and transformed constitute the aggregated effects of their action; clear and temporary dominances or hegemonies are rare constellations that cannot be empirically excluded.

The concept of "social relations of knowledge" was reinvented with regard to Ulrich Beck's concept of "relations of definition", a term that was formulated with regard to risk conflicts and risk discourses, and alluded to Karl Marx's "relations of production". Social relations of knowledge are the socially produced and historically situated configurations of claims of reality, or facticity and normativity, that span the local, national, transnational, and global horizon of what is seen as "social reality". This also includes, apart from the factual, the true, and the correct, definitions of what is beautiful, possible, good, bad, supernatural, transcendental, and so on. These kinds of relations of knowledge all occur as "objective reality". But like relations of production, they are an externalized product of human and socialized activity. They structure interpretations and modes of action, insofar as they are "realized" by social actors in appropriate acts of translation. And they can be changed by human, social practice, by events and problematizations. The concept of social relations of knowledge, therefore, incorporates what Michel Foucault understood as power-knowledge regimes. Concerning politics of knowledge, there is talk of sticking to two ideas: first, the process-and-change character of knowledge relations (it is always a matter of only temporary and only relatively stable constellations), and second, the active role of social actors who are concerned, in the context of problem areas and the processing of events, with production and change of relations of knowledge. Politics of knowledge, therefore, are not limited to the usually suspicious area of the political, nor are they reduced to conflicts about risky (technological) developments. Politics of knowledge policies take place, rather, in the most varied social fields of action, such as when some neighborhood community engages in collecting data about traffic, pollution, or gentrification, in order to make cases against the city's officials. They are an expression of the conflict-ridden and controversial nature of the social construction of reality. Objects of SKAD are, in Foucault's understanding, both general-public and special-interest discourses. They are investigated with regard to their speakers and agencies, their means, strategies, or patterns for meaning-making and establishing claims, and the effects of these. The analysis of special-interest discourses and the analysis of public discourses are both based on "rules" and resources; that is to say, on discourse structures that underlie the individual discursive events. Public discourses also consist of statement events that occur in widely differing places and times. They display typifiable regularities and may be understood – even if not as immediate interactions under conditions of co-presence – as processes of negotiation about the definition of the situation (Thomas and Thomas 1928). Here, we are not suggesting a process of argumentative consensus formation in the sense of Habermas' discourse ethics. "Negotiation" means, rather, conflictual constellations, a fight about the "reality of reality" which – using the most varied resources – is conducted as a symbolic battle. In this process, specific discourse coalitions and actors may gain the advantage over others. But the discursive formations that are found here cannot be understood (or if so, only in borderline cases) as the intended and controlled effect of individual actors. Both types of discourse – special-interest discourses and general-public discourses – are regarded by SKAD as discursive formations. Their "rules" and resources of meaning-making, their socio-historically situated protagonists, the knowledge that is codified in them, and its effects are all investigated.

Heuristics of analysis

SKAD proposes a number of terms to investigate the assumed existence of an actual formation of statements for the analyzable content of a discourse. The term *discourse* itself characterizes a structuring relationship that underlies scattered discursive events. It is precisely this that the concept of discourse is aiming for: providing a term for typifying disparate empirical and – if viewed as events – singular statements. The unity of the structuring relationship (i.e. the discourse) is a basic assumption in discourse observation, an indispensable research hypothesis. In the numerous but finite sequence of actual utterances (communications) discourse structures are reproduced and transformed by social actors through the contingency of the historical-situational conditions and concrete actions, while such actors pursue their particular everyday business in a more or less enthusiastic way and more or less in agreement. Discursive orders are the results of a *permanent communicative production* in singular speech and action events which form a series of discourse acts of a particular kind. These, however, are not understood as spontaneous and chaotic phenomena, but as interrelated, co-referencing, and structured practices. With this definition, discourses are interpreted as instances of factual, manifest, observable, and describable social practice in social arenas that is present in the most varied natural documents, in oral and written uses of language, in images, and – more generally – in signs. The realization of discourses takes place to a great extent in the communicative action of social actors. They underlie this action as orientation, and in this way become "real" as a structural and signification relationship. A leaflet, a newspaper article, or a speech in the context of a demonstration may exemplify a discourse of city politics in various concrete forms and with differing empirical range, but with the same statement value. Qualitatively important transformations of discourses may, in very rare cases, be related to a single event of this sort. Much more frequently, they arise from the sum total of discrepancies in a kind of change from the quantitative to the qualitative effect. Discursive events, actors, practices, *dispositifs*, and patterns of meaning-making thus constitute the components in the materiality of discourses. For that reason, they are briefly discussed here.[1]

(a) *Discursive events* (statement events): These constitute the typifiable material form of statements in which a discourse takes shape. An *utterance* (*énonciation*), in Foucault's sense, is the concrete semiotic or communicative event, and in itself it is unique and unrepeatable. In contrast to this, *statement* (*énoncé*) refers to the level of the typical and typifiable: The same statement can be found in quite different utterances and situationally unique forms. Singular linguistic utterances contain discourse fragments. Without statement events, there are no discourses; without discourses, statement events cannot be understood, typified, and interpreted and so cannot constitute any collective reality. Peter Wagner (1990), following Anthony Giddens, talks of "discourse structuring" when the empirical typifiable form of this kind of structural relationship gradually emerges from the scattered statement events. This type of structure is therefore both structured, as a result of past processes of structure formation, and structuring, in respect of the scope of future discursive events. What actually happens is not a direct consequence of structural patterns and rules, but the result of the actively interpretive behavior of social actors using these orientation patterns. The rules guarantee the common ground, the connection between interactive and communicative processes. Their realization depends on a (comparatively) creative and performative act on the part of the social actors who depend on resources, and use, interpret, and further develop them for their practical purposes, strategies, tactics, and contexts in order to carry out their "moves". We may therefore summarize discourses as follows: They make available normative rules for the (formal) mode of statement production (e.g. legitimate communicative genres); they provide rules of signification for the discursive constitution of the meaning of phenomena; and they mobilize action resources and material resources (*dispositifs*) for the creation and dissemination of meanings.

(b) *Social actors*: in their discursive practice, social actors *make use of* the rules and resources for the production of interpretations that are available in the form of discourses or they react to them as *addressees*. Only then does it become clear how we arrive at a more or less creative execution of such practices. SKAD does not focus on the (social) phenomenological reconstruction of typifiable acts of conscious performance. Nor does it target "actual" motivations or the (inner) subjectivity of the producers of statements. Instead it remains on the surface of what is stated. But it is not overly hasty to confuse the discourse level as a constraint on the possibilities and limitations of utterances with the actual interpretive and action practices of social actors. Social actors are addressees of stocks of knowledge and the embodied values, but they are also, in accordance with the social-historical and situated conditions, *self-reflective subjects* who — in their everyday sense-making and meaningful behavior — interpret social stocks of knowledge as sets of rules in a more or less independent way (Hitzler, Reichertz, and Schröer 1999, 11 ff.). Social actors (whether individual or collective) are related to discourses in several ways: As those who adopt *speaker positions* (i.e. *statement producers*) and speak within a discourse, as *addressees of the statement practice*, and finally as implicit "talked about" actors, (re)presented and positioned in and by the discourse at hand. The distinction between social actors, who exist, in the first instance, independently of or outside discourses, and their "discourse-specific" configuration, which is effected in the form of adopting speaker positions that were prepared or "conquered" in discourses, is helpful to social science discourse research. Only in this way can we be aware that speakers in a discourse do not turn up out of nowhere, that they are never involved in it in their "entirety", or that not every social actor can adopt a concrete speaker position. The sociological vocabulary of institutions, organizations, roles, and strategies of individual or collective *but always social actors* may be used for the relevant analysis of the structuring of speaker positions in discourses. They may also bring about a transformation of the structural conditions through their reflexive and practical interpretations.

With reference to the *addressing of human actors* that is undertaken in discourses at the level of their structuring of knowledge, one may speak of different *subject positions*. Here social actors are "called upon" in different ways — for example, as instigators of problems, problem figures, objects of essential intervention, or potential customers in need of specific services. The different possibilities of participation that can be formulated in the context of urban spatial politics constitute, in this sense, subject positions for involvement. Another example of this might be the talk of tourists or investors who find one or the other feature attractive in a particular city and who ought to be appropriately attracted or encouraged in their wishes. The manner in which addressees who are spoken to like this adopt appropriate subject positions, or "subjectify" themselves in terms of their elements and rationalities, is therefore not preordained, but merits targeted investigations. Between the discursively constituted or implicit self and the actual empirical modes of subjectification there is an important difference. In this, *dispositifs* play a major role; that is to say, the institutional and organizational infrastructures offering concrete situative settings for relevant types of programming in the shape of buildings, trainers, round tables, demonstrations, seminars, technologies of the self, practical guides, laws, participants, and so on.

As role players in or addressees of discourses, social actors then pursue institutional (discursive) interests as well as personal "projects" and "needs". In this, they use both legitimate and illegitimate strategies, tactics, and resources for action. But what is pursued as an interest, motive, need, or goal is equally the result of collective bodies of knowledge and discursive configurations, in the same way as the perception and assessment of the ways and means that are used. This should in no way be confused with the control of sequences of action or discourse production by actors and their intentions. Of course, habitually or deliberately completed actions take place under structural conditions, or rely on them, even though these were not produced or controlled by the actors themselves. And of course, equally obviously, action has both intended and unintended, or foreseen and unforeseen, consequences, and as structural effects these become preconditions for subsequent actions.

SKAD therefore suggests the following basic conceptual distinctions for the "human factor" in doing discourses:

- (individual or collective) *social actors*, who are socially constituted and who function (temporarily) as *speakers or addressees* in discourses;
- the *speaker positions* that are made available in discourses;
- the additional *personnel of discourse production* and *world intervention* that is related to the *dispositifs* of a discourse;
- the *subject positions* that are made available in discourses;
- the concrete *modes of subjectification*, with which social actors as addressees adopt such subject positions in (maybe rather selective) "ways of their own".

(c) *Practices*: The term *practices* is used to characterize generally conventionalized action patterns that are made available in collective stocks of knowledge as an action repertoire; that is, a more or less explicitly conscious and frequently incorporated knowledge of prescriptions or scripts about the "appropriate" manner for performing actions. This knowledge may arise, on the one hand, in areas of social practice – that is to say, with reference to specific action problems or causes – by means of experimental or scrutinizing actions. And it may then establish itself there and develop further. Under modern conditions of social de-traditionalizing as well as extended observation and the reform of social practice based on expert systems, this is also guided, in certain essential elements, by the elaboration of theoretical models of action (Giddens 1991). For the purposes of SKAD research, it is helpful to distinguish the following forms of practices.

Discursive practices refer to performed patterns of communication that are involved in a discourse context. In discourse research, unlike in linguistic genre research, these are not only of interest in respect to their formal sequential structure but also very much on account of the formation rules distinguished by Foucault, their use by social actors, and their function in discourse production. Discursive practices are observable and describable typical modes of action in statement production (communication), the execution of which, as a concrete action, requires the interpretive competence of social actors, and which is actively formed by social actors. This is similar to the relationship between a statement (as the "type" dimension) and a singular concrete utterance ("the token"). In the context of the orders and orderings of space (what Martina Löw calls "spacing", cf. Löw 2001) that we are interested in here, we may cite as examples the production of media reports or pamphlets, but also draft legislation in provincial parliaments, the formulation of questions at public hearings, or the different textual genres on the web which present visions and experiences of a concrete city.[2] While such discursive performances are more or less part of the public sphere, more special-interest discourses occur in "closed arenas" such as a city's development department or in academic urban sociology, smart city promotion hubs, etc.

SKAD makes a conceptual distinction between these practices and so-called *discourse-generated model practices*; that is, sample patterns for actions that are constituted in discourses for their addressees. These include, for example – if we stick to the example given above – recommendations for good or even "best practice" in citizens' participation in political and administrative decision-making and regulations for "correct use of space" (where it is or is not permitted to organize a barbecue or drink alcohol, where nudity is or is not permitted, what the correct way to ride a bicycle is, how one behaves appropriately in a public space, what type of participation is or is not acceptable, and so on). As with the subject positions mentioned above, one should not be overly hasty here in proceeding from a model practice to its actual realization.

Finally, a third type of practice is sometimes important, and this – in relation to whatever discourse is of interest – may be described as practices which exist before a given discursive concern in a variety of social fields. To clarify this with a further example: If assemblies of people (lectures or discussions) are an important form of discursive practice in local politics, they only work if people can be present. This assumes, for example, that comprehensive technologies of mobility and associated practices are also in place (flying, taking the train, buying tickets, and so on), but it is difficult to describe these as practices of a local-political discourse (in fact, they might be the result of discursive meaning-making performed long ago about future traffic infrastructures). But since such forms of practice may, in particular cases, be important for questions of discourse research (for instance, in the transition of modes of communication to Internet culture) they are also kept in mind by SKAD.

(d) *Dispositifs*: Discourses react to (more or less) self-constituted problems of meaning and action. In the context of their own processing, or prompted by discourse-external "problems", they produce "definitions of the situation" and thereby bring together concepts of action. The social actors who are carriers of a discourse create an appropriate infrastructure of discourse production and problem-solving that may be characterized by the term *dispositif* (I prefer this term instead of "apparatus"). *Dispositifs* are the real means through which a discourse exerts power. *Dispositifs*, as "instances" of discourse, mediate between discourses and fields of practice. A *dispositif* is either the institutional totality of the material, action-practical, personal, cognitive, and normative *infrastructure* of the production of a discourse or the *implementation* of "problem-solving" devices which it offers in a specific field of practice. This includes, for example, the legal determination of responsibilities, formalized modes of procedure, specific objects (e.g. religious objects), technologies, instances of sanctions, training courses, and so on. These complexes of measures are, on the one hand, both solid ground for and components of a discourse and, on the other hand, the ways and means by which a discourse intervenes in the world. For example, the dual system of waste separation is part of the *dispositif* of a specific discourse of waste (Keller 1998). In connection with the implementation of the *models of practice* generated in the discourse, we may include web brochures, the statistical and process-related logistics of the description and collection of waste, large containers, directions for waste separation, or contracts with the local authorities. We also include the relevant legal ordinances, the employees of Duales System Deutschland (DSD) (the leading German private household waste recycling company), the countless green dots (as part of the Grüne Punkt scheme – the signs on products indicating collection by DSD), and finally also the practices of waste cleaning and separation that people subject themselves to. With reference to the level of discourse (re)production we might mention the discursive interventions of the various agencies of leadership, spokespersons, and press contacts as well as the research units, all of which disseminate and legitimize a particular construction of the waste problem in their expert opinions, brochures, and so on. The consideration of *dispositifs*, in particular, indicates that SKAD is not only communication, textual, or image research, but that it also takes into account, in the sense of new developments in actor-network theory and similar positions, the heterogeneous materialities that underlie discourse production as well as those that emerge as effects of their occurrence. For this reason, it can also be realized as case study, observation, even focused ethnography, taking account of the interrelation of statement events, practices, actors, organizational arrangements, and objects as historical and social-spatial processes with a greater or narrower outreach. *Dispositifs* are produced by social actors to the extent that they institutionalize a discourse. In this we are concerned with *orders of practice* or appropriate *ordering processes and efforts*, the actual scope of which probably matches the discursively projected model only rarely and which are all of a more or less transitory nature. It is only in conjunction with the investigation of discursive construction and the mediation of knowledge that questions concerning the relationship of subjective reception or acquisition and societal knowledge are appropriate. The processing of relevant questions can, therefore, also be conducted in the form of an *ethnography of discourse*.

Methodology

SKAD insists that discourse research is an interpretive activity, a discourse about discourses (Keller and Clarke 2018). Like all discourse research, it needs hermeneutics; that is, a theory of interpretation. Data have nothing to say in themselves, but provide answers to the questions that one asks of them. In addition, SKAD follows basic theories of the understanding of meaning and the human use of symbols. "Hermeneutics" is in no sense an enterprise that is reduced to the understanding of subjectively intended meaning. Of course, such positions do exist. But since the mid-1990s the term *social science hermeneutics* (Hitzler and Honer 1997) has been used quite generally to refer to the goal of reflecting on scientific processes of data interpretation and clarifying this as a task of interpretation and construction. This is also true of forms of data analysis that focus on the surface of what is stated, including programs of analysis which indeed are not at all interested in the investigation of "intended meaning" or "intention".

If one understands SKAD, in the tradition of Foucault, as an investigative undertaking that targets the historical development, stabilization, and modification of discourses and their power effects, then this kind of undertaking inevitably contains a strong element of *reconstruction* – for how else could one describe the attempt to analyze how something became what we perceive it to be today? For this reason every genealogical perspective proceeds reconstructively. Of course, instances of deconstruction are also built in: Data are split up, relations are "destroyed" and re-established, the obvious is stripped of its obviousness and embedded in new concepts and perspectives. A reconstructive type of discourse analysis corresponds absolutely to what Foucault had characterized as his ethos and the task of criticism – the analysis of the historical contingency of so-called "objective" and "inevitable" constructions of reality. This is "enlightenment" in its very traditional sense – pursued in order to expand the action repertoire of societies. Deconstruction and reconstruction are analytical processes that go hand in hand within SKAD.

SKAD makes a plea for a link between discourse research and various analytical strategies of the interpretive paradigm and interpretive methods. The analytical moves may, on the one hand, be directed at the *materiality of discourses* expressed in practices, actors, and *dispositifs* and, on the other hand, at the various aspects of content of the *knowledge-related (symbolic) structuring* of statements and the order of the world. I speak of *interpretive analytics* to stress that discourse research may relate together a variety of data formats and analytical steps, and so, for example, it may combine comparatively classical sociological strategies of single-case analysis or case study with detailed close analysis of textual data. Another reason why I talk of interpretive analytics is that, unlike other approaches in qualitative social research, SKAD is not interested per se in a single document (such as a text) as a coherent unit of meaning-making in itself, but proceeds on the basis that a document of this type is only articulating fragments of one or more discourses. This is why it breaks down the material surface unity of the texts and utterances and sometimes attributes the results of its analytical fragmentation and detailed analysis to different discourses. From this emerges, step by step, the mosaic of the investigated discourse(s) – and this is undoubtedly one of the most important modifications to the routine processes of qualitative social research.

With reference to the analysis of content-symbolic structuring of discourses, we may distinguish interpretive schemes, classifications, phenomenal structures, and narrative patterns, and these may be understood as components of interpretive repertoires. Here we are concerned with general concepts which derive from the sociology of knowledge tradition or may be adjusted to fit. Furthermore, they are particularly suitable as bridging concepts for research interested in investigating the adaptation of discursively created knowledge of social (e.g. professional) practices and everyday life.

- Interpretive schemes are patterns for meaning-making in reference to phenomena, situations, events, and actions in the world. The human body, for instance, may be interpreted as a robust machine or as a fragile organic assembly. "Mother's love" may come about between protective, emotional care and places of refuge or from the obligation to develop the acquisition of competence in early childhood (to mention only two different patterns). Technologies may be interpreted as safe or as (fundamentally) risky. Urban neighborhoods may be seen as ghettoes or as bohemian; an infrastructure project may be viewed as an expression of gigantism or as a responsible investment in the future. Interpretive schemes link the factual with the normative, or arguments with examples and moral conclusions. The "pattern" element points to the aspect of what is typical not only in factual data but also, for example, in subject positions that are used in concrete interpretive action. Such types are manifest in a variety of tokens; that is, symbolic-material forms – as a cartoon, as a sentence or related group of sentences, as a photograph, or as a linked set of practices. Meanings occur in discourses not as loose and isolated semiotic particles, but in the form of such interpretive types. And interpretive schemes can be seen as collective products, as for instance discursive condensation of historical processes that have become elements in the social stock of knowledge. Discourses frequently use a number of interconnected patterns; they offer, simultaneously, locations for the generation of new schemes/frames or for the transformation of existing ones.
- A second approach to discourses is found in the investigation of the *classifications* (and then of the qualifications) of phenomena that are undertaken in and through them. Classifications are more or less developed, formalized, and institutionally stabilized forms and processes of social typification. They do not order "given" reality into the "right" categories, but rather create the experience of this reality. The normal course of everyday routines consists of an uninterrupted process of classification using appropriate elements of our collective stock of knowledge. Like all types of language use, the use of language in discourses classifies the world, dividing it into specific categories that underlie its experience, interpretation, and action. Between discourses there are competitions about such classifications; for example, about how urban districts are to be interpreted with regard to preservation orders, what counts as a green area, what degree of air pollution is tolerable, what counts as correct or reprehensible behavior, what kind of waste separation should be undertaken, and so on. Specific consequences in terms of action practice are bound up with this. Their effect ultimately depends on whether they are institutionalized in the form of appropriate *dispositifs* and thereby give guidance in terms of action

practice. The analysis of discursively processed classifications has so far only been realized in a rudimentary way in discourse research.

- In addition, the concept of *phenomenal structure* addresses a third complementary heuristic tool at the level of the content structure of discourses. It refers to the fact that discourses, in the constitution of their referential relations (their topic), designate different elements or dimensions of their subject and relate them to a specific form or constellation of phenomena. This is in no way about the essential qualities of a discourse object, but rather about the "relevant" discursive attributes. The analytical reconstruction of phenomenal structures focuses on two aspects: The *dimensional reconstruction* is related to the general composition of the phenomenon. The dimensions of which the phenomenon is discursively constituted may, in a particular discursive field, at a given moment in time and sociocultural space, resemble or differ from other competing discourses. The *content* of the dimensions reconstructed in the first step may vary considerably according to the situational-contextual cause of a discursive event and also between discourses. In this respect, SKAD aims to examine the rules and principles of what is possible or legitimate content and how these are formed. It does not aim to provide a simple summary of everything that is said in original citations, although these may well be used for purposes of presentation or illustration. Phenomenal structures change over the course of time. Appropriate search strategies, therefore, cannot focus merely on the "freezing" of a specific phenomenal structure at a given point in time, but they make the development, change, and comparison of phenomenal structures their research object. This means that phenomenal structures make it possible to represent the *statements* of a discourse, and from this many additional questions (about its genesis, constellation of antagonists, *dispositif* consequences) can be addressed.

- One final instance of the content form of discourses should be mentioned here: We may characterize as *narrative structures* those structuring devices of statements and discourses by means of which different patterns (frames), classifications, and dimensions of phenomenal structure are related to each other in specific ways. The discovery of narrative structures (plots, storylines, central themes) in discourses may look at principle or subsidiary stories, general or generalizing narrations, from illustrative documentary or evidential stories. Narrative structures are not just simple techniques for linking linguistic elements together, but must be considered as a "*mise en intrigue*" (Paul Ricœur), as a configurative act of linking disparate signs and statements in the form of narratives, a basic mode of the human ordering of world experience. They constitute (debatable) "ways of the world as it is" by organizing stories with performing actors and agents, events, challenges, successes and defeats, good and evil, and so on.

Finally, in connection with the setting up and "processing" of a data corpus in the context of empirical discourse research, we may consider analytical strategies such as theoretical sampling, minimal and maximal contrast, coding, and many others, as useful guidance. These concepts are relevant both to the selection of data for detailed analysis and the analytical combination of results (cf. Strauss 1987; Keller 2013).

The discursive construction of spaces

Space, knowledge, and power are interconnected in many different ways. Foucault, in an interview, refers to the specific modern reflection that began in the 18th century on the construction of cities, in which questions of architecture are linked with those of the government:

> One begins to see a form of political literature that addresses what the order of a society should be, what a city should be, given the requirements of the maintenance of order; given that one should avoid epidemics, avoid revolts, permit a decent and moral family life, and so on. In terms of these objectives, how is one to conceive of both the organization of a city and the construction of a collective infrastructure? And how should houses be built?
>
> (Foucault 1984/1982, 239)

Symbolic and material orders of the spatial occur largely via discourses. Such a discursive construction of spaces does not exclude taking into account the material (*dispositif*) dimensions, consequences, or effects of such constructions in analysis. For example, if a city council decides to position its town "better" in a ranking for ecotourism or the knowledge industries, this is certainly a discursive event and practice which generates material effects, as, for example, squares have to be laid out, rivers "naturalized", or "industrial estates" developed. Politico-economic discourses concerning the competition for economic investors may lead to rotten infrastructures, because industrial taxes will have to be abolished. From a worldwide political discussion concerning sustainable development and citizens' participation arise meeting and voting *dispositifs* for a Local Agenda 21, that perhaps have impacts on urban infrastructures. In the name of Christian values and Western cultural heritage, citizens are mobilized against the building of mosques. City districts are protected against gentrification or are "developed" by investors. With regard to the spatial, be it "nature" or "culture", there is a merging of symbolic orders and materialities of the most diverse kinds. The *discursive productions of the imaginary of a place* are undoubtedly one of the principle subjects of discourse-analytical investigations. This area of phenomena includes politico-administrative initiatives in city marketing as well as policies of the symbolic upgrading and downgrading of city districts or struggles over the siting of industries, buildings or infrastructures. Spaces, locations, and cities therefore are an expression of *relations of knowledge* and *politics of knowledge*. "Natural" and "built" spaces, for example, are shaped in multiple ways by the multiple knowledges of experts and citizens. The former might, for example, use scenario techniques and prognostics to produce the future of a city's infrastructures along "the demands of tomorrow", while the latter inquire into a neighborhood's local histories in a struggle for the maintenance of the "traditional" shape of a local place, etc. Such politics of knowledge include politics of knowing; that is, *dispositifs* which allow one to establish legitimate statements (like citizen research, big data research, etc.) as well as regimes of justification, which allow, for instance, for the ordering of evaluations of "best practices", "what has to be done", what should be considered "cultural heritage", what is not allowed to be touched. Whether it is a matter of the restoration of landscapes, architectural ideas for good family life, designs for traffic or lighting in public areas, or restrictions in the budgetary situation of cities and other communities, this all relates to relations of knowledge and politics of knowledge, in which meaning-making, "factual" knowledge, imaginations, justifications, and other elements of knowledge coincide. The potential of discourse-analytical approaches to the investigation of relevant processes and phenomena of spacing is far from being exhausted.

Notes

1 For further theoretical rationale, analytical ideas, and methodological implementation, cf. Keller (2010/2005, 2011, 2012, 2013) and Keller, Hornidge, and Schünemann (2018).
2 Other forms of spacing include producing (Lefebvre 1994/1974) and walking the city (De Certeau 1984/1980), everyday practices of symbolic ordering (Segaud 2010), or sensual experiences of a city's atmosphere (cf. Sansot 1973).

References

Berger, Peter L. 1967. *The Sacred Canopy: Elements of a Sociological Theory of Religion*. New York: Anchor Books.
Berger, Peter L., and Thomas Luckmann. 1966. *The Social Construction of Reality: A Treatise in the Sociology of Knowledge*. New York: Anchor Books.
Christmann, Gabriela B., ed. 2016. *Zur kommunikativen Konstruktion von Räumen: Theoretische Konzepte und empirische Analysen* [On the communicative construction of spaces: Theoretical concepts and empirical analyses]. Wiesbaden: Springer VS.
Christmann, Gabriela B. 2022 "The Theoretical Concept of the Communicative (Re)Construction of Spaces". In *Communicative Constructions and the Refiguration of Spaces*, edited by Gabriela Christmann, Hubert Knoblauch, and Martina Löw, 89–112. Abingdon: Routledge.
Christmann, Gabriela B., Hubert Knoblauch, and Martina Löw. 2022 "Introduction: Communicative Constructions and the Refiguration of Spaces". In *Communicative Constructions and the Refiguration of Spaces*, edited by Gabriela Christmann, Hubert Knoblauch, and Martina Löw, 3–15. Abingdon: Routledge.
de Certeau, Michel. 1984/1980. *The Practice of Everyday Life*. Translated by Steven Randall. Berkeley: University of California Press.
Foucault, Michel, ed. 1982/1973. *I, Pierre Riviere, Having Slaughtered my Mother, my Sister, and my Brother: A Case of Parricide in the 19th Century*. Translated by Frank Jellinek. Lincoln: University of Nebraska Press.

Foucault, Michel. 1984/1982. "Space, Power and Knowledge". In *The Foucault Reader*, edited by Paul Rabinow, 239–256. New York: Pantheon Books.
Foucault, Michel. 1986. "Of Other Spaces". Translated by Jay Miskowiec. *Diacritics* 16 (1): 22–27.
Foucault, Michel. 1991/1966. *The Order of Things: An Archeology of the Human Sciences*. London: Pantheon.
Foucault, Michel. 2010/1969; 1972. *The Archeology of Knowledge and The Discourse on Language*. Translated by A.M. Sheridan Smith. New York: Pantheon Books.
Giddens, Anthony. 1991. *Modernity and Self-Identity: Self and Society in the Late Modern Age*. Cambridge: University Press.
Hitzler, Ronald, and Anne Honer, eds. 1997. *Sozialwissenschaftliche Hermeneutik* [Social science hermeneutics]. Opladen: Leske + Budrich.
Hitzler, Ronald, Jo Reichertz, and Norbert Schröer, eds. 1999. *Hermeneutische Wissenssoziologie. Standpunkte zur Theorie der Interpretation* [Hermeneutic sociology of knowledge. Cases for a theory of interpretation]. Konstanz: UVK.
Keller, Reiner. 1998. *Müll – Die gesellschaftliche Konstruktion des Wertvollen.* [Waste – the social construction of value]. Opladen: Westdeutscher Verlag.
Keller, Reiner. 2010/2005. *Wissenssoziologische Diskursanalyse. Grundlegung eines Forschungsprogramms* [The sociology of knowledge approach to discourse. Grounds for a research program], 3rd ed. Wiesbaden: VS Verlag.
Keller, Reiner. 2011. "The Sociology of Knowledge Approach to Discourse (SKAD)". *Human Studies* 34 (1): 43–65.
Keller, Reiner. 2012. "Entering Discourses: A New Agenda for Qualitative Research and Sociology of Knowledge". *Qualitative Sociology Review* 8 (2): 46–55.
Keller, Reiner. 2013. *Doing Discourse Research*. Translated by Brian Jenner. London: Sage.
Keller, Reiner. 2018. "Michel Foucault: Discourse, Power/Knowledge and the Modern Subject". In *The Routledge Handbook of Language and Politics*, edited by Ruth Wodak and Bernhard Forchtner, 67–81. London: Routledge.
Keller, Reiner. 2019. "New Materialism? A View from Sociology of Knowledge". In *Discussing New Materialism: Methodological Implications for the Study of Materialities*, edited by Ulrike T. Kissmann and Joost Van der Loon., 151–170. Wiesbaden: Springer VS.
Keller, Reiner, and Adele E. Clarke. 2018. "Situating SKAD in Interpretive Inquiry". In *The Sociology of Knowledge Approach to Discourse: Investigating the Politics of Knowledge and Meaning-Making*, edited by Reiner Keller, Anna-Katharina Hornidge, and Wolf Schünemann, 48–72. London: Routledge.
Keller, Reiner, Anna-Katharina Hornidge, and Wolf Schünemann, eds. 2018. *The Sociology of Knowledge Approach to Discourse: Investigating the Politics of Knowledge and Meaning-Making*. London: Routledge.
Keller, Reiner, Hubert Knoblauch, and Jo Reichertz, eds. 2013. *Kommunikativer Konstruktivismus. Theoretische und empirische Arbeiten zu einem neuen wissenssoziologischen Ansatz* [Communicative constructivism. Theoretical and empirical work on a new approach in the sociology of knowledge]. Wiesbaden: VS Verlag.
Keller, Reiner, and Inga Truschkat, eds. 2012. *Methodologie und Praxis der Wissenssoziologischen Diskursanalyse. Vol. 1: Interdisziplinäre Perspektiven* [Methodology and practice of the sociology of knowledge approach to discourse. Vol. 1: Interdisciplinary perspectives]. Wiesbaden: VS Verlag.
Lefebvre, Henri. 1994/1974. *The Production of Space*. Translated by Donald Nicholson-Smith. Oxford: Basil Blackwell.
Löw, Martina. 2001. *Raumsoziologie* [Sociology of space]. Frankfurt am Main: Suhrkamp.

Sansot, Pierre. 1973. *Poétique de la ville* [Poetics of the city]. Paris: Klincksieck.

Segaud, Marion. 2010. *Anthropologie de l'espace. Habiter, fonder, distribuer, transformer* [Anthropology of space. To live, to establish, to distribute, to transform]. Paris: Armand Collin.

Strauss, Anselm L. 1961. *Images of the American City*. New York: Free Press.

Strauss, Anselm L. 1968. *The American City. A Sourcebook of Urban Imagery*. Chicago: Aldine.

Strauss, Anselm L. 1987. *Qualitative Analysis for Social Scientists*. Cambridge: Cambridge University Press.

Thomas, William I., and Dorothy S. Thomas. 1928. *The Child in America: Behavior Problems and Programs*. New York: Knopf.

Wagner, Peter. 1990. *Sozialwissenschaften und Staat. Frankreich, Italien, Deutschland 1870–1980* [The social sciences and the state. France, Italy, Germany 1870–1980]. Frankfurt am Main: Campus.

4 Digital media, data infrastructures, and space
The refiguration of society in times of deep mediatization

Andreas Hepp

Introduction

One of the core insights made by media and communications research is that "space" is a communicative construction and that changes in "spatial experience" relate to media change.[1] In recent years, there has been a particular focus on how the experience of space transforms alongside digital media and their infrastructures – and most recently on how the Internet and data processing reconfigure our sense of space. For example, some studies have focused on the "space of flows" (Castells 2000, 407–459), the spatiality of digital communications that is superimposed over the "space of places", the rearticulation of urban spatial experience through mobile digital media (Bull 2007), the material aspects of translocal mediated networking (Hepp 2009), or the representation of space in code and data (Kitchin and Dodge 2011). We can see all these studies – and many more – as examples of how the experience of space transforms, at least in part, with media change.

One concept that is widely used in the social sciences to address these connections is mediatization. Mediatization as a concept implies an experience everybody is acquainted with in his or her everyday life: Technical communication media saturate a growing number of social domains which are, at the same time, radically transforming themselves (Hjarvard 2013; Krotz 2007; Lundby 2014). More specifically, mediatization refers to the relationship between the transformation of media and communication on the one hand and culture and society on the other (Couldry and Hepp 2013, 197). Digitalization has seen us emerge into a new stage of mediatization which we can identify as deep mediatization: an advanced stage of the process in which all elements of our social world are intricately related to media and their underlying infrastructures (Couldry and Hepp 2017, 7, 34).

In this chapter, I want to take this discussion as a starting point to address the question of how deep mediatization relates to a fundamental refiguration of society. My particular focus is, therefore, *not* just the transformation of space and spatial experience alongside deep mediatization (see Couldry and Hepp 2017, 81–100). Instead, I am more interested in placing the analysis of digital

DOI: 10.4324/9780367817183-6

media, data infrastructures, and space into a broader context; namely, that of the general transformation of society within the confines of deep mediatization. At first glance, this may appear as a detour from the discussion of media and space. However, as I hope to make clear, this is not so much a detour as it is a broadening of perspective: The transformation of space and spatial experience appears as a particular dimension of the transformation of society. To this end, I take up the arguments that I developed in my most recent book *Deep Mediatization* (Hepp 2020) (especially those in Chapter 4), on which my following arguments are largely based.

This chapter is structured as follows: First, I briefly point out that we should not regard deep mediatization as a process that would be homogeneous within a society or even across societies. Rather, we need a domain-specific analysis if we want to understand the transformations stimulated by deep mediatization, and a figurational approach offers the most useful analytical tools to achieve this adequately. I develop a figurational approach to media and communications in order to explain the ways in which we can imagine a refiguration of society as part of deep mediatization. In my conclusion, I contextualize ideas related to media and space through these theoretical and analytical frameworks. My hope is that in this way I can demonstrate the usefulness of understanding the media-related transformation of space in the broader context of societal transformation as it is shrouded by the processes of deep mediatization.

The domain specificity of (deep) mediatization

As I have argued elsewhere (Hepp 2020, 56–99), a processual perspective on media is required if we want to understand deep mediatization with any real rigor. The need for a processual perspective is even more essential when, instead of isolating individual media, we are, in fact, examining the dynamics between different media. We live in a media environment that is characterized by a media manifold in which we can understand the influences of media only if we consider them in terms of their interrelations. If we take these dynamics seriously, it is less appropriate to begin research on deep mediatization by investigating a (single) medium. We must consider our approach inversely: A helpful starting point for researching deep mediatization is, paradoxically, *not* media themselves, but the social domains in which they thrive and, *in a second step*, the role of media in the construction of a social domain.

An understanding of society as separated into different domains has a long tradition in the social sciences. The argument generally goes that our present societies are characterized by ongoing social and cultural differentiation.[2] Classical theorists in the social sciences have stumbled on various terms to categorize society's wide assortment of separate domains. Max Weber, for example, used the term "*Wertsphären*" (Weber 1988/1919, 611) to reflect this differentiation. Pierre Bourdieu (1993) described processes of differentiation by analyzing differences within and across social fields. In systems theory, the concept of the (sub)system as described by Niklas Luhmann (2012, Vol. 2, 4–27), also used by Jürgen Habermas (1992/1981), seeks to describe social differentiation. Phenomenology places emphasis on different (small) life-worlds (Luckmann 1970, 587; Schutz 1962, 207–259), with a certain relationship to the social worlds of symbolic interactionism (Shibutani 1955, 566; Strauss 1978). More recently, Luc Boltanski and Laurent Thévenot (2006) argued for different orders of justification. Irrespective of which theoretical approach one takes, the lines between them emphasizes the differences and tensions between "sub-spheres" in (late) modern societies. This point of view is shared by mediatization research when emphasizing the domain specificity of mediatization.

Mediatization research investigates "domain specificity" with varying theoretical conceptualizations and different approaches to scale; for example, the discourse on the mediatization of different social fields that follows Bourdieu's understanding of societal differentiation (Couldry 2012, 144–153), or the discussion on the idea of different (sub)systems in the spirit of Luhmann (Kunelius and Reunanen 2016, 378–381), or the tendency to explore social worlds by adopting phenomenological and symbolic interactionism (Hepp and Krotz 2014, 6–9). The use of the term "social domain" does not mean to suggest that these different theoretical conceptualizations are the same. Rather, in using the less theoretically loaded term "domain", emphasis is placed on the overarching argument that mediatization differs from one social sphere to another.

At this point we move to what is called "non-media-centric media studies".[3] The idea of this perspective is "to 'decenter' the media, in our analytical framework, so as to better understand the ways in which media processes and everyday life are interwoven with each other" (Morley 2007, 200). While this approach has already been developed in regard to electronic media such as television and radio, it has additional relevance for digital media and their infrastructures: In a moment in which digital media are "everywhere", a focus on just *one* of them prevents us from understanding how they influence different social domains as well as individual human beings. Only by taking particular social domains and individuals' involvement in them as a starting point can we fully grasp what media "do". In this way, we can reflect on the processual dynamics of media as embedded in meaningful units of everyday practice.

However, in adopting this perspective, we are confronted with another question: In the moment when individual media cease to be the starting point of our research and we focus instead on social domains and their media ensembles, there is a need to clarify how we want to comparatively describe the media-related transformation of these different social domains. This is exactly the point at which a figurational approach becomes most relevant.

Figurations, communications, and media

For a long time in the social sciences, there has been a tendency to conceptualize each social domain as a stationary object that would surround the individual human being (Elias 1978, 13). Society is thought of as consisting of entities such as the family, school, the workplace, and the state, each arranging themselves "around" the individual and imposing varying degrees of regulation and governmentality on members of society. In opposition to these crude categorizations, Norbert Elias argued for what we can call a "figurational" approach. A figurational approach understands the individual and society not as separate entities but as fundamentally entangled with each other (Elias 1978, 129). The various institutions that make up society only exist in and through the social practices of individuals, and the individual only exists in light of the social relations he or she engages in. Society does not consist of entities external to and independent from the individual from which he or she is isolated. All social institutions are made up of individuals who are oriented to and linked with each other in diverse ways. This is what we can understand as webs of interdependencies or, as Elias (1978, 15) put it, figurations. If we follow Elias' train of thought, the traditional institutions of family, school, and workplace are no longer positioned *around* individuals but are constituted *as* figurations of individuals. Each individual lives at the intersection of the different figurations he or she is involved with and develops an identity through the subjective narration of the self on the basis of his or her involvements.

Figurations are kept together by a shared orientation of practice among those who are comprise them. An individual can be a family member, a school member or a member of various organizations; how he or she acts is mediated through their overall "doing" within the figuration. The relations in these figurations operate also as power relations, which, typically, have a certain stability in the sense that the roles of those in power have corresponding relations to those of the less powerful. The chief presupposes the employee, the officer presupposes the soldier, the chief physician presupposes the nursing staff, and so on. There is a balance of power (Elias 1978, 15) that is to be considered as part of the whole.

In all, the term "figuration" is a "simple conceptual tool to loosen [the] social constraint to speak and think as if 'the individual' and 'society' were antagonistic as well as different" (Elias 1978, 130). The idea is to think of individual and society as one. Figurations are constituted in processes of interweaving (Elias 1978, 130) in which the practices of the people involved are interdependent on and oriented toward each other. With figurations, the "behavior of many separate people intermeshes to form interwoven structures" (Elias 1978, 132). A figuration is constituted in the continuously changing pattern of interaction between all those involved.

One specific approach to the concept of figurations is that, as an analytical tool, they transgress the distinction between the levels of micro, meso, and macro.[4] The idea of figurations is to have *one* analytical concept that can be applied to dyad or triad relationships as well as larger entities such as communities and organizations or even societies as a whole. For example, a figuration can be a school class being built by pupils and teachers, it can be the service team at a bistro, a company, a city, or an entire state. Different figurations overlap with one another but are individually distinct in their members' orientations of practice and their related frames of relevance. To reconstruct figurations analytically, we can begin with the orientation of practice of the individuals who form them and analyze the chains of interdependence (Elias 1978, 131) present between those individuals.

Today, many figurations are constructed around media use. The figurations of collectivities (families, peer groups, communities, etc.) and organizations (media companies, churches, schools, etc.) are entangled with specific media ensembles – that potentially transform the figurations of which they are a part. Deep mediatization also makes new figurations possible, such as online gatherings in chat threads or various other platforms. Some figurations are even entirely constructed around media technologies. For example, collectivities of taste (Passoth, Sutter, and Wehner 2014, 282) represent the calculation of groups of individuals brought together because they share product interests on online stores such as Amazon.

From a media and communications research perspective, we can consider each figuration as a *communicative* one: When it comes to the *meaningful* construction of each figuration, communication practices are incredibly relevant. Figurations are typically articulated through practices of communication that take place across a variety of media. Family members, for example, can be separated in space but connected through multimodal communication such as (mobile) phone calls, email, and sharing on digital platforms, all maintaining the everyday dynamism of family relationships.[5] Organizations, considered as figurations, are kept together through the use of databases and communication across an intranet as well as printed flyers and other media for internal and external communication.[6] Individuals are involved in these figurations according to the role and position they have in their respective actor constellations. Doing media and communications research from a figurational approach, therefore, allows us to connect in a productive way perspectives on individuals and the social domains they are part of via their entanglement with media.

There are three core characteristic features that make up a figuration (see Couldry and Hepp 2017, 66 f.; Hepp and Hasebrink 2017):

- A figuration contains a certain *constellation of actors* that can be regarded as its structural basis; that is, a network of individuals interrelated and communicating with each other.
- Each figuration has dominating *frames of relevance* that serve to guide its constituting practices. These frames define the orientation in practice of the involved individuals and, therefore, the character of the figuration.
- Figurations are constantly rearticulated in *communicative practices* that are interwoven with other *social practices*. In their composition, these practices typically draw on and are entangled with a *media* ensemble.

The figurational approach begins with an understanding of practices as an "embodied doing".[7] This "doing" is based on what Giddens (1984, xxiii) called "practical consciousness", which is learned in highly contextualized ways as part of our socialization; that is, our "growing into society". Based on this learning process, practices can be realized in a meaningful way *without* being discursively accessible for the involved individuals; that is, the individual cannot explain what they are doing even though they know how to do it. This stands for communication as much as it does for any other human practice.[8] Practical consciousness as an embodied capacity is generally understood as know-how, skills, tacit knowledge, and dispositions and is related to an individual's habits. Most practices are rooted in this practical knowledge, which has its own potential for situational creativity. If and when a "doing" does not require the full mental capacity of the individual, this opens up space for creativity.[9] Practices are anchored in the body and cannot be described as a mechanical obedience to rules. In this sense, practices of communication – with media but also without – are also embodied and should be considered in terms of their interrelation with other forms of practice.[10] With deep mediatization social practices turn into a media-entangled and, therefore, object-related practice. It is in the change of practices through which media mold figurations.[11]

Following this line of reasoning, we can understand *practices of communication* as complex and highly contextualized patterns of "doing". Or to put it differently: Certain forms of communicative action build up complex practices of communication as they are realized in a manifold media environment. Communication involves the use of signs that humans learn and adapt to during their periods of socialization and which, as symbols, are for the most part entirely arbitrary. This means that the meaning of communicative practices largely depends on social conventions. Communicative practices are fundamental to the human construction of reality: We "create" the meaning of our social world through multiple communicative processes; we are born into a world in which communication already exists; we learn the characteristics of this social world (and its society) through the (communicative) process of learning to speak; and when we proceed to act in this social world, our practices are always communicative practices (Christmann 2016, 2022).

A figurational perspective on society

When we adopt a figurational approach to an analysis of society, it is insufficient to only consider individual figurations. We have to clarify, then, how different figurations relate to each other and build what we call societies. As Nick Couldry and I have outlined elsewhere (see Couldry and Hepp 2017, 72–76), there are two basic ways in which figurations are interwoven with society: first, through relationships between figurations and, second, by their meaningful arrangements.

A basic interrelation of figurations emerges through the *overlap of actors* who are involved in an actor constellation of more than one figuration. If we take the basic examples already discussed, an individual might be part of a family, a group of friends, a company where he or she works, or the neighborhood where they live. There are various connections between these different figurations as certain individuals are involved in more than one of them at a time. What we can learn from network analysis is that particular individuals are in a powerful position because of the number and kinds of figurations they are connected to. Manuel Castells referred to these actors as "switchers" (Castells 2009, 45), people that can easily shift from one figuration's actor constellation to another. This is evident in the world of business where, for example, powerful people are involved in the figurations of different supervisory boards. But we also find this in other domains, such as on a local level where powerful people are part of the inner circle of different associations. Following these connections between figurations provides an ideal starting point for gaining an understanding of how power relations work. Therefore, adopting a figurational approach doesn't only mean that we are reconstructing the fragile power balances within a figuration; it also means that we are reconstructing the power relations *between* figurations.

A more complex interrelation between figurations occurs when we consider the *figurations of figurations*.[12] A figuration of a figuration emerges when an entire figuration becomes part of an actor constellation of another figuration. This might sound overly abstract, but there are obvious examples. From a political economy perspective, we can consider corporations like Alphabet (Google) as figurations of figurations: This corporation is a complex figuration in which other companies – which we again can understand as figurations – are part of the overall actor constellation – which again has figurations of different departments and so forth.

The concept of figurations of figurations refers to the idea of "supra-individual actors" (Schimank 2010, 327–341): figurations such as organizations or communities that have their own agency; but when we take a closer look at them, they often turn out to be figurations of figurations – a company, for example, is in most cases a figuration of different departments, which are again figurations of their own; then there is the possibility that this company is a "subsidiary" of a "parent company", which would lead to another level of nesting figurations. Conversely, a figuration of otherwise unconnected individuals *as well as* other figurations can become the figuration of a supra-individual actor when the practices of those involved result "in an orderly whole and not only occasionally but systematically build upon one another in such a way that an overall objective is pursued" (Schimank 2010, 329, author's translation). This includes corporate actors such as companies and state agencies as well as collective actors such as social movements and communities.

In addition to the relations of overlapping actor constellations, figurations can relate to each other through *meaningful arrangements of figurations*.[13] This means that figurations and figurations of figurations do not just exist – however interlinked – beside each other, but rather discourse positions the respective figurations within society. Again, this can be best explained with some examples. We cannot understand the power of a state government, for example, as a certain figuration by analyzing only its actor constellations, practices, and frames of relevance as well as how its actors relate to the actor constellations of other figurations. It is just as important to consider society-wide discourses on political decision-making and the legal framework which both *position* the government at the center of the state executive. It is discourses like these that make governmental decisions binding. Meanwhile other figurations are positioned within a society because of overarching discourses: discourses about the nuclear family as the fundamental societal unit (in contrast to the diversity of other forms of living together and raising children); discourses about schools and universities as principal educational institutions (in contrast to self-learning and grassroots approaches to education); discourses about companies and corporations as the main institutions of economic value creation (instead of the contributions of cooperatives and state agencies), and so on. If we consider particular societies, we find many of these discourses inscribed into legal frameworks. In all these cases, it is not just about the meaning of a certain figuration as such; it is about the meaning of the *normative* arrangement of figurations within society as a whole.

As far as media are concerned, the meaningful arrangement of figurations also refers to what Nick Couldry (2012, 22) has called the "myth of the mediated center"; that is, the generally shared assumption that the media (as in the totality of mass media) offer privileged access to the society's center: Media communicate what is "going on" in society and in the world. If we follow Roland Barthes (2000, 109), a myth is not an object, a concept, or an idea, but a more general form or mode of signification. The myth of the mediated center is related to mechanical and electronic mass media institutions which have positioned themselves at the "center" of society. In essence, this myth is based on the construction that everything which is of importance in a society takes place in and is represented by mass media. The point here is not to say that the issues, events, and matters which are the subject of mass media are not important. The point is that this myth is a powerful principle of discursive construction that excludes other areas of society. With the ideas of a national public and national media systems, this myth became well established not only in Europe[14] but also in other regions of the world.[15]

Mass media have for a long time been the space where imaginaries of the meaningful arrangements of figurations have been constructed. But with deep mediatization, "traditional" mass media change radically when they become digital. This does not mean that mediated discourses about the meaningful arrangement of figurations would cease to exist. However, instead of digital media like social network sites becoming divorced from centrally produced media flows and offering an "alternative social center" to that offered by the media, today's platforms and centrally produced media become ever more closely connected (van Dijck, Poell, and de Waal 2018, 31–72). For example, Wikipedia became well known because of articles in journals or newspapers, Facebook became a main point of access for single articles from online newspapers, and television shows refer to online discussions and YouTube influencers. Deep mediatization does not necessarily work against the articulation of a mediated center, but media become a "site of a struggle for competing forces" (Couldry 2009, 447) in constructing a mediated center of society.

Transformation as refiguration

In sum, figurations are a concept that help us understand the ordered interweaving of humans and the shared meaningful orientation of their practices. With deep mediatization, figurations are entangled with digital media and their infrastructures. The point mediatization research is concerned with is less a reflection on figurations and their interrelatedness as such and more on their transformation over time. Transformation at this point refers to a more fundamental, structural shift of human relationships and practices, something more than mere change in the sense that tomorrow is somehow different than today. From a figurational point of view, we are talking here about *refiguration*.[16] Broadly speaking, refiguration refers to the transformation of figurations and their interrelatedness to society. Refiguration is more than a functional adjustment; rather, it is a process that is related to questions of power, tension, and conflict. Any refiguration also refers to the significance of powerful individual and supra-individual actors as well as the power of discursive constructions about what character figurations *should* take. It is not just a question of how, for example, organizations change when digital media are introduced. It is also a question of how they should change – and how they orient themselves to normative discourses when implementing digital media.

As my discussion up to this point shows, in times of deep mediatization we are confronted with a particular form of transformation which we can call *recursive transformation*. "Recursivity" indicates that rules are reapplied to the entity that generated them (Couldry and Hepp 2017, 217). In many respects, the social world has always been recursive, at least insofar as it is based on rules and norms: We sustain it, and repair it when problems arise, by replaying once again the rules and norms on which it was previously based.[17] However, with deep mediatization, recursivity intensifies in tune with its fundamental relation to technology. Many practices are now entangled with digital media, and the algorithms they are based on involve a new kind of recursivity. Human practice, when incorporating digital media and their infrastructures, leads to a continuous processing of data, which in turn is the basis for adapting these media. A continuous technology-based monitoring of social practices takes place, the change of which is inscribed in the further development of these technologies, which, in turn, can stabilize particular practices and question others. We can see this happening in the way platforms like Facebook function: User behavior on these platforms is continuously tracked, which not only leads to friend suggestions but is also the basis for generating new functions. The fact that we are dealing with digital media as a process drives this recursivity. Developers' visions of sociality play an important role here: implicit ideas of how society *should* be inscribed into algorithms, which are then reapplied to social practices (Hepp 2020, 30–40, 67–84). Through these development loops, the transformation of society is in many ways a transformation that occurs through digital media and their infrastructures.

Taking this move into a deeply recursive transformation, nonlinear approaches to media-related transformation become more relevant as they are able to grasp these loops. In this way, approaches to "media evolution"[18] or "domestication"[19] are widespread. Quite different in their origins, these approaches share the idea of describing media-related transformation not as a diffusion of innovations (Rogers 2003) but as a complex sequence of various circles of change interlinking the production and design of new technologies with their appropriation and use. While the idea of refiguration as a recursive transformation shares with these approaches a thinking in cycles of development, its emphasis is quite different: Approaches of evolution and domestication are primarily focused on transformation in relation to a single medium and the interplay between its production and appropriation. The idea of recursive refiguration emphasizes the cross-media character and technological anchoring of today's societal transformations (see Figure 4.1).

This figure starts with the argument that from an actor's point of view, the engagement of the large technology companies, state agencies, and pioneer communities result in five trends of deep mediatization: the differentiation of digital media, their increasing connectivity, media's growing omnipresence through mobile communication technologies, the accelerating pace of media innovation, and the rise of datafication (Hepp 2020, 40–52). These trends are first of all manifest in the media manifold of societies' media environments, but they become more specific in particular media ensembles of social domains like schools and communities as well as individuals' media repertoires. In all these

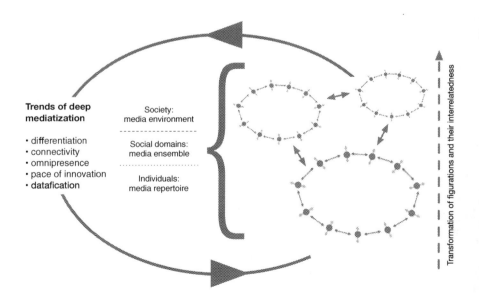

Figure 4.1 Refiguration as a circle of recursive transformation.
Source: Own representation.

cases, we must be aware that digital media are a process, institutionalizing and materializing human practices and generating the paradox of a constantly changing sense of stability.

However, as I have argued in this chapter, we cannot conclude that a uniform, linear transformation of society will emerge. Rather, it is always a concrete question of how certain figurations of people change alongside media change. What is decisive – as the right-hand side of Figure 4.1 demonstrates – is the way figurations change. Figurations are depicted as dots arranged in circles, with the dots visualizing humans as members of figurations. Their arrangement in circles is intended to illustrate the shared orientation in practice of people in their figurations, their frames of relevance, and to show clearly that the actor constellation of figurations is something more than an arrangement of pure networks. The arrows between the actors that form the circle of a figuration represent the practices that are constitutive for each figuration that is increasingly entangled with digital media and their infrastructures. The arrows pointing inwards and outwards visualize the power relations between the respective actors in relation to the figuration and its power balances, but also in relation to other figurations of which these actors are also part.

This visualization makes us aware of the complexity we are dealing with when we talk about refiguration. In order to grasp this complexity, internal and external perspectives on figurations are necessary: The *internal perspective* refers to the question of how individual figurations are transformed by deep mediatization. How do their actor constellations change? How do the underlying practices change? Are there changes in the frames of relevance and in the orientation of practice within the figuration as a whole? Are completely new figurations emerging? The *external perspective* is concerned with the question of the transformation of the interrelationship between figurations. What are the new interrelations between them? Which new figurations of figurations emerge? Are there shifts in the meaningful arrangements of figurations?

If one speaks of a "refiguration", these are the kind of questions that need to be discussed and clarified. Our outlook becomes increasingly complex, because we have to be aware that the changes take place not only within a society, but also across different societies. And we have to be aware that deep mediatization is only one aspect of the process of refiguration. Other metaprocesses of change – globalization, individualization, and commercialization are mentioned here as the main important examples – must also be taken into consideration. It is, therefore, always necessary to question the extent to which the transformation of digital media and their infrastructures is the driving force for change and where other driving forces may be more important (and maybe even the reason why media and their infrastructures themselves transform).

The semicircular arrows at the top and bottom of Figure 4.1 illustrate the overall recursiveness of the process of transformation. We cannot see the transformation of deep mediatization detached from the change of figurations and their interrelationship. To illustrate this, we can use a simple example: When individuals in their various figurations appropriate the already differentiated range of social media platforms, they support their connectivity and omnipresence as they generate data that are continuously processed; this glut of continuous data then stimulates and maintains these platforms' "innovation cycles". Therefore, the simple act of appropriating social media platforms can stabilize deep mediatization's core trends. However, the opposite is just as conceivable, at least in theory: Perhaps the individuals who form multiple figurations discard certain platforms without moving on to something else; in this scenario, the differentiation of digital media, their connectivity, omnipresence, pace of innovation, and increasing attachment to datafication could taper away.

From this perspective, the left side of Figure 4.1 can also be read as the cumulation of institutionalization and materialization: "New" media arise and are appropriated in certain figurations, but a more general stability arises when media-related institutionalizations and materializations emerge which then endure across different figurations and come together into overarching trends. And, as I have argued, because of their rootedness in algorithms, the loops of recursiveness tighten as deep mediatization progresses.

Conclusion

With this chapter, I set out to demonstrate how we can best describe the transformations associated with deep mediatization as a refiguration of society – a refiguration that has different characteristics depending on the social domain in which it takes place. In order to describe such transformations, it makes sense to develop an "internal view" on individual figurations and to analyze the transformations of their constellation of actors, their frames of relevance, and their constitutive practices that come about alongside their changing media ensemble. Alternatively, one can develop an "external view" that deals with the transformation of the interrelations of figurations in and across societies.

As this has shown, it makes sense to place an analysis of the transformation of space and spatial experience in just such an overarching perspective on the refiguration of society. Like deep mediatization in general, the transformation of space remains something that is first and foremost specific to individual domains. Precisely because they did *not* take this into account, many of the assumptions about a general spread of completely new network spaces, for example,[20] were too detached from the concrete transformations of deep mediatization to arrive at truly profound insights. A figurational approach means that general assumptions about refigurations are not so useful; rather, it is more expedient to examine particular refigurations in individual social domains and the individual relationships between them. Only in this way is it possible to arrive at reliable statements about the transformation of space.

With this in mind, the distinction of three kinds of basic patterns of transformation is particularly helpful when analyzing space and spatial experience. This relates, first, to patterns of the interrelatedness of figurations; second, to patterns in the transformation of existing figurations; and, third, to patterns in the emergence of new figurations (Hepp 2020, 115–144).

In times of deep mediatization, a *new interrelatedness of figurations* is evident in various respects. Digital infrastructures work across figurations, data are collected and analyzed from various figurations, and mythical discourses about how deep mediatization would change society exist globally. All this concerns more than mere questions of space, but, at the same time, always has something to do with its transformation: Today's digital infrastructures do not dissolve local rootedness; instead they afford an overreaching construction of social reality by means of automated data processing new spatial extensions. The spread of Airbnb, for example, and the influence of this platform on local processes of structuring spatiality (e.g. changes in neighborhoods through new rental models for tourists) only became possible through the existence of globalized digital infrastructures (Guttentag 2015). The mythical discourse of "digital purity" (Hepp 2020, 118) – an interrelating discourse that implies that digital technologies were immaterial, clean, and environmentally friendly – implicitly refers to space and spatiality: Imaginaries of data stored in the cloud (Mosco 2017), for example, are part of those kinds of constructions that push deep mediatization forward.

Furthermore, the *transformation of existing figurations* refers to questions of space. Examples of such transformations include the changing figurations of public debate, the transforming figurations of news production, and changing family figurations. In all these cases, their transformation is related to space: Today's public debate is partly delinked from the territorial structure of media's historical distribution areas (newspaper circulation and broadcasting, for example). Today, a mediated space for public debate is always, at least partly, deterritorial (Rigoni and Saitta 2012). For a long time, news production was restricted locally in broadcasters' and publishers' newsrooms. Today's news production takes place in much more varied figurations whose actor constellation spreads across different spaces and includes many actors that do not define themselves as journalists (Deuze and Witschge 2019). When it comes to families, one aspect of their transformation through deep mediatization is their translocal spread (in the case of migrants, this can occur across thousands of kilometers) alongside an intense communicative relatedness through digital media that makes new models of family life take on forms such as distant parenting (Madianou and Miller 2012).

Finally, the emergence of new figurations in light of deep mediatization is related to space. Think about "platform collectivities" (Hepp 2020, 138) – collectivities of humans that group around a digital platform, such as Uber drivers – which also represent a new form of spatial spread (related to globalized digital infrastructures). Another example is the financial markets which we can understand as a new, globalized space of trade that is purely based on digital media (Knorr-Cetina 2014). The same can be said of new forms of political gathering in the form of smart mobs and which can be thought of as a form of globalized connective action (Bennett and Segerberg 2013), as seen in Occupy Wall Street or Fridays for Future, which also represent new spatial models for the organization of political engagement.

The length of this chapter is limited so it has not been possible to go into too much detail. The examples I have laid out, however, should demonstrate that all these cases are not simply about spatial refiguration. To put it pointedly, we cannot understand the current transformation of space and spatial experience if we (a) do not consider it in relation to the progression of deep mediatization and (b) do not understand the transformation of space and spatial experience as part of a further-reaching refiguration of society. A figurational approach to deep mediatization should provide access to space and spatial experience that takes both points into account.

Notes

1 See, for an overview, Couldry and McCarthy (2004), Falkheimer and Jansson (2006) and Morley and Robins (1995). See also Christmann (2016, 2022) and Christmann, Knoblauch, and Löw (2022).
2 See Giddens (1984, 180–193), Hahn (2000, 14–24), Schimank (2013, 37–50, 131–149), and Winter and Eckert (1990, 142–151).
3 For more on this discussion on non-media-centric media studies, see Couldry (2005), Krajina, Moores, and Morley (2014), Moores (2016), and Morley (2009).
4 See Alexander et al. (1987), Ryan (2005), and Turner (2006).
5 See Greschke, Dreßler, and Hierasimowicz (2017) and Hasebrink (2014) as well as Lohmeier and Böhling (2017).
6 See Fredriksson, Schillemans, and Pallas (2015) and Fredriksson and Pallas (2017).
7 As far as this idea is concerned, I refer to the discussion on a practice approach in general but also that on media and communications research in particular; see Reckwitz (2002), Schatzki, Knorr-Cetina, and von Savigny (2001), and Couldry (2012).
8 However, methodologically, I do not share the position that we cannot gain access to practices and their meaning via interviews. Depending on the interview strategy, we can, in an indirect way, get access to (media-related) practices (of communication); for example, by asking questions about specific habits and everyday experiences (Klein, Walter, and Schimank 2017).
9 A good example of this is driving a car: As long as a novice driver has to concentrate entirely on shifting gears and using the clutch, driving is barely a part of his or her creative travel practice.
10 See Bourdieu (1977, 16–22) and Reichertz (2009, 118–120).
11 As the practice theorist Andreas Reckwitz put it, "writing, printing and electronic media mold social (here, above all, discursive) practices" (Reckwitz 2002, 253).
12 See Couldry and Hepp (2017, 73).
13 Again, see Couldry and Hepp (2017, 74–77) for a more detailed discussion of this concept.
14 Benedict Anderson (1983) has analyzed this in detail.
15 There are various historical analyses of this process taking place in Europe and beyond, supported by the emergence of mass media institutions and important national media events. See, for example, Martín-Barbero (1993), Scannell (1989), and Thompson (1995).
16 For a further reflection on the idea of refiguration, see Knoblauch (2017, 381–398) and Knoblauch and Löw (2017). While Knoblauch and Löw are interested in the

"spatial refiguration of the social world" and use the term "refiguration" to refer to the whole of society, my focus is the relationship between mediatization and the transformation of specific figurations.
17 This is one of the key arguments of ethnomethodology; see Garfinkel (1967) and Giddens (1984).
18 See Neuman (2010), Scolari (2013), and Just and Latzer (2017).
19 See Berker et al. (2006), Hartmann (2013), and Silverstone and Haddon (1998).
20 See, for example, the partly utopian analysis by Castells (2000) or early forms of web studies (Gauntlett 2000).

References

Alexander, Jeffrey C., Bernhard Giesen, Richard Munch, and Neil Smelser, eds. 1987. *The Micro-Macro Link*. Berkeley, Los Angeles: University of California Press.

Anderson, Benedict. 1983. *Imagined Communities: Reflections on the Origins and Spread of Nationalism*. New York: Verso.

Barthes, Roland. 2000. *Mythologies*. London: Vintage Books.

Bennett, W. Lance, and Alexandra Segerberg. 2013. *The Logic of Connective Action: Digital Media and the Personalization of Contentious Politics*. Cambridge: Cambridge University Press.

Berker, Thomas, Maren Hartmann, Yves Punie, and Katie J. Ward, eds. 2006. *Domestication of Media and Technology*. London: Open University Press.

Boltanski, Luc, and Laurent Thévenot. 2006. *On Justification: Economies of Worth*. Princeton, NJ: Princeton University Press.

Bourdieu, Pierre. 1977. *Outline of a Theory of Practice*. Cambridge: Cambridge University Press.

Bourdieu, Pierre. 1993. *The Field of Cultural Production: Essays on Art and Literature*. Cambridge: Polity Press.

Bull, Micheal. 2007. *Sound Moves: iPod Culture and Urban Experience*. London and New York: Routledge.

Castells, Manuel. 2000. *The Information Age: Economy, Society and Culture. Volume I: The Rise of the Network Society*. Oxford: Blackwell.

Castells, Manuel. 2009. *Communication Power*. Oxford: Oxford University Press.

Christmann, Gabriela B., ed. 2016. *Zur kommunikativen Konstruktion von Räumen: Theoretische Konzepte und empirische Analysen* [On the communicative construction of spaces: Theoretical concepts and empirical analyses]. Wiesbaden: Springer VS.

Christmann, Gabriela B. 2022. "The Theoretical Concept of the Communicative (Re) Construction of Spaces". In *Communicative Constructions and the Refiguration of Spaces*, edited by Gabriela Christmann, Hubert Knoblauch, and Martina Löw, 89–112. Abingdon: Routledge.

Christmann, Gabriela B., Hubert Knoblauch, and Martina Löw. 2022. "Introduction: Communicative Constructions and the Refiguration of Spaces". In *Communicative Constructions and the Refiguration of Spaces*, edited by Gabriela Christmann, Hubert Knoblauch, and Martina Löw, 3–15. Abingdon: Routledge.

Couldry, Nick. 2005. "Transvaluing Media Studies: Or, beyond the Myth of the Mediated Centre". In *Media and Cultural Theory*, edited by James Curran and David Morley, 177–194. London: Routledge.

Couldry, Nick. 2009. "Does 'the media' have a future?" *European Journal of Communication* 24 (4): 437–449.

Couldry, Nick. 2012. *Media, Society, World: Social Theory and Digital Media Practice*. Cambridge and Oxford: Polity Press.
Couldry, Nick, and Andreas Hepp. 2013. "Conceptualizing mediatization: Contexts, traditions, arguments". *Communication Theory* 23 (3): 191–202.
Couldry, Nick, and Andreas Hepp. 2017. *The Mediated Construction of Reality*. Cambridge: Polity Press.
Couldry, Nick. and Anna McCarthy, eds. 2004. *MediaSpace: Place, Scale and Culture in a Media Age*. London: Routledge.
Deuze, Mark, and Tamara Witschge. 2019. *Beyond Journalism*. Cambridge: Polity Press.
Elias, Norbert. 1978. *What Is Sociology?* London: Hutchinson.
Falkheimer, Jesper, and André Jansson, eds. 2006. *Geographies of Communication: The Spatial Turn in Media Studies*. Göteborg: Nordicom.
Fredriksson, Magnus, and Josef Pallas. 2017. "The Localities of Mediatization: How Organizations Translate Mediatization into Everyday Practices". In *Dynamics of Mediatization*, edited by Oliver Driessens, Göran Bolin, Andreas Hepp, and Stig Hjarvard 119–136. London: Palgrave Macmillan.
Fredriksson, Magnus, Thomas Schillemans, and Josef Pallas. 2015. "Determinants of organizational mediatization: An analysis of the adaptation of Swedish government agencies to news media". *Public Administration* 93 (4): 1049–1067.
Garfinkel, Harold. 1967. *Studies in Ethnomethodology*. Englewood Cliffs, NJ: Prentice-Hall Inc.
Gauntlett, David, ed. 2000. *Web.Studies: Rewiring Media Studies for the Digital Age*. London: Arnold.
Giddens, Anthony. 1984. *The Constitution of Society: Outline of the Theory of Structuration*. Cambridge and Oxford: Polity Press.
Greschke, Heike, Diana Dreßler, and Konrad Hierasimowicz. 2017. "Die Mediatisierung von Eltern-Kind-Beziehungen im Kontext grenzüberschreitender Migration" [The mediatization of parent-child relationships in the context of cross-border migration]. In *Mediatisierung als Metaprozess* [Mediatization as a metaprocess], edited by Friedrich Krotz, Cathrin Despotovic, and Merle-Marie Kruse, 59–80. Wiesbaden: VS Verlag.
Guttentag, Daniel. 2015. "Airbnb: Disruptive innovation and the rise of an informal tourism accommodation sector". *Current Issues in Tourism* 18 (12): 1192–1217.
Habermas, Jürgen. 1992/1981. *The Theory of Communicative Action. Volume 2: Lifeworld and System: A Critique of Functionalist Reason*. Boston: Beacon Press.
Hahn, Alois. 2000. *Konstruktionen des Selbst, der Welt und der Geschichte* [Constructions of the self, the world and the history]. Frankfurt am Main: Suhrkamp.
Hartmann, Maren. 2013. *Domestizierung* [Domestication]. Baden-Baden: Nomos.
Hasebrink, Uwe. 2014. "Die kommunikative Figuration von Familien: Medien, Kommunikation und Informationstechnologie im Familienalltag" [The communicative figuration of families: Media, communication and information technology in everyday family life]. In *Zukunft der Familie – Anforderungen an Familienpolitik und Familienwissenschaft. Tagungsband zum 4. Europäischen Fachkongress Familienforschung* [Future of the family – requirements for family policy and family science. Conference proceedings for the 4th European Conference on Family Research], edited by Marina Rupp, Olaf Kapella, and Norbert F. Schneider, 225–240. Opladen, Berlin, and Toronto: Verlag Barbara Budrich.
Hepp, Andreas. 2009. "Localities of diasporic communicative spaces: Material aspects of translocal mediated networking". *Communication Review* 12 (4): 327–348.

Hepp, Andreas. 2020. *Deep Mediatization*. London: Routledge.
Hepp, Andreas, and Friedrich Krotz, eds. 2014. *Mediatized Worlds: Culture and Society in a Media Age*. London: Palgrave.
Hepp, Andreas, and Uwe Hasebrink. 2017. "Researching Transforming Communications in Times of Deep Mediatization: A Figurational Approach". In *Communicative Figurations: Transforming Communications in Times of Deep Mediatization*, edited by Andreas Hepp, Andreas Breiter, and Uwe Hasebrink, 15–50. London: Palgrave Macmillan.
Hjarvard, Stig. 2013. *The Mediatization of Culture and Society*. London: Routledge.
Just, Natascha, and Michael Latzer. 2017. "Governance by algorithms: Reality construction by algorithmic selection on the Internet". *Media, Culture & Society* 39 (2): 238–258.
Kitchin, Rob, and Martin Dodge. 2011. *Code/Space: Software and Everyday Life*. Cambridge, MA: The MIT Press.
Klein, Juliane, Michael Walter, and Uwe Schimank. 2017. "Researching Individual's Media Repertoire: Challenges of Qualitative Interviews on Cross-Media Practices". In *Communicative Figurations: Transforming Communications in Times of Deep Mediatization*, edited by Andreas Hepp, Andreas Breiter, and Uwe Hasebrink, 363–386. London: Palgrave Macmillan.
Knoblauch, Hubert. 2017. *Die kommunikative Konstruktion der Wirklichkeit* [The communicative construction of reality]. Wiesbaden: VS Verlag.
Knoblauch, Hubert, and Martina Löw. 2017. "On the spatial re-figuration of the social world". *Sociologica* 11 (2): 1–27.
Knorr-Cetina, Karin. 2014. "Scopic media and global coordination: The mediatization of face-to-face encounters". In *Mediatization of Communication*, edited by Knut Lundby, 39–62. Berlin and Boston: de Gruyter.
Krajina, Zlatan, Shaun Moores, and David Morley. 2014. "Non-media-centric media studies: A cross-generational conversation". *European Journal of Cultural Studies* 17 (6): 682–700.
Krotz, Friedrich. 2007. "The meta-process of 'mediatization' as a conceptual frame". *Global Media and Communication* 3 (3): 256–260.
Kunelius, Risto, and Esa Reunanen. 2016. "Changing power of journalism: The two phases of mediatization". *Communication Theory* 26 (4): 369–388.
Lohmeier, Christine, and Rieke Böhling. 2017. "Communicating family memory: Remembering in a changing media environment". *Communications* 42 (3): 277–292.
Luckmann, Benita. 1970. "The small life-worlds of modern man". *Social Research* 37 (4): 580–596.
Luhmann, Niklas. 2012. *Theory of Society*. 2 vols. Stanford, CA: Stanford University Press.
Lundby, Knut. 2014. "Mediatization of communication". In *Mediatization of Communication*, edited by Knut Lundby, 3–35. Berlin and Boston: de Gruyter.
Madianou, Mirca, and Daniel Miller. 2012. *Migration and New Media: Transnational Families and Polymedia*. London: Routledge.
Martín-Barbero, Jesus. 1993. *Communication, Culture and Hegemony: From the Media to Mediations*. London, Thousand Oaks, and New Delhi: Sage.
Moores, Shaun. 2016. "Non-media-centric media studies and non-representational theories of practice". *New Media, Everyday Life and Social Change* 17 (2): 682–700.
Morley, David. 2007. *Media, Modernity and Technology: The Geography of the New*. London and New York: Routledge.

Morley, David. 2009. "For a materialist, non-media-centric media studies". *Television & New Media* 10 (1): 114–116.
Morley, David, and Kevin Robins. 1995. *Spaces of Identity. Global Media, Electronic Landscapes and Cultural Boundaries*. London and New York: Routledge.
Mosco, Vincent. 2017. *Becoming Digital: Toward a Post-Internet Society*. Bingley: Emerald Publishing.
Neuman, W. Russell. 2010. "Theories of Media Evolution". In *Media, Technology, and Society: Theories of Media Evolution*, edited by W. Russell Neuman, 1–21. Ann Arbor: University of Michigan Press.
Passoth, Jan-Hendrik, Tilmann Sutter, and Josef Wehner. 2014. "The Quantified Listener: Reshaping Providers and Audiences with Calculated Measurements". In *Mediatized Worlds: Culture and Society in a Media Age*, edited by Andreas Hepp and Friedrich Krotz, 271–287. London: Palgrave.
Reckwitz, Andreas. 2002. "Toward a theory of social practices. A development in culturalist theorizing". *European Journal of Social Theory* 5 (2): 243–263.
Reichertz, Jo. 2009. *Kommunikationsmacht: Was ist Kommunikation und was vermag sie? Und weshalb vermag sie das?* [Communication power: What is communication and what can it do? And why is it able to do that?]. Wiesbaden: VS Verlag.
Rigoni, Isabelle, and Eugénie Saitta, eds. 2012. *Mediating Cultural Diversity in a Globalized Public Space*. London: Palgrave Publishing.
Rogers, Everett M. 2003. *Diffusion of Innovations*, 5th ed. New York and London: Free Press.
Ryan, Michael. 2005. "Micro-Macro-Integration". In *Encyclopedia of Social Theory*, Vol. 1 (A–M), edited by George Ritzer, 501–503. Thousand Oaks, CA: Sage.
Scannell, Paddy. 1989. "Public service broadcasting and modern public life". *Media, Culture & Society* 11 (2): 135–166.
Schatzki, Theodore R., Karin Knorr-Cetina, and Eike von Savigny, eds. 2001. *The Practice Turn in Contemporary Theory*. New York: Routledge.
Schimank, Uwe. 2010. *Handeln und Strukturen. Einführung in die akteurstheoretische Soziologie*, 4. Aufl. [Action and structures. Introduction to actor-theoretical sociology, 4th ed.]. Weinheim and Basel: Juventa.
Schimank, Uwe. 2013. *Gesellschaft* [Society]. Bielefeld: Transcript.
Schutz, Alfred. 1962. *Collected Papers I: The Problem of Social Reality*. The Hague: Martinus Nijhoff.
Scolari, Carlos A. 2013. "Media evolution: Emergence, dominance, survival, and extinction in the media ecology". *International Journal of Communication* 7: 1418–1441.
Shibutani, Tamotsu. 1955. "Reference groups as perspectives". *American Journal of Sociology* 60 (6): 562–569.
Silverstone, Roger, and Leslie Haddon. 1998. "Design and the domestication of information and communication technologies: Technical change and everyday life". In *Communication by Design: The Politics of Information and Communication Technologies*, edited by Robin Mansell and Roger Silverstone, 44–74. Milton Keynes: Oxford University Press.
Strauss, Anselm. 1978. "A social world perspective". *Studies in Symbolic Interaction* 1: 119–128.
Thompson, John B. 1995. *The Media and Modernity. A Social Theory of the Media*. Cambridge: Cambridge University Press.
Turner, Jonathan. 2006. "Micro-Macro Theory". In *The Cambridge Dictionary of Sociology*, edited by Bryan S. Turner, 383–384. Cambridge: Cambridge University Press.

van Dijck, José, Thomas Poell, and Martijn de Waal. 2018. *The Platform Society: Public Values in a Connective World*. Oxford: Oxford University Press.
Weber, Max. 1988/1919. *Gesammelte Aufsätze zur Wissenschaftslehre*. 7. Aufl. [Collected essays on science teaching. 7th ed.]. Tübingen: Mohr Verlag.
Winter, Rainer, and Roland Eckert. 1990. *Mediengeschichte und kulturelle Differenzierung. Zur Entstehung und Funktion von Wahlnachbarschaften* [Media history and cultural differentiation. On the emergence and function of neighborhoods]. Opladen: Leske + Budrich.

5 Cities, regions, and landscapes as augmented realities

Refiguration of space(s) through digital information technologies

Gertraud Koch

Introduction

Information technologies are today ubiquitous. The universal use of mobile phones is one, perhaps the most visible, indicator of this, but this is nevertheless only a small part of a manifold and complex phenomenon. Information infrastructures, wired and wireless, are expanding their networks across the globe and provide a variety of modes for accessing information and for communicating. Global positioning systems (GPS), the web, satellite and mobile phone networks – even in the most remote corners of the world, such information infrastructures have been implemented successfully and enable more and more new forms of transmitting information and of communication,[1] leading to considerable changes in how one can experience and act in time and space. Still, by contrast to what was initially expected to occur in connection with the global coverage of digital information technologies (Meyrowitz 1985), the global flow of information has not led to a decrease in the significance of local or direct face-to-face communication. On the contrary, modes of connecting global information flows to localities in cities, regions, and landscapes have become manifold through the ubiquity of digital and locative media (Dourish and Bell 2014). Through these infrastructures, a variety of local information can be accessed and an extensive investigation of one's current position can be carried out in real time and with regard to a range of specific interests, bridging time and space in the process. Locative media play a key role for the spatiality of social practices and the refiguration of spaces, as outlined by Knoblauch and Löw (2017) as well as by Christmann (2016, 2022) and Christmann, Knoblauch, and Löw (2022).

The augmentation of spaces with information is a common and long-standing spatial practice that did not first emerge with the development of digital information technologies. Nevertheless, the extensive provision of these technologies has enormously increased the means for facilitating such augmentation, resulting in new attention being paid to this spatial practice. Adding information to spaces and augmenting them in this particular way has a long tradition; for example, in the installation of information and commemoration

DOI: 10.4324/9780367817183-7

boards, religious shrines and wayside crosses, artists' works and installations, and billboards and advertising pillars (Huhtamo and Parikka 2011; Huhtamo 2009). With digital information technologies, the options for augmenting spaces have been enhanced, and new, more flexible textures of information can be laid over spaces (Lindner 2008), such as directions being visually superimposed on the real scene on the display of a navigation system. Here, actual spaces dynamically blend with digital information in real time.

Meanwhile, this and similar augmented reality (AR) applications have become a rather common phenomenon in diverse areas of everyday life, such as museums, tourism, climate communication, sports and leisure activities, artistic interventions, marketing, and traffic management. Moreover, AR technologies engage not only one's sense of vision, but also one's hearing and potentially also one's sense of touch and smell (Bederson 1995; Dörner et al. 2013, 33 ff.).

AR as a technology provides particular means for the refiguration of spaces through sociotechnical practices. This contribution therefore explores the ways in which digital information technologies augment physical spaces. The technology of AR will be distinguished from the social reality emerging in the context of its application. This difference will be marked by using the plural for the sociotechnical constructions of spaces that merge AR technology with contexts of everyday life. Accordingly, the difference between the technical processes of providing information will be distinguished from the social processes. The latter always results from communicative intent and will thus be designated as such throughout the chapter. Still, both dimensions – the technical process of providing information and the social process of communicating it – are understood here as two aspects of the same sociotechnical setting. To understand how digital information technologies refigure spaces, one must start by reflecting on the spatial dimensions of two key concepts: AR and mixed reality. The technical definitions of AR and mixed reality use a vocabulary shared by social and cultural theory; in particular, the terms "virtual", "actual", and "real" require critical discussion and differentiation of their theoretical foundations. This is also true for the concepts "digital" and "analogue", which are used with varying connotations in different areas, as well as with fuzzily defined meanings in everyday language, and which therefore need specifying when used in academic research. After these conceptual clarifications, the chapter will continue with an overview of recent applications to which AR has been put. The main focus here will lie on how AR contributes to the social construction of reality and the ways such new socio-technological arrangements of AR demand a re-conceptualization of spatial theory.

Concepts and their spatial dimensions

Augmented reality and mixed reality: Merging actual and media spaces

AR belongs to so-called "mixed reality" and are therefore a fusion of virtual and actual environments. Actual environments, which are perceived without media, are different from virtual environments or cybernetic spaces, which are only experienced through media; for example, in computer game environments.

Different levels of the mediatization of spaces can therefore be distinguished along a continuum from reality to virtuality, as outlined conceptually by ergonomics researchers Paul Milgram and Fumio Kishino (1994). AR is located more strongly in actual environments, an example being a pilot wearing a data helmet and computer glasses that simulate a landscape lying ahead of him. On the other hand, augmented virtuality is located more strongly in virtuality; for example, in a virtual conference room with images of the participants visible by means of a webcam or a runner and tracked in real time via an Internet platform. Thus AR and augmented virtuality represent different intensities of mediatization on the reality–virtuality continuum. The input from digital media augments environments with digital information and thus changes our perception of them. Since wearable digital devices – smartphones, biosensors for tracking sports activities, Google glasses, etc. – allow ubiquitous and mobile computing when combined with wireless Internet, mobile phone networks, and GPS, the augmentation of spaces has become an increasingly relevant information technology. In essence, this consists of tracking technologies that follow an object moving in space, display technologies for merging physical and digital spaces, and input and interaction technologies, such as a smartphone's touchscreen or camera, as interfaces. As a media technology, AR is always working with spatial references and is thus materially connected to a particular space, or particular properties within it, either through sensors and transmitters (installed in spaces or the devices themselves) or through GPS data (Billinghurst, Clark, and Lee 2015). It is a socio-technological construction of social reality.

Virtual, actual, and real: The media character of mixed reality technology

Moving away from a technological to a social constructivist perspective on mixed reality, however, the opposition of "real" and "virtual" as poles of a continuum is not very convincing given that virtual environments are also part of reality and are thus as "real" as environments accessible without media support. The cultural and digital anthropologist Tom Boellstorff speaks about "actual" rather than "real" environments with the intention of introducing a new perspective on the different ways of being "real" and of constructing reality (Boellstorff 2008). With the term "actual", he shifts the emphasis to the material basis of constructing realities as the most crucial characteristic and distinctive element of both ends of the mixed reality continuum. While the "actual" is constructed materially with things, the "virtual" is constructed symbolically through media. It is perfectly apparent that virtual reality depends on material bases too, as has been pointed out by Marilyn Strathern. In her critique of the idea of a virtual society, she emphasizes the socio-technical quality of virtuality with its information technology infrastructures and devices (see Woolgar 2002, 302–313).

Acknowledging the socio-technical quality of "virtual spaces" converts them from spaces into subunits of digital media. Only metaphorically are virtual realities spaces; principally, they are media technologies with the capacity to refer to spatial dimensions in particular ways. We observe a multitude of spatial references in computer games, maps on the Internet, websites of cities, regions, and landscapes as tourist destinations, virtual tours through museums and collections, locative functions on smartphones and other digital devices, and packages equipped for tracking via QR codes or other information items. Such media developments are not random, but are directed by investment, motivation, and power relations (Williams 1992/1972; Bolter and Grusin 2000). In this context, the post-phenomenological approach of Don Ihde is also significant, as it emphasizes the role of media as a co-constructor of reality and highlights the way in which digital technologies shape the human perception of reality by transforming data into visualizations that then become meaningful through interpretive processes (Ihde 1993; Verbeek 2001).

Mass media, in particular those with international coverage, are "machineries of meaning" according to Ulf Hannerz, an anthropologist of globalization. This can be said of the Internet as well. Going beyond their traditional media function, digital media and Internet platforms provide new options for cultural production and circulation (Hannerz 1992). Audio, photo, video, text, documentation, fiction, or simulation may all be created and shared with a potential mass audience. This provides media amateurs with a means of public communication to an extent not previously known. On the whole, AR as a digital media technology has initiated a re-mediation (Bolter and Grusin 2000) of other mass media; that is, a reinvention of their uses and functions in an expanded media ecology. Today, the function of "traditional" mass media as machineries of meaning, produced and distributed by large global media companies, is challenged by digital media and their capacity as machineries of imagination to be (co-)created and motivated by the practices of "digital media users" themselves.

Digital and analogue

"Digital" has become a buzzword and a signifier for all kinds of information-technology-related innovation perceived as epoch-making (Negroponte 1998). In essence, it refers to an ongoing media change in the direction of computerization. Some of the proponents of such an understanding of digital media change even speak about "post-digitality", seeing the principle of digital media as ubiquitously established. From this perspective, the revolutionary phase is over and the digital belongs to the "natural" equipment of "digital natives", while the analogue is more and more integrated into digital environments. The digital is a system of binary distinctions. Media theorist Hartmut Winkler (2004, 118 f.) emphasizes the "isolating" nature of the processes in the medium of the computer, which does not allow for ambiguity, except when its results

80 *Gertraud Koch*

are subsequently interpreted by humans. In a media archaeology approach,[2] Wolfgang Ernst points out that for the question of the digital and how we study it today, the computer itself is the model and guides our inquiry of the digital. Within the computer, the digital is represented by a binary system – based on switches that are either "on" or "off", "one" or "zero" – and is paired with the so-called von Neumann architecture (Ernst 2004), introduced in 1945. In von Neumann architecture, the mode of a computer's operation is no longer built into hardware, but is based on software, allowing for quicker modification. The term "analogue" is often presented as the opposite to "digital". This is, however, a rather incomplete picture of the digital and a contested one, too, because it refers to the very narrow and specific idea of the digital as a synonym for information technology.[3] Nevertheless, digital media represent the convergence of all media types as well as an exponential acceleration of information transmission and real-time communication across the globe. It thus brings with it a historically new quality, bridging time and space (Williams 1992/1972). In many ways, digital information technologies provide new media and thus new means for augmenting physical spaces with information and communication.

Augmented reality as a socio-technological refiguration of spatial experiences and behavior

AR as a socio-technological construction of reality conjoins social and material dimensions of spaces in specific ways. This socio-technological conjunction by means of AR applications is explored in a broad variety of areas for the enhancement of physical spaces with information. The list of areas of application has been growing over the years; it holds such diverse areas of application as environmental planning, edutainment, games and artistic content, automotive safety, product development and manufacturing, the military, tourism and culture, geographic information systems (GIS), three-dimensional geodata, and the medical sector (Dubois et al. 1999; Sanna and Manuri 2016). This chapter cannot give a comprehensive overview of all AR applications, but provides a compilation of exemplary augmented realities emerging from the implementation of AR as a media technology in a specific spatial environment. Rather than looking at technological modes of implanting AR, it will address the different purposes and motivations for augmenting spaces through information and communication.

In urban planning, AR is explored as a new media format. It is more dynamic than nondigital models and allows for the recording of motion in spaces through the use of specialized devices in the form of tablets and screens that combine tangible and visual interfaces for three-dimensional visualization, supported by computer-aided design tools. Another application in this field is the augmentation and reconstruction of architecture through image-based modeling, rendering, and lighting. It provides new alternatives for the visualization of design ideas or of the appearance of a place in ancient times and, thus, provides additional conceptions to what was formerly represented in plans and models. AR technology is often a transitional format on the way to virtual reality representations (Fisher, Dawson-How, and O'Sullivan 2001; Folz, Broschart, and Zeile 2016; Zeile 2011).

The enhancement of modes for stipulating and sharing conceptions of spaces, and for envisioning past or future spatial settings, is also a strong motivational factor in the arts, culture, and tourism. Common examples for these fields of application are provided by automated tour guides, in and outside of museums, in the form of audio or visually augmented reality (Bederson 1995; Damala et al. 2008). Artistic interventions with AR use cities as canvasses for the appropriation and redefinition of urban spaces; for example, by hacking billboards and advertising screens to display noncommercial information (Biermann, Seiler, and Nunes 2011; Gaspar and Mateus 2015).

A key feature of AR is the enhancement of sensual experiences beyond those available in a particular spatial context (Demarmels 2011; Dörner and Steinicke 2013, 33 ff.), which is especially relevant to educational settings. Here, AR is introduced in a variety of subject areas; for example, to explore the mathematical relations between objects (Jaramillo et al. 2004; Filler, Ludwig, and Oldenburg 2010), in aesthetic education (Billinghurst, Clark, and Lee 2015, 209 f.), and in vocational training to facilitate learning at the workplace through its augmentation with digital information (Fehling 2017). The involvement of multiple senses is also a crucial motivation for the use of AR in marketing. This induces the closer attention and involvement of potential customers (Billinghurst, Clark, and Lee 2015, 217 f.).

Moreover, AR fosters the personalization of spaces in diverse ways. Blending spaces with digital content – for example, through monitor AR – provides new options for user-centered indexing and the opening up of spaces. In fact, it becomes quite a simple operation when information can be flexibly projected through AR into actual spaces. The perception of a space can be stipulated according to individual and group backgrounds. More playful leisure-oriented artistic spatial interventions also become possible; for example, in the projection of a digital image of oneself onto a sculptural base, replacing the original figure. The computer game Pokémon GO is another example of the individual- and group-oriented opening up of spaces by AR. Players collect digital game figures virtually positioned in public spaces such as parks, squares, trees, and much else besides.

A further motivation for the implementation of AR is the reconnaissance of spaces in unclear territory, often for military purposes but also with relevant applications in automotive safety, such as for identifying pedestrians in the dark through night vision (Sanna and Manuri 2016). In these fields, the guiding motivation for developing AR solutions is the superiority of sensor and tracking technologies that are above human perception capacities and the liberation from dependency on human attention in a situation of fuzzy information.

In the course of this, the fluidity of the boundaries between AR, augmented virtuality, and virtual reality are to be considered. Augmented realities are maybe not the most relevant application that mixes digital information and actual spaces at the current state of technological development. Augmented virtuality now seems to be more frequently present in everyday life, most visibly in the diverse tracking applications and their documentation on Internet platforms: health data, fitness data from biosensors, transaction data from joggers, boats, logistic goods, and all kinds of other belongings in the Internet of Things, traffic data on Google Maps, sensor-based mapping in GIS, medical applications, smart city applications, and so on. The tracking of data and their visualization on Internet platforms is relevant in many areas of life.

The large variety of AR applications offers new options for the visualization of design ideas or of a place in past times, and they thus provide methods of representation that go beyond static plans and models. The visualization of virtual content in actual spatial contexts together with real-time motion is a mode of sharing conceptions of spaces that makes them available to experience-oriented perception and discursive negotiation. They are an enhancement of sensual experiences and information beyond those present within a space, which provides people with further options for action. Sometimes, as already noted, AR applications are installed because of the superiority of sensor and tracking technologies by comparison with human perceptual capabilities or to support humans in situations when information is unclear or present in overwhelming quantities. AR is a field of intense exploration and further applications will emerge. At present, augmented virtuality's blending of actual, real-time information on digital platforms seems more prevalent than AR. Since the boundaries along the mixed reality continuum are fluid, augmented virtualities have been considered here too.

Conclusion: Augmented reality and mixed reality in spatial theory

Digital images, graphics, texts, and information are being merged with the physical spaces of everyday life, and these spaces are being placed in new contexts of interpretation, sense-making, knowing, and imagination. Although AR technologies are spreading slowly, they are gradually becoming part of everyday life. It is therefore possible that people sharing a particular space will experience it in different ways as a result of diverse augmentations. Media permeate today's spaces in manifold ways, giving them a specific socio-technical character that has not yet been considered in socio-spatial theory. AR and augmented virtuality are a socio-material infrastructure that relates actual and virtual entities to one another. This can be viewed as a kind of hypertextualization of cities, regions, and landscapes; it links spaces with digital information via interfaces, providing access to further materials for sense- and meaning-making. The implementation of mixed reality, as sociotechnical and symbolic structures, is a particular spatial practice that at the same time facilitates others, including those illustrated above. The particular contribution of AR as a media technology to augmented realities as socio-material constructions of space calls for additions to spatial theory in three dimensions: the material, the symbolic, and the practical.

Socio-technological dimensions of mixed reality

The material dimensions of AR cannot be overlooked. They are a precondition for augmenting actual spaces with virtual content. Digital information technologies are necessary, either in the form of data infrastructures and sensor technologies that furnish spaces (Internet hotspots, energy-charging stations, etc.) or as mobile devices for accessing information (such as mobile phones, head-mounted displays, or glasses). The city with its specific living spaces, everyday life, and urban qualities is first refigured by the digital infrastructures of AR and can then be experienced through them. With these technologies, the material structure of the city provides specific forms for living and experiencing its spaces as well as for expressing oneself as a citizen or visitor. At the same time, inhabitants must acquire specific knowledge and new skills for dealing with the new technologies – besides simply being able to use them – that require users to keep an eye on updates, new apps, data security, functionality of devices, business models, and the price development of new technologies. Spatial theory considers the material dimensions of cities, regions, and landscapes conceptually in various ways: Such conceptual approaches include the materialization of the social in architecture and urban development (Bourdieu), the habitus and the inner logic (*Eigenlogik*) of cities in analogy to the incorporation of socio-material conditions in the human habitus (Berking and Löw 2008; Lindner 2008), spacing as materialization of meaning within and outside spaces (Löw 2013), and infrastructure studies as the study of how materiality and social practices refer to each other (Bowker et al. 2010; Horst 2013). They are important starting points for further theorizing on how mixed reality refigures spatial properties and spatiotemporal relations.

Symbolic dimensions of mixed reality

The making of spatial hypertexts through augmented realities and augmented virtualities enhances the bandwidth of symbolic expression and thus of discursive utterances, contributing to ways in which a city is imagined by designing and sharing new narrative spaces about places (Liestol 2011). These narrative spaces create imaginations and make them available as experiences in and about spaces, as the actual and the imaginary space are accessed in the same location. The connection of actual and fictional information in real-time motion and their multisensory character provide an immediacy to the experience, a quality that is exceptional in comparison to other media content. Mixed reality is an efficient means of sharing space-related information and conceptions with others and, thus, of making them a subject of discourse. Here, it provides textures for approaching cities, regions, and landscapes in a way that communicates points of view while opening up experiences to sense- and meaning-making processes. AR as a texture may thus provide the means for developing shared understandings of spaces and their future development; AR therefore also provides exploratory spaces of a remixed reality (Lindlbaur and Wilson 2018).

It provides infrastructures for envisioning and negotiating conceptualizations of future development and uses of a space. For an integration of the symbolic dimension into spatial theory, studies are required that facilitate an empirically grounded understanding of what has so far been discussed philosophically under the umbrella of post-phenomenology.

Practices of mixing realities in spaces

AR sociotechnical infrastructures and spatial hypertexts can implement structures that allow new spatial practices within a space (such as the AR-based gaming scenarios of Pokémon GO in urban areas) and merge urban and virtual gaming spaces (de Souza e Silva and Sutko 2009). The appropriation of space is guided by the technical means and their availability. Spaces are experienced differently when AR-related technologies are implemented and then refer back to practices, such as the augmentation of spaces with screens at stations displaying information about the time of the next available means of transport, based on real-time tracking of each individual vehicle.

Furthermore, telepresence, digital proximities, and cocooning can interfere with face-to-face situations in public spaces and may turn them into private spaces; for instance, when we distance ourselves through media usage: listening to music with headphones on a train, staring at one's laptop in a café, talking on one's mobile phone on a park bench (Licoppe 2004; Licoppe and Inada 2008). More than one spatial context may be present in a local setting due to multiple mobile media sources for translocal connections that augment spaces with information from elsewhere. This creates AR too, either with AR technology or through ubiquitous computing and mobile media. The appropriation of spaces through such practices as described by Lefebvre is highly mediated today (Lefebvre and Nicholson-Smith 1991). The presence of many simultaneous socio-spatial contexts in one local setting is to be considered a form of AR as well since, even though not technically connected through tracking and locative functions, connections are made by humans. Thus the coordination of switching between multiple telepresent contexts, private and public, is necessary. Additionally, new conventions for the use of these technologies must be developed.

Theorizing the spatial dimensions of mixed reality depends very much on the areas in which it is applied. Each area of application – environmental planning, education, the tourism and cultural sectors, the military, gaming, product development, and marketing – are embedded in particular socio-spatial temporal contexts.

Notes

1 Depending on the theoretical orientation, Neuberger understands the term "communication" as either a subordinate concept or as a subsection of interaction. Communication and interaction therefore need to be differentiated. Interaction

refers to the potential of media technology, and different technologies each enable different degrees of interaction (Neuberger 2007). Accessing information from Internet platforms via mobile phones is therefore a form of mass media communication, as are newspapers. Of course, in comparison to newspapers, the virtual world offers much more choice and possibility for participation through communication. Since mass media and interpersonal communication are both present on the Internet, though, each particular case must be considered separately.

2 Media archaeology is interested in historical traditions that have contributed to the emergence of a media phenomenon in current times, and it understands these developments as contingent, discontinuous, and distributed across time and populations, with no direct genealogies expected (Huhtamo and Parikka 2011).

3 "Digital" actually has a rather different meaning to this. The digital as a concept was present in the world long before the computer was invented. "Digital" means the use of definite signs that are of a particular type and finite in number. An alphabet is thus digital. Often, and maybe mostly, the digital and the analogue are related, such as in the case of a sundial on which a shadow moves with analogue continuity or a clock face displaying discrete values. The digital principle is here realized in an analogue material setting. The alphabet on paper and the early vacuum tube computer are good further examples of this relation (cf. Schröter and Böhnke 2004).

References

Bederson, Benjamin B. 1995. "Audio Augmented Reality: A Prototype Automated Tour Guide". In *Conference Proceedings Of Mosaic Of Creativity: CHI' 95 Conference On Human Factors In Computing Systems*, edited by Irvin R. Katz, Robert Mack, and Linn Marks, 210–211. Denver, CO: ACM Press.

Berking, Helmuth, and Martina Löw. 2008. *Die Eigenlogik der Städte: Neue Wege für die Stadtforschung* [The intrinsic logic of cities: New ways for urban research]. Frankfurt am Main: Campus.

Biermann, B.C., Jordan Seiler, and Chris Nunes. 2011. *The AR | AD Takeover: Augmented Reality and the Reappropriation of Public Space*. Columbia: University of Southern Carolina.

Billinghurst, Mark, Adrian Clark, and Gun Lee. 2015. "A Survey of Augmented Reality". *Foundations and Trends in Human-Computer Interaction* 8 (2–3): 73–272.

Boellstorff, Tom. 2008. *Coming of Age in Second Life: An Anthropologist Explores the Virtually Human*. Princeton, NJ: Princeton University Press.

Bolter, David Jay, and Richard Grusin. 2000. *Remediation: Understanding New Media*. Cambridge, MA: MIT Press.

Bowker, Geoffrey C., Karen Baker, Florence Millerand, and David Ribes. 2010. "Toward Information Infrastructure Studies: Ways of Knowing in a Networked Environment". In *International Handbook of Internet Research*, edited by Jeremy Hunsinger, Lisbeth Klastrup, and Matthew Allen, 97–117. Dordrecht: Springer.

Christmann, Gabriela B., ed. 2016. *Zur kommunikativen Konstruktion von Räumen: Theoretische Konzepte und empirische Analysen* [On the communicative construction of spaces: Theoretical concepts and empirical analyses]. Wiesbaden: Springer VS.

Christmann, Gabriela B. 2022. "The Theoretical Concept of the Communicative (Re) Construction of Spaces". In *Communicative Constructions and the Refiguration of Spaces*, edited by Gabriela Christmann, Hubert Knoblauch, and Martina Löw, 89–112. Abingdon: Routledge.

Christmann, Gabriela B., Hubert Knoblauch, and Martina Löw. 2022. "Introduction: Communicative Constructions and the Refiguration of Spaces". In *Communicative Constructions and the Refiguration of Spaces*, edited by Gabriela Christmann, Hubert Knoblauch, and Martina Löw, 3–15. Abingdon: Routledge.

Damala, Areti, Pierre Cubaud, Anne Bationo, Pascal Houlier, and Isabelle Marchal. 2008. "Bridging the Gap between the Digital and the Physical: Design and Evaluation of a Mobile Augmented Reality Guide for the Museum Visit". In *Conference Proceedings of DIMEA 2008, 3rd International Conference on Digital Interactive Media in Entertainment and Arts*, edited by Sofia Tsekeridou, Adrian David Cheok, Konstantinos Giannakis, and John Karigiannis, 120–127. New York: ACM.

Demarmels, Sascha. 2011. "Als ob die Sinne erweitert würden (...). Augmented Reality als neue semiotische Ressource in der multimodalen Kommunikation" [As if the senses are being expanded (...). Augmented reality as a new semiotic resource in multimodal communication]. *KODIKAS/CODE: Ars Semiotica* 34 (3–4): 34–51.

de Souza e Silva, Adriana, and Daniel M. Sutko. 2009. *Digital Cityscapes: Merging Digital and Urban Playspaces*. Bern: Peter Lang.

Dörner, Ralf, and Frank Steinicke. 2013. "Wahrnehmungsaspekte von VR" [Perceptions of VR]. In *Virtual and Augmented Reality (VR/AR). Grundlagen und Methoden der Virtuellen und Augmentierten Realität* [Virtual and augmented reality (VR/AR). Basics and methods of virtual and augmented reality], edited by Ralf Dörner, Wolfgang Broll, Paul Grimm, and Bernhard Jung, 33–61. Heidelberg: Springer-Vieweg.

Dörner, Ralf, Wolfgang Broll, Paul Grimm, and Bernhard Jung. 2013. *Virtual and Augmented Reality (VR/AR): Grundlagen und Methoden der Virtuellen und Augmentierten Realität* [Virtual and augmented reality (VR/AR): Basics and methods of virtual and augmented reality]. Heidelberg: Springer-Vieweg.

Dourish, Paul, and Genevieve Bell. 2014. *Divining a Digital Future: Mess and Mythology in Ubiquitous Computing*. Cambridge, MA: MIT Press.

Dubois, Emmanuel, Laurence Nigay, Jocelyne Troccaz, Olivier Chavanon, and Lionel Carrat. 1999. "Classification Space for Augmented Surgery, an Augmented Reality Case Study". In *Proceedings of Interact '99*, edited by A. Sasse and C. Johnson, 353–359. Edinburgh: IOS Press.

Ernst, Wolfgang. 2004. "DEN A/D-Umbruch aktiv denken: medienarchäologisch, kulturtechnisch" [Thinking actively about THE A/D-upheaval: Media-archaeologically, cultural-technical]. In *Analog/Digital – Opposition oder Kontinuum? Zur Theorie und Geschichte einer Unterscheidung* [Analog/digital – opposition or continuum? The theory and history of a distinction], edited by Alexander Böhnke and Jens Schröter, 49–66. Bielefeld: transcript.

Fehling, Christian Dominic. 2017. "Erweiterte Lernwelten für die berufliche Bildung. Augmented Reality als Perspektive" [Expanded learning worlds for vocational education and training. Augmented reality as perspective]. In *Lernen in virtuellen Räumen. Perspektiven des mobilen Lernens* [Learning in virtual spaces. Perspectives of mobile learning], edited by Frank Thissen, 125–142. Berlin: Walter de Gruyter.

Filler, Andreas, Matthias Ludwig, and Reinhard Oldenburg. 2010. *Werkzeuge im Geometrieunterricht: Vorträge auf der 29. Herbsttagung des Arbeitskreises Geometrie in der Gesellschaft für Didaktik der Mathematik vom 10. bis 12. September 2010 in Marktbreit* [Tools for teaching geometry: Lectures at the 29th autumn conference of the working group Geometry in the Society for Didactics of Mathematics from 10 to 12 September 2010 in Marktbreit]. Hildesheim: Franzbecker.

Fisher, Bob, Kenneth Dawson-How, and Carol O'Sullivan. 2001. "Virtual and Augmented Architecture (VAA' 01)". In *Conference Proceedings of the International Symposium on Virtual and Augmented Architecture (VAA' 01), Trinity College, Dublin, 21–22 June*, edited by Bob Fisher, Kenneth Dawson-Howe, and Carol O'Sullivan, 5–17. Berlin: Springer.

Folz, Steffen, Daniel Broschart, and Peter Zeile. 2016. "Raumerfassung und Raumwahrnehmung – aktuelle Techniken und potenzielle Einsatzgebiete in der Raumplanung" [Spatial acquisition and perception – current techniques and potential areas of application in spatial planning]. In *REAL CORP 2016: SMART ME UP! How to Become and How to Stay a Smart City, and Does this Improve Quality of Life? 21st International Conference on Urban Planning and Regional Development in the Information Society*, edited by Manfred Schrenk, Clemens Beyer, Kai-Uwe Krause, Peter Zeile, and Wolfgang W. Wasserburger, 541–550. Hamburg: CORP.

Gaspar, Miguel Belbut, and Artur Mateus. 2015. "Augmented Reality Sculpture Bases for Public Space". In *Conference Proceedings of the ARTECH 2015: 7th International Conference On Digital Arts*, edited by J. Bidarra, T. Eca, M. Tavares, R. Leote, L. Pimentel, E. Carvalho, and M. Figueiredo, 39–44. Lamas-Cadaval: ARTECH-International.

Hannerz, Ulf. 1992. *Cultural Complexity: Studies in the Social Organization Of Meaning*. New York: Columbia University Press.

Horst, Heather A. 2013. "The Infrastructures of Mobile Media: Towards a Future Research Agenda". *Mobile Media & Communication* 1 (1): 147–152.

Huhtamo, Erkki. 2009. "Messages on the Wall: An Archaeology of Public Media Displays". In *Urban Screens Reader*, edited by Scott McQuire, Meredith Martin, and Sabine Niederer, 15–28. Amsterdam: Institute of Network Cultures.

Huhtamo, Erkki, and Jussi Parikka. 2011. *Media Archaeology. Approaches, Applications, and Implications*. Oakland: University of California Press.

Ihde, Don. 1993. *Postphenomenology: Essays in the Postmodern Context. Studies in Phenomenology and Existential Philosophy*. Evanston, IL: Northwestern University Press.

Jaramillo, J. E., P. Esteban, N. Alvarez, J. Restrepo, and H. Trefftz. 2004. *Augmented Reality: A Space for the Understanding of Multi-Variate Calculus*. Medellín: EAFIT University.

Knoblauch, Hubert, and Martina Löw. 2017. "On the Spatial Re-Figuration of the Social World". *Sociologica* 11 (2): 1–27.

Lefebvre, Henri, and Donald Nicholson-Smith. 1991. *The Production of Space*. Oxford: Blackwell.

Licoppe, Christian. 2004. "'Connected' Presence: The Emergence of a New Repertoire for Managing Social Relationships in a Changing Communication Technoscape". *Environment And Planning D: Society and Space* 22 (1): 135–156.

Licoppe, Christian, and Yoriko Inada. 2008. "Geolocalized Technologies, Location-Aware Communities, and Personal Territories: The Mogi Case". *Journal of Urban Technology* 15 (3): 5–24.

Liestol, Gunnar. 2011. "Situated Simulations Between Virtual Reality and Mobile Augmented Reality: Designing a Narrative Space". In *Handbook of Augmented Reality*, edited by Borko Furht, 309–319. Berlin: Springer.

Lindlbaur, David, and Andy D. Wilson. 2018. "Remixed Reality: Manipulating Space and Time in Augmented Reality". Paper 29 in *Conference Proceedings of CHI 2018 – Conference on Human Factors in Computing Systems, Montreal, 21–26 April*, edited by Regan Mandryk, Mark Hancock, Mark Perry, and Anna Cox, 1–13. New York: ACM.

Lindner, Rolf. 2008. "Textur, Imaginaire, Habitus: Schlüsselbegriffe der kulturanalytischen Stadtforschung" [Texture, imaginary, habitus: Key terms in cultural-analytical urban research]. In *Die Eigenlogik der Städte. Neue Wege für die Stadtforschung* [The intrinsic logic of cities. New ways for urban research], edited by Helmuth Berking and Martina Löw, 83–94. Frankfurt am Main: Campus.

Löw, Martina. 2013. *Raumsoziologie* [Sociology of space]. Berlin: Suhrkamp.

Meyrowitz, Joshua. 1985. *No Sense of Place: The Impact of Electronic Media on Social Behavior.* New York: Oxford University Press.

Milgram, Paul, and Fumio Kishino. 1994. "A Taxonomy of Mixed Reality Visual Displays". *IEICE Transactions on Information and Systems* 12 (12): 1321–1329.

Negroponte, Nicholas. 1998."Beyond Digital". *Wired* 6 (12). http://web.media.mit.edu/~nichoals/Wired/WIRED6-12.html

Neuberger, Christoph. 2007. "Interaktivität, Interaktion, Internet: Eine Begriffsanalyse" [Interactivity, interaction, Internet: A conceptual analysis]. *Zeitschrift für Publizistik* 52 (1): 33–50.

Sanna, Andrea, and Federico Manuri. 2016. "A Survey on Applications of Augmented Reality". *Advances in Computer Science: An International Journal* 5 (1): 18–27.

Schröter, Jens, and Alexander Böhnke. 2004. *Analog/Digital – Opposition oder Kontinuum? Zur Theorie und Geschichte einer Unterscheidung* [Analogue/digital – opposition or continuum? The theory and history of a distinction]. Bielefeld: transcript.

Verbeek, Peter-Paul. 2001. "Don Ihde: The Technological Lifeworld". In *American Philosophy of Technology: The Empirical Turn*, edited by Hans Achterhuis and Robert P. Crease, 119–146. Bloomington: Indiana University Press.

Williams, Raymond. 1992/1972. *Television: Technology and Cultural Form*. London: Routledge.

Winkler, Hartmut. 2004."Medienmentalitäten. Analog und digital unter Gender-Aspekt" [Media mentalities. Analogue and digital from a gender perspective]. In *Analog/Digital – Opposition oder Kontinuum? Zur Theorie und Geschichte einer Unterscheidung* [Analogue/digital – opposition or continuum? The theory and history of a distinction], edited by Jens Schröter and Alexander Böhnke, 117–134. Bielefeld: Transcript.

Woolgar, Steve. 2002. *Virtual Society? Technology, Cyberhole, Reality*. Oxford: Oxford University Press.

Zeile, Peter. 2011. "Augmented City – erweiterte Realität in der Stadtplanung" [Augmented city – Augmented reality in urban planning]. *Bauwelt* 24: 34–39.

6 The theoretical concept of the communicative (re)construction of spaces

Gabriela B. Christmann

Introduction

As already stated in the introduction to this volume, there are indications that in the course of globalization, mediatization, and digitalization processes, as well as of increased mobilities and migration flows, a comprehensive "refiguration of spaces" has taken place – processually – since the 1960s (Christmann, Knoblauch, and Löw 2022). This refiguration is characterized, it is assumed, by moving more and more in the direction of deterritorialized and decentralized spatial constructions – to name just a few of the fundamental changes in the course of refiguration (Knoblauch and Löw 2020, 282 f.). In this context, it is important to emphasize that the refiguration of spaces should not be understood as a disruptive break with previously dominant spatial constructions. Rather, it is to be understood as a processual change that takes place incrementally, not least because it is based on communicative action by subjects or members of society who 'reconstruct' previous spatial orders. The theoretical approach of communicative (re)construction of spaces presented here aims to formulate how the small steps of reconstructing spaces can be conceptualized within the broader refiguration of spaces.

The premise of a social construction of space has been widely accepted. Attempts to elaborate this premise *theoretically* have mainly focused on factors such as knowledge (including the attribution of meaning) and action (see, e.g., Lefebvre 1991; Giddens 1984; Löw 2016; Thrift 2007). Only slowly did an awareness develop that communication or communicative action should also be considered (see Paasi 1989; Healey 1992; Lees 2004; Pott 2007). In *empirical* spatial research, it has long been obvious that spatial transformations (e.g. in urban development) are often accompanied by extensive (public) communication processes. By comparison, the theoretical conceptualization of such processes is still weak today. There are only few theoretical approaches that treat communication as a factor in spatial construction processes, and the few that do exist are inspired either by Luhmann's theory of autopoietic systems (Pott 2007) or by Foucault's post-structuralist discourse analysis (Glasze and Mattissek 2009). However, while taking various communications into account, they see them,

DOI: 10.4324/9780367817183-8

rather, as media within a systemic or structural generation of meaning. The actions of subjects are of little importance to this process.

In contrast, the theoretical approach of the communicative (re)construction of spaces proposed here is both communication *and* action oriented. Moreover, it is firmly anchored in the thinking of the sociology of knowledge. In this context, knowledge is understood as a socially mediated and accepted meaning that is considered 'certain' and typically guides action (Löw and Knoblauch 2021). The approach is based on the idea that (re)constructions of spaces cannot be grasped without attributions of meaning by actors. It also takes into account the fact that materiality — for example, in the form of bodies or physical objects — participates in action and, in doing so, shapes the (re)construction of spaces. Above all, the processual nature of the (re)construction of spaces is considered. Accordingly, spatial constructions are conceptualized as dynamic, more or less fluid phenomena. The theoretical approach thus allows one to conceptualize not only how spatial constructions emerge and solidify or institutionalize, but also — as the term (re)construction suggests — how existing spatial constructions are modified or restructured. Last but not least, the potential simultaneity of different social constructions of space for one and the same spatial unit is considered, since ascriptions of meaning, communicative action, and material arrangements in relation to a spatial unit can differ depending on the social group. This phenomenon is also discussed under the concept of relational space (see, especially, Löw 2016). In summary: *Communication, action, knowledge,* and *materiality* are regarded as central dimensions in the (re)construction of spaces. Furthermore, spatial (re)constructions are considered in their *processuality* and *relationality*.[1]

In order to theoretically develop the idea of the communicative construction and ongoing reconstruction of spaces, the approach proposed here makes use of universal — basically constructivist — social theories and theories of society that can address the dimensions mentioned above. Nevertheless, the approach is to be understood as a theory of medium range, because it does not intend to focus on universal social processes, but rather on specific ones; namely, space-related social processes. Initially, to keep things simple, the transfer of these theories to spaces, as well as the conceptual development of the same, is carried out using the example of small spatial units that might also be termed 'places'. This does not mean that the proposed approach is limited to places. Rather, the approach is intended to be general enough to represent constructions of larger spatial units.

Specifically, the approach is based on considerations of the following social theories and theories of society:[2] social constructivism (Berger and Luckmann 1966), communicative constructivism (Knoblauch 2020), and the sociology of knowledge approach to discourse (SKAD, Keller 2013). While the strength of social constructivism lies in the fact that it is able to show how reality constructions in situations involving face-to-face action are consolidated, the significance of communicative constructivism lies in the fact that it can grasp the dynamization in (re)construction processes via the element of (physically realized) communicative action. With SKAD, it is possible to consider the entanglement of communications as well as discursive negotiation processes in highly institutionalized public contexts. The element of *dispositifs* contained in the concept also allows us to take a look at instruments by which discursively constructed orders of knowledge are socially established and material designs are brought about. This chapter unfolds as follows: In the next section, cornerstones of the universal theories already mentioned are presented in order to be able to take up fundamental theories from these approaches in the third and fourth sections, where they are transferred to processes of the (re)construction of spaces and developed further. Conceptualization of the space-related theoretical approach is accomplished in two stages: First, the process of the initial communicative construction of a space is laid out (in "The communicative construction of space"). There, the historical emergence and consolidation of an institutionalized space is outlined, starting from the subjective interpretations of 'historical' subjects. Second (in "The communicative *re*construction of space"), based on the model of the historically created, institutionally consolidated space, processes of the communicative *re*construction of space, also known as spatial transformation processes, are examined by looking at the role of individual actors, groups of actors, networks, and governance constellations as well as of small and large public spheres. There, the way in which already existing spatial constructions are negotiated, contested, modified, or restructured is developed in theoretical terms. In some final remarks, the methodological implications of the theoretical considerations for empirical analyses are reflected upon.

Theoretical foundations

The aim of this section is, as stated before, to provide a focused outline of the basic assumptions of the above-mentioned theoretical approaches to the envisaged project. Social constructivism, communicative constructivism, and SKAD will each be considered in turn.

Berger and Luckmann's approach focuses on the question of how it is possible "that subjective meanings become objective factualities", or how "human activity should produce a world of things" (Berger and Luckmann 1966, 18). By way of their theory of the *social construction of reality*, the authors answer this question – which is interesting from the perspective of spatial theory, as it alludes not only to immaterial but also to material objectivations – as follows: Intersubjectively shared interpretations of reality (a term which is used as a synonym for knowledge) are the result of a dialectical process of externalization, objectivation, and internalization.

The theoretical starting point is the externalization of subjective meaning; that is, at the beginning of the process, there are subjects who express their interpretation or reaction with regard to a certain phenomenon by way of action – mainly, according to this approach, linguistic action. Language plays a central role in Berger and Luckmann's (1966, 36 f., 64) theoretical model, because the authors see in it an objectifying function. Only by way of linguistic expressions (i.e. verbal communication) can subjective externalizations be made accessible to other subjects; only in this way is it possible to lastingly attribute common meanings to certain objects. Consequently, although the authors are also aware of the significance of nonverbal communication and of material objects in construction processes, they do not pay systematic attention to them (Berger and Luckmann 1966, 36). In their opinion, linguistic institutionalizations and legitimizations are much more important in the process of objectivation (Berger and Luckmann 1966, 61 f.). These elements are what make it possible to stabilize and secure social reality. The authors point out explicitly that reality constructions – as soon as they have become stable entities and have their legitimacy secured – face the individual in the form of objects. In the course of socialization processes, individuals finally internalize the social constructions of reality, which in turn influence those individuals (see Berger and Luckmann 1966, 173 ff.). To summarize: In the context of social constructivism, one holds language primarily responsible for the process of the social construction of reality, given its objectivating power.

This is viewed differently in *communicative constructivism*, as proposed by Knoblauch (1995, 2001, 2013, 2020; Knoblauch and Steets 2022). There, the concept of communication or communicative action is the focus of attention. Keller, Knoblauch, and Reichertz (2013, 14) understand communicative action as mutually interrelated action that makes use of a variety of different signs; that is, not only linguistic, but also non-linguistic signs, and even material objects in the form of bodies, objects, media, and technological or cultural artifacts. In this context, "communication is not only understood as the means by which people purposefully send messages and try to control others, but communication is always also the human practice by which identity, relationship, society, and reality are simultaneously established" (Keller, Knoblauch, and Reichertz 2013, 13). While the concept of language (understood as a central means of communication that, with the help of a semantic system, establishes a certain shared knowledge) in social constructivism includes a comparably inflexible structure or durability, the overarching concept of communicative action in communicative constructivism has the advantage that it can make the dynamics of action and restructurings or negotiations of reality constructions more comprehensible. It is furthermore based on the assumption that communicative action produces and conveys knowledge and that "at the same time social structures [are] created and reproduced" (Knoblauch 1995, 5). Of further interest in communicative constructivism is that materiality, in the form of bodies and things, is regarded as an integral part of communicative action. The body in particular is taken into account, because it is the only thing through which meaning can be made socially visible (Knoblauch 2013, 29). With this orientation, the approach comes close to considerations central to theories of practice and actor-network theory.

In addition, as mentioned above, discourse-theoretical considerations that Keller (2001, 2008, 2013, 2022) has presented in the context of SKAD are of importance to the theoretical concept proposed here. And it should be mentioned that SKAD has become an integral part of the overall approach of communicative constructivism. On the one hand, SKAD is inspired by Foucault (1994): What is Foucaultian in this context is the structural-theoretical interest in how intersubjectively shared knowledge orders and power structures emerge within the framework of discourses. This said, however, SKAD differs from Foucault's approach in that it does not focus exclusively on the unintended dynamics of knowledge genesis that are detached from actors, but rather takes an action-theoretical perspective as its basis. From the very beginning, Keller pursued the goal of further developing the social constructivist approach from the point where it is a matter of objectifying interpretations of reality (knowledge). In contrast to social constructivism, however, the focus is not on face-to-face situations, but on institutionally formalized processes of discursive reality construction: The actions of collective actors, including media actors, are systematically examined within complex, institutionalized social structures (Keller 2001, 126). From this perspective, discourses are conceived of as an ensemble of different communicative actions that are thematically related to each other and, as a consequence, result in the thematic bundling of knowledge elements, or the conjunction of interpretations of reality. They are furthermore regarded as dynamic — potentially contested — negotiation processes both within small and large public spheres.

Keller assumes not only that discursive processes produce knowledge orders, but also that discourses with their knowledge orders may influence social processes — even in physical-material forms. Central in this context is the concept of the *dispositif*, originally developed by Foucault, which allows for a bridging of the gap between knowledge orders and materiality (Foucault 2013, 35, 1978). Similarly to Foucault, Keller (2008, 258) understands *dispositifs* as instruments — for example, in the form of personal equipment, specific institutional measures, and/or material objects — by way of which specific orders of knowledge can be enforced or implemented in society. With their help, work is done on the transformation of knowledge orders as well as of manifest social orders. A *dispositif*, as an ensemble of ideal and material things, is thus used to structure not only forms of knowledge, but also social relationships and material object worlds.

When it comes to the question of how the construction of reality is socially constructed, Keller thus attempts to theoretically grasp the connection between communicative action, knowledge (orders), and materiality. However, while Knoblauch, in the context of the communicative construction of reality, considers materiality in connection with the corporeality of subjects and the contribution of material objects in mutually related actions (and basically does so in immediate as well as medially communicated action situations), Keller, in his concept of the discursive construction of reality, points to *dispositifs* that are a type of (material) resource for action by collective actors in more or less highly institutionalized social contexts and which are used instrumentally for the social manifestation of knowledge orders.

94 *Gabriela B. Christmann*

In all three approaches, it is obvious that the concept of relationality – that is, the idea of a potential simultaneity of different constructions of reality with respect to an object – is given. In social constructivism, this is – implicitly – the case, because there different subjective interpretations of reality form the starting point of the approach. As Poferl (2009, 242) remarks, "this way ... the path has been cleared to basically recognize that social reality ... and its (multi-) perspectivity depend on ways of interpreting [it]". The same idea can be found in communicative constructivism. In SKAD, the simultaneity of different perspectives on an object is much more clearly expressed, to the extent that the assumption that discourses are contested and that different interpretations of reality struggle for a power of interpretation and social establishment play a role.

The dimension of processuality is also taken into consideration in all approaches. While social constructivism focuses more on processes of establishing and consolidating a social construction of reality, communicative constructivism focuses rather on the dynamics of and modifications to existing socio-physical arrangements, and discourse concepts are, as Knoblauch (2001, 212) puts it, "dynamic-diachronic" in nature. Already in Foucault's works are the analysis of discourses aimed at the reconstruction of historical processes, including the historical genesis of knowledge orders, as well as how they changed over the course of history.

The communicative construction of space: From subjective interpretations of space to socially shared space

Using the example of an imagined spatial unit, termed 'Space A', this section aims to theoretically trace the path from subjective interpretations of space to a socially shared space, the latter to be understood as an ensemble of immaterial and material constructions that has grown historically in the course of social processes, is widely shared in a social context, and has experienced institutional consolidation, even though very different subjects with different ways of imagining the space took part in it. Furthermore, the resulting social construct is conceived as an 'initial' construction, hypothetically starting from a tabula rasa and leading by stages to an institutionalization and, at the hypothetically assumed 'end', to a commonly shared reality construction. This happens, of course, in the knowledge that consolidations of reality constructions may be changed again – that is, transformed or reconstructed – at any time. Only the second part of this theoretical approach is this dealt with systematically (see "The communicative *r*econstruction of space"). Prior to this, the space-related action and interpretation by individual subjects and the communicative construction of intersubjectively shared and institutionalized space within a social context are clarified.

Space-related action and interpretation by individual subjects

The starting points are – as already indicated – historical subjects who are thought of as 'first constructors' (see Figure 6.1). Subjects are understood

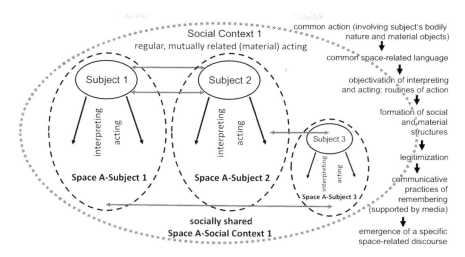

Figure 6.1 From subjective interpretations of space to socially shared space.
Source: Own representation.

as thinking and acting human beings who relate to their world (Löw and Knoblauch 2021). A historical Subject 1 acts in a spatial environment, which it explores on the basis of its embodied nature and sensory equipment and that it perceives as a surrounding space. This space is referred to in the following as Space A. There, the subject, in the course of his or her actions, perceives and brings together in a certain way the surfaces, objects, plants, animals, but also other subjects, as well as their modes of action and social orders; they assign them to Space A, thus attributing certain meanings to it, and on this basis develop certain space-related interpretations of reality and, at the same time, modes of action. Only through these subjective achievements, which can also be described as "synthetizing operations" (after Löw 2016, 159), does this space become existent for the subject. From its own subjective perspective, the historical Subject 1 thus gains a specific idea of the surrounding space. At the same time, it can to a certain extent shape this space materially within the framework of its available actions. This space is termed Space A of Subject 1 (= reality of Space A–Subject 1).

Subject 1 is not alone, however. The historical Subject 2, located in the same spatial environment, by way of acting and interpreting also has specific experiences of their environment and so develops their own space-related modes of action and interpretations (= reality of Space A–Subject 2). The same applies to other subjects (= realities of Space A–Subject 3, Space A–Subject 4, etc.). Each subject initially has its own space-related modes of action and interpretations of reality. Due to the different subjective perspectives – as is the basic idea behind relational concepts of space – there is not 'a' space as such, but variations of this space that exist for the individual subjects, each in a specific way. Subjects act communicatively in various ways, sometimes in cooperation with one another. Such actions can be nonverbal, involving interaction with the space: using it in a certain way, 'occupying' it, or (if external conditions allow) materially changing or shaping it, for instance. But other actions can establish verbal forms of communication about the space, externalizing implicitly (in the case of nonverbal communicative action) and/or explicitly (in the case of verbal communicative action – i.e. of speaking about space) their subjective space-related interpretations of reality.[3] Löw (2016, 158) calls that which might be considered the spatial effect of acting subjects "spacing". Spacing can, for example, involve "erecting, building, or positioning" (Löw 2016, 158). (Social) goods, humans, or living beings are placed and arranged in space. Löw (2016, 159) rightly states that in the

> everyday action of constituting space ... there is a simultaneity of synthetizing operations and spacing .... In fact, building, erecting, or placing, i.e. spacing, is not possible without synthetizing operations, i.e. without at the same time connecting the surrounding social goods and humans to spaces.

Operations of synthetizing and spacing are to be regarded here as space-related communicative actions that condense into spatial constructions. At the level of the individual subjects described here, however, these constructions – as already indicated – only have the status of externalizations of *subjective* spatial constructions. Individual subjective reality constructions of space tend to differ from each other. Nevertheless, individual subjects are confronted with the externalizations of other subjects and must accommodate them – provided they (wish to) live together in one space.

The communicative construction of intersubjectively shared and institutionalized space within a social context

Subjects do not stand in isolation, but are constituent parts of a social context. A social context develops in the regular, mutually related (material) actions of subjects (involving the subjects' embodied nature and material objects), as well as in dense linguistic internal communications. It consists of dense communicative relationships between the subjects (= Social Context 1). Within a social context, the subjects thus engage with the actions of others as well as with their expressed interpretations of reality. Typically, the *space-related* actions and interpretations of others are also there observed, mutually adapted, negotiated, and – to a certain degree – processed into jointly shared space-related modes of action and interpretations of reality which, until further notice, become valid for that social context. These collectively generated and socially shared space-related ways of acting and interpreting form the reality of Space A-Social Context 1.

In this context, importantly, objectivations also take place. They emerge, for example, through the development of a shared space-related language. By means of the latter, specific and socially shared attributions of meaning are lastingly established. This means, for example, that concepts are established by means of which interpretations of space within the social context are typically discussed. The effect of linguistic definitions should not be underestimated. Knowledge produced in this way acquires in this social context the character of an objectified and consolidated reality construction of Space A.

However, a common language in relation to space is only one aspect of the process of objectivation. Over the course of time, the reality construction of the social context related to 'the' space is further institutionalized in that jointly shared knowledge receives additional consolidation, corresponding space-related routines of action are developed, and social structures, including physical-material structures, are formed. In the sense of Läpple (1991, 196 f.), an institutionalized and normative system of regulation emerges, which mediates between the material substrate of 'the' space and the group practice of its appropriation and use. Against this background a specific spatial 'regime' emerges (Löw and Knoblauch 2021). The resulting structures are reproduced in the further actions of the subjects.[4] In other words, social structures do not – analytically speaking – confront the subjects in a simply polarized manner, but are produced, endorsed, and consolidated by the subjects in regularly occurring actions and, as such, provide the orientation for further action.

This does not disguise the fact that from the perspective of the subjects, institutionalizations or structures can be perceived as objectivations; that is, as phenomena that are objectively given and face the subjects. This is especially the case with members of a social milieu who were not involved in the original construction process, such as those from subsequent generations or foreigners. Societies have developed strategies of legitimization for this. In the context of legitimizations, patterns of justification are created for the specific constructions of space, with which new members of society are introduced to its specific orders of knowledge and modes of action, as well as its social and physical-material structures.

Processes of objectivation in the form of action routines, linguistic definitions, institutionalizations, and legitimizations thus lead to increasing consolidation of the construction of space in a social context.

Also constitutive for the formation of a highly institutionalized space – which, as mentioned above, is understood as a historically evolved ensemble consisting of an immaterial and a material construction of space – are socially shared memory (Assmann and Assmann 1993) and communicative practices of remembering. This refers to communicative action by which members of the social context constantly ascertain what is significant for 'their' space: the physical-material structure of what they perceive as typical for 'their' space (e.g. a certain landscape), the material shape they have given to 'their' space throughout history (e.g. through changes in the landscape, the construction of buildings, perhaps with specific architectural features), the important events that have taken place there, the people who worked there, the objects that were created there, the ways of acting, habits, and customs that are typical there, and so on. Communicative practices of remembering occur in nonverbal and/ or verbal forms, such as in the form of material symbols (e.g. monuments), of visual communication (e.g. pictures), of oral or written narratives, or other forms of (media) communication. It is through regular communicative acts of remembering in the social context, which refer to Space A in a typical and recurring way and that are usually underpinned and emphasized by, for instance, local media, that a specific space-related discourse emerges. In discursive processes, knowledge orders emerge, which are further consolidated due to typical communicative actions recurring in a specific way. By means of *dispositif* structures created by the subjects for the upholding of knowledge orders, such as regulations, institutions, personnel equipment, and/or material objects, the created knowledge orders do not remain merely mental constructs, but are implemented socially and materially. If one applies SKAD and the *dispositif* concept to the conceptualization of space, a space is thus – historically speaking – the result of the previous space-related discourses and *dispositif* structures of participating subjects that have now become manifest.

The communicative *re*construction of space: On spatial transformation processes

Space-related constructions of reality must not be considered static, however, even if they are highly institutionalized and take material shape, such as in the form of architectural designs. In the course of general social shifts due to, for instance, demographic, economic, or technical developments, changing environmental and climatic conditions, evolving habits and lifestyles, or (new) needs, social problems, or even crisis-like phenomena with spatial implications, constructions of space can be questioned, modified, or adjusted. Of course, this particularly applies to the processual refiguration of spaces in view of globalization, mediatization, and digitalization processes. In fact, constructions of space in modern societies are constantly undergoing processes of transformation and thus of *re*construction for various reasons. Physical-material features can themselves be abandoned, reused, modified, or torn down. In the following, the question of how *re*constructions of space take place in communicative action will be conceptually developed.

The starting point of this theoretical section is not a tabula rasa, but rather an existing, highly institutionalized space. As described above, it is a historically established space created through processes of communicative action, which must now be thought of as the space of a functionally and socially differentiated society, a society that has different social fields (e.g. politics, administration, economy, civil society) as well as complex social, institutional, organizational, and power structures. Furthermore, this space is to be viewed within a structure of various other (e.g. political-administrative, sociocultural, global) constructions of space that may surround and possibly even penetrate or overlap it.

In the example case Space A, its specific social context (= Space A-Social Context 1) could be a district in a city – if, for pragmatic reasons, one starts out from a small spatial unit – but it might well also encompass a whole city, and so on. As already mentioned, Space A-Social Context 1 is part of broader spatial constructions that have also historically emerged in processes of communicative action, within the framework of corresponding social contexts (within a district, a region, a nation, a supra-nation, or a world society). In fact, Space A-Social Context 1 can be brought into a relationship – of whatever kind – with these frameworks in the context of the communicative actions of the members of society. Accordingly, as in the previous section, individual subjects are again understood as acting subjects and are taken as the starting point for communicative *reconstruction* processes – even though Space A must now be seen as a highly institutionalized, complex, and multifaceted social construct. Subjects themselves must also now be seen as socialized members of society. However, this does not mean that they are to be understood exclusively as products of society. Since they typically generate meaning and shape objects materially, they are above all producers of society (Berger and Luckmann 1966, 89). Early on, in a contribution to social mobility, Luckmann and Berger (1964) point out that the subject is, on the one hand, determined to a great extent by the specific history and culture of a society. On the other hand, however, they emphasize that new possibilities for the development of the subject have arisen as a result of processes of mobility, realities offered by the mass media, and the pluralization of worldviews in modern societies. The subject selects from the 'market' of different interpretations, configures them in novel ways, and thus creates something unprecedented. Against this background, the subject can be considered a producer of original interpretations and modes of action; it may potentially develop something new and thus contribute to transformations.

In view of the elaborate functional and social differentiation within complex societies, it must also be taken into account that the subject acts within the framework of societal institutions that they have incorporated in the form of institutionally specific social expectations. That is, a subject acts according to social roles[5] and may have access to role-specific – symbolic or material – resources. This socialized role-subject will be referred to as a 'societal actor' or, in the following, simply as an 'actor', and is thus understood as a socially acting and interacting subject who holds particular points of view and is bound to certain social structures in their actions (Löw and Knoblauch 2021).

It becomes clear in this part of the theoretical approach that, in contrast to that of the previous section, theories of society play a stronger role. Nevertheless, as mentioned above – analogous to the historically conceived 'initial construction' of space by historical subjects – processes of the *reconstruction* of an institutionalized space by individual societal actors and groups of actors are considered first (in the subsection below). Only then (in the second subsection) do theoretical considerations follow on networks and governance constellations – that is, on more complex constellations of societal actors – whereby governance constellations are understood as networks in which actors from different societal fields (e.g. politics, administration, economy, civil society) convene to (purposefully) coordinate spatial transformations (Christmann

2010). Finally, (in the last subsection) communicative *re*constructions of space in the public sphere are taken into account, not least in the context of space-related (media) discourses.

Spatial transformations as communicative reconstructions of space: Individual societal actors and groups of actors

Typically, individual societal actors (here: Individual Actor 1, 2, and 3, for instance) may instantiate space-related actions and/or interpretations, which, compared to established routines of action and interpretation, contain modifications, reveal something novel, or even a break with the past (see Figure 6.2). As a rule, these societal actors do not act in isolation, but are integrated into a social context, such as a group of actors, and thus engage with other individual actors who think and act in similar ways. Some individuals might play a particularly active role within the framework of groups of actors and, thus, be given or attributed a prominent social position. Due to certain forms of knowledge, strategies of action, communication skills, institutional anchoring, and/or resource endowments, they may act as key individuals who are particularly capable of driving on the development and implementation of new modes of action and interpretation within groups of actors (and sometimes even beyond).

As members of Space A–Social Context 1, however, individual societal actors and groups of actors must also deal with the existing dominant spatial modes of action and interpretations that constitute Space A, since Space A has unfolded a power of interpretation on the basis of the objectified, institutionalized, and legitimately established orders of knowledge, and due to the routines of action associated with them. Within the actions and internal communications of the actor group (here: Actor Group 1), new space-related modes of action and the interpretations of individual actors – more or less consciously in confrontation with previously existing spatial practices – are exchanged, coordinated, and jointly transformed into common interpretations and modes of action that are valid for the members of this group until further notice. The new modes of action and knowledge thus developed concerning Space A is the reality of Space $A^{transformed}$ of Actor Group 1.

The common reality construction developed within the group forms the basis for their further space-related actions and knowledge, which become institutionalized over the course of time. The group externalizes its new modes of action and interpretation, because it is also not isolated, but stands in a social context and in exchange with other groups of actors assigned to the spatial environment. These other actor groups (here: Actor Groups 2 and 3, for instance) go through the same processes, but this does not mean that they develop the same altered spatial realities of Space A. It is likely that specific realities will develop within each particular group (= reality of Space $A^{transformed}$ of Actor Group 2, and reality of Space $A^{transformed}$ of Actor Group 3). At the same time, however, it is possible that at least partially common realities regarding Space A are produced.

As stated above, Space A does not simply exist objectively as such. Rather, following Löw (2016), we must assume a relational space. But while Löw defines relational space primarily in the physical sense – as temporally constituted "relational arrangements of bodies that are incessantly in motion, whereby the arrangements themselves are constantly changing" (Löw 2016, 131) – here, space is additionally regarded as a relational knowledge construct, for it owes its existence not least due to the attributions of meaning by actors that might differ from each other depending on the group. This may have consequences for their space-related actions inasmuch as the actors (intend to) shape 'the' space – against the background of different attributions of meaning – through different arrangements of living beings and goods, potentially giving rise to conflict.

Spatial transformations as communicative reconstructions of space: Networks and governance constellations

Actor groups that maintain regular social relations with other actor groups (or their members) – through representatives (i.e. delegated actors) or as a whole – form a network (here, Network 1). An example of such a network could be an association of local civil society actor groups who convene to jointly change certain qualities of 'their' place. It could also be an association of representatives coming from different administrative areas to work on a collaborative spatial-development concept. Networks are characterized by regular action and communication relationships – usually in the context of joint meetings; that is, where communication is direct. This is where old and new space-related modes of action and interpretation of the various actor groups involved are negotiated. The group representatives are each confronted with the actions and interpretations of other groups of actors, process them, reject some of them and take a firm stand against them, accept some of them, carry them into their group, and together modify the actions and interpretations previously typical for the actor group or jointly develop new ones and carry them into the network, and so on. Through such processes of communicative exchange between actor groups within a network, a (to a certain extent) jointly shared new construction of space emerges on the level of the network (= reality of Space $A^{transformed}$ Network 1).

However, different groups of actors in a network may be compatible in different ways due to a certain degree of still different space-related interpretation and action patterns and due to differently developed communicative relationships; for example, the interpretations and actions of Actor Group 1 may be easily compatible with those of Actor Group 2, but at odds with those of Actor Group 3. As a result, in addition to the new constructions of space that are to a certain extent shared, there may also be different distributions of certain modes of action and interpretation within the network.

This is even more complex in the context of networks known as governance constellations. Here, actors from very different functional areas of society

102　*Gabriela B. Christmann*

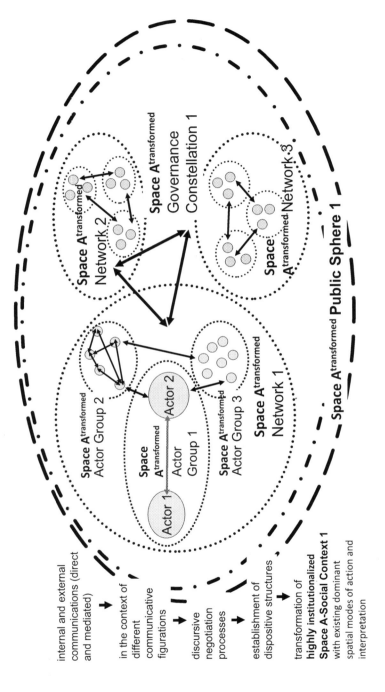

Figure 6.2 The communicative reconstruction of space.
Source: Own representation.

try conscientiously and reflexively to advance spatial transformation processes together (Christmann 2010).

Functionally differentiated societies are characterized, as mentioned above, by the fact that they are divided into branches such as politics, administration, planning, economy, civil society, and so on, to name only the most important ones. Each of these functional areas has certain structural peculiarities.[6] To some extent, this is reflected in the heterogeneity of representatives typically involved in governance constellations: Depending on their affiliation to a functional area of society and to a specific organization belonging to it, representatives can thus bring along specific space-related knowledge backgrounds, problem definitions, task understandings, and modes of action – against the background of the modes of action, communication, knowledge and role structures established there. Each representative may activate specific rationalities, interests, and objectives as well as specific powers and resources.

Despite this heterogeneity and the resulting complexity, space-related governance constellations are created specifically for a desired spatial-transformation process (Governance Constellation 1). They are designed to develop, by means of negotiation and coordination processes, socially binding common modes of space-related interpretation and strategies for action with regard to concrete future spatial transformations. This is considered necessary by societal actors, since far-reaching space-transforming actions, especially when it comes to physical-material and infrastructural but also social aspects, are typically considered to be of high societal relevance locally: Third parties might be affected to a high degree. Far-reaching space-transforming actions (whether taken by a mayor, a municipal planning authority, an industrial company, or civil society actors) cannot therefore simply be implemented at will. There is thus an expectation that such action will be planned and coordinated with other actors before it is implemented. For certain types of space-transforming action (e.g. for building), institutional regulations have even been created in the course of lengthy social processes (e.g. construction law), which more or less precisely prescribe planning and coordination processes.

Governance constellations are here characterized, similarly to the networks mentioned above, by regular action and communication relationships[7] – usually in the context of meetings; that is, in situations involving direct communication. In addition, such coordination processes can be supported by certain kinds of media communication, such as e-governance and e-participation. In both direct and mediated communication, old and new space-related modes of action and interpretation of participating actors from various functional areas are negotiated. The actors are each confronted with the actions and interpretations of other actors (from different socially functional areas), process them, reject and oppose some, accept and absorb others into their functional area, and modify the actions and interpretations typical to their area or develop new ones and introduce them in turn to the governance constellation, and so on. Through such processes of communicative action between actors of a governance constellation, a (to a certain extent) commonly shared, altered construction of space at the level of the governance constellation (= reality of Space A^{transformed} Governance Constellation 1) is created, which becomes a guiding force and is institutionalized and legitimized for further space-related action.

As already indicated, however, this does not hide the fact that developing jointly shared action goals and strategies for spatial transformation in governance constellations is structurally more difficult than in the previously described – comparatively more homogeneous – networks and actor groups. Deep-seated differences between the space-related interests, interpretations, and/or actions of societal actors from different functional areas of society cannot simply be bridged, renegotiated, or transformed – owing first of all to the comparably low communication frequency within governance constellations and the typically short periods available for negotiation. Conflict is therefore a structural given. It might remain latent, but can also be dealt with openly. In the latter case, it can be constructively reversed in more or less protracted negotiation processes, at least for some participants, and lead to compromise; or it can escalate and, in extreme cases, lead to the failure of a governance constellation. Above all, not all modes of space-related interpretation and action represented within a governance constellation have the same opportunities to assert themselves. Instead, power constellations and resource endowments play a role. Due to institutional regulations established by society, political and administrative actors have a formal, legitimate decision-making power by virtue of their office. By contrast, civil society actors, for example, do not have decision-making powers, but can withdraw trust from political and administrative actors and symbolically deny legitimacy. In principle, power constellations and their associated symbolic resources can thus shift during the negotiation process. Contrary to various theories of power, which assume that power is a kind of substance that an actor type or institution either has or does not have, and that also has a certain static nature, it makes sense to assume with Elias (1978) that power is always to be understood as being located in relationships, as fluctuating, and thus as performing a balancing act.

In the preceding considerations, individual societal actors, actor groups, networks, and governance constellations were regarded as social units in their own right in order to be able to describe processes of communicative reconstruction of space for each of these units from an analytical perspective. It has already become clear, however, that these social units can be interconnected: An individual societal actor can belong to one or several actor groups; a group of actors can be part of one or several networks; representatives from actor groups and/or networks can be members of a governance constellation.

Spatial transformations must be thought of in terms of even more complex social structures, which can be briefly outlined thus: (i) On the one hand, individual societal actors, groups of actors, and networks *can act independently of one another*, running in parallel or at different times, as individual social units that transform space by developing and implementing their own new modes of action and interpretation with respect to Space A; (ii) on the other hand, individual societal actors, groups of actors, and networks can develop new space-related modes of action and interpretation in the form of *interrelated social action together with the other social units*; (iii) furthermore, *governance constellations* that are characterized by their ability to coordinate spatial transformations of greater scope *can work within a narrower core group*; and (iv) they *can also extend their focus beyond the narrower core group* and maintain broader communicative exchange with other actors. Among the interrelated actions occurring between different social units, complex – processual and interdependent – interrelationships emerge, which can be described as "communicative figurations" after Hepp (2013, 84–89), following Elias (1978, 141 f.), since they are essentially realized through intermeshing (direct and mediatized) communicative forms.

Just as conflicts are likely to occur within social units (e.g. in networks) when it comes to developing jointly shared new modes of action and interpretation with regard to a space, this is also the case *between* different social units; that is, in the interrelationships between communicative figurations.[8] The different spatial units' new spatial modes of action and interpretation and the constructions of spaces that emerge from these can thus result in conflict. Some social units might attempt, together with other selected social units, to enforce their respective construction of space in the public sphere. In doing so, they can, if necessary, stand in opposition to other social units. Incidentally, especially in the case of mediatized and digitalized communicative action – which has not been treated systematically here so far, but should not be neglected – one should also assume implications for the communicative reconstruction of spaces. For a long time, social actors in all societal fields have been increasingly exposed to media and technology in both analogue and digital forms (Hepp 2020), and there is increasing evidence that mediatized and especially digitalized communication may result in different experiences, forms of knowledge, ways of acting, social processes, and possibly also in different constructions of spaces. This argument is illustrated by the fact that social actors can be (virtually) 'present' in several places simultaneously and that, depending on the (digital) media they use, they are able to act in various forms of translocality. Against this background, the ways in which social actors communicatively reconstruct spaces change fundamentally. Knoblauch and Löw (2017, 3) therefore argue that mediatization and digitalization should be seen as essential elements in the processual refiguration of spaces.

Spatial transformations as communicative reconstructions of space: Public spheres and (media) discourses

But let us return to the collective actors interacting with each other and consider their – quite conflictual – actions in the context of the public and media discourses of which they become a part. Actor groups, networks, and governance constellations that initially operate in small public spheres as part of their internal communication usually address other actors or local residents with their space-related modes of action and interpretation, thus addressing a larger public. Depending on the group of actors, network, or governance constellation, this takes place via specific ensembles of – direct and media-based – forms of communication.[9] In the understanding of such actors, these activities are also referred to as public relations. Such forms of communication can range, for example, from a public lecture, a citizens' meeting, a panel discussion, a festival, an artistic or cultural event, or a collective walk through an urban space. It can take place via posters, exhibitions, flyers, brochures, and articles in city or local newspapers as well as in online, e-governance, or e-participation forums, besides a variety of social media manifestations and classic public relations work. Through such forms of outwardly directed communication to other actors and residents, a public sphere (here, Public Sphere of Space A) is created, in which a public discourse on Space A is constituted.

This space-related discourse is a contested field with regard to its themes. Prior themes (or space-related modes of interpretation) that may have become dominant in Space A in the context of earlier communicative figurations and negotiation processes are questioned and renegotiated alongside newly emergent ones. Groups of actors, networks, governance constellations, and the communicative figurations arising from them attempt, by and large strategically, to shape the discourse on Space A thematically (in accordance with their space-related modes of interpretation), to establish corresponding orders of knowledge, and to insist on their implementation in action and material arrangements. In addition, they can accrue *dispositif* structures which, from their perspective, can be helpful for the further establishment of 'their' space-related discourse topics and their practical implementation. The establishment of such a *dispositif* structure can include, for example, the appointment of a person for public relations work, the recruitment of further supporting actors and networks, the creation of specific institutions, the enforcing of certain legal regulations, or a special arrangement of material objects. Insofar as several different groups of actors, networks, and governance constellations act in parallel as communicative figurations, there can be several different but highly interrelated discourse topics and *dispositif* structures that attempt to constitute and shape the respective space: those that are in opposition to one another (that compete) and those that support each other (that form a coalition).

Local mass media also play a role in this process. They do not simply function as arenas of discourse or news relays that take up and pass on to their audiences the space-related, external communications of groups of actors, networks, or governance constellations. Rather, they appear as specific – powerful – actors due to journalistic actions such as news selection and news staging, and they can have a considerable influence on the further public negotiation of specific discourse topics. Although these various discourse topics are brought into a local public sphere through local mass media or social media, not all societal (discourse) actors and topics are heard there. In short, here too, power constellations shape the process of space-related communicative reconstructions.

Within the framework of public communications and the discursive negotiations of various space-related themes – by groups of actors, networks, and/or governance constellations as well as by local mass media or social media – multiple collective reconstructions of space compete at the level of the local public sphere of Space A. However, these reconstructions of space are partly intertwined and can be shared to a certain extent between different communicative figurations within the area of overlap. What we can thus observe are multiple realities of Space A^{transformed} in the Public Sphere A.

Supra-regional, national, or international media and their contents can also be of importance for the communicative construction and reconstruction of Space A. In comparison to the local public sphere of Space A, corresponding media and their news constitute a large supra-regional public sphere. Supra-regional, national, and international media offer societal actors and inhabitants who (among other things) assign themselves to Space A knowledge of other spaces (e.g. of villages, cities, regions, countries, supra-nations, the world as a whole, and even outer space), a knowledge that the actors and inhabitants cannot have obtained only from direct experience, but which can nevertheless be directly relevant to Space A. In this context, these media can point out regional, national, or global processes (economic, cultural, social, or religious, for instance) that can play a role for Space A. Of course, such other spaces or processes do not objectively exist as such. Rather, the media provide multiple media constructions of other spaces and supra-regional processes that are fed by, among other things, the knowledge of experts. Actors and inhabitants of Space A process these constructions. Together with a locally available, individual practical knowledge of such spaces, which – as already mentioned – is only available to a limited extent, such spaces are made to endow particular qualities, extensions, and positions in relation to Space A. That is, they become spaces that are characterized in a certain way; they become associated or alien spaces, small or large spaces, near or distant spaces, surrounding or adjoining spaces, or spaces from which one distances oneself, and so on. Regional, national, or global processes are turned into processes that in a certain way influence Space A or that may have interdependencies with its processes. Via media constructions of other spaces, actors and inhabitants of Space A can see their space in a new light. Through them, they can be stimulated to construct new ways of interpretation, action, and material arrangements (such as establishing or dismantling borders, cooperating with the surrounding area, or sealing themselves off).

Importantly, media (but also outsiders who temporarily or permanently enter Space A) may communicate a picture (i.e. space-related interpretations) of Space A that is foreign to the actors and inhabitants of Space A. These too are constructions of space to which actors and residents relate, which they further process communicatively, and to which they grant a place of one kind or another in their own construction of space. At the level of the delimited public sphere, Space A is thus positioned and qualified in relation to other spaces within a framework of communicative action. Since other spaces, like Space A, are also constantly transforming, and since this is communicatively processed in public spheres as well, corresponding communications about this can – in addition to the internal transformation impulses described in detail above – act as external impulses for new space-related modes of interpretation and action as well as for changed material arrangements in the case of individual societal actors, groups of actors, networks, and governance constellations in Space A.

Final remarks: Methodological implications of the approach of communicative (re)constructions of space

If one considers the theoretical reflections developed above, especially those of the previous section, for the analysis of spatial transformation processes, and particularly for the processual refiguration of spaces, the empirical question arises of how, in individual cases, the dynamics of space-related communicative action in (heterogeneous) constellations of actors, the communicative negotiations of space-related knowledge orders in the context of discourses, and the development of *dispositifs* and the inclusion of material objects in action occur. Which forms and patterns of space-related communicative actions are characteristic for which actor constellations and communicative figurations, how conflicts take place, and how spatial transformation processes happen against this background – these are just a few research questions that could arise from the theoretical approach.

Connected to this is the methodological question of how communicative reconstruction and, as part of this, the refiguration of spaces can be methodologically investigated. It is argued that such a historic, dynamic, and comprehensive research subject requires a complex research design in methodological terms and that an "ethnographic discourse analysis" (Christmann 2014) would meet the requirements. Consequently, a combination of two comprehensive methodological concepts – the ethnographic one and the discourse-analytical one – is considered necessary. By means of the ethnographic approach, it is possible to comprehend forms and content of space-related communicative actions – and, on this basis, space-related transformations – in groups, networks, governance constellations, and communicative figurations of the present. To some extent, it is also possible to reconstruct past phases of space-related transformation through interviews. The discourse-analytical approach allows for the (historical) analysis of space-related discourse topics, their discursive negotiations, and the thus-developing knowledge orders, as well as their changes in small and large public spheres. The object of a *dispositif* analysis – as a possible part of discourse analyses – requires more than the investigation of public discourses, because it is necessary to consider a multitude of instruments and strategies by means of which certain knowledge orders are transformed and practically implemented. For this purpose, an ethnographic approach with participatory observation and additional qualitative network analyses is again helpful; for example, when it comes to the analysis of actor constellations, support networks, and modes of action that work toward the implementation of new space-related modes of interpretation and action. At least for the present, material spatial transformations can also be traced via forms of observation (using special visualization methods such as mapping). For material-spatial transformations that go back further in time, analyses of appropriate documents and discourses that contain visualizations of spatial arrangements will need to be carried out.

To summarize: From a methodological point of view, the approach of the communicative (re)construction of spaces – which, as stated at the beginning, is to be understood as a tool for investigating the processual refiguration of spaces – thus requires an interweaving of methods with which it is possible to scrutinize in detail the communicative action of social actors in their complex communicative figurations in the past and present.

Notes

1 The theoretical approach was first developed on the basis of empirical work carried out in the context of two research projects on "Urban Pioneers in Neighborhoods" (2009–2011, 2012–2014) funded by the Leibniz Institute for Research on Society and Space (Erkner, Germany). In four different urban neighborhoods, the project investigated how spatial transformation processes have taken place in the past and present and what role urban pioneers and their networks have played with their communicative actions. A first version of the approach was published in Christmann (2015). The contribution printed here is a substantially revised version of that approach. It was developed as part of theoretical work at the Collaborative Research Center 1265 "Re-Figuration of Spaces" at the Technische Universität Berlin, Germany (funded by the German Research Foundation under project no. 290045248).

2 Social theories are approaches that deal with the foundations of subjects and their knowledge and reciprocal social action, usually using the example of face-to-face relationships (e.g. theories of action). Theories of society deal with highly institutionalized forms of action of (collective) social actors, with discourse orders and their social implications, or with the formation of systemic structures (e.g. discourse theories, systems theories).

3 Spatial action is often accompanied by verbal communication that makes this action explicit to others. However, nonverbal and verbal space-related action can each also occur in isolation.

4 This is a process that can also be described using Giddens' (1984) structuration theory. The concept of "structuration", consisting of the conceptual components "structure" and "a[c]tion", points to the fact that action and structure may not be seen as opposing phenomena, but rather as mutually related elements of an action process.

5 See Berger and Luckmann (1966, 74), who understand "roles" as follows: "It can readily be seen that the construction of role typologies is a necessary correlate of the institutionalization of conduct. Institutions are embodied in individual experience by means of roles."

6 The functional areas themselves can be further subdivided in many different ways. For example, they may be segmentally structured (in the area of spatial planning, for instance, a distinction can be made between municipal, regional, and state planning) and/or hierarchically structured (e.g. in the form of superordinate and subordinate authorities); furthermore, there might be ideological or milieu-specific differentiations (e.g. in the party political system and in civil society).

7 Governance constellations as well as social groups and networks can, incidentally, also be regarded as collective actors. Collective actors are characterized by the fact that they develop spatial constructions in a coordinated and cooperative manner

against a background of shared knowledge and common modes of action (Löw and Knoblauch 2021).
8 Against this background, "multiple spatialities" may emerge as different or even divergent spatial constructions informed by differently situated social action references. As a rule, multiple spatialities are associated with different spatial regimes (Löw and Knoblauch 2021).
9 According to Hepp (2013, 89), each communicative figuration (e.g. in the form of a network) is constituted by: (i) its specific forms and patterns of communication and, among these, (ii) its specific forms of media communication, (iii) its typical actor constellations, and (iv) its typical thematic framings.

References

Assmann, Aleida, and Jan Assmann. 1993. "Schrift und Gedächtnis (Nachwort)" [Writing and memory (epilogue)]. In *Schrift und Gedächtnis. Beiträge zur Archäologie der literarischen Kommunikation* [Writing and memory: Contributions to the archaeology of literary communication], edited by Aleida Assmann and Jan Assmann, 265–284. München: Fink.
Berger, Peter L., and Thomas Luckmann. 1966. *The Social Construction of Reality: A Treatise in the Sociology of Knowledge*. Garden City, NY: Anchor Books.
Christmann, Gabriela B. 2010. "Kommunikative Raumkonstruktionen als (Proto-) Governance" [Communicative constructions of space as (proto-)governance]. In *Governance und Raum* [Governance and space], edited by Heiderose Kilper, 27–48. Baden-Baden: Nomos.
Christmann, Gabriela B. 2014. "Investigating Spatial Transformation Processes: An Ethnographic Discourse Analysis in Disadvantaged Neighbourhoods". *Historical Social Research* 39: 235–256.
Christmann, Gabriela B. 2015. "Das theoretische Konzept der kommunikativen Raum(re)konstruktion" [The theoretical concept of the communicative (re)construction of spaces]. In *Zur kommunikativen Konstruktion von Räumen* [On the communicative construction of spaces], edited by Gabriela B. Christmann, 89–117. Wiesbaden: Springer VS.
Christmann, Gabriela, Hubert Knoblauch, and Martina Löw. 2022. "Introduction: Communicative Constructions and the Re-Figuration of Spaces". In *Communicative Constructions and the Refiguration of Spaces*, edited by Gabriela Christmann, Hubert Knoblauch, and Martina Löw, 3–15. Abingdon: Routledge.
Elias, Norbert. 1978. *What is Sociology?* New York: Columbia University Press.
Foucault, Michel. 1978. *Dispositive der Macht* [*Dispositifs* of power]. Berlin: Merve Verlag.
Foucault, Michel. 1994. *The Order of Things*. New York: Vintage Books.
Foucault, Michel. 2013. *Lectures on the Will to Know*. Basingstoke: Palgrave Macmillan.
Giddens, Anthony. 1984. *The Constitution of Society: Outline of the Theory of Structuration*. Cambridge: Polity Press.
Glasze, Georg, and Annika Mattissek, eds. 2009. *Handbuch Diskurs und Raum* [Handbook of discourse and space]. Bielefeld: transcript.
Healey, Patsy. 1992. "Planning through Debate: The Communicative Turn in Planning Theory and its Implications for Spatial Strategy Formation". *Town Planning Review* 63: 143–162.
Hepp, Andreas. 2013. *Medienkultur. Die Kultur mediatisierter Welten* [Media culture: The culture of mediatized worlds]. Wiesbaden: Springer VS.

Hepp, Andreas. 2020. *Deep Mediatization*. London and New York: Routledge.
Keller, Reiner. 2001. "Wissenssoziologische Diskursanalyse" [Sociology of knowledge approach to discourse]. In *Handbuch Sozialwissenschaftliche Diskursanalyse. Band 1* [Handbook of social-science-based discourse analysis. Volume 1], edited by Reiner Keller, Andreas Hirseland, Werner Schneider, and Willy Viehöver, 113–144. Opladen: Leske + Budrich.
Keller, Reiner. 2008. *Wissenssoziologische Diskursanalyse* [Sociology of knowledge approach to discourse]. Wiesbaden: VS Verlag.
Keller, Reiner. 2013. *Doing Discourse Research: An Introduction for Social Scientists*. London: Sage.
Keller, Reiner. 2022. "The Symbolic Construction of Spaces: Perspectives from a Sociology-of-Knowledge Approach to Discourse". In *Communicative Constructions and the Refiguration of Spaces*, edited by Gabriela Christmann, Hubert Knoblauch, and Martina Löw, 36–56. Abingdon: Routledge.
Keller, Reiner, Hubert Knoblauch, and Jo Reichertz. 2013. "Der Kommunikative Konstruktivismus als Weiterführung des Sozialkonstruktivismus" [Communicative constructivism as a continuation of social constructivism]. In *Kommunikativer Konstruktivismus* [Communicative constructivism], edited by Reiner Keller, Hubert Knoblauch, and Jo Reichertz, 9–21. Wiesbaden: Springer VS.
Knoblauch, Hubert. 1995. *Kommunikationskultur* [Communication culture]. Berlin and New York: de Gruyter.
Knoblauch, Hubert. 2001. "Diskurs, Kommunikation und Wissenssoziologie" [Discourse, communication, and sociology of knowledge]. In *Handbuch Sozialwissenschaftliche Diskursanalyse. Band 1* [Handbook of social-science-based discourse analysis. Volume 1], edited by Reiner Keller, Andreas Hirseland, Werner Schneider, and Willy Viehöver, 207–224. Opladen: Leske + Budrich.
Knoblauch, Hubert. 2013. "Grundbegriffe und Aufgaben des kommunikativen Konstruktivismus" [Basic concepts and tasks of communicative constructivism]. In *Kommunikativer Konstruktivismus* [Communicative constructivism], edited by Reiner Keller, Hubert Knoblauch, and Jo Reichertz, 25–47. Wiesbaden: Springer VS.
Knoblauch, Hubert. 2020. *The Communicative Construction of Reality*. London and New York: Routledge.
Knoblauch, Hubert, and Martina Löw. 2017. "On the Spatial Re-Figuration of the Social World". *Sociologica* 11 (2), 1–27.
Knoblauch, Hubert, and Martina Löw. 2020. "The Re-Figuration of Spaces and Refigured Modernity – Concept and Diagnosis". *Historical Social Research* 45 (2): 263–292.
Knoblauch, Hubert, and Silke Steets. 2022. "From the Constitution to the Communicative Construction of Space". In *Communicative Constructions and the Refiguration of Spaces*, edited by Gabriela Christmann, Hubert Knoblauch, and Martina Löw, 19–35. Abingdon: Routledge.
Läpple, Dieter. 1991. "Essay über den Raum" [Essay on space]. In *Stadt und Raum* [City and space], edited by Hartmut Häußermann, Detlev Ipsen, Thomas Krämer-Badoni, Dieter Läpple, Marianne Rodenstein, and Walter Siebel, 157–207. Pfaffenweiler: Centaurus.
Lees, Loretta. 2004. "Urban Geography: Discourse Analysis and Urban Research". *Progress in Human Geography* 28 (1): 101–107.
Lefebvre, Henri. 1991. *The Production of Space*. Cambridge: Blackwell.
Löw, Martina. 2016. *The Sociology of Space: Materiality, Social Structures, and Action*. New York: Palgrave Macmillan.

Löw, Martina, and Hubert Knoblauch. 2021. *Re-Figuration von Räumen. Fortsetzungsantrag für den Sonderforschungsbereich 1265* [Re-Figuration of Spaces. Continuation Application for the Collaborative Research Center 1265]. Berlin: Technische Universität Berlin. [Unpublished manuscript].

Luckmann, Thomas, and Peter L. Berger. 1964. "Social Mobility and Personal Identity". *European Journal of Sociology* 5 (2): 331–344.

Paasi, Ansi. 1989. "The Media as Creator of Local and Regional Culture". In *The Long-Term Future of Regional Policy – A Nordic View*. Report on a Joint NordREFO/OECD seminar in Reykjavik, 151–165. Helsinki: NordREFO/OECD.

Poferl, Angelika. 2009. "Orientierung am Subjekt?" [Orientation toward the subject?]. In *Handeln unter Unsicherheit* [Acting under uncertainty], edited by Fritz Böhle and Margit Weihrich, 231–264. Wiesbaden: VS Verlag.

Pott, Andreas. 2007. "Sprachliche Kommunikation durch Raum – das Angebot der Systemtheorie" [Linguistic communication through space – what systems theory offers]. *Geographische Zeitschrift* 95: 56–71.

Thrift, Nigel. 2007. *Non-Representational Theory: Space, Politics, Affect*. London: Routledge.

7 Eliciting space

Methodological considerations in analyzing communicatively constructed spaces

Martina Löw and Séverine Marguin

Introduction

Any interviewer who has attempted to ask people what meaning they attribute to spaces will probably have had the sort of experience we have had in various research projects. People are virtually incapable of giving information about spaces when asked to do so. Most seem unable to say ad hoc how spaces guide bodies in channels, or how bodies are integrated into spatial arrangements, and few are capable even of giving an exact description of the material environment, especially if an interviewer asks them to supply one from memory. Whether we are managers or travelers, cultural entrepreneurs or hairdressers, spaces appear to inhabit an area of experience we know a great deal about in practical terms, but this knowledge is hardly accessible to the discursive consciousness of the layperson.

This does not apply in the same measure to places that can be specifically named. People asked to introduce themselves will often not only give their name, but also provide as additional information the city they come from (Myers 2006). "I'm Nick from Kirkham", or "My name's Mike Hannah, and I'm from Preston". Mentioning the place one comes from along with one's name is considered basic information for communication. Mentioning concrete places allows for people to be spatially positioned without spaces having to be concretely described.

Interaction studies of mobile telephone communication have produced similar findings. Not only do people localize themselves to set up the conversation, they might also – as Ilkka Arminen and Alexandra Weilenmann (2009) have found – convey enticing spatial information prior to extending an invitation.

> For instance, mentioning that one is at the beach can open a discussion about what to do next, or presenting the nightclub as having a very long queue configures that place as popular, and a potential place to go to.
> (Arminen and Weilenmann 2009, 1920)

DOI: 10.4324/9780367817183-9

Their thesis is that the description of places enhances emotional intensity in mobile telephone communication. The authors see descriptions of places as a resource in communication, particularly when invitations are extended or offers made.

Taken together, these three findings – that where a person comes from is standard information on who that person is; that space is used as an emotional amplifier in communication; and that people have little comprehension for actually providing information about space – suggest the following thesis: that speech as a routine aspect of action is regularly (which means to say not always but often) inherent in the dynamics of spatial constructions and that the speaker is aware of the speech act itself but not of its effects in forming space.

Furthermore, communicative action comprises more than only speaking. It relates just as much to body language and to the relevance of objects in an arrangement. As spaces involved in communicative action also emerge from the manner in which subjects mutually relate to one another and to objects, spaces thus also become meaningful in that they become a part of communication through subjective, physical experience (Christmann 2016, 2022; Christmann, Knoblauch, and Löw 2022).

From a methodological perspective, the question poses itself of how spaces arising in communicative action can be investigated when speaking about space presents a problem to many laypersons. How can knowledge about spatial construction be gained from group interviews and discussions even though many people are only aware of the construction of spaces in practical terms? How can mappings be used in order to support the processes of making gains in knowledge?

This chapter explores several possible social science approaches to space without making any claims to comprehensiveness.[1] Not considered are, for example, anthropological methods or go-alongs that seek to understand spatial constructions through observation. It is much more our aim to present pragmatic, resource-saving, and creative approaches, reflecting from a methodological perspective on both verbal and image-based instruments and their operationalization in both the surveying and the analytical phases. We begin here in the first section with secondary analyses of interviews in order to give an example of how productively incidental spatial narratives in interviews dealing with other issues can be interpreted for spatial analysis. Following on from this, we show how helpful implicitly or explicitly communicated knowledge about places and regions in (focus) group discussions is for the comprehension of the significance of action and spaces. In the second section, we place the focus on mapping procedures, particularly the productive interrelation of the graphic and the spoken or written. We see drawings as a chance, in the process of visualization, of loosening up the blockages in speaking about space. In presenting the methodological approach, it becomes increasingly apparent that the collection and interpretation of data itself forms a space-constituting action situation.

Before coming to the first instrument – the narrative interviews – we elucidate the theoretical framework within which we are working, inasmuch as it is decisive to how, from what perspective, and with what focus the research instruments are employed. The relation of space and communicative action is explored more thoroughly elsewhere (cf. Knoblauch and Steets 2022; Christmann 2022). We therefore limit ourselves to a short note on our point of departure: It is now taken for granted in the social sciences that spaces are relational in nature. This means that they are understood not as absolute values, but as structures (Malpas 2012). Space is defined (in a very general sense) as a complex of relations between potential objects, which as an institutionalized structure both determines and is changed by practice. If we accept this basic idea, then space can be defined in a sociological sense as a relational arrangement of living beings and social goods at places (Löw 2016; see also Knoblauch and Steets 2022). It is useful here to distinguish analytically between spacing and synthesis (Löw 2016) as two aspects of the construction of space. Space comes into being by connecting elements in such a way that they are perceived as a communicative form (synthesis) and by positioning these elements (spacing). Spacing is, according to Knoblauch (2017), in its basic form a triadic relation in which the actions of subjects (and their positions or places) remain dynamically related to one another. Put briefly, every analysis of space addresses the fact that communicative action is formed not only in a subject-subject relation, but is also rather tied together with objectivation. Objectivations might be fleeting examples of reification such as gestures or institutionalized placements and connections of objects to spaces that create an interpretable, objectivized meaning. As the establishment, building, or positioning of social goods and people occurs through the spatial effects of acting subjects, we identify spatial constructions themselves as communicative.

Eliciting by talking

Narrative interview: The willy, for example

All interviews contain information about spatial constructions in everyday life, even when they are conducted with other aims in mind, and can be used to understand commonplace communicative constructions of space. The interview situation is, indeed, itself a spatial setting that can be interpreted, but for the comprehension of everyday spatial constructions, it is the transcribed text that serves above all. It is even of methodological help for the understanding of the relevance of space to daily life to speak in interviews about thematic areas that do not explicitly address space and to interpret these in the light of spatial constructions. Alternatively, secondary analyses can equally be conducted from preexisting interview material. We illustrate this with an example interview taken from the context of a study on prostitution. In many instances, sexual services in prostitutional contexts begin with the washing of the man as a "self-evident element in a sequence of action" (Ahlemeyer 2002, 155; Löw and Ruhne 2011). In the following sequence, a brothel keeper attempts to convey how matter-of-factly a colleague treats a client:

> For example, last Saturday I was here briefly. You won't believe it, but I was sitting here and listened in a bit. She was in the bathroom with him and said, "come on, show me your willy". [Laughs] Charming she is. She deals with men so naturally.

We already know from communication in hospital settings that genitalia can be cause for embarrassment. As a rule, the situation can be fraught long before a nurse embarrasses herself, and everyone else, through ineptitude and deviation from routine. Birgit Heimerl (2006) has very precisely traced the choreography of exposure in hospitals. The awkwardness lies not only in touching the exposed body of a patient in the presence of clothed, healthy people, but also in the gender constellation of female nurse and male patient. In hospital, the rule is that if men feel embarrassed in front of nurses, it is a sign of effeminacy, while if they are not embarrassed enough, they are soon considered lewd.

In a brothel, it might be assumed that the second risk would not arise. In fact, the sentence "show me your willy", as a communicative act accompanying the spatial act of washing, marks a shift in power. In the act of washing, the woman takes a measure of control over the situation. The prostitute uses the opportunity to check the penis for signs of disease and hence to reduce the risk of infection through sexual intercourse. In the context of a controlled activity, treating the penis lightly as a "willy" can be interpreted as active de-dramatization of the practice of inspection. In interviews, prostitutes repeatedly stressed how important control over washing is for them. They want to know that their customers are properly washed, but implementing a practice of cleaning before the sexual act is socially far from being a matter of course. If, in everyday life, a physical encounter between two people is construed as "intimate", showering or washing prior to sexual intercourse is possible but by no means necessary. In prostitution, the act of washing routinely precedes sexual intercourse. The prostitute uses this opportunity – quite in keeping with our knowledge of nursing practices – to demonstrate and gain control. By talking, she also gains the opportunity to de-dramatize her action and embed it again in everyday life. As her colleague remarks, she treats men naturally.

Now space comes into play. For the question remains why paying men would put up with this. What is decisive is that, as Renate Ruhne convincingly argues (in Löw and Ruhne 2011), we construe prostitution in every regard as an "other" space. If the real world prevails in one kind of space and prostitution waits in another, some form of passage is needed between them. In the interviews, men describe the ritual of cleaning as relaxing, as a transition, as a shaking off of external space. Through the act of cleaning, the prostitutional actors construct a dual spatial pattern with an external space – "world" – and an internal space – "prostitution". It is this construction that allows acts in the internal space to appear legitimate that would not be sanctioned in the external space – and the consequences of this construction concern not only the practices of sexuality, but also and above all the legal and working conditions of sex workers.

Generalizing this example from a methodological point of view, we are dealing with a doing (washing) and a saying (willy) which together constitute a reality. The two persons involved harmoniously agree to a practice in the pursuit of quite different, gender-specific purposes. Although the result, the production of a two-world idea as spatial construction, is in practice consciously perceived, it is seldom discursively available. Space comes into being by connecting elements in such a way that they are perceived as a common structure and by positioning these same elements. In this case, space comes into being in an internal-external construction, which does not simply attribute a female component to the internal dimension and a male component to the external dimension; inasmuch as the existence of the internal dimension leads to other rules applying here than to those outside, and in a society that categorizes almost all commercial activities in training formats, it results in sex work being considered an intuitive activity. The acting subjects place themselves in relation to this synthesis.

Space and place can no longer be understood as being "already given" when an interaction begins; the communicative action of producing spaces has to be seen as part of speaking and bodily positioning (Broth 2008; Mondada 2009).

Such examples help us to understand how synthesizing and spacing can occur in linguistic and bodily coordination and are synthesized through the mediation of complex meaning constructions. However, just as often, the construction of spaces in speech is not coordinated through positioning.

Focus groups: Imaginary placing

A to-date largely neglected instrument for the analysis of spatial constructions are imaginary, often translocal positionings of individuals or groups of people through contextual information in language (dialects) or in conversation (e.g. indications of place of origin). Particularly in group discussions, participants regularly use incidentally provided indications of location (e.g. the street from which they come) or linguistic colorations of dialect in order to meaningfully react to one another. Communicative action among participants can again be sociologically interpreted to understand cultural constructions of space.

Alfred Lameli (2009) investigates the extent of spontaneous knowledge among linguistic laymen in localizing dialects. It appears that most people, even without speaking a dialect, can relatively correctly localize dialects on a map. This was the case both for the group of just over 16-year-olds under study as well as for an adult control group. According to the author, the linguistically retrievable knowledge that relatively untraveled young people with low dialect identification show about how people speak in different areas can be attributed to their associating regions with personalities known from television, such as Helmut Kohl, Franz Beckenbauer, Angela Merkel, Pope Benedict XVI, Udo Lindenberg, and so on, and by notions about language areas gained from dialect comedies. What is more, dialect areas center around cities. For example, respondents identified Kassel as the focal point for a manner of speaking exemplified by a speech sample recorded in a northern Hesse town 60 kilometers from the city.

In this case, neither the decline in dialect competence nor perceivable spatial dissonances (the former Pope speaks his Bavarian dialect in Rome; we imagine Angela Merkel in Berlin, but don't know where she is right now, etc.) prevent space being constructed as relevant through the imaginary positioning of figures in relation to places. Here, too, a relative relevance system is used (positions concentrated through synthesis to form spaces). Decisive is that, in absentia, the complex interplay between synthesis and spacing has to rely on the media of language and image to reproduce spatial structure. This does not mean that spacing is irrelevant for synthesis. In the sentence "I am Nick from Kirkham", or a mobile phone call about an idyllic beach, or the ability of young people to describe how people speak in Bavaria because they have heard the (former) Pope on television – in all three speech acts, the bodily presence of the speaker is not irrelevant. Nick may make sure his origins are known in order to cope better with an unnerving round of introductions, the person on the telephone addresses emotions through spatial descriptions, and young people integrate themselves into a system of regional differentiation.

Communicative actions are embedded within spaces through consciously or unconsciously transmitted information about places and regions. Translocal spaces thus particularly extend themselves when those places and regions mentioned in these texts lie beyond the immediate vicinity of an action situation. The reference to current and earlier spaces that one has had experience of are important producers of meaning. A person, a situation, or an action, through the additional knowledge of space, all contribute to meaning. The full significance of actions can thus be better comprehended through social scientific analysis. Even those spaces that lend meaning to communicative action can in this way be reconstructed. In this connection, a space gains efficacious shape (e.g. an administrative region) that is not congruent with actual spacing, even though the speech act configures the action situation.

How a region or an object is spoken about is, of course, also important information for interpretation. In most everyday situations, however, we make use of relational constructions to put space into words. We say, for instance, that "the ball is in front of the car". But it is important to note that there is always an alternative way of putting it, such as "the ball is to the left of the car" (see, in detail, Levinson 2003, 24 ff.). From the point of view of space theory, it is important to note that the first speech act ("the ball is in front of the car") expresses the spatial relationship between the ball and the car. In the second speech act, by contrast, the position of the speaker is integrated into what is communicated. The statement then makes sense only if I recognize that I am looking at a structure in which a ball is lying to the left and a car is standing to the right. If I say that the ball is lying to the left of the car, I give far stronger expression to the fact that I am standing here as an observer who is describing a spatial arrangement. By contrast, a clearer dissociation through the use of an abstract reference system is evident in "the ball lies to the west".

Cultural differences are also relevant here. Stephen C. Levinson (2003; see also Levinson and Wilkins 2006) shows that spatial relations are portrayed linguistically very differently from one culture to another. Whether, for example, positioning is marked by a preposition (in, at, on, under) or shown by a verb, and thus conceived of as a movement formation, indicates both that spatial structures can be very differently constructed from a cultural point of view and that typical spatial relations are fundamentally structured through language (Levinson and Wilkins 2006, 4 ff.). In Central America, in New Guinea, and in Nepal, we find languages whose speakers know only a fixed system of north, south, east, and west for conceiving of and expressing positionings, so, as Clifford Geertz (1973) writes, anyone in Bali who cannot say which direction is north is simply considered mad. Western languages all utilize both relational and absolute reference systems to describe relational arrangements.

We must be clear about the methodological consequences. Since the subject matter of sociology is society, a social structure in constant flux, it requires a relational concept of space in order to describe the institutionalized patterns of ordering. An absolutist concept of space would not be helpful. However, if we work with a relational concept of space, we can distinguish various reference systems for communication about spaces in everyday speech: the absolute, relational synthesis of social goods, or the relational synthesis of social goods with the linguistic marking of the speaker's position. Drawing this distinction helps in analyzing communication to understand the role of the speaker in constituting space.

Eliciting space by drawing

Social science empirical research has to date concentrated on the interpretation of text. Qualitative methods above all interpret written data (such as transcribed interviews, group discussions, or field notes). Images, maps, sound, and so on hardly belong among the usual sources for the interpretation of the environment, despite the recent formation of the field of visual research methods, with particular relevance of photography (Rose 2011, 2014; Traue 2013) and videography (Knoblauch, Tuma, and Schnettler 2014). The practice of drawing still remains largely under-examined in social science exploration of space, although in other spatial sciences (such as architecture and urban planning), it has long since played an important role.

How does communicative action change in the research setting when graphic instruments are included in observation or questioning? And what findings about space can be produced by such means that would not otherwise be obtained? To answer these questions, the tool of mappings is introduced; as a graphic record, mappings possess spatial relevance per se.[2] Beyond the social sciences, and explicitly in sociology, mapping currently enjoys a certain currency and does so in a range of disciplines: Various mapping concepts are discussed and their methods employed in cultural studies (Schmidt-Lauber and Zechner 2018), (critical) geography (Cosgrove 1999; Rekacewicz 2013a, 2013b; Dodge 2016), historiography (Rankin 2016; Siegel and Weigel 2011), and anthropology (Hammarlin et al. 2009; Munk and Jensen 2014; Roberts 2016). We are of the conviction that spatial social science research can profit from these current, stimulating, multidisciplinary discourses on mapping.

Consistent with the approach of critical geography, we prefer the concept of mappings to that of maps, for the reason that it places the focus on process rather than on the "finished object of the map" (Cosgrove 1999, 1). Following Sybille Krämer, we understand mappings as "operative images" (Krämer 2008, 94) that constitute "the thing portrayed and that enable one to operate with it" (Krämer 2018, 23). Alongside critical geographers (Harley and Markham 1989; Wood and Fels 1992), we understand mappings as a co-construction of observed reality.[3] In this sense, they form important objectivations from the research process, which in the (re)construction of everyday spaces are reflected upon as well as used. We find it particularly appealing to combine (for the social sciences, novel) visual methods such as mapping with the core competence in textual interpretation – or put another way, to concentrate in the research setting on the interrelationship between the graphic and the spoken and written.

In the following, we show how mappings can assist in communicating (about) spaces. In order to empirically account for the spatially constitutive triad of subject-subject-objectivation, instruments are required that can capture the materiality of the space-constituting objectivation. In this regard, mappings offer promise in that they enable a (potentially complete) survey of the built environment.

In contrast to interviews, where the research situation is relatively fixed and routine – one person poses the questions and another answers them – mapping processes form the most varied of communicative action situations that require some unravelling here: Depending on who draws, says, or asks what, different communication settings for a graphic elicitation on the topic of space will arise. To this end, three instruments are introduced here:

- *mental mapping*, in which the act of drawing is performed by the interviewee;
- *mapping analyses*, in which the act of drawing is carried out by the researcher;
- *collaborative mapping elicitation*, in which the act of drawing alternates between the researcher and the subject.

Mental mapping: Spaces of researching

The geographical method of mental mapping (also known as cognitive mapping) aims to collect the subjects' spatial perceptions on the basis of drawings (Lynch 1960; Venturi, Scott Brown, and Izenour 1972; Shobe and Banis 2010; Smiley 2013; Götz and Holmén 2018). The classic researchers, such as Lynch or Venturi, developed the potential of the method as a quantitative analytical tool with which the importance of a place is determined by the frequency of mentions made by the subject or the graphically skewed spatial presentation of the subject is compared against the "true" perspective and to-scale cartography. In the geographical literature, following this tradition, the employment of templates is recommended with the aim of standardizing, and thus making comparable, the collected data (Gueben-Venière 2011). Such a closed process offers little possibility for the surveying of signification and meaning-positing, though. In the following, the example of an academic research project on the impacts of space on the production of knowledge (Marguin, Rabe, and Schmidgall 2019) shows what chances are offered to qualitative spatial research by an open mental mapping procedure.

In this project, we used an investigation protocol with a blank sheet of paper – that is, without a template such as a floor plan – and various colored pencils. We asked participants about the localization of their everyday research practices. Our initial aim was to generate drawings as "spatial narratives" (Dangschat 2014, 975) about their working context. More than just a list of places, though, the method allowed us to grasp the participants' understanding of space. In the analysis, we distinguished two understandings, a topological one and a multi-scalar one, each referring to a different form of relationality.

The topological understanding shows various places on a scale of measurement, positioned in relation to one another as on a map or the ground plan of a building (Figure 7.1a). Rather unexpectedly, questioning did not lead to such topological representations, but rather to further spatial constructions that one can describe as multi-scalar (Figure 7.1b). Characterized by the inclusion of various scales of measurement within the same drawing, these show the simultaneous synthesizing of different spaces nested within each other: The writing desk forms one space, the book on the writing desk forms another space, and within the picture, the drawing also forms a space.

Both representations indicate the dynamic character of the spaces of research, with alternating places (in the city, within buildings) or in the same place (with leaps between various scales of measurement).

The method of mental mappings – to the extent that they are carried out without a template – appears relevant to issues of analyzing scales of measurement (Lepetit 1993).[4] The choice of scale, much more than a simple arithmetic relation to reality, presents a specific perspective that gives an indication of the knowledge produced (Orain 2016). In that the chosen scale determines the selection, encoding, and prioritization of the subjects' drawn information, its analysis allows for insight into the structuring of the subjects' spatial knowledge. In our case there were, for instance, indications of the individual synthesizing processes but also of the levels of mobility of the subjects (e.g. whether their place of work is limited to one location or spans a number of places). Here it is important, however, to make no reference to scales of measurement in the questioning, but rather to formulate questions that are as free as is possible from references to scale.

The invitation to draw has a double-edged aspect for the interviewed subject, in that it both provides a stimulus and can provoke inhibitions. On the one

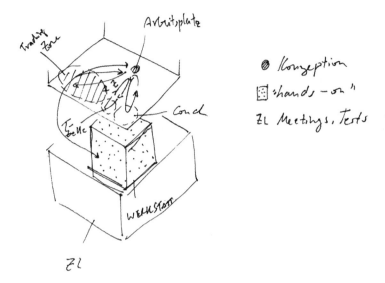

Figure 7.1a Topological understanding of space.
Source: Séverine Marguin, Henrike Rabe, and Friedrich Schmidgall.

hand it supports the elicitation of spatial knowledge, the act of drawing making their thoughts "visible" on the page – both for the researcher and for the interviewed subjects themselves. The filtering, prioritization, and arrangement of thoughts are reflected upon "aloud" by the interviewed subject (Krämer 2018), which often leads to their experiencing a eureka moment that turns out to be insightful for the investigation.

On the other hand, subjects often complain that they are unable to express the complexity of their experience through drawing, leading to frustration. One needs to be careful to consider the disparities in subjects' graphical representations when analyzing drawings. Researchers should not allow themselves to be influenced by the (to their taste) more "attractive" drawings. It is therefore important to lay the focus on the connection between the spoken and the drawn, as what the interviewed subject is unable to draw can possibly be expressed verbally, while what they are already able to sketch might be of somewhat marginal interest in their own interpretation. A further danger exists in the possibility that the drawn answer might prove very metaphorical while, at the same time, little is said about space. In this case, space has been used simply

Eliciting space 123

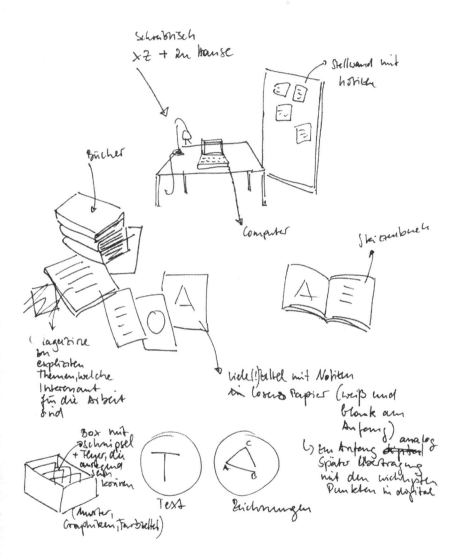

Figure 7.1b Multi-scalar understanding of space.
Source: Séverine Marguin, Henrike Rabe, and Friedrich Schmidgall.

as a helpful analogy for other issues. In such a case, prepared follow-up questions directly related to objectivation can bring about reification.

Having presented a research tool requiring the act of drawing on the part of the interviewed subject, we shall now take a closer look at research situations in which the researchers themselves take their pens in hand.

Mapping analysis: Personal spaces in an open space

Mapping analysis relates to researchers' collective evaluation situations based on mappings. Questions in this context might be: What findings can be brought by a graphic translation of data in a geo-referenced two-dimensional space? And what challenges are implied by such a translation?

We see the gain from the practice of mapping analysis in the attempt to spatialize and superimpose visually different types of data and media (not only drawings but also diagrams, plan bases, photography, statistical data, ethnographic data). Besides the processual aspect, it seems important to point out the relevant function of integration or the articulation of heterogeneous data through mapping.

In order to develop a methodological discourse pertinent to sociology, we propose a confrontation with the existing, rich debates on the triangular integration of qualitative and quantitative data (Creswell 2015), specifically on the technique of "joint display", understood as the joint or concomitant display of heterogeneous data for their integration (Kuckartz 2017; Creswell and Plano Clark 2011).[5] Of Kuckartz's three integration strategies (primary data integration, results integration, and sequential integration), we focus here on the integration of primary data, which is the most problematic but also the most interesting strategy – the other two integration techniques would primarily refer in this context to visualization.

We used such visual integration methods for data in the research project "ArchitekturenExperiment". In the area of territory analysis (Goffman 1971; Hall 1969), we aimed to draw the personal, group, and shared territory of individual scientists in a shared, open space. With the intention of using data from participant observation, mappings of movements and interactions, autophotography, systematic photographic documentation, and documentation of spatial arrangements, we first jointly composed an analogous spatial display for simultaneously viewing the data (Figure 7.2).

We then combined these different data into one single floor plan in order to reveal the spatial structure of the shared space – or, as Corner says, to reveal the unknown and the invisible (Corner 1999; see also Amoroso 2010). In the process, we switched from a juxtaposition to a superimposition of various datasets, in the sense of a "layered display". As a basis, we took the floor plan, showing the spatial arrangement of social goods such as walls, tables, chairs, waste bins, roll containers, pinboards, and so on. We superimposed the manual mappings of movements and interactions that had been collected over the course of some weeks. From this, we were able, in a preliminary stage of interpretation, to draw

Eliciting space 125

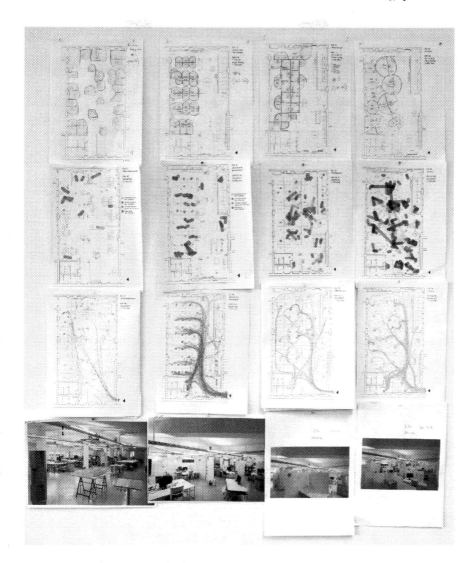

Figure 7.2 Analogous joint display.
Source: Séverine Marguin, Henrike Rabe, and Friedrich Schmidgall.

up zonings. We then confronted these initial drawings with further data, such as auto-photography, which provided information from the participants themselves on how they perceived the extent of their workplace. This allowed us to distinguish conflict zones through tactful spatial bargaining, but also to reveal the role of specific artefacts such as the lunchbox for the territorial marking of personal space (Figure 7.3).

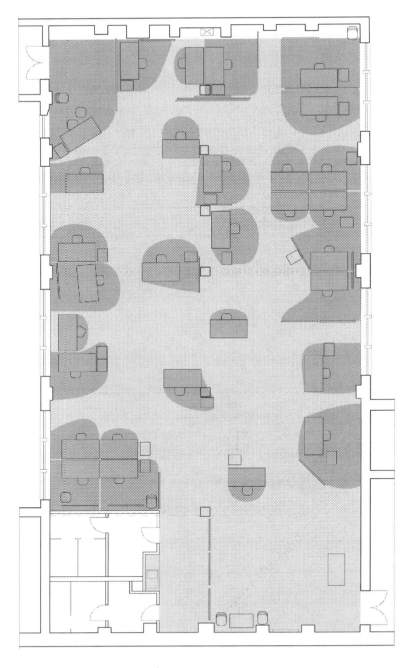

Figure 7.3 Personal territory analysis.
Source: Séverine Marguin, Henrike Rabe, and Friedrich Schmidgall.

These mappings were a good basis on which to accomplish further analysis; for example, in accordance with the disciplinary background of the researcher present in the open space. It is apparent, for example, that researchers in the humanities carry out the negotiation and appropriation of their personal territory differently to engineers or designers (Marguin, Rabe, and Schmidgall 2019). The personal territory of humanities researchers is accessed much less frequently than that of designers, as though the invisible threshold is much higher. Graphic data thus enable important findings on the relationship between space and academic cultures.

Such visual methods of analysis are tied to manual challenges, however, in that the mappings are produced by the researchers themselves. While mappings help to synthesize and concentrate data, it is also necessary that the chosen scale and the graphic language be reflected on critically during interpretation or that it be used as a gateway to understanding. The teachings on graphic semiology by the French cartographer Jacques Bertin (1980, 1983)[6] enable reflection on how to determine the reception of our own graphic (with regard to color, shape, and size), which has, in his view, to allow the content (the order of information) to correspond to its visualization (the visual order) (Bertin 1980, 34). Edward Tufte also expresses this idea of graphic integrity, when the visual representation of the data is consistent with its numerical representation (Tufte 2001, 51 ff.). The authors insist here that mappings can and must be taken in instantaneously as a result of their clear graphic language (cf. also in Bertin 1980 the difference between the [successful] *"cartes à voir"* and the [failed] *"cartes à lire"*). From a sociological perspective, we do not see the necessity of an instantaneous reception, and especially not if this graphic imperative leads to a too-pronounced reduction in complexity. In order that it give no false impressions, the creation of such a mapping nevertheless requires precise reflection on what message is meant to be seen or read from it. To this end, data sessions in which the creation process of a mapping is discussed intersubjectively among the researchers are indispensable.

A second challenge concerns the difficulty of graphically implementing a relational understanding of space. A mapping, even if emphasis is laid on its processuality, presents a static image. In this sense, mapping reifies represented space as a network of places, but neglects the dynamic aspects of the spatial construction. This is closely dependent on the issue of temporality: How can the dimension of time be integrated into a mapping? Interesting attempts to integrate time into cartographic productions already exist in geography and urban research, whether through the production of a sequence of mappings (cf. the development of the Ukrainian border, Eckert 2017) or, in the case of digital mappings, through the embedding of a timeline into the maps (cf. the development of the Berlin project-space scene, Marguin 2011).

However, even if these mapping projects demonstrate temporal change, they often only form container spaces. The rigidity of mappings does not, in fact, only relate to the issue of time, but equally to the difficulty of visually representing sociality. As Harley formulates it: "Maps as an impersonal type of knowledge tend to de-socialize the territory they represent. They foster the notion of a socially empty space" (Harley 2001, 81). Mapping, in contrast to classical cartography, thus offers the potential for integrating various data types. One can refer here to the mapping project "Residing in the Hidden", which focuses on the topic of the hostel industry in Berlin, and the forms of concealed housing that come with it (Kelling and Pelger 2021). In one final, large map, the narratives of refugees were integrated together with the spatial, organizational, and social systems of Berlin's hotel industry in order to provide insight into their habitation practices, their negotiation of privacy, and their movements through the city. In the overlapping of quantitative and qualitative data (as well as of language and drawing), social and spatial processes are able to be brought together simultaneously in one graphic manifestation.

Collaborative mapping elicitation: Accessing an art institution

Work with mappings offers the further possibility of animating participants, by means of maps, to speak and perhaps draw (or draw upon). Following the example of photographic elicitation (Rose 2007), one can speak here of mapping elicitation. Here, however, we are talking not of any kind of map, but of mappings that have been produced by researchers from their preliminary findings and placed before the subjects. This form of reflection on the researchers' interim results by the target group being investigated can be described as a "collaborative research approach" (Niewöhner 2014) inasmuch as it enables a conceptual co-construction of results with the subjects. In this sense, the method displays similarities to such popular mapping practices as participatory, critical, counter, and collective mapping, which lie at the intersections between art, activism, and social movements and (where applicable) academia (Halder and Michel 2018, 13).

The research project "Mapping Accessibilities of the Haus der Kulturen der Welt – in the World" (Marguin and Pelger 2021)[7] places emphasis on the generation of findings by such methods. In an initial stage, mapping analyses of accessibility to Berlin's culture institutions were carried out at various levels (building, surroundings, city, world). During the second stage, we allowed visitors to the various culture institutes to react to and work on the preprepared mappings in the context of a workshop. For example, in the run up to the workshop, a Nolli map[8] of buildings' surroundings was used to interpret the relationship between public and private space around the institutes. As part of the hands-on workshop, the participants placed power structures at the center of their observations and drawings. The intersubjective analysis of the surrounding landscape led to the jointly developed conclusion that the Haus der Kulturen der Welt is to be interpreted as a "cultural institution in the shadow of the government district" (Figure 7.4).

Methodologically, it is relevant to ask to what extent this result was influenced by the processing of the primary data in the form of a Nolli map. The question always arises in the course of using such a method, to what extent

Figure 7.4 The Haus der Kulturen der Welt in the shadow of the government district. Source: Marc Volk.

the preprepared mappings, serving as a means of eliciting responses, is supportive, channeling, or determining. In the present case, the preprepared Nolli map, on which public areas were presented as accessible or inaccessible inner and outer spaces, steered discussion toward the materiality of the demarcations between public and private. At the same time, it was precisely as a result of this awareness that the spatial proximity of the governmental district could be made the subject of discussion.

Another question is in what way the mapping process itself presents a particular space-constituting communicative action situation. Spatial visualizations are shown through gestures on paper as well as constructed by hand movements above and beyond it (Figure 7.5). It could be observed in the workshop how a group was able to "engage with the many aspects of everyday life [such as] thoughts, feelings, and experiences that are simply 'unspeakable'" (Moss and Irving 2018, 274). Drawing, as well as the impossibility of drawing, provoked discussion among the interviewed subjects and researchers about the space being investigated.

In the context of negotiating one's perceptions (among the interviewees themselves, but also between interviewee and researcher) an intersubjectivity was achieved. Mappings are thus more than simply an illustration or visual representation of facts. They can contribute essentially to gains in knowledge in research when it is a matter of understanding spaces in their socio-materiality.

Figure 7.5 Collaborative mapping elicitation.
Source: Marc Volk.

Conclusion

In this chapter, we have presented two methods for eliciting space: talking and drawing. Through interpreting interviews or group discussions, one can gain access to the structures of actors' knowledge and experience. Many statements only have meaning for their speakers because subliminal spatial constructions (such as inside–outside) underlie them. Individual positionings (such as "the ball is in front of the car") are often described, whose implicit spatial relation can be interrogated, including in order to understand the position of the speaker in a sequence of events being remembered. Places are often mentioned because they evoke the spatial imagination of the listener (in the case of city names or places culturally imbued with emotion, such as beaches) and thus enable information about social constructions of space to be given. In group discussions in particular, spatial relations can be interpreted from reactions to embedded speech acts (such as dialects).

Likewise, mapping presents an instrument with much potential in the most varied of communicative research settings for sociological research into space, because an abundance of possible interpretations arise out of the interrelation between the drawn and the spoken. The method of open mental mapping ("open" in the sense of being free of a scale of measurement) enables spatial representations to be brought forward whose analysis can provide fundamental information on the spatial knowledge of the subject (perspectives, scope, relationality). Spatial patterns can be discovered through mapping analyses as a result of the graphic superimposition of a layered display. In this sense, they are a suitable tool for categorizing and typifying spatial construction. Collaborative mapping elicitation allows the visual focus to be intensified by way of the selected mode of presentation of the preprepared mappings (e.g. an axonometric drawing). It also allows, for instance, the materiality of built space to be placed in the foreground of questioning or analysis in a way that could only with difficulty be achieved through purely verbal surveying tools.

Experimenting methodically with mapping continues to raise many issues. Nevertheless, new insights into data and spatial constructions can be won through reflective encounters with these challenges. Or, as Krämer puts it, mapping does not shut representationality and relativity *out*, but rather *in*:

> The relativity of the methods of presentation (projection, scale, selectivity, …) becomes the condition of the possibility of representing something on a map, in such a way that the object represented can at the same time be intervened in and operated on with this object.
>
> (Krämer 2018, 21)

In this sense, mappings take on the role of an orientation tool for spatial elicitation.

Notes

1 The chapter presents findings of the Collaborative Research Center 1265 "Re-Figuration of Spaces" at the Technische Universität Berlin, Germany. It is funded by the German Research Foundation under project no. 290045248.
2 We would like here to thank the Working Group "Hybrid Mapping Methods" of the Collaborative Research Center 1265 "Re-Figuration of Spaces", in which researchers at Technische Universität Berlin and the Leibniz Institute for Research on Society and Space in Erkner collaborate. The group served as an important source of inspiration and discussion in the preparation of this chapter. For more information see: https://www.sfb1265.de/en/research/method-lab/working-group-hybrid-mapping-methods/
3 In the debate surround representation (Goodman 1976), in which mapping is characterized as lying between transparency (as an instrument for measuring the world, following classical geography) or opacity (as an instrument for creating the world, following critical geography), we position ourselves among the constructivists. This means that, methodologically, we should closely follow the process of reconstruction.
4 A critical view of the employment of scale in analysis is offered by a contribution from Smith (2009): "Urban Studies without 'Scale'".
5 These observations were developed together with Nina Baur, Jörg Stollmann, and Dagmar Pelger. In addition, the Mapping as Joint Spatial Display conference was organized at the Collaborative Research Center 1265 "Re-Figuration of Spaces" of the Technische Universität Berlin in November 2018.

6 We could also cite Kevin Lynch's formatting, with circles, asterisks, stars, and thick versus thin lines to demarcate primary and secondary elements (Amoroso 2010, 48).
7 The project is a cooperation between the Chair of Urban Design, the Institute for Architecture, and the Institute for Sociology at the Collaborative Research Center 1265 at the Technische Universität Berlin. Involved in the project were Séverine Marguin and Dagmar Pelger with architecture master students Fadi Esper, Aaron Geier, Jörn Gertenbach, Muhannad Ghazal, Olga Juutistenaho, Andres Reyes Kutscher, and Anna Lesch.
8 The Nolli map uses a figure-ground representation of built space, with blocks and buildings shaded in a dark poché and (enclosed) public spaces left white. It was developed by the Italian architect Giambattista Nolli in the 18th century.

References

Ahlemeyer, Heinrich W. 2002. *Geldgesteuerte Intimkommunikation. Zur Mikrosoziologie heterosexueller Prostitution* [Money-driven intimate communication. On the microsociology of heterosexual prostitution]. Gießen: Psychosozial-Verlag.
Amoroso, Nadia. 2010. *The Exposed City: Mapping the Urban Invisibles*. London and New York: Routledge.
Arminen, Ilkka, and Alexandra Weilenmann. 2009. "Mobile Presence and Intimacy: Reshaping Social Actions in Mobile Contextual Configuration". *Journal of Pragmatics* 41 (10): 1905–1923.
Bertin, Jacques. 1980. "Voir ou lire" [Seeing or reading]. In *Cartes et figures de la terre: 2–8* [Maps and figures of the earth: 2–8]. Paris: Centre Georges Pompidou CCI.
Bertin, Jacques. 1983. *Semiology of Graphics: Diagrams, Networks, Maps*. Redlands, CA: Esri Press.
Broth, Mathias. 2008. "Seeing through Screens, Hearing through Speakers: Managing Distant Studio Space in Television Control Room Interaction". *Journal of Pragmatics* 41 (10): 1998–2016.
Christmann, Gabriela B., ed. 2016. *Zur kommunikativen Konstruktion von Räumen: Theoretische Konzepte und empirische Analysen* [On the communicative construction of spaces: Theoretical concepts and empirical analyses]. Wiesbaden: Springer VS.
Christmann, Gabriela B. 2022. "The Theoretical Concept of the Communicative (Re) Construction of Spaces". In *Communicative Constructions and the Refiguration of Spaces*, edited by Gabriela Christmann, Hubert Knoblauch, and Martina Löw, 89–112. Abingdon: Routledge.
Christmann Gabriela B., Hubert Knoblauch, and Martina Löw. 2022. "Introduction: Communicative Constructions and the Refiguration of Spaces". In *Communicative Constructions and the Refiguration of Spaces*, edited by Gabriela Christmann, Hubert Knoblauch, and Martina Löw, 3–15. Abingdon: Routledge.
Corner, James. 1999. "The Agency of Mapping: Speculation, Critique, and Invention". In *Mappings*, edited by Denis Cosgrove, 213–300. London: Reaktion Books.
Cosgrove, Denis, ed. 1999. *Mappings*. London: Reaktion Books.
Creswell, John W. 2015. *A Concise Introduction to Mixed Methods Research*. Los Angeles: Sage Publications.
Creswell, John W., and Vicki L. Plano Clark, eds. 2011. *Designing and Conducting Mixed Methods Research*. 2nd ed. Los Angeles: Sage Publications.

Dangschat, Jens S. 2014. "Räumliche Daten" [Spatial data]. In *Handbuch Methoden der empirischen Sozialforschung* [Handbook of methods of empirical social research], edited by Nina Baur and Jörg Blasius, 973–979. Wiesbaden: Springer Fachmedien.

Dodge, Martin. 2016. "Cartography I: Mapping Deeply, Mapping the Past". *Progress in Human Geography* 41 (1): 89–98.

Eckert, Denis. 2017. "L'Ukraine ou les contours incertains d'un Etat européen" [Ukraine or the uncertain contours of a European state]. *L'espace politique* 33 (3). https://journals.openedition.org/espacepolitique/4411

Geertz, Clifford. 1973. "Deep Play: Notes on the Balinese Cockfight". In *The Interpretation of Cultures: Selected Essays*, 412–454. New York: Basic Books.

Goffman, Erving. 1971. "The Territories of the Self". In *Relations in Public: Microstudies of the Public Order*, 28–61. New York: Basic Books.

Goodman, Nelson. 1976. *Languages of Art: An Approach to a Theory of Symbols*. 2nd ed. Indianapolis, IN: Hackett Publishing.

Götz, Norbert, and Janne Holmén. 2018. "Introduction to the Theme Issue: 'Mental Maps: Geographical and Historical Perspectives'". *Journal of Cultural Geography* 35 (2): 157–161.

Gueben-Venière, Servane. 2011. "How Can Mental Maps, Applied to the Coast Environment, Help in Collecting and Analyzing Spatial Representations?" *EchoGéo* 17. https://journals.openedition.org/echogeo/12625

Halder, Severin, and Boris Michel. 2018. "Editorial: This Is Not an Atlas". In *This Is Not an Atlas: A Global Collection of Counter-Cartographies*, edited by Kollektiv Orangotango+, 12–25. Bielefeld: transcript.

Hall, Edward T. 1969. *The Hidden Dimension*. New York: Anchor Books.

Hammarlin, Mia-Marie, Jonas Frykman, Bo Rothstein, and Isabell Schierenbeck. 2009. "Sense of Communitiy. Trust, Hope and Worries in the Welfare State". *Ethnologia Europaea* 39 (1): 5–74.

Harley, J. Brian. 2001. "Maps, Knowledge, and Power". In *The New Nature of Maps: Essays in the History of Cartography*, edited by Paul Laxton, 51–82. Baltimore and London: Johns Hopkins University Press.

Harley, J. Brian, and Beryl Markham. 1989. "Deconstructing the Map". *Cartographica* 26 (2): 1–20.

Heimerl, Birgit. 2006. "Choreographie der Entblößung: Geschlechterdifferenz und Personalität in der klinischen Praxis" [Choreography of exposure: Gender difference and personality in clinical practice]. *Zeitschrift für Soziologie* 35 (5): 372–391.

Kelling Emily, and Dagmar Pelger. 2021. *Mapping Re-Figurations: Studio Project (A) Residing in the Hidden*. Catalogue Seoul Biennale Global Studio.

Knoblauch, Hubert. 2017. *Die kommunikative Konstruktion der Wirklichkeit* [The communicative construction of reality]. Wiesbaden: Springer VS.

Knoblauch, Hubert, and Silke Steets. 2022. "From the Constitution to the Communicative Construction of Space". In *Communicative Constructions and the Refiguration of Spaces*, edited by Gabriela Christmann, Hubert Knoblauch, and Martina Löw, 19–35. Abingdon: Routledge.

Knoblauch, Hubert, René Tuma, and Bernd Schnettler. 2014. *Videography. Introduction to Interpretive Videoanalysis of Social Situations*. Frankfurt am Main: Peter Lang.

Krämer, Sybille. 2008. *Medium, Bote, Übertragung. Kleine Metaphysik der Medialität* [Medium, messenger, transmission. Small metaphysics of mediality]. Frankfurt am Main: Suhrkamp.

Krämer, Sybille. 2018. "'Kartographischer Impuls' und 'operative Bildlichkeit'. Eine Reflexion über Karten und die Bedeutung räumlicher Orientierung beim Erkennen" ['Cartographic impulse' and 'operational imagery'. A reflection on maps and the importance of spatial orientation when recognizing]. *Zeitschrift für Kulturwissenschaft* 12 (1): 19–32.

Kuckartz, Udo. 2017. "Datenanalyse in der Mixed-Methods-Forschung: Strategien der Integration von qualitativen und quantitativen Daten und Ergebnissen" [Data analysis in mixed-methods research: Strategies for the integration of qualitative and quantitative data and results]. *Kölner Zeitschrift für Soziologie und Sozialpsychologie* 69: 157–183.

Lameli, Alfred. 2009. "Die Konzeptualisierung des Sprachraums als Teil des regionalspezifischen Wissens" [The conceptualization of the language area as part of regional knowledge]. *Zeitschrift für Germanistische Linguistik* 37 (1): 125–156.

Lepetit, Bernard. 1993. "Architecture, géographie, histoire: usages de l'échelle" [Architecture, geography, history: Uses of scale]. *Genèses* 13 (1): 118–138.

Levinson, Stephen C. 2003. *Space in Language and Cognition: Explorations in Cognitive Diversity*. Cambridge: Cambridge University Press.

Levinson, Stephen C., and David P. Wilkins, eds. 2006. "The Background to the Study of the Language of Space". In *Grammars of Space: Explorations in Cognitive Diversity*, 1–23. Cambridge: Cambridge University Press.

Löw, Martina. 2016. *The Sociology of Space: Materiality, Social Structures, and Action*. New York: Palgrave Macmillan.

Löw, Martina, and Renate Ruhne. 2011. *Prostitution – Herstellungsweisen einer anderen Welt* [Prostitution - ways of making another world]. Frankfurt am Main: Suhrkamp.

Lynch, Kevin. 1960. *The Image of the City*. Cambridge, MA: MIT Press.

Malpas, Jeff. 2012. "Putting Space in Place: Philosophical Topography and Relational Geography". *Environment and Planning D: Society and Space* 30 (2): 226–242.

Marguin, Séverine. 2011. "Interaktive Karte über die Berliner Projekträume seit 1970" [Interactive map of the Berlin urban projects since 1970]. http://www.projektraeume-berlin.net/interaktivekarte/index.php

Marguin, Séverine, and Dagmar Pelger. 2021. *Mapping Re-Figurations. Studio Project (C) Mapping Accessibilities of an Art Institution*. Seoul: Catalogue Seoul Biennale Global Studio.

Marguin, Séverine, Henrike Rabe, and Friedrich Schmidgall. 2019. *The Experimental Zone*. Zürich: Park Books.

Mondada, Lorenza. 2009. "Emergent Focused Interactions in Public Places: A Systematic Analysis of the Multimodal Achievement of a Common Interactional Space". *Journal of Pragmatics* 41 (10): 1977–1997.

Moss, Oliver, and Adele Irving. 2018. "Imaging Homelessness in a City of Care: Participatory Mapping with Homeless People". In *This Is Not an Atlas: A Global Collection of Counter-Cartographies*, edited by Kollektiv Orangotango+, 270–275. Bielefeld: transcript.

Munk, Anders, and Torben Elgaard Jensen. 2014. "Revisiting the Histories of Mapping". *Ethnologia Europea* 44 (2): 31–47.

Myers, Greg. 2006. "'Where Are You From?' Identifying Place in Talk". *Journal of Sociolinguistics* 10 (3): 320–343.

Niewöhner, Jörg. 2014. "Raum: anthropologische Perspektiven" [Space: Anthropological perspectives]. In *Theorien in der Raum- und Stadtforschung: Einführungen* [Theories in

spatial and urban research: Introductions], edited by Jürgen Oßenbrügge and Anne Vogelpohl, 14–23. Münster: Westfälisches Dampfboot.
Orain, Olivier. 2016. "Le rôle de la graphique dans la modélisation en géographie. Contribution à une histoire épistémologique de la modélisation des spatialités humaines" [The role of graphs in geographical modeling. Contribution to an epistemological history of modeling human space]. In *Modélisations et sciences humaines: Figurer, interpréter, simuler* [Modeling and humanities: Figuring, interpreting, simulating], edited by Claude Blanckaert, Jacqueline Léon, and Didier Samain, 215–268. Paris: L'Harmattan.
Rankin, William. 2016. *After the Map. Cartography, Navigation, and the Transformation of Territory in the Twentieth Century*. Chicago: The University of Chicago Press.
Rekacewicz, Philippe. 2013a. "Aéroports, de l'espace public à l'espace privé" [Airports, from public to private space]. *LE MONDE diplomatique*, Février, 13–16. https://www.monde-diplomatique.fr/2013/02/REKACEWICZ/48733
Rekacewicz, Philippe. 2013b. "Cartographie Radicale" [Radical mapping]. *LE MONDE diplomatique*, Février, 15. www.monde-diplomatique.fr/2013/02/REKACEWICZ/48734
Roberts, Les, ed. 2016. *Deep Mapping*. Basel: MDPI.
Rose, Gillian. 2007. "Making Photographs as Part of a Research Project: Photo-Elicitation, Photo-Documentation and Other Uses of Photos". In *Visual Methodologies: An Introduction to the Interpretation of Visual Materials*, 237–256. London: Sage Publications.
Rose, Gillian. 2011. "The Question of Method: Practice, Reflexivity and Critique in Visual Culture Studies". In *The Handbook of Visual Culture*, edited by Ian Heywood and Barry Sandywell, 542–558. London: Berg Publishers.
Rose, Gillian. 2014. "On the Relationship between 'Visual Research Methods' and Contemporary Visual Culture". *The Sociological Review* 62 (1): 24–46.
Schmidt-Lauber, Brigitta, and Ingo Zechner. 2018. "Mapping. Begriff und Verfahren" [Mapping. Concept and procedure]. *Zeitschrift für Kulturwissenschaften* 12 (1): 11–18.
Shobe, Hunter, and David Banis. 2010. "Music Regions and Mental Maps: Teaching Cultural Geography". *Journal of Geography* 109 (2): 87–96.
Siegel, Steffen, and Petra Weigel. 2011. *Die Werkstatt des Kartographen: Materialien und Praktiken visueller Welterzeugung* [The cartographer's workshop: Materials and practices of the visual production of the world]. Paderborn: Fink.
Smiley, Sarah L. 2013. "Mental Maps, Segregation, and Everyday Life in Dares Salaam, Tanzania". *Journal of Cultural Geography* 30 (2): 215–244.
Smith, Richard G. 2009. "Urban Studies without 'Scale': Localizing the Global Through Singapore". In *Urban Assemblages: How Actor-Network Theory Changes Urban Studies*, edited by Ignacio Farías and Thomas Bender, 73–90. London: Routledge.
Traue, Boris. 2013. "Visuelle Diskursanalyse. Ein programmatischer Vorschlag zur Untersuchung von Sicht- und Sagbarkeiten im Medienwandel" [Visual discourse analysis. A programmatic proposal for the investigation of the visual and sayable in media change]. *Zeitschrift für Diskursforschung* 2 (1): 117–136.
Tufte, Edward. 2001. *The Visual Display of Quantitative Information*. 2nd ed. Cheshire, CT: Graphics Press.
Venturi, Robert, Denise Scott Brown, and Steven Izenour. 1972. *Learning from Las Vegas*. Cambridge, MA: The MIT Press.
Wood, Denis, and John Fels. 1992. *The Power of Maps*. New York: Guilford Press.

III
Empirical studies

8 Digital urban planning and urban planners' mediatized construction of spaces

Gabriela B. Christmann and Martin Schinagl

Introduction

Urban planning has a long history of using media to better describe, analyze, anticipate, communicate, and more clearly visualize processes of urban development in its structural, economic, social, and ecological dimensions. While analogue media has been a part of the planning process since the very beginning (for instance, in the form of city models, posters, and exhibitions), digital technologies were first employed in the 1970s (Lampugnani, Frey, and Perotti 2005). Since the 2010s their use has increased enormously due to the continuous improvements made in planning tools, to the extent that one can speak of a boom in the field (BMVI 2015, 3).

We take it as a given that digitalization has an impact on planning practice and, therefore, on the ways in which spaces are "constructed"; that is, planned, conceived of, and designed. In this respect, we follow the theory of mediatization developed in the field of communication science (cf. Krotz 2007; Hepp 2020). This proceeds from the observation that historically speaking, in societies the world over there has been an increasing application of ever newer media, and in more recent times of *digital* information and communications technologies, and that the tendency is for all segments of society to be swept up in this development. Bound together with this observation is the assumption that the communicative actions of actors have been changed in the course of increasing digitalization, which in turn leads to changes in the ways in which life and work are experienced, and thus in the "reality constructions" of actors (Berger and Luckmann 1966). Against this backdrop, and in light of comprehensive globalization processes, Knoblauch and Löw (2020) work on the basis that a process of large-scale refiguration of spaces has occurred.

When one translates these assumptions onto the actions of planners, the empirical questions arise of how processes of digitalization have developed in urban planning, what changes they have produced for planning activities, and to what extent altered spatial constructions can be observed (Christmann 2016, 2022; Christmann, Knoblauch, and Löw 2022). These questions have yet to be systematically researched in the social sciences. To date, studies (mostly from planning sciences) on digital tools in urban planning have largely tended to be

DOI: 10.4324/9780367817183-11

descriptive and pragmatic. Generally, these studies have focused on reporting experiences with digital processes and suggested possibilities for optimization (for an example of this, cf. Krause 2015). Considerations from the perspective of spatial theory are entirely absent.

The following contribution addresses this gap in the research. Initial results will be presented from an empirical investigation that pursues the overarching research questions: What changes can be observed in the actions of planners with regard to the globally unfolding processes of digitalization – through the use of digital planning tools, such as geographic information systems (GIS) or computer-aided design (CAD) – and what implications do these have for the communicative construction and refiguration of spaces? Digital urban planning will be analyzed using selected cases in New York City (North America/USA), Lagos (Africa/Nigeria) and Frankfurt (Europe/Germany).[1] We are conscious of the fact that despite worldwide developments in information and communications technologies and the international diffusion of planning tools, specific national planning systems and urban planning cultures can exert their own influence on planning practice. The focus of our analysis nevertheless goes beyond the various contexts and cultures to explore the possible common features in the actions of planners that can be ascribed to digitalization.

Our understanding of planning follows that of Ellwein (1968, 13) and Streich (2011, 16) as a systematic design for an urban and architectural order, taking place before the implementation of a project on the basis of all available, relevant knowledge. In contrast to a broader concept of planning that relates in general to urban development processes (structural, economic, social, ecological), urban planning can also focus in particular on the design of ensembles of buildings. In such cases, it shares a proximity to architecture. Since in cities the design of green spaces and public parks is also a requirement, the planning of open spaces also belongs to urban planning.

Within urban planning, one can differentiate between *structural* planning and *design* planning: The former focuses on the functional elements of a city (such as buildings, parks, and traffic routes) and aims to account for their future requirements, while the latter is tasked with shaping the aesthetic composition of the city. Both kinds of planning are nevertheless intertwined in concrete urban planning processes. If one takes Ellwein's (1968, 13) concept of planning seriously – that is, as design on the basis of all available relevant knowledge – and is aware of the complexity of urban planning, it stands to reason that planning is only possible on the basis of comprehensive information in the form of extensive and diverse urban data, maps, land registry information, etc. Even before the invention of the computer, analogue forms of information media were used. With the introduction of digital information and communications technologies, however, an all-encompassing structural change has occurred (Batty 1991; Pinto 2014).

Increasingly, in order to support the working processes of *urban structural planning*, planning information systems have been developed to make spatial data, maps, and models available in digital form. Information is here processed in such a way as to facilitate monitoring (i.e. accounts of historical and current processes) and the prediction of future developments as well as to better assess the specific planning requirements of a particular area (Wegener 2001; Shen 2012). Among the most important planning information systems belong GIS, which provide data on existing building structures, social processes (such as population and traffic development), microclimatic conditions (such as fresh airflow), and potential hazards (such as floodplains) for further processing. On the basis of the data obtained, computer-aided mapping can then be used to create and update maps, which in turn can be transferred to CAD applications for design use (Berchtold and Krass 2009).

Digitalization has made inroads in *design planning* too. Here, the focus is on the design of concrete spatial structures and the aesthetic formation of urban building ensembles. The analogue methods that once existed in urban planning have long since been transferred to computer systems and further developed in the form of applications such as CAD and computer-aided architectural design. These have revolutionized urban design. Such applications offer not only digital design methods, but also methods of presentation that bring to life the aesthetic qualities of architectural design by means of vivid simulations. Here one can differentiate above all between two-dimensional simulations (which abstract spatial depth) and three-dimensional simulations (which convey three spatial dimensions) (Yin and Shiode 2014; Lovett et al. 2015; Czerkauer-Yamu and Voigt 2016).

The methodological approach of the research project will be sketched out in the following section. Next we shall present, first, an overview of the central findings on the development of digitalization processes in spatial planning. In this context, we shall report on what changes, in both planning practice and in planners' spatial constructions, can be seen to have occurred as a result of digitalization (see the third section). This is then the basis on which, taking the examples of structural planning and the use of GIS (see the fourth section) and design planning and the application of CAD (the fifth section), we will explore in greater depth how planning practice has been molded by digitalization, what characterizes digital practice, and what implications this has for spatial constructions. The chapter will be rounded off with a summary pursuing the question of the extent to which one can, on the basis of the data, speak of a refiguration of spaces.

Methodological approach

To select the cities for investigation, as well as the urban planning agencies and authorities situated within them, the following criteria were drawn up: The cities must have distinguished themselves within their country or continent with regard to digitalized urban planning. The planning agencies and authorities to be selected from each city must have long-term experience with digital tools and have completed numerous urban design projects that have employed them. The USA, especially New York City, is considered throughout the world to be a pioneer in digital planning (Al-Kodmany 2002). Nigeria (with Lagos) and Germany (with Frankfurt) are cases that had in the past made less progress compared to New York, but which since the 2000s have caught up significantly. Lagos, the largest city in Africa, has been described in the literature as a case of dynamic development in Africa (Adeoye 2010), in which a digital planning strategy was devised. Frankfurt is well known in German digital planning for the openness to experimentation of its urban planning authorities.

As both digitalization processes in urban planning and changes in planning practice and planners' spatial constructions are treated here as objects of investigation, the research encompasses a number of dimensions and is therefore rather complex, requiring a combination of several methods.

To examine the course of digitalization processes in urban planning, interviews took place with acknowledged experts in the USA, Germany, and Nigeria who were able to provide information regarding central developments from the beginnings of digital planning up to the present (Bogner, Littig, and Menz 2009). Milestones in the process were thus reconstructed and initial evaluations concerning the possible outcomes of planning practice were made. Beforehand, and accompanying the interviews, documents were collected (including the relevant literature) in order to carry out corresponding documentary research (Prior 2003). In this way, the interviews could be better prepared, information obtained better classified, and the interview data further supplemented.

For the investigation of planning practice and the spatial constructions connected to it, focused ethnographies were undertaken in the selected cities and planning institutions from 2018 to 2020 (Knoblauch 2005). The ethnographies are "focused" in the sense that, in the tradition of workplace studies (Suchman 1987, 2000; Knoblauch and Heath 1999; Knoblauch 2000; Ammon 2013; Farías 2013), they concentrated on the working situations and communicative transactions marked by digital technologies and tools. In this chapter, the findings will thus be presented above all from the perspectives of the application of GIS in structural planning and the use of CAD in design planning. Alongside participatory observation, which allowed us to gain authentic insight into the concrete planning activities of the actors investigated (Angrosino 2007), ethnographic interviews were undertaken (Spradley 1979). Here, in order to gain a better understanding of specific activities, the focus was on spontaneous questions that could be posed directly to the actors being observed in the situation under consideration. In addition, guided interviews were carried out with the actors at a later point (Hopf 2000) to collect, in more concentrated form, their experiences, perceptions, and reflections related to digital tools in urban planning.

For the analysis of all this data, a grounded theory analysis procedure was employed. The approach of grounded theory originally described how an "object-related" theory could be developed out of empirical data. As is well known, this initially rather conceptional approach has since been elaborated into a method of data analysis (Strauss and Corbin 1997) in which three coding techniques are used sequentially: open, axial, and selective coding. In principle, this method is suitable for the analysis of the most varied kinds of data and allows even larger bodies of data to be opened up to analysis relatively quickly.

Digitalization processes and changes in planning practice and spatial constructions: An overview

The reconstruction of digitalization processes in the field of urban planning has revealed that discourse on new technologies and the planning of urban spaces has been evolving since as long ago as the 1950s. Certainly, the term "digitalization" was not yet in use, but surrounding the topic of "cybernetics" at this time, new technological possibilities were being hypothetically discussed. There were even experimental attempts to use digital technologies for planning purposes involving the creation of initial, computer-based drawings. In the 1960s and 1970s, while additional digital tools for planning were indeed developed, their application remained rather experimental. Not until the mid to late 1980s did more developed technologies find a foothold in planning practice. This occurred principally in the USA and initially only sporadically, owing to the issue of cost for planning agencies in acquiring and using such technologies. In addition, the tools were from a technological point of view still far from fully mature. It was not until the 1990s that a more wide-scale dissemination of digital tools could be seen in American and European, as well as in African planning offices, though a boom in their use had to wait until the 2010s.

In the case of Lagos (Nigeria), it can be seen that digitalization occurred rather differently than in the USA or in Europe: First, financial aspects continue to hamper the acquisition of digital tools; and, second, owing to the city's pressing need to fundamentally record and map the large planning area, other technologies tend to be used. There is great interest in drone technologies there, while efforts in the USA and in Europe aim to network existing databases and improve GIS.

As an interim conclusion, it can be noted that digitalization was already anticipated in the 1950s. It thus entered into "planning thought" earlier than has been presumed. By contrast, in "planning practice" – for both technological and financial reasons – digitalization has developed slower than anticipated. In addition, when viewed globally, the processes of digitalization in planning continue today to demonstrate asynchronicities. There are pioneers and early and late adopters. Not least of all, digitalization can, depending on the planning context (for instance, that of a megacity), exhibit differences in their technical focus (drone technologies vs. the optimization of GIS databases).

But to what extent has planning practice been altered by the course of digitalization processes? Our analyses show that clear changes have occurred following the establishment and further technological development of digital tools. Most striking are the *changes in the division of labor* and the *increase in translocal actions* or *spatially distributed work* in planning agencies and institutions.

Occupational groups such as typists and technical draftsmen have become redundant, their tasks being assumed by planners themselves owing to the availability of easy-to-use tools, such as word-processing and drawing programs. At the same time, new occupational groups, such as geoinformatics specialists, have been created that have no background in planning, but work in planning agencies due to their specialist knowledge with regard to digital technologies and applications. What has increased substantially are the demands on visualizations of planning products, especially (though not only) in the form of digital visualizations. Increasingly, renderings are expected: These are aesthetically appealing graphics or videos of a specific planning product, created with some effort on computers in the form of two- or three-dimensional virtual presentations. These must likewise be produced by specialists able to combine their knowledge of visualization with spatial forms.

Planning agencies increasingly work together with others translocally, something enabled by ever-improving information and communications technologies. This means that not a few (if not yet all) planning agencies are supra-regionally, internationally, or globally active and function together with other agencies or branches as if in "one" office. An example from our data is a planning agency with branches in New York City, London, and Shanghai. Here, a planning team distributed among the three locations works together on one project in Southeast Asia. Only a part of the team is required to be at times at the target location. From their different work locations, staff on the team have access to a shared server structure, shared digital planning tools, and the necessary information and communications technologies. These enable distributed work on the project and even, in some cases, the coordination of simultaneous work on individual files.

In light of these changes in planning practice, one can see first of all that a refiguration of working spaces and processes has occurred: Planning teams no longer work in a shared office. The planning of urban spaces is often achieved by spatially dispersed team members who – and this is remarkable in the field of spatial planning – plan spaces with which they themselves are hardly, or not at all, directly acquainted.

A further change reported by planners is the *increasing complexity of their actions*, resulting from the ever more complex tasks that digital tools enable. Elaborate visual presentation of planning products (in the form of renderings, for instance) are today a "must-have" for planning agencies. The complexity of tasks is thus increased, because visualizations need not only to be produced or commissioned, but must also be systematically integrated into a communications strategy.

Communicating with stakeholders has markedly diversified and increased in both direct and digital forms. Owing to the availability of the most diverse range of tools enabling exchange with stakeholders, it is now expected that such contact is accordingly maintained.

A further factor is the constant accrual of geodata platforms and other spatially oriented databases. It is expected that ever more data are processed in the course of spatial planning in order that the planning product is optimized as far as possible, on the basis of such data, for its intended use.

It therefore appears that a direct viewing by planners themselves of the space being designed is becoming rarer, while, conversely, the forms of knowledge and data about such spaces, owing to communication with stakeholders and, above all, the use of GIS, has grown vast and become more complex. A comprehensive datafication has taken place, within which context the most diverse aspects of specific places have been transformed into computerized data. On this basis, it has become possible to map the most varied aspects of a place (such as the built structure, retail infrastructure, traffic and visitor flows, fresh airflows, occurrences of heatwaves, etc.) that "overlap" and, depending on the project, might all be pertinent to planning actions. But what implications does this have for the spatial constructions of planners? This is the question the next section will address in more detail.

Altered spatial constructions I: Geographic information systems and spatial layers

In the following, we shall illuminate how planners in structural planning work in particular with GIS and examine what experiences and consequences result with regard to the construction of spaces.

Through a combination of software and the relevant databases, GIS – as already mentioned above – allow the most diverse kinds of spatial information to be collected, analyzed, and positioned in relation to one another. For a spatial analysis, geographical data, usually in tabular fashion, are combined and visualized in the form of a map. One interview partner even labeled GIS a "spatial calculator", because, like a calculator, it functions by means of an input-output procedure; that is, after the input of data, visualized geo-referenced results are computed and made visible in a virtually constructed space. In the process, the tabular data are combined with one or more "layers". GIS thus merges layers and arranges them either on a map (based on a square, or other polygonal, grid) or in a three-dimensional model.

There are prerequisites to using this technology, however: It must first be carefully learned; for instance, from video tutorials. This is true for both the GIS software itself and for working with layers, whose logic a user must thoroughly understand if they wish to integrate them meaningfully into their planning practice. By merging layers, spatial relationships and patterns can be identified that will support planners in their decision-making processes.

"Layers" are clearly not a new phenomenon in spatial planning. Already in the 18th century, the landscape architect Humphry Repton (1752–1818) had the idea of integrating a range of spatial aspects (or layers) into one visualization with the aid of tracing paper (cf. Rogger 2007). This technique had its limits, however, and more complex layered structures could not yet be represented. "Layering" together with the introduction of GIS in the late 1970s is thus still considered a relatively young technology for representing large-scale urban or nonurban landscapes (cf. Corner 1999, 235).

The superimposition and connecting together of data enables the analysis and interpretation of complex spatial orders and dynamics. Conversely, complex situations can be dismantled layer by layer in order to map out certain elements. For instance, combining census data on social diversity, real estate and its spatial use, and services and placing such data in relation to each other enables one to understand and visualize unequal distributions of services within an urban neighborhood. The visualization then provides a data-based overview, allows precise analyses to be made, and suggests where planning intervention is necessary. One of our interview partners expresses it thus:

> *Well, we normally cannot, with our intellectual capabilities, I believe, understand what all this ... what kind of impact this has, and so one can break it down to various layers. Maybe there are people who can do that ... [estimate] rental prices or something. And perhaps you have a good intuition for it, but perhaps not. And then maybe you get it right, maybe you don't. But I believe you then, as a planner, reach decisions where you don't really know what the impact will be.*
>
> (Interview 1)

An understanding of socio-spatial relations can be to some extent gained on the basis of one's own experience and knowledge of local circumstances. Planners can develop "a good intuition" for things in this way. It is then this "intuition" – that is, the knowledge that is bound to a particular person – that underlies planning decisions. The above statement suggests, though, that the more complex the relations, the more difficult it appears to be to rely on "intuition".

With GIS, individually contingent intuition is superseded. Where spatial synthesizing operations are (co-)constructed through automated layering procedures, the individual planner's spatial knowledge of an area takes a back seat. GIS thus becomes an epistemological tool and displaces the spatial experiences of planners. As a digital planning tool, it thus points the way to gains in knowledge and practices and influences how spaces are understood. Spatial synthesizing operations are becoming more systematic with increasing processing power, enabling a continually greater complexity that could not be achieved with analogue technologies. Spatial and local knowledge are not "intuited", but calculated, and they are available translocally, beyond the boundaries of any one place itself.

Through this epistemological tool, an understanding of space is generated that has, on the one hand, an enabling effect on planning practice; on the other hand, it harbors limitations as to what spatial knowledge it can generate (cf. Boon and Knuuttila 2009). GIS does indeed solve complex spatial problems with apparent effortlessness, merely by means of data processing and representation (Koch 2004, 13). This nevertheless occurs within a logic of layers specific to GIS, as is succinctly – and critically – noted in the following remark:

The worldview of a GIS is layered. All the things that happen together, somehow happen separately though in the same place. ... That is part of the logic, of the way our data is structured. I will collect data on this thing and on this thing and I will do that separately. And then just smash them together but never actually bring them together.

(Interview 2)

Ultimately, the use of "layers" relies on the automated conglomeration of data originating from a variety of different actors and institutions. What the quotation only hints at is that data of varying quality, and arising from different surveying methods, are collated and processed even though they in fact have nothing in common. GIS databases are thus highly "polycontexturalized" (Knoblauch and Löw 2020, 272). For the planning process, this means that planners, when they want to get an idea of a planning area and need to make planning decisions on this basis, will find very heterogeneous references for action.

Free and publicly accessible open data assembled by GIS users by collaborative, networked means are, in particular, emblematic of the polycontextural and translocal character of spatial data. There is also the fact that GIS, due to the means by which they function, are dependent on an elaborate data infrastructure and on exchange between various institutions. Where this goes smoothly, it opens up the possibility of spatial planners accessing constantly updated and enhanced databases. In those places we investigated, however, there were obviously significant differences with regard to the opportunities to access such data. On the one hand, institutional networks and data consistency are a basic prerequisite for the meaningful application of GIS; on the other hand, though, these are not to be found equally everywhere (cf. Wilson 2017).

As has been shown, the practices of "experiencing" and "planning" space by means of GIS software are, in current (preparatory) structural planning, to a large extent digitalized and have led – because they are produced through automation – to new spatial constructions in the form of virtual "layers". Through "layers", highly datafied, polycontextural, and (ideally) translocally available spatial knowledge is automatically synthesized. The basis of digital planning is thus different to that of analogue practice, in which planners are instead required to relate to a planning space firsthand, physically and cognitively, even if they are at the same time supported by methods of abstraction in the form of plotting, producing, and reading maps. It is something quite different to walk through parts of a city and to receive impressions and visualize information through being physically present than it is to access a space through GIS and digital mapping services. While planners' analogue spatial constructions always involve abstraction, it is not an automatically synthesized abstraction.

The issue of physical and performative aspects of integrating digital technologies and applications, and the implications for planners' spatial constructions, will be further pursued in the following section, using the example of planning with the assistance of CAD.

Altered spatial constructions II: Computer-aided design and perspectivation from the mouse and keyboard

In the overview of changes in planning practice provided above, it was mentioned that CAD programs have displaced the occupation of technical draftsmen at the level of planning agencies. By this was meant those who had specialized in the rather executive, and less creative, activity of graphically translating sketches and specifications into accurate plans. Gone with them are such analogue tools of the design process as the light table. Paper sketches still exist, but they are integrated in such a way as ultimately to serve a digital end product.

Within our interviews, especially with younger planners, the "digitalization" of "drawing" tended to be positively framed: It is more efficient, precise, and expedient to the design process.

> *We get a lot more time to actually think and work. ... When I was in college, I used to draw on vellum with ink. So, if my ink blotted somewhere, I couldn't throw the drawing away, I had to scrape off the ink .... It was very hard to do this; you were very careful. There was a bit of care that you couldn't do it again. You thought hard about one solution and you made just one solution. Now with most of my [digital] tools doing most of my drawing very quickly ..., I have come to a point to spit out five solutions.*
>
> (Interview 3)

> *It makes no sense to make a master plan by hand. ... [It] is particularly abysmal when a partner sits themselves down and traces out another plan by pen. Of course this makes no sense.*
>
> (Interview 1)

Both implicitly and explicitly, quality is ascribed to drawing by hand. The practice of drawing, merging with physical action, is associated with a particular sensory and cognitive grasp of the visual and material design product (a map, for instance). It requires above all specific knowledge about how one draws. The architect must

> *generally first know how to draw before they get involved in this sort of [digital] world, where you can, I think, ... be led astray and get entangled. ... Because when they are a kind of "old school" architect, who has drawn a lot by hand, then they also sort of do it the same way with such a tool. Cause they know roughly where they want to be.*
>
> (Interview 1)

According to this, manual drawing allows one to relate to the design in a certain sensory way and reduce complexity. At the same time, one remains bound to one particular scale. The quotation describes how the experience of manual drawing is translated to one's work with CAD software. Pen and tracing paper suggest certain modes of action which, alongside their restrictions and depending on the level of individual skill developed, allow certain freedoms in the design process. The division between digital and analogue "worlds" may be understood here as the difference between tool-dependent, epistemological approaches. Computer technology is ascribed a higher complexity, which in turn requires a higher degree of reflexivity to be able to work with. The term "old school" points to generational differences between designers who tend to draw more by hand and thus belong more to the older generation of architects and those who have learned from the start to design using digital tools. In order to know how one designs digitally – that is, to arrive "where one wants to be" – one must learn once again to draw. The "arriving" seems, under the conditions of increased complexity, to demand greater reflexivity, or else one "loses" oneself.

If one were to observe only the physical actions involved in the use of CAD, it would be noticed that the majority consist of clicking and typing. The digital logic of connecting point to point is effected through mouse commands and by entering coordinates – and not by drawing a line per se. In addition, the drag-and-drop function for objects and elements allows one to create, move, edit, and undo changes made to geometric bodies. By performing these physical actions, the architect deals with the materiality and quality of surfaces and software programs. As practices tied to epistemological tools, they fit into the communicative processes of planning in a meaningful way.

The practical knowledge formed through the use of CAD software is thus a part of the planners' socio-technological fabric of things, people, rules, and practices. That is, the programs and devices are integrated meaningfully into actions. Drawing, therefore, as a sensually experienceable technology providing a physical and cognitive means of navigating this fabric of people and things, goes hand in hand with certain perspectivations. This is reflected in the comments of one planner, regarding work with CAD: "*You are working on a kind of a flat surface and you are in digital land*" (Interview 4). The quotation suggests that despite the two-dimensional environment, various perspectivations are possible, whether through zooming in and out or through the fluid alteration between various sections and levels of scale. Scale and original size do not lose relevance for planning, but the process of designing frees itself from its former rigidity, in contrast to drawing on a sheet of paper or creating designs in the form of models. In the use of CAD, planners' spatial constructions are thus more dynamic and, above all, multiple in their perspectives.

The virtual inspection of three-dimensional environments generated by CAD software can, in addition, convey a vivid impression and allows changes of perspective and, thus, a "*testing of spatiality*" (Interview 5). It is not yet possible to conclusively elucidate how the promise of digitalization in planning will shape the built environment. In fact, as one Berlin planner reports, digitally designed models have given the impression of being "*more organically*" formed. According to her, analogue architecture models have its limitations. This has resulted in such arrangements as at Potsdamer Platz, which viewed from above are indeed interesting and attractive, she says, looking out onto the site from the high-rise office building in which the interview is being conducted. But, she continues, when one walks through the square, the forms are not well matched.

Summary and conclusions

Our analyses show that digital technologies and applications have been established in urban planning since the 1990s, but that they only achieved high technical proficiency and internationally widespread dissemination during the 2010s. It was also revealed that in the course of digitalization since the 1990s, a process of change has occurred in planning practice. Increasingly, members of a planning team assigned to any one project are spatially dispersed (perhaps even around the globe) between different places of work. Translocally organized planning actions are made possible through shared server structures, digital tools, and preexisting information and communication technologies. In addition, ever more stakeholders are being incorporated into the planning process. Forms of analogue and digital communication, through which exchange among stakeholders can take place, are increasingly diversifying and increasing in number. Elaborate digital visualizations of planning products (for instance, in the form of renderings) are becoming ever more important for their use in external communications (cf. also Christmann, Bernhardt, and Stollmann 2020). In light of these developments, one can speak of a refiguration of forms of work and work spaces.

Considering digital planning in more detail, a large-scale datafication of spatial realities can be seen to have taken place. Urban spaces have entered the digital world and continue to be further structured from the computer. For planners, the amount of working data has increased enormously; the kinds of data involved are diverse and highly complex. Planners have to process more aspects of space than ever before – this is a task that could hardly be managed without the use of digital planning tools. With the aid of digital tools, the different – datafied – layers that compose the spatial reality of a place, as well as the overlapping of these layers, can now be virtually mapped. In this way, "virtualized" constructions of space arise that form the basis of further planning processes. Through the digitally achieved connections made between various spatial layers, there emerges in digital planning a high degree of spatial polycontexturalization.

Even if increasing digitalization can be observed in planning practice, and signs of a refiguration of spaces in the form of translocal actions and the polycontexturalization of spatial constructions can be discovered, the process of refiguration nevertheless does not appear to be complete. It appears much more that analogue practices continue to exist and remain common, whether for data collection and the analysis of locations (such as in the form of site visits) or for analogue forms of visualizing planning products (such as models or manual drawing). Traditional planning practice still exists, but it is being increasingly permeated by digital forms. Generational change in the planning professions, leading to a predominance of "digital natives", will possibly accelerate this process.

Note

1 The project is entitled "Digital Urban Planning" and forms part of the Collaborative Research Center 1265 "Re-Figuration of Spaces" at the Technische Universität Berlin, Germany. It is funded by the German Research Foundation under project no. 290045248. The sub-project is being conducted at the Leibniz Institute for Research on Society and Space, Erkner, Germany.

References

BMVI (Bundesministerium für Verkehr und digitale Infrastruktur). 2015. *Stufenplan Digitales Planen und Bauen* [Step-by-step plan for digital planning and building]. Berlin: BMVI.

Adeoye, Anthony A. 2010. *Lagos State Geoinformation Infrastructure Policy (LAGIS) as a Tool for Mega-City Development: Opportunities and Challenges.* XXIV FIG International Congress 2010: Facing the Challenges – Building the Capacity, Sydney, April 11–16.

Al-Kodmany, Kheir. 2002. "Visualization Tools and Methods in Community Planning: From Freehand Sketches to Virtual Reality". *Journal of Planning Literature* 17 (2): 189–211.

Ammon, Sabine. 2013. "Wie Architektur entsteht. Entwerfen als epistemische Praxis" [How architecture is made. Designing as epistemic practice]. In *Wissenschaft Entwerfen. Vom forschenden Entwerfen zur Entwurfsforschung der Architektur* [Design science. From research-based design to architectural design research], edited by Sabine Ammon and Eva Maria Froschauer, 337–362. München: Wilhelm Fink Verlag.

Angrosino, Michael. 2007. *Doing Ethnography and Observational Research.* London: Sage Publications.

Batty, Michael. 1991. "New Technology and Planning: Reflections on Rapid Change and the Culture of Planning in the Post-Industrial Age". *The Town Planning Review* 62 (3): 269–294.

Berchtold, Martin, and Philipp Krass. 2009. "Digitale Räume. Neue Möglichkeiten der Planung" [Digital spaces. New possibilities of planning]. *PLANERIN* 9 (5): 5–8.

Berger, Peter L., and Thomas Luckmann. 1966. *The Social Construction of Reality.* Garden City, NY: Doubleday.

Bogner, Alexander, Beate Littig, and Wolfgang Menz, eds. 2009. *Experteninterviews: Theorien, Methoden, Anwendungsfelder* [Expert interviews: Theories, methods, fields of application]. Wiesbaden: VS Verlag für Sozialwissenschaften.

Boon, Mieke, and Taria Knuuttila. 2009. "Models as Epistemic Tools in Engineering Sciences: Philosophy of Technology and Engineering Sciences". In *Handbook of the Philosophy of Technological Sciences*, edited by Anthonie Meijers, 693–726. North-Holland: Elsevier.

Christmann, Gabriela B., ed. 2016. *Zur kommunikativen Konstruktion von Räumen: Theoretische Konzepte und empirische Analysen* [On the communicative construction of spaces: Theoretical concepts and empirical analyses]. Wiesbaden: Springer VS.

Christmann, Gabriela B. 2022. "The Theoretical Concept of the Communicative (Re) Construction of Spaces". In *Communicative Constructions and the Refiguration of Spaces*, edited by Gabriela Christmann, Hubert Knoblauch, and Martina Löw, 89–112. Abingdon: Routledge.

Christmann, Gabriela B., Christoph Bernhardt, and Jörg Stollmann, eds. 2020. "Visual Communication in Urban Design and Planning: The Impact of Mediatisation(s) on the Construction of Urban Futures". *Urban Planning*, Special Issue, 5 (2). https://doi.org/10.17645/up.v5i2.3279

Christmann, Gabriela B., Hubert Knoblauch, and Martina Löw. 2022. "Introduction: Communicative Constructions and the Refiguration of Spaces". In *Communicative Constructions and the Refiguration of Spaces*, edited by Gabriela Christmann, Hubert Knoblauch, and Martina Löw, 3–15. Abingdon: Routledge.

Corner, James. 1999. "The Agency of Mapping Speculation, Critique and Invention". In *Mappings*, edited by Denis Cosgrove, 213–300. London: Reaktion Books.

Czerkauer-Yamu, Claudia, and Andreas Voigt. 2016. "Spatial Simulation and the Real World: Digital Methods and Techniques in the Context of Strategic Planning". In *The Routledge Handbook of Planning Research Methods*, edited by Elisabete A. Silva, Patsy Healey, Neil Harris, and Pieter Van den Broeck, 348–363. New York and London: Routledge.

Ellwein, Thomas. 1968. *Politik und Planung* [Politics and planning]. Stuttgart: Kohlhammer.

Farías, Ignacio. 2013. "Epistemische Dissonanz. Zur Vervielfältigung von Entwurfsalternativen in der Architektur" [Epistemic dissonance. On the multiplication of design alternatives in architecture]. In *Wissenschaft Entwerfen. Vom forschenden Entwerfen zur Entwurfsforschung der Architektur* [Design science. From research-based design to architectural design research], edited by Sabine Ammon and Eva Maria Froschauer, 77–108. München: Wilhelm Fink Verlag.

Hepp, Andreas. 2020. *Deep Mediatization*. London and New York: Routledge.

Hopf, Christel. 2000. "Qualitative Interviews – ein Überblick" [Qualitative interviews – an overview]. In *Qualitative Forschung. Ein Handbuch* [Qualitative research. A handbook], edited by Uwe Flick, Ernst von Kardorff, and Ines Steincke, 349–360. Hamburg: Rowohlt.

Knoblauch, Hubert. 2000. "Workplace Studies und Video: zur Entwicklung der visuellen Ethnographie von Technologie und Arbeit" [Workplace studies and video: On the development of the visual ethnography of technology and work]. In *Münchner Beiträge zur Volkskunde, Band 26: Arbeitskulturen im Umbruch: zur Ethnographie von Arbeit und Organisation* [Münchner contributions to folklore, Volume 26: Work cultures in transition: On the ethnography of work and organization], edited by Irene Gotz and Andreas Wittel, 159–174. München: Waxmann.

Knoblauch, Hubert. 2005. "Focused Ethnography". *Forum: Qualitative Social Research* 6 (3): Art. 44.

Knoblauch, Hubert, and Christian Heath. 1999. "Technologie, Interaktion und Organisation: Die Workplace Studies" [Technology, interaction and organization: The workplace studies]. *Schweizerische Zeitschrift für Soziologie* 25 (2): 163–181.

Knoblauch, Hubert, and Martina Löw. 2020. "The Re-Figuration of Spaces and Refigured Modernity – Concept and Diagnosis". *Historical Social Research* 45 (2): 263–292.

Koch, Tom. 2004. "The Map as Intent: Variations on the Theme of John Snow". *Cartographica: The International Journal for Geographic Information and Geovisualization* 39 (4): 1–14.

Krause, Kai-Uwe. 2015. "Standards in der Planung" [Standards in planning]. *PLANERIN* 15 (3): 47–49.

Krotz, Friedrich. 2007. *Mediatisierung. Fallstudien zum Wandel von Kommunikation* [Mediatization. Case studies on the transformation of communication]. Wiesbaden: Springer.

Lampugnani, Vittorio M., Katia Frey, and Eliana Perotti. 2005. *Anthologie zum Städtebau* [Anthology on urban planning]. Berlin: Gebr. Mann Verlag.

Lovett, Andrew, Katy Appleton, Barty Warren-Kretzscmar, and Christina von Haaren. 2015. "Using 3D Visualization Methods in Landscape Planning". *Landscape and Urban Planning, Special Issue: Critical Approaches to Landscape Visualization* 142: 85–94.

Pinto, Nuno Norte. 2014. *Technologies for Urban and Spatial Planning*. Hershey: IGI Global.

Prior, Lindsay. 2003. *Using Documents in Social Research*. London: Sage.

Rogger, André. 2007. *Landscapes of Taste: The Art of Humphry Repton's Red Books*. London: Routledge.

Shen, Zhenjiang, ed. 2012. *Geospatial Techniques in Urban Planning*. Berlin and Heidelberg: Springer.

Spradley, James. 1979. *The Ethnographic Interview*. New York: Holt, Rinehart and Winston.

Strauss, Anselm, and Juliet M. Corbin. 1997. *Grounded Theory in Practice*. Thousand Oaks, London and New Delhi: Sage Publications.

Streich, Bernd. 2011. *Stadtplanung in der Wissensgesellschaft. Ein Handbuch* [Urban planning in the knowledge society. A handbook]. Wiesbaden: VS Verlag für Sozialwissenschaften.

Suchman, Lucy. 1987. *Plans and Situated Actions: The Problem of Human-Machine Communication*. Cambridge: Cambridge University Press.

Suchman, Lucy. 2000. "Embodied Practices of Engineering Work". *Mind, Culture, and Activity* 7 (1–2): 4–18.

Wegener, Michael. 2001. "New Spatial Planning Models". *International Journal of Applied Earth Observation and Geoinformation* 3 (3): 224–237.

Wilson, Matthew W. 2017. *New Lines: Critical GIS and the Trouble of the Map*. Minneapolis: University of Minnesota Press.

Yin, Li, and Narushige Shiode. 2014. "3D Spatial-Temporal GIS Modeling of Urban Environments to Support Design and Planning Processes". *Journal of Urbanism: International Research on Placemaking and Urban Sustainability* 7 (2): 152–169.

9 Centers of coordination refigured?
Control of synthetic space

René Tuma and Arne Janz

Introduction

This chapter aims to understand the interrelated processes of mediatization and the changing synthesis of space visible in control rooms. It presents preliminary insights drawn from an ongoing study.[1] An empirical starting point for the research were current developments observed in, but not limited to, "smart cities" in which new forms of the control of space are being presented in paradigmatic form. These new developments aim to integrate algorithmic computation into control systems and are a central part of socio-technological, spatially distributed systems. The infrastructures, as well as the interactions, within complex (not only urban), socio-technological and infrastructure systems are monitored and managed in increasingly complex control rooms or "centers of coordination". Those centers that were present in traditional infrastructure systems are now changing. They are increasingly equipped with advanced information and communication systems to monitor, record, and regulate specific processes within a controlled area. This entails management of infrastructures such as traffic control, energy supply, and waste management; but surveillance and policing are also increasingly controlled by automated systems – or at least such developments are envisioned. An important aspect is centralization within polyfunctional centers, in which formerly divided functions, also known as "sectors" of management, are joined to form integrated systems. Both developments, the automation and the integration of systems, are correlated and lead to increasingly mediated communication. In the planning and ongoing installation of such new control systems, we do not observe a mere technological shift, but rather one that is connected to changing daily interactions and activities within and outside the centers. Importantly, the relational character of control and controlled spaces is emphasized by changing interrelations and communication technologies. Many new technologies, such as the 5G wireless standard and various digital platforms, change both the means and the forms of management and control. Not only do they enhance established forms of computing and representation of space, but, being embedded into the world, they rapidly redefine and redesign the spaces and infrastructures that surround human actors.

DOI: 10.4324/9780367817183-12

In this regard, there are various processes that should be expected: first, the integration of formerly separated sectors or domains of control and infrastructural tasks within one localized system or control room (polyfunctionality of control centers); and, second, the integration of complex digital systems with increased degrees of agency (algorithms) and increased availability of information (big data).

Control rooms

What is a control room?

Control rooms and centers of coordination are institutionalized architectural and technological spaces where professionals manage and control routine processes necessary to keep spatially distributed (open or enclosed) systems operational.

Generally, there are several terms: Centers of coordination, control rooms, and control stations are widely used within the field. Control rooms involving continuous surveillance are distinct from crisis rooms or situation centers/rooms, which are more focused on decision-making in emergency situations. Centers focusing on a specific "security-related" topic are often labeled as operations centers (such as network operations centers, security operations centers, emergency operations centers, fusion centers, joint operations centers, and social media command centers) or are sometimes referred to as environments (for instance, the "command, control, communications, computers, intelligence, surveillance, and reconnaissance" (C4ISR) environment).[2]

As these specialist terms are confusing and overlap with one another, we differentiate between three broad types, appropriate to current developments.

First, there is the dominant form of monofunctional control room, usually embedded into organizations that manage a specific task (such as the police, surveillance, fire services) or infrastructure (such as power networks, water distribution systems, etc.).

Second, in relation to situations exceeding routine capacity, designated crisis or situation rooms are retained within the premises of second parties. Even where control rooms are intended for one infrastructural system or public service, very often other organizations will utilize them. The Berlin Police, for example, have constantly staffed workspaces at the center of Berlin's public transport services (BerlinerVerkehrsbetriebe) as well as the traffic control centers (Verkehrsregelungszentrale) responsible for private automotive traffic. The prevalently monofunctional control rooms are thus in many cases not merely so characterized, but can already be understood as at least oligo-functional.

In the third case, several organizations are housed at one center. The degree of integration varies, the simplest being "multicenters" of coordination that generally work independently on their tasks. London's Surface Traffic and Transport Operations Centre, studied by Luff et al. (2017), is one example of this kind. Here, bus service management, metropolitan police, and traffic management are gathered in one place while continuing to work independently in most situations. Depending on the number of participating organizations and how their functions relate, we term these oligo- or polyfunctional centers of coordination.

Newer developments aim at more integrated centers, strongly supported by automation and big data systems and with interconnected infrastructures. These new, integrated centers seek to reduce the need for (staffing) resources. What unites all the different types of control centers is that they create a special material relation to the controlled spaces.

Existing studies on control rooms

An important line of research into centers of control has emerged due to the interdisciplinary link between ethnomethodological interaction analysis and the emerging interest in interaction between human actors and computer systems. The fields of computer-supported collaborative work and workplace studies (cf. Heath, Knoblauch, and Luff 2004) have developed a rich body of ethnographic studies in a variety of research fields such as airports (Goodwin and Goodwin 1996), the London Underground (Heath and Luff 1992; Luff et al. 2017), air traffic control rooms (Suchman 1997), ambulance control in Manchester (Martin, Bowers, and Wastell 1997), and camera surveillance (Berndtsson and Normark 1999). This research field, which also has an interest in participating in the design of such systems, highlights the social and cooperative aspects of work involving "human–computer" interaction in control rooms.

These studies highlight the processes of interaction and show the means by which control room workers achieve their work, especially with regard to how problems are routinely identified and resolved. Workers are shown to be constantly "monitoring" the actions of other members in the control room, visually, bodily, or by listening. Actions and the planning of further actions are made reciprocally available to others. These insights into the social dimension of work within control rooms has provided a major stimulus to the design of such systems, and most studies address how technologies (ranging from slips of paper to closed-circuit television – commonly known as CCTV – installations) are embedded into those practices and used as a resource in supporting shared understanding. In contrast to other studies of work, the control room studies focus on the interactions within large, distributed sociotechnical systems and identify control rooms as centers of coordination that allow work on shared systems to be done remotely, coordinating multiple different views of a service. Multilocal coordination between these centers and external points of control (such as the drivers of underground trains) has increasingly become the focus.

From mono- to polyfunctional centers

Classic control rooms have usually focused on one "function" or "sector"; this means they have usually focused on managing a specific infrastructural service. The function is related to the tasks and design of the controlled infrastructure.

This infrastructure is usually itself a sociotechnical system; that is, it is instituted as an organization. For example, a fire service control room is responsible for processing incoming emergency calls and distributing and managing the resources of the local service. Examples of other systems are the management of the water-pumping infrastructure or of underground railway lines. Those control rooms, addressing one specific sector, can be called monofunctional, while more newly integrated control rooms that manage several sectors can be understood as polyfunctional.

A number of recent developments in the regulation, control, management, and surveillance of (urban) infrastructures are important for understanding the changing character of control rooms. First, new digital technologies and integrated systems promise to allow for a reduction of staff in control rooms. Within the field, a shortage of qualified personnel is currently an issue (for financial reasons). From interviews with control room suppliers and operators, we derive that the science-fiction-influenced designs of recent control centers is intended to attract and retain new and young employees. Visual similarities with the bridge of the Spaceship *Enterprise* are both a selling point (on the supplier side) and an incentive in recruiting new employees (on the operator side).

Newer attempts and developments in the field focus on joining formerly dispersed control rooms. Several organizations attempt to bundle their efforts, managing different infrastructure systems, such as water supply and disposal, and power networks or other energy networks, as well as public (emergency) services such as the fire service, police, or emergency medical services. The developments we observe aim at an integration of those different control rooms within "polyfunctional" coordination centers. This development is especially apparent in the advanced urban control centers that are architecturally as well as infrastructurally designed and planned at the drawing board. Examples of such planned (smart) cities are Songdo (South Korea) and Shenzhen (China), where the most recent centralization efforts have already been realized. But preexisting cities such as Rio de Janeiro (Brazil) or Glasgow (Scotland) are also being equipped with such polyfunctional control rooms. The Centro de Operações in Rio is a control center that integrates approximately 30 organizations.[3] The Glasgow Operations Centre integrates significantly fewer organizations. Nevertheless, CCTV, traffic management, police, emergency services, community enforcement, and security services are united under one roof.[4] These centers are advertised as employing smart integration and use of data and, ultimately, as offering the promise of increased security.

Another development is the transgression of the classical understanding of control rooms. Some control room suppliers are already developing concepts that seek to abstain from human-operated control rooms altogether, reducing them to mostly technological systems in which only the service technician need access the systems data on demand. Such concepts already exist in attenuated form. Service providers such as the Critical Infrastructure Competence Centre (CCI) specialize in transferring shifts from other control rooms to their own control center. If, for example, there is so little to do at night in the waterworks of a small town that it is normally not worthwhile to have someone on site, then the CCI can take this shift over. The CCI implements monitoring software in the corresponding control room that then monitors the control room of the waterworks via a mobile network. In the event of a fault, the CCI can itself intervene in the event of minor issues or otherwise instruct a service technician on standby to rectify the problem. Most efforts, however, do not lead to a replacement of the personnel, but rather are supportive and shift the tasks from mere observation to handling problematic cases. A current example of such systems can be found in Santander in Spain, where parking spaces, waste containers, and so forth are being equipped with sensors to create a more convenient and efficient urban lifestyle. Those systems still have flaws, however: The automated waste collection system in Songdo is not working as planned, and Santander has also reported trouble with faulty sensors.

The data produced and integrated in such systems is not only a result of the sensors that provide an overview of spatial ordering but also of additional data from automated processes. Centers integrate not only coordination tasks, but also data resources, which leads to our assumption that control centers are not only polyfunctional but also polycontextural.[5]

Theoretical perspective

To encapsulate the changes undergone in control rooms, we refer to the concept of refiguration. In order to explain this, we need to clarify a number of important theoretical foundations. In general, we understand control rooms and controlled urban spaces by means of a relational concept of space (Löw 2012). This means that we do not apply conventional "container models" of space, but rather focus on the processes and practices by which spaces are "(re)constructed" (Christmann 2013, 2016, 2022; Christmann, Knoblauch, and Löw 2022). We consider two social processes able to capture new arrangements analytically: (i) the accomplishment of synthesis and (ii) place making, or spacing (Löw 2012, 159 f.). Societal changes are understood when one observes the new forms in which spaces are synthesized and what new dynamics of spacing emerge.

In our study, this leads to a research perspective from which we not only focus on the design and architecture of the "room" itself, but on the actions that are performed within it and their effects, on the mediatization that interrelates the room with other spaces, and on the changes that such a "fluid network" undergoes (cf. Latour 2003). Our argument is that the general processes of such networks are changing and becoming increasingly complicated due to mediatization. This is due to an overarching process that can be termed "refiguration".

Refiguration is a term that, based on the above-mentioned relational concept, focuses on how, since the 1960s, new forms of space making and synthesis have developed. This chapter focuses in particular on the dimension of how control rooms contribute to these wider changes as well as how they can be understood as a part of new relational forms. They are an especially interesting example, as they are explicitly built to control spatially distributed systems, they centralize control and the specific use of technology, and media in these infrastructural figurations can be addressed to allow detailed scrutiny of those processes. In detail, our empirical research sought to understand social orders through a model of communication able to integrate the symbolic dimension with the material, bodily, and spatial dimensions. The underlying social theory of communicative constructivism (Knoblauch 2019) allows for an understanding of the empirical processes of change in social orders as part of a process of refiguration (see Knoblauch and Steets 2022). The subjective dimension of perception of and knowledge about space is as relevant as the dimension of spatial interrelations as they are manifested in interaction and communication as well as in built and material technologies and architectures.

Refiguration is a processual concept that takes communicative actions as linkages that have recently become increasingly mediatized. New forms of communication give rise to new forms of order that are established materially as well as in discourse and subjective knowledge and practices. One of the underlying assumptions used in our project to record these changes is that the constitution of space is increasingly characterized by mediated action (Knoblauch and Löw 2020). Through the increasing mediatization of ("communicative") action, action in such contexts can be described as increasingly synthetic, especially since digitalization has been the driving factor. The relationship between control center and controlled space becomes increasingly mediated, and thereby fluid, in the newly digitalized and integrated centers. For example, advanced communication technologies, sensor networks, area-wide CCTV installations, and other resources providing "nonspecific" data are interpreted, combined, and used for various tasks to intervene in the space under control. New technologies allow for extended scope in local face-to-face interaction but, at the same time, place the demand on actors to manage different scales actively and to reflexively integrate the interpersonal with the other dimensions. The concept of "synthetic situations" (Knorr-Cetina 2014) addresses and empirically demonstrates similar changes through the example of global finance trading (Knorr-Cetina 2012). However, contrary to the relatively space-independent trading floors, the phenomenon we observe in control centers is characterized by an emphasis on spatial action. In those synthetic situations the space does not (almost) disappear, as is apparently the case for financial markets (Knorr-Cetina 2012). We argue that the transformation of face-to-face situations into synthetic situations, highlighted by Knorr-Cetina, is also of consequence for the specific forms of spatial construction. Combined with the idea of relational space, we put forward the argument that the construction extends the "synthesis" (Löw 2012), making mediated objectivation an essential part of this process, and not only for the aspect of space making. "Synthetic actors" (Knorr-Cetina 2014) increasingly intervene in the construction of space in a regulating and controlling manner and are thus an active part of "spacing" (i.e. placement) practices. The fact that communication within a center, as well as between the center and the controlled outside space, is almost exclusively by means of technological equipment and digitalized images indicates that space is no longer merely a social-construction process that is carried out between subjects and (analogous) arrangements. Just as the digitalized representation of external space takes effect in the control center, the control center affects the outside space. In the following, we make a first attempt to show that synthetic situations are reproduced and to show how the supposedly traditional and "digital" contexts are intertwined. In the following parts, we present three examples, the first of which highlights the traditional form and communicative work in a monofunctional control room (Example 1). Building on this, we compare two examples that show the current developments toward polyfunctional control centers, address the integration of algorithms as synthetic actors (Example 2), and then draw attention to integration problems as well as organizational and alternative solutions that arise when introducing such new control centers (Example 3).

Work in monofunctional and polyfunctional centers

Example 1: Work in monofunctional centers

To give an impression of the work done in a traditional monofunctional center, we now show a short excerpt from one typical sequence of work. In this example, the center is responsible for taking emergency calls and dispatching police units in a major German city. A typical routine task is shown first. Here, a police officer accepts an incoming call and transforms the statements of the caller into manageable information using the software forms on her screen (see Figure 9.1).

After receiving the initial information, she checks again for the location in the city, the street, and enters it into the input field on the left screen. The information is compared against the city map, which dynamically shifts to the precise spatial location identified, allowing for a targeted inquiry. After recording the telephone number, she records details of the offence and enters the code for narcotic abuse along with other information. These are now displayed in the list in the center screen. The case is now closed for the officer in the emergency reception and is processed further by colleagues in the opposite part of the room, the so-called dispatch section.

The architecture of the room is deliberately designed in such a way that the division of labor is already present in the spatial arrangement (see Figure 9.2). Incoming cases are processed in the emergency call reception area and passed into the system to be taken up shortly afterwards on the other side of the room by an official with dispatch tasks.

On the other side of the room, in the dispatch area, the information collected reappears (see Figure 9.3). A colleague verbalizes the information (two male persons handling drugs) previously entered by the policewoman. The recipient officer then uses her communication resources to clarify whether a radio car or a special police unit should take over the case.

Centers of coordination refigured?   161

(1.) **Types street name. Location appears on the map to the right.**
[Types the circumstances into the field on the left-hand monitor]

(2.) **Input**
"2 males at the entrance to the park"
"Yelling and using drugs"
"Children present" –
"[Name]"

(3.) **Presses ENTER → The text is transferred to the comment field.**
[Moves the mouse and clicks ACCEPT, sending the case to be dispatched]

(4.) **The case "NARC" appears on the schedule in the upper part of the middle monitor** – showing cases yet to be dispatched. Simultaneously, at the top of the left-hand monitor, a red signal indicates a NEW case. (...)

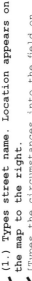

Figure 9.1 Incoming call.
Source: Arne Janz and René Tuma.

162 *René Tuma and Arne Janz*

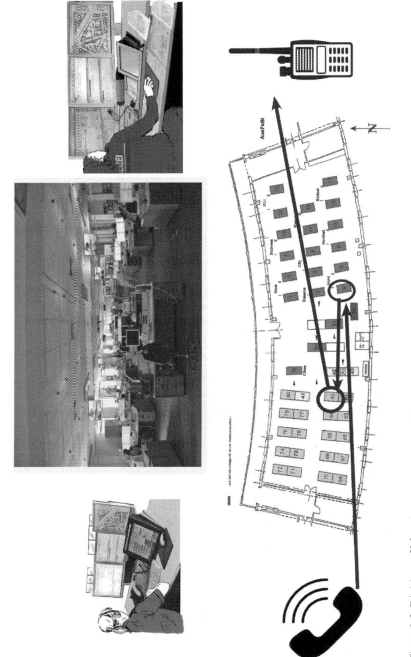

Figure 9.2 Division of labor in emergency reception.
Source: Arne Janz and René Tuma.

Centers of coordination refigured? 163

```
Translation of illustration text:
[Clicks on the NEW button on the left monitor,
which then displays the information entered by her
colleague]
```

[Turns to the monitor]

[Selects a number, then takes up the receiver]

[At the same time, takes the mouse and clicks. She types something into the upper field of the window and then maintains her position]

`[Someone comes to the telephone]`

Yes, good afternoon, (unintelligible – presumably her name) here, central dispatch.

I've a question: Are you interested in, um, narcotics users, um, or (unint.) with children present? (unint. – time and ... Hmm, pffff)

Well, it won't be any faster if I send a radio car, (unint. – we haven't) much success. So, hopefully, or do you already have a special assignment?

Yes, and so (unint.) not sure if somewhere (unint. – you can ask that) you can call again and then I'll send the radio car over, (Yes) yes. And it's in the Schinkenstraße 23 (2s.) there are just two males at the entrance to the park (2s.). Um, they look to be handling drugs and yelling and have, um, probably somehow, um, drugs wrapped in plastic and children are apparently there. Mr Kaja is troubled about it and wanted to make a report. (2s.) Yes? Thank you (unint.) Bye [Hangs up the receiver]

Figure 9.3 Dispatch.
Source: Arne Janz and René Tuma.

It is particularly interesting that division of labor is organized here but, at the same time, the urban space and the resources available to the police are represented – and made utilizable – by various reference objects. The dispatcher can keep track of the time schedule and the current actions on the map or order screen while at the same time making direct contact with colleagues on site via a digital telephone and radio system. But the events in general also remain available to her as a background stream, so she constantly overhears the conversations of colleagues in her vicinity. Her interaction space, which refers to various connections to the outside world, is integrated into the room architecture of the office, in which certain tasks are assigned to certain workstations.

The police provide an example of a classic, monofunctional control room. This means that only one sector is addressed, and one specific task is managed. The center is built and organized around the task of managing incoming emergency calls and distributing units within urban space. The participants use the information provided by the callers and city maps as well as information about the positioning of mobile units. When further information is needed, they rely on gathering such information by calling or radioing the responsible parties. The mediatization in this case uses traditional forms of communication, which means that the controlled space is only represented by maps and indirect information gathered via phone and verbal communication, and control is exerted by informing local police teams and informing other organizational units. There are plans to merge this control room with, for example, the fire service, but the management of other municipal services and infrastructure (transport companies, water, electricity, etc.) remains separately coordinated.

However, in the case of major crises, separate crisis centers are used. Representatives of the concerned organizations and political persons in charge are gathered here to exchange information and manage the situation. The different participating parties often use different technical and mapping systems, terminology, knowledge, and practices. As the infrastructure systems are connected, this is a complicated communications problem, for which new systems of visualization are required.[6]

Work in polyfunctional centers: Algorithmic control and integration of functions

In larger global cities, technological developments and concepts that can be encapsulated under the umbrella term "smart city" are currently being pushed forward. It is in such cities that integrated and algorithmically optimized control systems are being installed. An international race for the implementation of such concepts has begun, and development is especially well advanced in Asia. Songdo in South Korea can be viewed as a prime example of a fully integrated city, according to its own description. Built and designed completely from scratch, traffic, surveillance, refuse collection, security services, and much more are controlled via a uniform infrastructure. In Europe, too, some cities are planning steps in this direction. Such systems promise a more economic and ecological use of resources, smoother management, and a faster response to events. On the other hand, these systems, primarily based on pervasive and ubiquitous forms of sensors (and CCTV), which track the movement of individuals, traffic, and other infrastructure-relevant changes in the urban "system", are based on a generalized surveillance of space. To deal with the many sources of information in these prototype centers, automatic monitoring and control systems are used. For example, during a field trip to South Korea, on a guided tour through a polyfunctional traffic control center, we learned about a social scoring system for bus drivers. The bus drivers have a points contingency that is valid for 3 years. Among other things, drivers automatically have points deducted if they do not maintain a minimum distance of 5 minutes from the bus driving the same route in front of them. If a bus driver loses a full contingency of points before the end of the 3 years, they lose their bus driving license. Technologies are also being tested in German control rooms intended to automatically recognize relevant events.

The German city of Mannheim, for example, is experimenting with systems that highlight certain movements between passersby (punches, etc.). Even if these digital control projects and visions of the future are currently considered "cybernetic utopias" (or dystopias, from a more critical perspective), much effort is being put into establishing such systems and reducing the currently still prevalent issues with automatic systems and their limited scope. Their ongoing emergence is an expression of a digital-algorithmic refiguration of spatial control.

Besides the significant criticism of the deployment of universal surveillance articulated in many surveillance studies and diagnostic publications, there is a further aspect to it: The use of new technologies to integrate different systems does not simply substitute human agency, but rather produces new complexity by transferring digital information generated by sensors in the controlled space into a center of control in "real time". This information needs, however, to be interpreted and used for the planning of actions. Algorithmic calculations are then applied to the flow of incoming data, and statistical and more advanced methods (often utilizing machine learning, frequently dubbed "artificial intelligence") are used to process these data. Though most of these systems are still in development, they are able to deal with some tasks; but our observations show that their deployment mostly leads to new problems that can only be curbed by the control room staff acting communicatively.[7] Some of our field visits to former "role model" control rooms show that the systems are less used than intended, being replaced, for instance, by staff returning to conventional and mundane means of coordination such as instant messengers, smartphones, and radio. Some advanced polyfunctional control centers are already present in smart cities, however. They house a number of organizations and are usually dominated by giant screens on which hundreds of cameras, maps, and sometimes graphs are intended for surveillance use. Our field trips and interviews show, nevertheless, that they are usually not used for the work intended, with staff contending that nobody can follow these streams of information permanently. We therefore argue that polyfunctional control centers mostly serve the public image of the respective institutions, whereas algorithmic systems work in the background or are used to direct the staff attention. The aim is therefore to trace the specific relevance and decision bases inscribed within the systems and, at the same time, to investigate how these are interpreted "in front of the screen" and translated into actions by users.

Example 2: Algorithmic control in a polyfunctional center

The following example gives an insight into the work of a large Asian control area that is part of an "intelligent transport and information system" and has some aspects of the newer technologies that we described above as synthetic actors. Data from CCTV, seismic sensors in bridges, thermal sensors in roads, smoke detectors in tunnels, images from traffic cameras, and global positioning system (GPS) data from public transport buses and their passengers converge at the control center and are monitored, partly automatically by algorithms and partly by control room personnel. These various sensors are also contrasted with technical control instruments, such as fire-extinguishing systems, barriers, and nozzles with which chemicals can be sprayed onto roads to prevent ice formation in urban areas and to control other problems that occur. The available data is used mostly for traffic regulation and control, but also to detect vibrations in bridges or fires in tunnels and to close their access roads as quickly as possible with the help of barriers, thus preventing major incidents or even disasters.

The main task is the control of inner-city traffic flow (see Figure 9.4). With the help of sensors at traffic lights and GPS data from buses, the system calculates the average speed of traffic on a given road section and then uses this data to automatically adjust the traffic light system. In order to optimize traffic flow, algorithms that permanently monitor the average speed intervene in the external area via signal control, a recommended speed being displayed at the traffic lights themselves. The cameras are not permanently monitored for traffic control, but as soon as the algorithm detects a drop in average speed to below a certain threshold, the system automatically directs the attention of the staff to the cameras in the affected area. The control room staff are then requested to locate the cause of the traffic jam. In such cases, the staff will, for example, keep an eye out for broken-down vehicles, accidents, or people who are on the road without permission.

Another part of the everyday routine is the work of parking provision. In this area, a system is deployed to detect cars parked in prohibited spots. Hempel (2007) has studied traditional forms of such systems in London, based on the monitoring by staff of video footage in London. In our example from Asia, a system using cameras attached to public buses provides this information to the center, which deploys mobile units (on bicycles) to give tickets to cars that block a spot for longer than 5 minutes and are recorded by the automatic

Centers of coordination refigured? 167

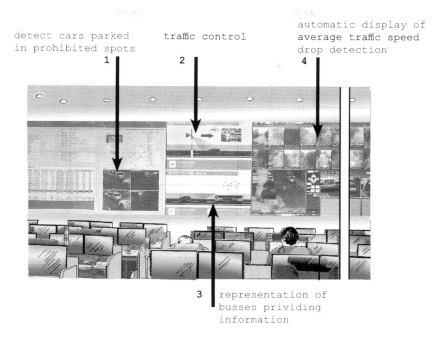

Figure 9.4 Monitoring inner-city traffic flow.
Source: Arne Janz and René Tuma.

systems several times. The system is designed to allocate tickets directly, based on the registration number of the vehicle, but as these are sometimes covered or otherwise illegible, mobile units remain necessary.

This case shows the influence of digital systems: the use of computer-generated data featuring elements of polycontexturality (integration of video, sensors, and other information sources), which is still divided into specialized tasks (ticketing on bus lines) due to work practices. There is no centralized control of all urban aspects, and digital systems require communicative work both within the room and out in the city – highlighting the interrelatedness of both spheres. In this case synthetic actors actively and effectively intervene in the urban space, and control room personnel are therefore participants in "synthetic situations". They manage the system through effective interventions in urban space, such as by sending rescue vehicles to the scene of an accident, switching traffic lights to divert traffic away from such a scene, or, in the event of an accident in a tunnel, closing its access barriers, activating the fire-extinguishing system if necessary, and thus preventing a disaster.

The algorithms that process and compare data on the basis of digital images of exterior space also, on this basis, take effect to intervene in that space in a regulating and controlling manner. (In practice, we have not yet observed the use of self-learning algorithms, merely those that make predefined "if-then" decisions). If further regulation is not possible, because some variable measured by the system falls below a certain threshold, the system brings the corresponding images to the attention of staff and thus also effectively intervenes in the space within the control center by creating relevance. Synthetic actors here are no longer just programs that represent an interface between a supposed inside and an outside, but an active part of the placement practice and thus of the constitution of the space. By "placing" or spacing, they synthesize the outside and the inside into a synthetic space of control – the control center. Conversely, urban space is also a synthetic space that contributes to the spatial constitution through this technological synthesis (performance) and spacing. Following Löw, one could speak of a mediatization of spacing and synthesis.

Example 3: Organizational integration in a polyfunctional center

In contrast to the "traditional" monofunctional control room that is based on representation as well as radio and phone communication (Example 1), and the polyfunctional control center that heavily draws on algorithmic control and automatization (Example 2), this example presents the case of a distinctly polyfunctional center. Here, however, the integration is not achieved on the basis of new technologies and mediatization, but rather through a fallback to traditional communication which maintains the organizational division. This third example comes from work in a Latin American control room that focuses primarily on city management. Here, more than 25 organizations are united under one roof, including gas and water suppliers, waste management companies, and traffic control alongside a police department and the military police. The center has a special focus on traffic and public safety. In addition, countless traffic cameras and CCTV are used in social hotspots. Information is mainly obtained via camera images, but also via reports from outside, such as from patrolmen. If traffic jams are detected on the traffic cameras, the traffic control center can intervene in the outside area and recommend detours via sign lights. The police permanently monitor the social hotspots using video cameras. Depending on the day, time, and occasion, 10 to 20 people each monitor three cameras, 24 hours a day, 7 days a week.

While one might assume that control rooms would reduce in size and that the functions of individual organizations would grow more interconnected, Paul Luff et al. (2017), for example, show that the trend for work in these multi-organization centers increasingly appears to resemble the workplaces of open-plan offices; that is, every employee at their workplace performs their job and is not dependent on micro interactions with their colleagues next door (Luff et al. (2017). This impression is reinforced by the smart city hype of recent years, in which control rooms are referred to as the "brain" of the city or as "integrated" operations centers (Knoblauch, Janz, and Schröder 2021).[8] We assume that this claim is due to marketing strategies and efforts toward uniting the control rooms of different organizations under one roof. All participating organizations share in common the fact that they existed 30 years prior and that they manage "core infrastructures" of large cities.

However, our analysis shows that supposed smart integration, through the use of algorithms and automated data exchange, does not occur in this way, at least not in the center observed. Here, the police and the military police are two separately operating organizations; should an exchange between each be necessary, this happens via face-to-face communication. The center as a whole could therefore be described as polyfunctional. The individual organizations operate self-sufficiently as far as possible and only come together for meetings that take place twice daily for about 15 minutes. The case is even more ironic, as the smart system formerly installed by a major technology player in the field has been abandoned by the local staff and replaced by the use of smartphones with consumer-oriented smart messengers (each operator has several smartphones connected individually to specific subunits) as well as conventional digital radio.

The CCTV system is used extensively, but our observations show how very often the ambiguous picture and video feeds require interpretation and checking against accounts from units present on site. We therefore argue that contrary to the promised aims of this smart project, the integration actually achieved cannot be described as increasingly drawing on algorithms and mediatization, or as polycontextural (Knoblauch, Janz, and Schröder 2021). Rather, as observed in the workplace studies of the 1990s, classic micro interactions and "overhearing" practices are still noticeable. As our research is ongoing, we are not yet sure whether this "failure" is due to local idiosyncrasies, the "problems and drawbacks" of the ongoing process of adaptation to new technologies, or if the promised integration is generally not able to fulfil the demands of everyday work.

Conclusion

The distinctions between the different forms of center are still fluid and overlapping. Even in some monofunctional centers (at least in routine operation) communication is exclusively based on technological devices, as was evident in Example 1 (German police). The polyfunctional coordination centers of advanced, smart city projects tend to be formed from a juxtaposition of different organizations. This interlinkage is manifested through technology, spatial order, and work and communication practices. However, in some of the polyfunctional centers (at least in routine operation), new processes in which synthetic actors are integrated and effect urban space can be observed. In the example of the South Korean control center, we have shown how synthetic actors are utilized to monitor digitalized representations of external space, to synchronize video findings from CCTV, and to detect parking offences. Furthermore, these technological systems are theoretically able to issue parking tickets directly.

Thus, in control centers that deal with urban infrastructures, the relevant "material arrangement" of the city is reflected in digitized form. These digital images are partly monitored, analyzed, and interpreted by human actors and partly by synthetic actors (such as algorithms and programs), and on the basis of these images, they intervene in space. The entire process of monitoring, regulation, and control is planned to take place on the basis of technological systems. Urban space, as well as the control room, increasingly exists as a synthetic space when there are sensors, cameras, traffic lights, and barriers located in the city. On the basis of digital images of external space, data synthesis is enabled and thus so too is regulation and control – in turn, directly effecting elements of external space.

These mediated relations are essential parts of spatial refiguration. We use the concept of synthetic space to capture the new forms of spatial relations enacted by control rooms intervening in the controlled spaces. The concept of synthetic spaces we propose here preliminarily draws on Knorr-Cetina's concept of synthetic situations, but highlights its spatial aspects. Its specific forms are characterized by modes of communication that are spatially structured. Knorr-Cetina distinguishes different forms, starting with the conventional form described as response presence (originating with Goffman 1982, 2) which is then changed by the new types of mediatization into forms of direct reaction presence, or the new "scopic" re-action presence. Even if these forms overlap in our data, since the systems do not (yet?) function as promised, some basic references to these synthetic spaces can already be found. The combination of the integration of new technologies that combine mediatization with algorithmic control, allowing the development toward synthetic spaces and the integration of control rooms into polyfunctional centers, has a combined effect that can be grasped with the concept of polycontexturalization.

However, certain limitations and the importance of traditional forms of communication can still be seen to exist in control rooms in our examples. The integration of existing organizations, with their own specific organizational structures, seems to be especially complex, as our initial analyses of the Latin American case (Example 3) shows. Here, it is more a case of organizational coexistence than of proper integration, in which data from the individual organizations would be exchanged, processed, and manipulated via databases and algorithms. If exchange between the organizations occurs, then it takes place face to face.

Is there a spatial refiguration? Do control centers synthesize translocal places into spaces? The idea that these places overlap and are completely synthesized does not completely capture the specifics of our case. On the one hand the controlled spaces, watched by sensors and CCTV, are medially connected with the control rooms in real time. Their multitude and complexity has an effect on the construction of the interior space and vice versa. For example, external space can be monitored by video cameras, and the images can be controlled in the control center, from which place someone in the external space can be instructed to intervene in a certain situation (like a gathering of people). This synthesis does not directly overlap but is, rather, the result of communicative processes. Our ongoing analysis gives hints that the management of the distinction between these spaces (made visible in the methods of understanding what is occurring, by sending personnel to a location to gather information, etc.) is constitutive for the figuration between controlled space and control room. The spaces are separate from each other, but can interact via technological equipment and personnel. On account of the new forms of mediatization, this new figuration can be understood as synthetic spacing.

Notes

1 This chapter presents results of the project entitled "Centers of Coordination: The Polycontexturalisation of Power in Control Rooms". It forms part of the Collaborative Research Center 1265 "Re-Figuration of Spaces" at the Technische Universität Berlin, Germany, and is funded by the German Research Foundation under project no. 290045248. The research group consists of Hubert Knoblauch, Arne Janz, Joshua Schroeder, and René Tuma, each participating in empirical research and theoretical discussion. Additional fieldwork and important insights have been contributed by Leon Hempel. We also wish to thank our student assistants Elisabeth Schmidt and Aris Harkat.
2 Cf. https://constanttech.com/installation-types/command-control-centers
3 Cf. http://cor.rio/institucional/
4 Cf. http://futurecity.glasgow.gov.uk/ops-data/
5 For the concept of polycontexturality, see Knoblauch, Janz, and Schröder (2021).
6 For a project experimenting with new forms of visualization, see Hahne et al. (2013).
7 Often an interface manager is employed to deal with that task (see Hempel 2020).
8 This Latin American city has also previously had the honor of being nominated the world's smartest city.

References

Berndtsson, Johan, and Maria Normark. 1999. "The Coordinative Functions of Flight Strips: Air Traffic Control Work Revisited". In *Conference Proceedings of GROUP '99: International ACM SIGGROUP Conference on Supporting group Work, Phoenix (Arizona, USA), November*, edited by Stephen C. Hayne, 101–110. New York: ACM.

Christmann, Gabriela B. 2013. "Raumpioniere in Stadtquartieren und die kommunikative (Re-)Konstruktion von Räumen" [Urban pioneers in neighborhoods and the communicative (re)construction of spaces]. In *Kommunikativer Konstruktivismus: Theoretische und empirische Arbeiten zu einem neuen wissenssoziologischen Ansatz* [Communicative constructivism: Theoretical and empirical work on a new sociological approach], edited by Reiner Keller, Hubert Knoblauch, and Jo Reichertz, 153–184. Wiesbaden: Springer VS.

Christmann, Gabriela B., ed. 2016. *Zur kommunikativen Konstruktion von Räumen: Theoretische Konzepte und empirische Analysen* [On the communicative construction of spaces: Theoretical concepts and empirical analyses]. Wiesbaden: Springer VS.

Christmann, Gabriela B. 2022. "The Theoretical Concept of the Communicative (Re) construction of Spaces". In *Communicative Constructions and the Refiguration of Spaces*, edited by Gabriela Christmann, Hubert Knoblauch, and Martina Löw, 89–112. Abingdon: Routledge.

Christmann, Gabriela B., Hubert Knoblauch, and Martina Löw. 2022. "Introduction: Communicative Constructions and the Refiguration of Spaces". In *Communicative Constructions and the Refiguration of Spaces*, edited by Gabriela Christmann, Hubert Knoblauch, and Martina Löw, 3–15. Abingdon: Routledge.

Goffman, Erving. 1982. "The interaction order". *American Sociological Review* 48: 1–17.

Goodwin, Charles, and Marjorie Goodwin. 1996. "Seeing as a Situated Activity: Formulating Planes". In *Cognition and Communication at Work*, edited by Yrjö Engeström and David Middleton, 61–95. Cambridge: Cambridge University Press.

Hahne, Michael, Thomas Becker, Marie Bartels, and Renate Lieb. 2013. *Simulation von intersektoriellen Kaskedeneffekten bei Ausfällen von Versorgungsinfrastrukturen unter Verwendung des virtuellen 3D-Stadtmodells Berlins (SIMKAS-3D). Projektabschlussbericht der Technischen Universität Berlin* [Simulation of intersectoral cascade effects in case of failures of supply infrastructures using the virtual 3D city model of Berlin (SIMKAS-3D). Final project report of the Technischen Universität Berlin]. Hannover: TIB.

Heath Christian, and Paul Luff. 1992. "Collaboration and Control: Crisis Management and Multimedia Technology in London Underground Line Control Rooms". *Computer Supported Cooperative Work* 1 (1): 69–94.

Heath, Christian, Hubert Knoblauch, and Paul Luff. 2004. "Tools, Technologies and Organizational Interaction: The Emergence of Workplace Studies". In *The SAGE Handbook of Organizational Discourse*, edited by David Grant, Cynthia Hardy, Chiff Oswick, and Linda Putnam, 337–358. London, Thousand Oaks, and New Delhi: Sage.

Hempel, Leon. 2007. "Zur Evaluation von Videoüberwachung" [On the evaluation of video surveillance]. In *Surveillance Studies. Perspektiven eines Forschungsfeldes* [Surveillance studies. Perspectives of a research field], edited by Nils Zurawski, 117–147. Opladen: Budrich.

Hempel, Leon. 2020. "Vom Oligoptikon zum Poligoptikon: Zur Koordination gleichzeitiger Zeitstrukturen in digitalen Umgebungen" [From oligopticon to poligopticon: On the coordination of simultaneous time structures in digital environments]. *Zeitpolitisches Magazin* 36: 19–28. www.zeitpolitik.de/pdfs/zpm_36_0720.pdf

Knoblauch, Hubert. 2019. *The Communicative Construction of Reality: Knowledge, Communication and Society*. Abingdon: Routledge.

Knoblauch, Hubert, and Martina Löw. 2020. "The Re-Figuration of Spaces and Refigured Modernity – Concept and Diagnosis". *Historical Social Research* 45 (2): 263–292.

Knoblauch, Hubert, and Silke Steets. 2022. "From the Constitution to the Communicative Construction of Space". In *Communicative Constructions and the Refiguration of Spaces*, edited by Gabriela Christmann, Hubert Knoblauch, and Martina Löw, 19–35. Abingdon: Routledge.

Knoblauch, Hubert, Arne Janz, and David Joshua Schröder. 2021. "Kontrollzentralen und die Polykontexturalisierung von Räumen" [Control centers and the polycontexturalization of spaces]. In *Am Ende der Globalisierung. Über die Re-Figuration von Räumen* [At the end of globalization. On the re-figuration of spaces], edited by Martina Löw, Volkan Sayman, Jona Schwerer, and Hannah Wolf, 157–182. Bielefeld: transcript.

Knorr-Cetina, Karin. 2012. "Skopische Medien: Am Beispiel der Architektur von Finanzmärkten" [Scopic media: Using the example of the architecture of financial markets]. In *Mediatisierte Welten: Beschreibungsansätze und Forschungsfelder* [Mediatized worlds: Descriptive approaches and research fields], edited by Andreas Hepp and Friedrich Krotz, 167–195. Wiesbaden: VS.

Knorr-Cetina, Karin. 2014. "Scopic Media and Global Coordination: The Mediatization of Face-to-Face Encounters". In *Mediatization of Communication*, edited by Knut Lundby, 39–62. Berlin: De Gruyter.

Latour, Bruno. 2003. *PARIS: VILLE INVISIBLE* [Paris: Invisible City]. [Virtual book available from Bruno Latour's website, photographs by Natalie Hermant and web design by Patricia Reed.] www.bruno-latour.fr/virtual/index.html

Löw, Martina. 2012. *Raumsoziologie* [Sociology of Space]. Frankfurt am Main: Suhrkamp.

Luff, Paul, Christian Heath, Menisha Patel, Dirk vom Lehn, and Andrew Highfield. 2017. "Creating Interdependencies: Managing Incidents in Large Organizational Environments". *Human–Computer Interaction*, 33 (5–6): 544–584.

Martin, David, John Bowers, and David Wastell. 1997. "The Interactional Affordances of Technology: An Ethnography of Human-Computer Interaction in an Ambulance Control Centre". In *People and Computers XII*, edited by Harold Thimbleby, Brid O'Conaill, and Peter J. Thomas, 263–281. London: Springer.

Suchman, Lucy. 1997. "Centres of Coordination: A Case and Some Themes". In *Discourse, Tools and Reasoning: Essays on Situated Cognition*, edited by Lauren B. Resnick, Roger Säljö, Clotilde Pontecorvo, and Barbara Burge, 41–62. Berlin: Springer.

10 Architectures of asylum

Negotiating home-making through concrete spatial strategies

Philipp Misselwitz and Anna Steigemann

Introduction

This article draws on an ongoing investigation of spatial appropriations in refugee camps in Berlin.[1] The theoretical framework that guides this volume acknowledges the (re)construction of spaces as multidimensional, involving communications, social, and spatial practices as well as knowledge, materiality, and processes. The extreme case of a refugee camp setting, however, confronts us with situations in which neither the possibility of direct verbal communication between subjects, nor a shared understanding of routines, values, or norms, or a socially shared cultural space, can be taken for granted.

Under these conditions, spatial and material appropriations initiated by refugees transforming a standardized shelter into de facto homes should be considered as a means by which they engage in communicative construction of spaces, often substituting for other, more or less obstructed forms of exchange via language or verbal communication. Camp management, social workers, or security personnel equally engage by choosing or resisting application and enforcement of norms and standards and by tolerating or insisting on the reversal of specific appropriations. The socio-spatial practices of refugees and other actors therefore become a complex arena of conflictual negotiations between residents and the regulatory regimes that define and revise shelter and camp planning standards, but which also communicate (existential) needs and the search for inclusion and acceptance.

We understand the communicative construction of space as distinctively practice based and grounded in concrete material and spatial realities (Christmann, Knoblauch, and Löw 2022; Christmann 2016, 2022). This chapter draws on a novel combination of spatial and social research methods required to decode such communication through the materials and spaces of selected camp settings. We argue that the relevance of this approach extends beyond humanitarian settings and could indeed be considered key to better understand the communicative construction of spaces in societies that are increasingly shaped by translocal relations, migration, and diversity. We start by briefly outlining the specific theoretical framework and sensitizing concepts that

DOI: 10.4324/9780367817183-13

guided our research. Here, we draw mainly on the work of Michel de Certeau and his likening of spatial practices to language, in that they can be understood as structuring communicative interactions. We also refer to more recent scholars who have provided the concept of social practices and argued for a praxeological turn in the social sciences (Reckwitz 2002; Schatzki 2001, 2010) and, more recently, in urban studies (Shove and Trentman 2018; Shove, Pantzar, and Watson 2012), to extend their conceptual work to the spatial dimension of social practices. We also draw on work that has analyzed and interpreted the meaning of spatial changes and domestic alterations initiated by inhabitants of dwellings and, more directly related to the context of refugee and migrant practices, we draw on the interpretation of arrival practices in refugee camp settings as processes of re-subjectification and self-assertion (Agier 2011) or in relation to "home-making" (Brun and Fabós 2015). Spatial practices are described here as part of conflictual negotiation processes, through which migrants and refugees engage with spatial orders imposed by humanitarian planning regimes. Reframing negotiations that inform concrete spatial outcomes through the concept of the communicative construction of spaces can help to further our understanding of the communicative power of spatial practices in general.

After laying out the theoretical framework, we describe the context of Berlin refugee accommodation as a research setting. In the empirical section, we discuss architectural ethnographies of the concrete spatial strategies negotiated between refugee residents and management and security personal as communicative constructions. This method allows us to precisely trace the material and spatial alterations of residents, the local management practices of Berlin's Tempohomes (LAF 2017), and the perspective of those of Berlin's centralized authorities responsible for defining norms, regulations, and management codes that provide an institutionalized pre-structured setting for negotiated spatial outcomes. We draw on a range of interview transcripts, spatial mappings, visual recordings, and ethnographic memos to show in detail how conflictual negotiations around everyday spaces can be understood as (nonverbal) communicative construction of spaces, characterized by conflicting assumptions, misunderstandings, and clashing rationalities as well as genuine attempts to reach out and learn from the other. This conversation, taking place by material means, is acted out through various tactics such as shifting frontiers and testing new ground on behalf of refugee residents, a variety of responses ranging between the enforcing of rules and establishment of boundaries, and softer approaches such as tolerating or simply ignoring experimental rule bending. In our conclusion, we speculate on the broader significance of including material and spatial constellations within the concept of communicative construction of spaces and outline ways in which this context could, beyond camp settings, help to build understanding of space-making within urban environments increasingly shaped by diversity and migration.

The communicative power of spatial practices: A theoretical framework

Our research is based on the assumption that making space is in itself a meaningful communicative practice. Space- and place-making do not primarily rely on direct verbal communication, but can rather be understood as the product of negotiations in which different norms and values and behavioral codes, but also the individual means, resources, and materialities at hand, are mobilized by various actors to alter given spatial constellations. The way diverse actors engage in such nonverbal negotiations can be understood as concrete spatial practices, including bodily enactment and performance, as well as spatial tactics to rearrange and design spaces according to one's needs and preferences. Michel de Certeau (1985, 129 ff.) writes that spatial practices have a clear and immediate "uttering function" – they are the equivalent to what the speech act is to language. Spatial practices are a "process of appropriation of the topographic, [...] they are a spatial realization of the site, [...] [they imply] relationships among distinct positions, i.e. pragmatic contracts in the form of movements". Building on de Certeau, we conceptualize communication as practice based in order to draw attention to everyday social life in refugee accommodation, run by mostly routinized actions, intentional or not, whose communicative power and ordering structure is often overlooked.

More recently, Theodore Schatzki (2001, 2010) and Andreas Reckwitz (2002) have argued for a praxeological turn in the social sciences. Following Schatzki, practice can be understood as combining four dimensions – practical understanding, rules, teleoaffective structures, and general understanding – which enable the knowledgeable but often routinized performance of a practice (Schatzki 2001; Steigemann 2017, 2019). In a similar vein, Reckwitz defines practices as

> a routinized type of behaviour which consists of several elements, interconnected to one another: Forms of bodily activities, forms of mental activities, "things" and their use, a background knowledge in the form of understanding, know-how, states of emotion and motivational knowledge.
> (Reckwitz 2002, 249)

A "simplified" and more empirically applicable version of practice theories is developed by Shove et al. (2012), conceptualizing practices as doings and sayings, involving not only specific meanings and competencies, but also artefacts or things. This involvement of materials and their embeddedness in concrete spaces and contexts add a first spatial layer to social practices.

Schatzki's (2003) definition of practice also acknowledges spatial context; in particular, his more recent "site ontology" more explicitly includes the spatio-temporal setting of practices, addressing material and immaterial entities and their relation to each other, which then constitute the practices' respective meanings, orders, and arrangements (Everts, Lahr-Kurten, and Watson 2011,

324; Steigemann 2017). He claims that the best way to approach the nature of social life and the character of its transformation "is to tie social life to something called 'the site of the social'". Spatial practices are thus inherently social practices and vice versa, assembling people, artefacts, things, and organisms (Schatzki 2001). Refugee accommodations explored in this article can thus be understood as comprising material and immaterial aspects of the social, which are in constant flux – temporally and spatially unfolding sites, according to the respective "timespaces" and enmeshed practices (Schatzki 2003, 226). From this derives a rather dynamic, activity-orientated understanding of space and place, existing only within and through activities, while the activities themselves also only occur within these arrangements (Everts et al. 2011, 327; Steigemann 2017, 2019).

The spatial methods of architectural and urban research offer opportunities for further elaboration and empirical grounding of the spatial and material dimensions of practice theories. Considering social and spatial practices as integrated (intentional or routinized) actions can help to better understand designing, constructing, rearranging (improvised, makeshift, or existing preinstalled) furniture, adapting and reorganizing shelters into multifunctional spaces, or negotiating the extension of containers and purchase of additional furniture – as all combine more strategic, intentional, and routinized actions (see Everts et al. 2011; Reckwitz 2002; Schatzki 2001, 2010). Often, a variety of practices coexist, each of which forms interdependent relations between the hardware of dwelling (cutlery or tools, beds, tables, etc.), distributions of competence (between humans and nonhumans), the emergence of home as a project, and, with them, new patterns of interactions and emotional attachments (Shove et al. 2007a, 2007b, 4; Steigemann 2017).

In this chapter, we use this praxeological approach not only to explore spatial appropriation within refugee accommodation on an empirical level, but also to argue the case for the particular relevance of a (spatial) praxeological approach for understanding the communicative construction of spaces in general. The spatial knowledge mobilized in such practices is conceptualized as including the (socialized) experience of space, ideas about space, and emotions and affective states connected with space. Our ethnographic studies of "implicit" bodily, habitualized, and routinized practices focus on physically and materially objectified spatial knowledge, deliberately reaching beyond linguistic articulation. We also focus on institutional knowledge resources imparted through standardized rule systems (e.g. building regulations), which equally condition ideas, arrangements, and management practices (cf. Knoblauch and Löw 2020). Our work also draws on an emerging body of critical camp studies within urban and architectural research. Two perspectives have been prevalent. First, scholars have scrutinized the techno-managerial arrangements of camp settings, which often result in dehumanizing, exploitative power systems. This is addressed, for instance, by Giorgio Agamben (1998, 78), who describes the refugee camp as the "the absolute, pure, impassable biopolitical space", in which control over life and death can be practiced (cf. Dalal et al. 2018). Here, the excessive control and disciplinary power that limits the practices and appropriative agency of camp residents can be seen as derived from the political otherness of refugees entering the new places of asylum as unwanted, undesirable others (Agier 2011; Said 2002). The apparatus of norms, codes, structures, and routines mobilized in Berlin Tempohomes expresses itself in specific spatial practices that inform the design and management approaches explored through empirical examples in this chapter. We draw at times on our own recent work on the design innovations that inform the planning of new refugee camps in Berlin, which have resulted in the ambivalent outcome of well-designed yet more controlling and disciplining environments, resulting in the further limitation of power and means by which refugees can engage in space-making practices (Dalal et al. 2018).

A second perspective, however, has focused on the agency of refugees to resist and, at times, subvert disciplinary regimes. Camp residents, rather than silently succumbing to the premeditated managerial and organizational structuring of daily life in a camp, tend to develop their own counter strategies to negotiate its spaces and structures. These practices, in which refugees engage in the co-production of spaces and subvert models of control and exclusion, are what we refer to as refugee agency. Cities and urban areas can play a vital role in facilitating refugee agency through their heterogeneity, autonomy, and the rich and complex environments they offer (see, e.g., Alshadfan 2015; Arous 2013; Fawaz 2016). "Even refugee camps themselves, where control and disciplining is given a wider scope to be exercised, are appropriated and reshaped through refugee agency" (Dalal et al. 2018, 65).

During their arduous journeys, refugees employ spatial practices to meet basic daily needs and, wherever possible, to rebuild livelihoods – a bundle of practices which can be understood as home-making in limbo (Brun 2001, 19; Boer 2015, 500 f.). While basic needs and survival are key, exile is also a search for a sense of self and belonging. Gupta and Ferguson argue that

> in a world of diaspora, transnational culture flows, and mass movements of people, the idea of culturally and ethnically distinct places becomes stronger. Consequently, people invent homes and homelands in the absence of territorial, national bases – not in situ, but through memories of, and claims on, places they can or will no longer corporally inhabit.
> (1992, 10; see also Boer 2015, 500 f.)

In previous work, we revealed that spatial practices are also key to urbanizing refugee camps and turning them into homes (Steigemann and Misselwitz 2020; Misselwitz 2009). For instance, Romola Sanyal (2011) has explained how, despite the policing practices and attempts to maintain the temporal nature of the camp, refugees most often manage to urbanize their accommodations through the incremental practice of building under cover of their tents and bribing policemen. Palestinian refugees in Lebanon, for instance "are active agents in the creation and consolidation of their community even under conditions of duress" (Sanyal 2011, 885). Hence, with a focus on the communicative power of spatial practices, and recognizing the importance of agency in addressing the social life and spatialities of camps, many urban studies scholars "called for alternative theorizations of the camp than the one offered by Agamben, where control and agency are both equally, and sometimes ambiguously, recognized and addressed" (Dalal et al. 2018, 65) (see, for instance, Isin and Rygiel 2007; Katz 2017; Oesch 2017).

Power, control, and agency as exercised through camp planning and the counter strategies they provoke remain underexplored and, we argue, require a stronger focus on micro-spatial settings with their particular materialities and social practices. By focusing on spatial production and appropriation as sets of practices, based on skills and stocks of knowledge gained in multiple contexts and sites prior to and during the refugees' journey but also on arrival in places of asylum, we explore the communicative power of spatial practice. The planning, design, and management practices of the camp operators and the political and administrative units that commissioned them, and the appropriation, design, and place-making practices of the accommodation residents can be understood as a power-permeated spatial communication. Following the spatial appropriation process communicates and reveals the constantly shifting negotiation processes and power relations between management regimes and the residents carving out spaces of autonomy and self-determination.

Context and key actors

In Germany, unlike many other European countries, local municipalities are the key administrative level responsible for designing and managing refugee accommodation. This high degree of decentralization leads to a considerable variation in policy, organizational routines, and design responses between German cities. In 2015, when Syrian refugees arrived en masse for the first time, institutions were slow to respond and bureaucratic routines evolved only gradually. While many refugees were initially housed in co-opted school gymnasiums, vacant buildings, hotels, or emergency tents, the Berlin State Office for Refugee Issues (Landesamt für Flüchtlingsangelegenheiten, LAF 2017) eventually succeeded in "normalizing" housing for refugees by means of temporary container solutions. The containers were first used in 2016 in so-called LaGeSo villages (often also referred to as "container villages") to house 2,200 residents. As the solution proved to be insufficient and costly, the LAF embarked on an improved container-based design solution for 18 additional sites – the Tempohomes. In contrast to the two-story LaGeSo villages, Tempohomes only have a single ground floor, based on small apartment-like units of three containers including cooking and bathroom facilities. The Tempohome sites were eventually also equipped with porches and outdoor infrastructure such as playgrounds, plant boxes, or communal facilities. In 2019, all 24 sites were surrounded by fences and guarded by security teams, that control access and are managed by various independent contractors on short-term management contracts.

A significant criticism of Berlin's refugee accommodation strategy has been directed toward the decision to segregate refugee housing from other affordable housing schemes in the city and to choose often peripheral, poorly serviced locations, which activists and researchers have called "campization" (Kreichauf 2018). Indeed, hostilities have been most frequent in those locations where Tempohomes or LaGeSo villages were placed within neighborhoods of predominantly low-income residents with infrastructural deficiencies. Although pragmatic reasons such as availability of space and cost may often contribute to the choice of location, they result in problematic and constraining institutionalized contexts within which communicative construction of everyday spaces (including homes) unfold.

However, our case studies also reveal the importance of differentiating between the techno-managerial order – as formalized norms which condition container design and arrangements, internal furnishings, and the overall layouts of Tempohomes as well as numerous rules and guidelines structuring everyday spatial routines – and the way they are applied, interpreted, and at times also suspended by local management staff. Here, we draw on Lipsky's concept of street-level bureaucrats (1971, 2010), which, as will be seen later on, perform a key role in spatial negotiations with refugee residents.

At the time of writing (early 2020), the future of the sites remains uncertain; some were "vacated" (LAF 2019) of refugees, while others are still occupied. Built according to temporary-use regulations, the sites were licensed and zoned to be dismantled by the end of 2019. But the construction of more durable housing solutions for refugees designed since 2016 – so-called MUFs (from Modulare Unterkünfte für Flüchtlinge, or modular accommodation for refugees) – are significantly behind schedule, and it can be assumed that the majority of container-based solutions will remain in place for several years to come (cf. Dalal et al. 2018). Official figures account for 77,423 registered asylum seekers in Berlin, out of which about 21,000 are housed in official refugee accommodation (LAF 2019).

Spatial negotiations

In this section, we describe examples which show how institutional spatial practices (standardized norms and rules) mediated through local management staff (street-level bureaucrats in the service of the LAF) provoke diverse refugee responses. The cases show how their different rationalities inform contrasting spatial practices that produce conflict and negotiations and, thus, highlight the communicative nature and qualities of spatial practices and appropriation processes, bringing to the fore the key role spatial tactics and material constellations assume in this mostly nonverbal negotiation. We focus primarily on the factors that affect the emerging spatial-material constellations and analyze how refugees respond to and challenge given spatial orders through spatial practices, such as appropriation or alterations, which provoke reactions from the managers and security personnel and, yet again, counter reactions from the residents. We argue that these cycles of responses and counter responses grow into mutually communicating and hybrid spatial and material configurations that bridge institutional norms and the subjective desire to turn shelters into homes. We also argue that these spatial negotiations, often local and situative improvisations, are also indirectly able to change the managerial approaches of the administration.

Our ethnographic research in Berlin's refugee accommodation took place between March 2018 and January 2020. Research methods included open, conversational, and informal interviews, walk-alongs, drawings, co-mapping workshops with residents, and their visual interpretation of pictures of their previous and current places of residence. Most of the joint drawings of refugees' spaces and spatial practices and interview quotations come from interviews with 10 camp residents, most of whom were male, middle-aged, and traveling alone. However, we also interviewed couples, families, and all other household constellations. Most women interviewed lived with either a partner or children; we rarely encountered lone-traveling women or girls. Interviews were transcribed and analyzed, following a grounded theory methodology (Strauss and Corbin 1997; Glaser, Strauss, and Strutzel 1968), going back and forth between analyzing interview and observation material, linking them back to our underlying assumptions, and sensitizing concepts on spatial practices, home-making, and spatial knowledge.

One interview partner, Iman, remembered the harsh and inhumane conditions that refugees had had to endure for several months back in 2014: "The hall was very big and furnished with beds only. About 300 people living next to each other! How is that possible?! What would happen if I want to take off my headscarf?" To overcome this issue, she and her family moved two bunk beds so that they were adjacent to one another and used the sheet to demarcate the boundaries of their private space. The lower beds would be used by her and her daughters, while one of the upper ones would be used by the husband. The second upper bunk was used to store luggage and family equipment. Moreover, Iman explained:

> There was no space to pray – the whole room was exposed and everyone could see you! So the neighbors started putting sheets between their beds to make extra rooms for praying. But the police[2] didn't like it. ... They got upset because they said they want to always be able to check between the beds. So we only put [out] the sheets when we wanted to pray and then we took them off again.

Another interviewee reflected on his individual response to these conditions (see Figure 10.1):

> We put mattresses on the ground. ... The beds we were supposed to sleep on, we put around. We were the first to do this as we needed our private space. But then the people liked it and started to do the same too! ... I installed them in a circle ... and covered it with sheets so we can change our clothes inside it. It became like a separate room.

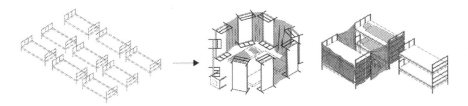

Figure 10.1 Roofless rooms allowing privacy.
Source: Philipp Misselwitz and Anna Steigemann.

Many other interviewees reported similar strategies to appropriate material resources at hand for establishing a physical boundary between "their" shelter and those of other neighboring refugees. Bed linen or blankets were fixed around beds to form screens. Interviewees reported that the local management initially resisted such self-provisioned structures and forced their dismantling, citing fire hazards and safety rules. Overwhelmed by the persistence of the residents, some local managers would be forced to turn a blind eye and ignore violations of rules, while others, especially during periodical visits from higher levels within the bureaucracy, continued to enforce them. Negative press coverage of "chaotic and overcrowded-looking halls" exerted additional pressure, and one of the first purpose-built emergency accommodations in Berlin – the vacant Tempelhof hangars – included aluminum-coated walls forming small, albeit roofless, rooms allowing the inhabitants some privacy.

By the end of 2014, criticism of the inhumane and overcrowded conditions in emergency homes, including at Tempelhof, as well as several scandals involving corruption and mismanagement forced the Berlin Senate and its administrative units to rethink both administrative management and to develop new accommodation strategies for refugees. This resulted in the aforementioned "container villages" (Figure 10.2) composed of stacked containers and placed in mostly peripheral locations in the city. The task force had managed to bypass complicated and dilatory planning laws by designating the structures as temporary; that is, limited to a 3-year period of use. However, this temporary character, both as sets of regulations but also especially in temporary architectures and physical features, communicates this ephemerality constantly to residents. Within the individual 2.5 meter by 6 meter containers, stacked on two levels along internal access corridors, and equipped with standardized furnishings, residents were strictly forbidden to make any alterations such as decorating walls, rearranging or installing additional furniture, etc. However, when we visited two container villages in 2018 and 2019, all shelters had been considerably transformed: Many container units had had additional curtains attached to the inside of the door in an attempt to minimize the impact of unannounced visits or the gaze of curious passersby in the corridor; other containers included individually acquired furniture, such as sofas and armchairs, and were at times heavily decorated with flowers, wall hangings, self-made curtains, and TV

Architectures of asylum 183

Figure 10.2 Container villages.
Source: Philipp Misselwitz and Anna Steigemann.

sets. The most common amendments to rooms remained the rearrangement and appropriation of beds. Several families clustered beds to create a space of closeness and security. Some of the beds also functioned during the day as large seating and play areas. Other families put mattresses against the walls during the day to free up space for eating or receiving guests or as a play area for children. When questioned, interviewees often stated that such practices were already common back home in Syria, referring to their lost homes.

Shortly after constructing six container villages for a total of 2,200 refugees, LAF staff proudly reported that a key lesson from problems with the earlier container villages had been incorporated: The new single-story arrangement was based on the concept of three 2.5 meter by 6 meter container units, facing each other along internal access "streets". The LAFs reference to "apartment"-like units consisting of a central container with entrance, kitchen facilities, and bathroom/toilet, giving access to two adjacent containers which include single or bunk beds, a small table, and metal cupboards demonstrates an attempt to include what had been learned from local appropriation practices and to address conflicts that had evolved around shared communal kitchens and bathrooms in the container villages. Although the "apartments" were to encourage self-reliance, rules specified that all furniture must remain within the unit, and decoration and additional furniture was discouraged. All shelters were to remain ready to be vacated at any moment and given over to new residents. Should a decision over an asylum application be negative, residents would be expected to be deported back to their home country. In the event of a positive decision, residents would be expected to move to accommodation outside the Tempohome. Beyond flexibility, the strict limitation on any alterations was also considered to ensure sustainability of the initial investment. Frequent and unannounced control visits were conducted and fines imposed on occasions where rules had been violated.

When visiting families or individuals in "their" Tempohome units in 2018 and 2019, it became clear to us that the LAF had not succeeded in controlling self-provisioning. Spatial appropriations within and around the units flourished to an even higher degree than in the earlier container villages. The extent to which residents had managed to transform and adapt the container settings to their needs of home-making, despite institutionalized constraints, was striking. Some residents had decided to move all the beds into one container, turning it into one collective bedroom, and to use the other container as a living room. As much as scarce financial means allowed, residents had bought curtains or additional cutlery, carpets, and cushions or furniture, relying on the tolerance and leniency of the camp management. Figure 10.3 illustrates how drawings can help to analyze the manifold subjective (individual or family-based) responses and tactics mobilized to appropriate and adapt the found situation of a standardized shelter with standardized furniture into what many residents referred to as their homes.

Yet in what seems like a space of limited self-determination and autonomy, rupture can occur at any time through visits of security guards or the camp

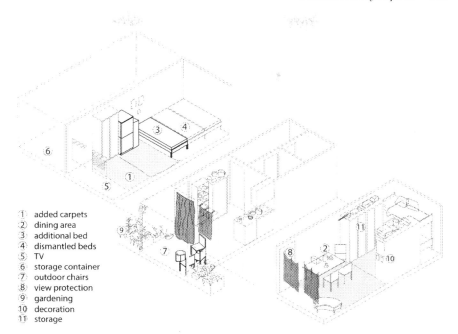

1. added carpets
2. dining area
3. additional bed
4. dismantled beds
5. TV
6. storage container
7. outdoor chairs
8. view protection
9. gardening
10. decoration
11. storage

Figure 10.3 Adaptations of standardized shelters.
Source: Philipp Misselwitz and Anna Steigemann.

management, resulting in fines and the demand that furniture or decoration be dismantled, citing fire risk or other violations of the design code. One interview partner complained:

> *I don't like this picture in my room. Imagine that we are not allowed to change anything here without the permission of the social worker! Therefore, I wrap it with plastic sheet because I don't like to see it … and when I know that they [social workers] are coming to visit, I remove the sheets beforehand.*

When asked if they are allowed to screw or put nails in the walls, Fatema said that the families had developed a technique (revealing both emergent and disseminated spatial knowledge) of fixing spoons between joins in the structure of the containers:

> *I need to have a curtain here. … Sometimes I am cooking and don't want to close the door, but also don't want people to see me from outside, but the management doesn't allow us to put screws in the container walls. So I learned this from Abeer! She told me, just bring a spoon and hook into the curtain and the container. … Haha, this is not the only place – we use it everywhere to hang things around!*

Figure 10.4 Additional curtains to obstruct the gaze of curious passers-by.
Source: Philipp Misselwitz and Anna Steigemann.

Seeking to minimize the impact of unannounced visits or to obstruct the gaze of curious passersby traversing the internal "streets", window shutters were mostly lowered or additional curtains fixed, contravening fire regulation rules (Figure 10.4).

Particularly striking was the appropriation of the entrance porches specifically fitted retrospectively by the LAF (2017) to existing Tempohomes in 2017 and later included in the new design standard. The porches were intended as a means to prevent disorderliness around the entrances owing to the tendency of residents to place shoes, bikes, or outdoor furniture loosely around the entrance (Figure 10.5). Now they had become welcome support structures offering even more opportunities for spatial adaptation. Many residents had closed off the porches with blankets or found plastic sheeting to transform them into thresholds between the "public" access street and the private interior of their container. Yet there are other ideas of home that can be negotiated using the porch as a material infrastructure.

Such appropriations communicate to us the longing for a stable and safe home; they are the nonverbal expression of presence, identity, needs, and

Architectures of asylum 187

Figure 10.5 Porches to prevent disorderliness around the entrances.
Source: Philipp Misselwitz and Anna Steigemann.

rights, which is bound to collide with the nonverbally communicated control articulated through the rules and codes of Tempohomes. The multiple conflicts resulting from this has led to the emergence of gray zones, although the overall hierarchy of power remains mostly unchallenged. While LAF staff often prefer to call Tempohomes "villages", this rhetoric serves to camouflage the reality of dependence, control, monitoring, and unilateral rule setting. The persistent control and reduced window for self-expression and for communicating needs also extends to social mixing approaches taken by LAF and local management teams. When asked whether social organization and the formation of social hierarchies among Tempohome residents was encouraged, a local manager replied:

> *We do not want refugees to group within their own language and cultural groups. We also do not want to privilege certain individuals over others. Refugees have to learn to live in Germany, according to our values where everybody is the same, where people from many nationalities and religious groups live peacefully side by side – not segregated. If they don't learn it here, when should they learn it?*

While fostering integration is the declared paradigm of LAF – it has devised the concept of an integration ladder, leading from dependence toward higher levels of autonomy and self-organization – the statement reveals the degree to which integration is understood as an assimilative paradigm when applied to practical camp management. Managing camp life is seen as an educative task communicated through appropriate design, rules, and regulations, preparing successful asylum seekers for life in the "proper" city. Hence, the architecture appears to serve as a means to an end, describing a landscape of "proper" living and preparing refugees for assimilation into German life.

However, when observed from the perspective of how control and refugee agency are nonverbally communicated, the planning outcomes are much more ambivalent. Spatial practices initiated by refugees constantly test the limits of what is allowed, tolerated, ignored, and, at times, also culminates in acts of open resistance. A male interviewee explained:

> *Security guards here always ask us to bring the furniture inside, but where? They are only doing what they are asked to do. There is no place for this table inside. When we know that someone from LAF will come to visit the camp, we take our furniture inside, and then we take it out after they leave. Even the carpet, despite the cold, is forbidden to be placed on the floor under the pretext of fire protection. It is our habit to sit on the ground with the family to eat, for example. We can't do everything they say, life … is different from what they think and plan.*

The Tempohome at Columbiadamm, now partly dismantled, was opened in December 2017 for refugees who had previously endured a residence in the former hangars of the neighboring airport building. When conceiving its design, the LAF responded to previous criticisms voiced by refugees, activists, and the press of earlier container villages; this led to the expansion of the Tempohome design standard to explicitly include outdoor facilities and public spaces. Costly design efforts were made to cover cables as well as water and heating pipes between the containers that could not be laid underground. An expensive solution was devised including open-space furniture, such as pergolas, seats, and benches. However, as we show in a previous paper (Dalal et al. 2018), these well-intentioned design innovations have remained rather underused, or appropriated for more banal purposes such as hanging washing, running contrary to the initial design purposes. The official explanation we received from the management team for this "rejection" was that "people [are] living now in this container settlement, who couldn't close a door behind them in 3 years. They spent years in emergency accommodation and were turned into totally dependent people there"; they also said that the design is intended to help change the residents back into "independent, autonomous, and responsible people", as one social worker expressed it. However, the "education" and "socialization" of adult and youth residents to become "responsible citizens" (in the social worker's words) through clean and aesthetic design solutions in effect continued and intensified the controlling and disciplining while further reducing spaces of self-provisioning and appropriation. Our own reading of why public spaces remained empty and underused was rather different from the official reasoning given by the camp management. The vacant public spaces and the surrounding signs and posters specifying behavioral rules are part of a disciplining design and management concept which, by design, seeks to reduce scope and wriggle room for "disorderly" practices by refugees, with residents resorting to the tactics of boycott and appropriation.

Conclusions

The cases cited illustrate how spatial practices exercised and reinforced by a powerful institution, on the one hand, and somewhat rebellious refugee residents, on the other, engage in a series of dialogues in which spatial and material resources could be considered key means of communication. The rationale of the institution is to provide a highly controlled environment with the ambiguous dual function of paternalistic care – preparing refugees for integration into German society – while also ensuring that those residents that do not receive asylum or lose their asylum status can be deported at any time to their country of origin. Control, here, means social and societal control in Deleuze's sense (drawing on Foucault's work) but also managing and organizing everyday life – throughout the camp space (Deleuze 1992; Foucault 1977). As communicatively constructed and maintained through rules, regulations, and the physical spaces and artefacts within the camps, control is, here, seen as more than mere disciplining, but instead as involuntary participation in "mechanisms of control that are equal to the harshest of confinements" (Deleuze 1992, 4), as a "spirit" of the place that turns social systems into quantifiably measurable entities, stripping residents of their individuality in the process.

Refugees, on the other hand, engage in spatial practices and spatial appropriation to express and communicate their individuality and choice, and they voice their claims at times when they are least expected or permitted to do so. Practices serve to adjust found settings in line with pragmatic daily routines, such as sleeping, cooking, and eating, or to increase privacy. But practices also serve as a memory for reliving what has been lost or as a testing ground for new aspirations for home in a new host country. Thus, the spatial practices and claims to rights, integration, and acceptance are not always bluntly or verbally expressed – as described in this chapter, but also through performativity (cf. Häkli, Pascucci, and Kallio 2017) and subtle negotiation with controlling regimes (Sanyal 2011). In camp settings, refugees' everyday lives and their respective everyday practices leave trajectories that can be mapped, while the controlling and provision regimes also aim to make these everyday practices traceable and thus controllable. But we found that most of the observed spatial practices also go beyond the "mappable" and "traceable". Rather, they entail an appropriative and sense-making quality that is only revealed when described by the subject of the spatial practice themselves. The quality and meaning of spatial appropriation processes (e.g. for a sense of home or belonging) are constantly nonverbally enacted, negotiated, and renewed. Just as with verbal communication, in the course of making oneself at home in camps, the residents enact spatial practices, but also discard them and invent others; they improvise, favor, alter, and abandon certain spatial elements (de Certeau 1985). Spatial practices can thus be conceptualized as a set of nonverbal communicative practices that (re)configure new spaces. Refugees transform

> every spatial signifier into something else. ... And while, on the one hand, [they make] only a few of the possibilities set out by the established order effective ..., on the other hand [they increase] the number of possibilities ... and interdictions.
>
> (de Certeau 1985, 130)

This underlines that spatial practices work just like language, constructing, reconstructing, and deconstructing meaning, norms, and values. For instance, redesigning a container intended to serve as a mere bedroom (as practiced in the previous homes) so that sleeping and living spaces were separated. Refugees thus create what de Certeau calls discontinuity, by using space in ways different to those originally planned and by altering it through new uses and the respective practices needed to carry out those uses associated with home-making, such as installing a samovar, dining, and having chats while sitting on a carpet instead of around a table on chairs.

The cases described show how both sets of actors – refugees and state bureaucrats – engage in a communicative relationship enacted through a variety of means: Employees choose to enforce rules, tolerate violations, or simply ignore such violations; refugees choose to adapt to rules, exploit loopholes, or test and, if possible, expand the boundaries of their self-provisioning spaces. Both contribute, albeit in different and highly asymmetrical ways, to the communicative construction of spaces.

Communication through spatial practices can be rather direct and immediate or highly indirect, such as in the rewriting of norms and design codes by the LAF in response to perceived problems and conflicts with refugee residents. In this indirect communication, the power and positions of those engaged in writing codes and norms are rarely questioned or changed. Yet our research has revealed that local camp managers have developed highly diverse approaches for interpreting, applying, and reinforcing norms and regulations. Following Lipsky's concept of street-level bureaucracy (Lipsky 2010), the research has also revealed the agency and leverage of individuals employed by camp management organizations who interact with refugee residents on a daily basis. This everyday interaction produces locally specific "negotiated outcomes" in terms of the adaptation of shelters (interior and exterior) or open spaces (removing or replacing furniture, applying interior decoration, enclosing spaces between shelters, etc.).

To conclude, the extreme case of camps reveals how concrete spatial strategies that alter the material constellations of shelters and open spaces can be regarded as a de facto substitute for the inability to draw on language, shared routines, and values, and as a result of the lack of means to directly and meaningfully engage with their neighbors, camp management, or indeed the regime that defines norms and regulations. We would argue that the insights drawn from this, however, can also shed light on the role of the physical and material dimension of the communicative construction of spaces in more ordinary settings. Verbal language is grounded and complemented by the possibility of providing or altering physical structures or of imposing or rejecting norms and values that structure our everyday lives.

Notes

1 This chapter presents results of the project entitled "Architectures of Asylum: Appropriation Processes in Refugee Accomodation". It forms part of the Collaborative Research Center 1265 "Re-Figuration of Spaces" at the Technische Universität Berlin, Germany, and is funded by the German Research Foundation under project no. 290045248. We wish to thank our interview and fieldwork partners, who allowed us to take part in their embattled everyday lives. We are also grateful to our team members – Ayham Dalal, Aline Fraikin, and Antonia Noll – and to the German Research Foundation (DFG) – Project number 290045248 - SFB 1265 – for their financial support, and for offering us an inspiring research environment at the Collaborative Research Center.
2 The interviewee referred to the local security personnel tasked to enforce security guidelines as the "police".

References

Agamben, Giorgio. 1998. *Homo Sacer: Sovereign Power and Bare Life*. Stanford, CA: Stanford University Press.
Agier, Michel. 2011. *Managing the Undesirables: Refugee Camps and Humanitarian Government*. Cambridge: Polity Press.
Alshadfan, Razan. 2015. "The Trends of Housing Transformation in Border Cities Hosting Refugees: The Case of Mafraq City". Unpublished master's thesis. Faculty of Architecture, Stuttgart University, and Ain Shams University, Stuttgart and Cairo.
Arous, Rasha. 2013. "Refugee Setting and Urban Form and Governance: The Predicament of Syrian Refugees in Navigating Cairo's Urban Spaces and the Complexities of Governance in Turbulent Times". Unpublished master's thesis. Faculty of Architecture, Stuttgart University, and Ain Shams University, Stuttgart and Cairo.
Boer, Roselinde D. 2015. "Liminal Space in Protracted Exile: The Meaning of Place in Congolese Refugees' Narratives of Home and Belonging in Kampala". *Journal of Refugee Studies* 28 (4): 486–504.
Brun, Catharine. 2001. "Reterritorializing the Relationship between People and Place in Refugee Studies". *Geografiska Annaler: Series B, Human Geography* 83 (1): 15–25.
Brun, Catherine, and Anita Fabós. 2015. "Making Home in Limbo: A Conceptual Framework". *Refuge* 31 (1): 5–17.
Christmann, Gabriela B., ed. 2016. *Zur kommunikativen Konstruktion von Räumen: Theoretische Konzepte und empirische Analysen* [On the communicative construction of spaces: Theoretical concepts and empirical analyses]. Wiesbaden: Springer VS.
Christmann, Gabriela B. 2022. "The Theoretical Concept of the Communicative (Re) Construction of Spaces". In *Communicative Constructions and the Refiguration of Spaces*,

edited by Gabriela Christmann, Hubert Knoblauch, and Martina Löw, 89–112. Abingdon: Routledge.
Christmann Gabriela B., Hubert Knoblauch, and Martina Löw. 2022. "Introduction. Communicative Constructions and the Refiguration of Spaces". In *Communicative Constructions and the Refiguration of Spaces*, edited by Gabriela Christmann, Hubert Knoblauch, and Martina Löw, 3–15. Abingdon: Routledge.
Dalal, Ayham, Amer Darweesh, Anna Steigemann, and Philipp Misselwitz. 2018. "Planning the Ideal Refugee Camp? A Critical Interrogation of Recent Planning Innovations in Jordan and Germany". *Urban Planning* 3 (4): 64–78.
de Certeau, Michel. 1985. "Practices of Space". In *On Signs*, edited by Marshall Blonsky, 122–145. Baltimore, MD: Johns Hopkins University Press.
Deleuze, Gilles. 1992. "Postscript on the Societies of Control". *October* 59: 3–7.
Everts, Jonathan, Matthias Lahr-Kurten, and Matt Watson. 2011 "Practice Matters! Geographical Inquiry and Theories of Practice". *Erdkunde* 65 (4): 323–334.
Fawaz, Mona. 2016. "Planning and the Refugee Crisis: Informality as a Framework of Analysis and Reflection". *Planning Theory* 16 (1): 1–17.
Foucault, Michel. 1977. *Discipline and Punish*. Translated by A. Sheridan. New York: NY Vintage.
Glaser, Barney G., Anselm L. Strauss, and Elizabeth Strutzel. 1968. "The Discovery of Grounded Theory: Strategies for Qualitative Research". *Nursing Research* 17 (4): 364.
Gupta, Akhil, and James Ferguson. 1992. "Beyond 'Culture': Space, Identity, and the Politics of Difference". *Cultural Anthropology* 7 (1): 6–23.
Häkli, Jouni, Elisa Pascucci, and Kirsi Pauliina Kallio. 2017. "Becoming Refugee in Cairo: The Political in Performativity". *International Political Sociology* 11 (2): 185–202.
Isin, Engin F., and Kim Rygiel. 2007. "Abject Spaces: Frontiers, Zones, Camps". In *Logics of Biopower and the War on Terror: Living, Dying, Surviving*, edited by Elizabeth Dauphinee and Christina Masters, 181–203. Basingstoke: Palgrave Macmillan.
Katz, Irit. 2017. "Between Bare Life and Everyday Life: Spatialising Europe's Migrant Camps". *Architecture_MPS* 12 (2): 1–20.
Knoblauch, Hubert, and Martina Löw. 2020. "The Re-Figuration of Spaces and Refigured Modernity – Concept and Diagnosis". *Historical Social Research* 45 (2): 263–292.
Kreichauf, René. 2018. "From Forced Migration to Forced Arrival: The Campization of Refugee Accommodation in European Cities". *Comparative Migration Studies* 6 (1): Art. 7.
LAF (Landesamt für Flüchtlingsangelegenheiten). 2017. "FAQ zu den Tempohomes auf dem Tempelhofer Feld" [FAQ about the Tempohomes on the Tempelhofer Feld]. www.berlin.de/laf/wohnen/allgemeine-informationen/tempohomes-faq/
LAF (Landesamt für Flüchtlingsangelegenheiten). 2019. "Qualitätssicherung" [Quality control]. www.berlin.de/laf/wohnen/informationen-zum-betrieb-von-unterkuenften/qualitaetssicherung/
Lipsky, Michael. 1971. "Street-Level Bureaucracy and the Analysis of Urban Reform". *Urban Affairs Quarterly* 6 (4): 391–409.
Lipsky, Michael. 2010. *Street-Level Bureaucracy: Dilemmas of the Individual in Public Services*. New York: Russell Sage Foundation.
Misselwitz, Philipp. 2009. *Rehabilitating Camp Cities: Community Driven Planning for Urbanised Refugee Camps*. PhD dissertation submitted to the University of Stuttgart.
Oesch, Lucas. 2017. "The Refugee Camp as a Space of Multiple Ambiguities and Subjectivities". *Political Geography* 60: 110–120.

Reckwitz, Andreas. 2002. "Toward a Theory of Social Practices: A Development in Culturalist Theorizing". *European Journal of Social Theory* 5 (2): 243–263.
Said, Edward. 2002. "Reflections on Exile". In *Reflections on Exile and Other Essays*, edited by Edward Said, 173–186. London: Granta Publication.
Sanyal, Romola. 2011. "Squatting in Camps: Building and Insurgency in Spaces of Refuge". *Urban Studies* 48 (5): 877–890.
Schatzki, Theodore R. 2001. "Practice Minded Orders". In *The Practice Turn in Contemporary Theory*, edited by Theodore R. Schatzki, Karin Knorr Cetina, and Eike E. von Savigny, 50–63. London: Routledge.
Schatzki, Theodore R. 2003. "A New Societist Social Ontology". *Philosophy of the Social Sciences* 33 (2): 174–202.
Schatzki, Theodore R. 2010. *Site of the Social: A Philosophical Account of the Constitution of Social Life and Change*. Pennsylvania, PA: Penn State University Press.
Shove, Elizabeth, and Frank Trentmann, eds. 2018. *Infrastructures in Practice: The Dynamics of Demand in Networked Societies*. London and New York: Routledge.
Shove, Elizabeth, Mika Pantzar, and Matthew Watson. 2012. *The Dynamics of Social Practice: Everyday Life and how it Changes*. London: Sage.
Shove, Elizabeth, Matthew Watson, Martin Hand, and Jack Ingram. 2007a. *The Design of Everyday Life*. Oxford: Oxford University Press.
Shove, Elizabeth, Matthew Watson, Martin Hand, and Jack Ingram. 2007b. "Products and Practices: Selected Concepts from Science and Technology Studies and from Social Theories of Consumption and Practice". *Design Issues* 23 (2): 3–16.
Steigemann, Anna. 2017. "Social Practices in a Café: Community through Consumption?" *Geographica Helvetica* 72 (1): 45–54.
Steigemann, Anna. 2019. *The Places where Community is Practiced: How Store Owners and their Businesses Build Neighborhood Social Life*. Wiesbaden: Springer VS.
Steigemann, Anna, and Philipp Misselwitz. 2020. "Architectures of Asylum: Making Home in a State of Permanent Temporariness". *Current Sociology* 68 (5): 628–650.
Strauss, Anselm, and Juliet M. Corbin. 1997. *Grounded Theory in Practice*. Thousand Oaks, London, and New Delhi: Sage Publications.

11 Over the counter

Configuration and refiguration of ticket-sales conversation through institutional architectures for interaction

Heiko Hausendorf

Introduction

This chapter addresses the mundane phenomenon of social and institutional change at railway stations.[1] You might meet such change when you enter a station and go to buy a ticket at the counter – only to find there is no longer a "counter", but instead a "service center". Take, for instance, the Basel Swiss National Railway Station (SBB CFF FFS) and its former row of window-pane counters in the station's main hall (Figure 11.1).

Figure 11.1 already documents a historic site. Some time after our recordings were made (in 2014), a discount supermarket with serve-over counters took the place of the row of ticket-sales counters. The closely packed, cabin-like window-pane counter (or *Hinterglasschalter* in technical terminology) placed centrally within the station's main hall has, in fact, been dying out not only in Basel SBB but at other Swiss and European railway stations too. Consequently, tickets are now exclusively available from a different area in the station that is not part of the main hall, but is situated in a separate open-space-like area known as a "service center" (Figure 11.2). You might consider this architectural transition a change of minor relevance to what goes on during ticket sales. You might even suggest, reasonably enough, that the counter has vanished from the new setting since there are still other places with bars ("counters") where clients can be served by SBB agents. We are, therefore, required to clarify our notion of the *counter* and its functionality in ticket-sales conversation: What makes a counter a special and unique place for service, and how does its architecture configure what is going on *over the counter*? Finally, what is the type of social interaction that the counter is built for? This is what this chapter is about.

What I wish to demonstrate is that we have undergone a refiguration of the ticket-sales setting at railway-station counters concerning the design of the interior and the use of both technological hardware and software. We see open-space-like service areas replacing the old-fashioned row of more or less contained and separated cabin-like counters that have obviously come to be regarded as outdated (respectively referred to in the following as *closed* vs. *open* counter settings). This refiguration affects not only the material world but also

DOI: 10.4324/9780367817183-14

Figure 11.1 Basel SBB Railway Station: A former row of counters.[2]

Figure 11.2 Basel SBB Railway Station: A service center with ticket sales.

the social (and ideological) world of what *service talk* is meant to be in modern society: The participants adjust their communicative activities; that is, their speaking and listening, their approach to each other, their gaze and posture, and their gestures and movements according to the new setting, as we shall show in the empirical part of the chapter. There can be no doubt that social interaction is involved, and we would accordingly like to know more about the communicative nature of what is actually becoming refigured over the counter and how service talk manifests under the new design. We shall study if and how the nature of the social encounter changes along with the shape of the counter as its built and, so to speak, "natural" home (Goffman 1961).[3]

Focusing on conversation over the counter and its still-continuing social and spatial refiguration, the chapter touches on a couple of *sociological* discussions. These have to do with broader social transformations in nonproductive industries and a change in institutional architectures for interaction across various modern organizations that are part of a far-reaching process of modern (or postmodern) social and institutional change (cf. Knoblauch 2017, for instance). There is some evidence that a massive transformation of the spatial organization of sociality has taken place in the last decades. The very notion of "refiguration", used before in a more descriptive sense, is accordingly used to refer to a process of "spatial transformation of contemporary society" which is assumed to have started in the 1970s (Knoblauch and Löw 2017). It fits nicely into this global diagnosis that the kind of change at railway-station counters that we are dealing with can, in fact, be dated back to the late 1970s and early 1980s when the first manifestations of "service centers" began to spread across a number of different public institutions (take, as another example, the emergence of "citizens' offices" in public services). Our aim in studying current changes in the social setting of ticket-sales conversation is, therefore, to zoom in on snapshots of this broader process of socio-spatial refiguration. In line with the previously cited refiguration approach, refiguration is understood both socially and spatially, and what we are interested in is the interplay of sociality and spatiality. The physico-material world of space will accordingly prove to be a thoroughly *social* one, and the social world of communication, vice versa, a thoroughly *spatial* one.

The chapter also addresses a couple of recent *linguistic* questions generally connected with issues of "interactional space" in conversation analysis (cf., for instance, Mondada 2009; Schmitt 2013; Hausendorf 2003; and from the workplace studies tradition, Hindmarsh and Heath 2000). Within this tradition, the role of spatiality as a resource of interaction in general, and that of architecture for interaction in particular, have only sporadically been accounted for (cf. LeBaron and Streeck 1997; Hausendorf, Mondada, and Schmitt 2012; Hausendorf, Schmitt, and Kesselheim 2016). This is thus a desideratum of current research in conversation analysis and video-based multimodal interaction analysis (Knoblauch et al. 2006), the more so as the study of "architecture(s) for interaction" seems to allow for promising links to research in recent sociologies of space and architecture (cf., for instance, Löw 2001; Fischer and Delitz 2009; Schroer 2007). Focusing on the example of the counter and its current transformation, the present chapter aims to take a step forward in this direction.

In what follows, we shall start with some reflections on architecture as a resource for situational anchoring in face-to-face interaction. The notion of architecture for interaction will be introduced in order to account more precisely for architectural manifestations as communicative forms suited to suggest certain types of social interaction. We shall then return to the counter in order to illustrate what architecture concretely affords social interaction. This will clarify the notion of *counter* and show what makes it a special and unique place for social exchange. In doing so, we shall show that the counter configures social interaction and describe how it does so. Having studied the classical *con*figuration, we shall finally turn to the current *re*figuration of the counter setting, comparing aspects of ticket-sales interaction – namely the opening sequence and the work on the client's request – across the closed- and open-counter settings. In doing so, we shall draw on empirical studies at a number of different Swiss railway-station counters.

Architecture for interaction: Configuring interaction through architecture

In what follows, I shall demonstrate that "architecture" can be addressed from an interactionist point of view that draws on Goffman's sociology of interaction

(Goffman 1961, 1967) and its reformulation within sociological systems theory (Luhmann 1984, 2005; cf. Hausendorf 2015). We need, therefore, to go somewhat further in order to elaborate how architecture for interaction relates to the general assumption of space as a communicative construction (Christmann 2016), as well as other related concepts of space, following the so-called *spatial turn* (Günzel 2017). This forms the theoretical part of the chapter. To begin with, my argument is that face-to-face interaction should be considered a social subject in its own right. It manifests a type of communication that is bound to the participants' co-presence. This is anything but new, but also anything but trivial, for there are other types of communication (such as reading and writing) that do not depend on co-presence (of authors and readers) but rather on social, historic, and media-dependent alternatives to co-presence (such as the readability of texts; Hausendorf et al. 2017). We are therefore emphatic in the view that face-to-face interaction is a special case of communication. Communication is understood as the superordinate concept referring to sociality, regardless of whether it depends on co-presence, membership, or reachability of participants.[4]

Due to the constraint of co-presence, face-to-face interaction necessarily implies some sort of situational anchoring as to the question of *who* is involved *when* and *where*. Within linguistic pragmatics, this kind of anchoring has long been regarded a prerequisite of interaction due to given parameters of the so-called speech situation (cf. Hausendorf 2013). In contrast to this conception, situational anchoring should be introduced as a genuine interactive task so that the speech situation appears to be a genuine interactive achievement performed within and through social interaction. In other words, it is through means and forms of situational anchoring that the speech situation actually comes into being. As far as space and spatiality are concerned, we have accordingly to assume that space (in whatever characterization) is a communicative construction in the strict sense: Being a crucial part of the speech situation's localities (as components of the participants' *here*), space and spatiality are constantly brought about through the participants' perception, movements, and actions in terms of co-orientation, coordination, and cooperation. This is the meaning of "doing space" as it has been introduced with respect to the communicative construction of space(s) across different media and settings (Jucker et al. 2018).

Having clarified this starting point, we can go further with regard to the resources of situational anchoring. This is where architecture re-enters the scene. There can be no doubt that the interactive achievement of the speech situation depends on input that in itself does not depend on social interaction. The construction of space in interaction is not a *creatio ex nihilo*, but refers to resources that can be taken up by the participants when doing the co-orientation, coordination, and cooperation. *Natural language* is perhaps the most prominent resource of this kind (at least for linguists) that participants can make use of; for instance, to secure joint attention, to refer to something *here* or *there*, or to clarify positions within a spatially ambiguous environment. Another resource often taken for granted is the human *body*; that is, *embodied* resources for sensory perception, movement, and cognition (take, for instance, the booming concept of "embodiment" in social interaction research; Streeck, Goodwin, and LeBaron 2011; Reber and Gerhardt 2019). Humans are, as Luhmann puts it, the "sensors of interaction" (Luhmann 1984, 558). As such, they are *mobile* and *intelligent* sensors.

Besides natural language and the human body as interaction resources, there is *architecture*. Although it forms an especially powerful resource for social interaction in general, and for situational anchoring in particular, architectural resources have – in contrast to verbal and bodily ones – largely been ignored in social interaction research. With the exception of some isolated studies (such as that by LeBaron and Streeck 1997), built space has scarcely attracted attention as a subject in its own right. This comes as no surprise. Aside from methodological restrictions, architecture is not as transient as the spoken word, but stable and durable. In this sense, it is said to be a "heavy" medium (Fischer 2009) that cannot be broken down so easily by reconstructive methodology. Accordingly, one might find it difficult to deal with architecture while postulating the interactive achievement of space. After all, might we not be well advised to accept that space is already a given when turning to architecture? To avoid such a misleading notion, I propose treating architecture – widely understood as the built, furnished, and/or designed environment (cf. Lawrence and Low 1990) – as the manifestation of a genuine type of communication that systematically differs from face-to-face interaction. Contrasting with face-to-face interaction, communication through architecture does not depend on co-presence (of, let's say, architects and users), but on *usability cues*. Architecture is considered to consist of usability cues in terms of built-in spatial features that allow for ways of use and, more than this, give hints not only to possible forms of use, but also probable and most likely ones. By means of such cues, architecture suggests usage forms that range from the basics of human sensory and motor behavior to sophisticated activities within highly differentiated social practices. More precisely, and according to the broad range of usage, I suggest differentiating between architectural cues: navigation cues; reading cues; and participation cues.

Navigation cues address embodied human sensory techniques and motor activities in a self-evident way. They suggest where to look and where to turn to, where to go and where to stop, where to walk and where to sit, where to pass by and where to stay, where to enter and where to leave – in short, how to *navigate*; that is, how to orient yourself as a mobile sensor. It is what architecture affords users in a basic sense of sensory-perception-related and body-movement-related us*ability*: Indications of walk-on-ability, stand-on-ability, go-through-ability, climb-on-ability, sit-on-ability, look-at-ability, take-hold-of-ability, and so on. Put in this way, navigation cues are similar to what has effectively been introduced as "affordances" by J. Gibson in the context of ecological psychology (Gibson 1977). Navigation cues lack external preconditions in terms of users' expert knowledge and familiarity with certain places and their cultures, but they should not be simplified and reified as givens. Instead, they have to be related to users' perceptual and motor skills.

As the terminology already indicates, *reading cues* take a step in the direction of further requirements. They address readings of architectural manifestations in terms of architectural semiotics (with elements such as "doors", "windows", "rooms", "steps", "tables", "chairs") and accordingly depend on users' reading competences in terms of what can be understood as a sort of "architectural literacy". Architectural items such as the ones just mentioned not only afford navigation cues, but are loaded with certain meanings, which is the reason why we can refer to them according to a vocabulary of more or less technical terms and why there is something like a readability of space (cf. Hausendorf and Kesselheim 2016).

This is not yet the whole story. There are *participation cues* that go further, with indications of social practices beyond those that can be found and gleaned by lexicon inspection. Participation cues are typically embedded in far-reaching contextualizaton cues (Gumperz 1982). They give hints not only of a more or less context-free architectural meaning, but of a certain communicative framework that relates to participation and to sharing in a certain social practice beyond mere navigating and reading. Participation cues accordingly address not only mobile and intelligent human sensors, and not only readers, but *members* of communities of practice. They call on social belonging and bear a certain type of social appeal – for those who are familiar with these social practices. Participation cues, therefore, are the most demanding usability cues: They depend on navigation and reading cues, but provide them with an overall social meaning. They call for *understanding* in a deeper sense. Institutional architectures ("churches", "hospitals", "university buildings", "court rooms", etc.) are abuzz with participation cues of this kind so that situating oneself in such a space already implies social positioning in terms of rights and duties (Hausendorf and Schmitt 2018).

It is by means of usability cues that architecture can be imagined to configure social interaction in a highly effective, but at the same time highly inconspicuous way. It goes without saying that *configuration* does not mean *determination*. Usability cues cannot prevent participants from using architectural affordances, items, and frameworks in a quite unpredictable and so to speak "creative" way. But due to the assumption of architectural usability, it is possible to account systematically for the everyday phenomenon in which people start participating in a differentiated social practice without any kind of prior understanding or agreement. This is what our concept of architecture for interaction is about. Built-in architectural navigation cues, reading cues, and participation cues constitute extremely strong and robust resources for situational anchoring, so it takes extra work to override them.

As a general term for usability cues, architecture for interaction stands for a concept of architectural resources that is suited to replace the idea of architecture as a given material world (as still seems to be the case in Barker's "behavior setting"; Barker 1968). A railway-station counter is indeed a physical object in the material world, independent of communication. But its built-in usability cues produce a specific architecture for interaction out of this physical object, referring to communication by pointing to a moment of *use*. The communicative manifestation accordingly lies in the architectural forms themselves: They realize *usability* cues which ensure certain forms of navigation, reading, and participation can be made accountable; that is, they can be reliably and dependably expected whether they take place or not. This is the *social* relevance of architecture for interaction. It implies a stand-alone subject of research (Hausendorf and Schmitt 2016). The analytic task, then, is to reconstruct usability cues from architectural forms. As such, they are durable and solid (in contrast to the spoken word), which means that they can be documented through video recording, photography, and ethnographic consideration. This is what we shall turn to in some detail in the next section.

What the "counter" affords social interaction: Architecture analysis from an interactionist point of view

Let us now turn more concretely toward our approach to architecture for interaction. The *counter* can be taken as a complex arrangement of usability cues that have proven to answer genuine communicative problems connected with ticket-sales conversation. What kind of architectural arrangement are we talking about when referring to the notion of *counter*? Before returning to the railway-station counter, we shall start off by inserting a few rather arbitrary examples of other counters in the material and social world (author's collection):

Note that in Figure 11.3 the notion of the counter appears in the data itself: "Dieser Schalter ist geschlossen" (This counter is closed). "Schalter" is the German term for "counter"; "guichet" and "sportello" are the corresponding

Figure 11.3 Mobile tent-show counters (Zurich Sechseläutenplatz).

Figure 11.4a Counter on public transport boat (Società Navigazione del Lago di Lugano).

Figure 11.4b Detail (turning device).

expressions in French and Italian. There is a rich variety of architectural forms of "counter" as can be seen in Figure 11.4a and b, which document a counter on a public transport boat on Lake Lugano (CH) and show a (mostly open) door that transforms the room beyond into a counter for selling and buying tickets for the boat trip.

When I took these pictures and was seen by the skipper, he immediately closed the door, put on his captain's hat, and proudly positioned himself behind the counter – which nicely illustrates the official atmosphere that obviously comes along with built-in counter-like architecture. A more recent counter setting can be viewed in Figure 11.5, showing a counter at the new Kunstmuseum (art gallery) Basel.

202 *Heiko Hausendorf*

Figure 11.5 Kunstmuseum Basel (main building).

Note that in this case, the counter setting is referred to as a "Kasse" ("cash desk": "Gerne bedienen wir Sie an der Kasse nebenan [/] We will be pleased to assist you at our second cash desk"), which gives a hint at its functional characteristics of selling and buying (an exchange of money). In its appearance, the counter accordingly, and not by chance, resembles a ticket machine. Despite the variations, these settings have in common that there is a window pane between the participants which includes a kind of aperture or hatch. With regard to this built-in transfer device, the counter setting may be described as "semi-permeable" (Marcel Naef, personal note). These characteristics, in particular, are of relevance when we turn to the open service area at Zurich Hauptbahnhof (the central station; see Figures 11.6a and b):

There can be no doubt that this is the location for ticket sales. But the window panes and, along with them, the transfer mechanism are missing. What has survived the transition is a place to stand at and to lean on. The area outside and in front of the counter is equipped with a kind of "bar" (mostly some 1.5 meters high) to lean on, to put things on, or to take things from. There is a continuous surface between those *in front of* and those *behind* that modifies the clear-cut separation of *inside* and *outside*: There is no closed interior space entirely separated from the publicly accessible area. Finally, the area within and behind the counter is equipped to serve as a complex workplace (with computer, pay office equipment, and other office furnishings).

Figure 11.6a Zurich Hauptbahnhof, open service area: Bird's-eye view.

Figure 11.6b Zurich Hauptbahnhof, open service area: Participants' perspective.

To sum up, the most striking architectural characteristics of the counter can be abstracted as follows:

1. The counter defines two spatial positions: You are either *in front* of or *behind* the counter.
2. The counter defines a spatial interior: You are either *within* or *outside* the counter.
3. The counter defines limitations of accessibility and permeability: You cannot enter the area behind the counter, but objects can be passed through and can accordingly be transferred at the counter.
4. The counter defines a place to arrive at, to stop, and to stay: There is a sort of shelf to lay things down and to lean on in front of and outside the counter.
5. The counter defines a place to work: There is a complex workplace behind and within the counter.

204 *Heiko Hausendorf*

Note that this list of characteristics holds true for all settings illustrated before, no matter whether a glass pane is present or not. But it becomes clearer that the glass pane with its built-in transfer device is the most obvious material sediment of communicating limited accessibility and permeability (cf. 3 in the list above). It is the striking component of an architecture of limited access and a built-in solution to requirements of separation on the one hand, and requirements of exchange on the other. It transparently manifests the difference between *inside* and *outside* and contributes essentially to the counter as a distinctive place (as distinct from bars, desks, and reception areas).

Having said this, we shall now return to the Zurich Hauptbahnhof counters in the counter hall in order to explain more precisely the social and communicative implications. To begin with, there are but two possible spatial positions according to items 1 and 2, above, that appear to be social positions as well. To be *in front of* the counter obviously means to be *outside* the institution the counter belongs to (see Figures 11.7a and b):

To approach the counter, to arrive at the counter, and to stop *in front of* the counter accordingly means that you make yourself accountable as the next, as the imminent, and, finally, as the current *client* and *customer*.[5] By contrast, to be *behind* the counter obviously means to be *inside* the institution and to be accountable as an *agent* and *officer* able to use the workplace and its technical affordances (see Figure 11.7c). The counter is the place where the institution, in this case the SBB CFF FFS, provides a special interface allowing for contact with respect to a certain service. Taking seriously the architectural constraints,

Figure 11.7a In front of and outside the counter, from a distance.

Figure 11.7b In front of and outside the counter, close-up.

Figure 11.7c Behind and inside the counter.

Figure 11.8 The transfer device as a turntable.

customers are hindered from entering the institution and are kept outside. Contact is restricted to a transfer device that allows for exchange of (small) objects. Figure 11.8 shows the kind of transfer device that is built in at Zurich Hauptbahnhof counters:

Most obviously, the transfer device is more than a sort of hatch or gap. It is a sophisticated technical achievement which makes it possible to exchange objects instantaneously from inside to outside without actually opening something. Note that it is this technical achievement that comes very close to the etymological original of the German expression "Schalter", in terms of a locking device that can be shifted (Kluge and Seebold 2011, 794). It is the counter in the original narrower sense of "shifter" that not only allows for an exchange of objects, but which materializes the social expectation of an exchange service. Thus, an exchange service appears to be the materialized rationale of any conversation that might arise at the counter. Due to this materialized social expectation, the turning mechanism becomes a closing device: Starting to operate the mechanism, in principle, signals that the encounter between client and agent has commenced its final phase. It can, in principle, function as a device for opening up a closure.[6]

Note that the turning mechanism can only be operated from the inside (using the knob visible in Figure 11.8). Accordingly, it is a built-in feature ensuring that it is the agent who decides when it is time to start the final transfer and to open up a closure of the conversation. S/he is, incidentally, also the one who decides when it is time to open up the encounter: There is a button inside the counter that has to be pressed by the agent in order to signal that s/he is available for the next client. There can accordingly be no doubt that the counter constitutes an *architecture of asymmetry* that clients come across whenever they approach the counter. Both clients and agents can be expected to behave in accordance with this asymmetry. The counter with its transfer and turning mechanism is most likely the strongest participation cue in this setting: It calls on the participants' familiarity with the membership categorization devices of *client* and *agent* as well as with the kind of transaction that allows for an exchange of money and tickets.

Put this way, the counter appears to be the historical precursor to the modern ticket machine: It provides an outer surface to be operated and used together with a slot for exchange, and therefore tends to restrict the interaction to the purpose of transfer. There is a difference, however: Over the counter there is a human. Instead of usability and readability cues, there is social interaction between client and agent – including all kinds of expansions, side sequences, small talk, and whatever social interaction might arise. What the counter architecture affords social interaction is, nevertheless, the orientation toward ticket sales in terms of turn-by-turn exchange and transfer. The turning mechanism is a unique *technical* manifestation of this *social* expectation: that the encounter merges in a concurrent exchange of money and tickets. It materializes the kind of expectation to which the client, when s/he initiates a request, and the agent, when s/he begins working on the request, are oriented, as will be demonstrated in the next section.

The counter architecture maybe tells the story of how ticket-sales conversation has been standardized and differentiated over the decades in order to allow for the most efficient and somehow official way of acquiring a ticket without getting too close to the agent (in a spatial *and* in a social sense). Those who experienced the introduction of counter architectures in newly built representative railway-station concourses (in the second half of the 19th century) might have been astonished and alienated in a similar way to how we, relatively recently, might have been astonished and alienated when the first ticket machines made their appearance at the same stations in the 1980s.

Getting your turn and getting served: Social interaction and its configuration and refiguration at Swiss railway-station counters

Architecture for interaction cannot prescribe and determine what occurs among those present in a certain architectural setting. Its analysis is an attempt in its own right and can by no means replace the study of social interaction itself. We shall, therefore, move on to social interaction at the counter in the remainder of this chapter. To begin with, we shall have a look at exemplary openings at the closed-counter setting in order to briefly demonstrate how social interaction can effectively make use of the counter's architectural usability cues. The opening of conversation over the counter will turn out to be a multi-modal achievement that heavily relies on the architectural usability cues of the setting. We shall then follow up the conversation and look at the way(s) in which the client's request is dealt with by the agent. Focusing on this sequence of service talk, it turns out that there is a significant change in social interaction that goes along with the change from the closed- to the open-counter setting.

Getting your turn at the counter: How architecture configures the opening of social interaction

When and how does ticket-sales conversation start? The question seems easy to answer so long as we restrict ourselves to the first words that can be heard when client and agent start to engage in talk. A look at the following examples (each one cut off after the beginning of the request) will give an impression of these first words at the counter:

Extract 1 / transcription First words with greetings and request

(1) BSoct_WIN_sch5_L_pers2_gespr8	(2) ZH_oct_WIN_Sch10_R_pers2_gespr18
1 SBB: GUEte tag [good day]	1 SBB: GrüeZI [hello [local dialect]]
2 KUN: guete TAG [good day]	2 KUN: GRÜEzi [hello]
3 Eh nach sankt marGREte ersti klAss eifach [uh, to [toponym] first class one-way]	3 SBB: WAS hetet sie gern? [what would you like?]
(3) ZH_oct_OPEN_sch16_L_pers2_new_gespr7	(4) ZH_oct_WIN_Sch10_R_pers3_gespr12
1 KUN: hallo [hello]	1 SBB: grüeZI [hello]
2 SBB: hallo grüezi [hello]	1 KUN: grüeZI: [hello]
	2 SBB: BITteschön [please]
3 KUN: grüezi [hello]	3 KUN: folgendes problem [following problem]
4 SBB: grüezi [hello]	
5 KUN: ähm ich hab NUR eine kurze frage [um, I just have a short question]	

The verbal transcript suggests an easy answer to the problem of openings: The beginning of social interaction is the equivalent of the first line of the transcript. But if we ask whether something interesting has maybe gone on *before* speaking and listening, the transcript immediately proves a dumb document. In some cases, it nevertheless allows for the observation that something has indeed been

208   *Heiko Hausendorf*

going on before so that we are prompted to take into account the setting and the situation in which these first words are spoken.

Extract 2 / transcription First words referring to the situation

(5) BSoct_WIN_sch6_L_pers1_4
 	
1 KU1: grüezi wohl [hello]
2 SBB: grüezi [hello]
3 KU1: ma gseht das nit
         immer ob
         beim wenn der
         frei isch
         [you can't be
         sure when
         it is free]
	(6) ZH_oct_OPEN_sch16_L_pers1_new_
	    gespr3
	1 SBB: GR[Üezi wo:hl] [hello]
	2 KUN: [grüezi WOHL] [hello]
	         etz han ich das Erscht
	         grad gseh
	         [I've just noticed it]

(7) BSoct_WIN_sch5_L_pers2_gespr9
1 SBB: schalter FÜNF bitte [counter five please]
2   (3.0)
3 SBB: schalter FÜNF [counter five]
4   (5.0)
5 SBB: schalter FÜNF isch frei [counter five is free]
6   (4.0)
7 SBB: grüeZI [hello]
8 KUN: guete TAG (-) [good day]
9   chan ich Au scho HÜT für am SAMStig (---)
         billiE chaufe nach!ZELL! im wiesental [may
         I already buy a
         ticket for Saturday to [toponym] today?]	

In these cases, the participants comment on what is visible at the counter and in this way give some sort of account of what was going on and perhaps went wrong before the verbal opening (Examples 5 and 6). The same holds for those cases in which there is a precursor of greeting on the agent's side: A (repeated) exclamation such as "*schalter FÜNF bitte (3.0) schalter FÜNF (5.0) schalter FÜNF isch frei*" (in Example 7) gives us a hint that getting your turn may be a problem at the counter. It even becomes apparent that getting your turn is a problem that in most cases has already been solved when the verbal transcript starts. Pursuing this idea, we shall return to the counter as the social home our verbal openings have been extracted from.[7]

The Zurich window-pane setting is characterized by a line of counters within the counter hall. The front of the queue is quite far off from the counters we have chosen to record, as can be seen in Figure 11.9.

The key elements of the setting are the front of the queue, the counters at which conversations have been recorded (Numbers 10 and 11, the last ones visible in Figure 11.9), and the electronic monitor displaying vacancies, placed above the counter opposite the front of the queue.

Over the counter 209

Figure 11.9 Zurich Hauptbahnhof, counter hall.

Let us now study a concrete case in order to trace back the very beginning of social interaction within this setting.

Extract 3 / video part 3.1 (ZH_Win_Sch10_Pers2_Gespr14)

Image 3.1 (34:08:12) Next client has just left the front of the queue.

We join the action at the point when the agent has pressed a button to signal his availability on the monitor opposite the front of the queue. It then takes approximately 5 seconds for the client to become visible on our recordings. We see the client (circled in Images 3.1 and 3.2), who we know will be heading to

210 *Heiko Hausendorf*

Image 3.2 Officer is still busy.

Counter 10. When she has started to move out of the queue and has gradually come into the field of view of the agent, the latter is still busy with other things (see Image 3.2). He seems to routinely anticipate that it will take some time for the next client to come into *his* sight and he himself comes into *her* sight. So, there is no face-to-face interaction between customer and officer at this very moment.

Our videos allow for the progression of her trajectory and the very moment of mutual perception to be precisely tracked. There seems to be a critical "focal zone" (Streeck 1983, 56) of proximity within which both participants adapt and adjust themselves to be noticed by each other. This zone depends on the particular spatial conditions for visual perception during the customer's approach: on passing the visual obstacles at the counter front and coming closer along the acute-angled route from queue to counter. As can be seen in the next extract (Video part 3.2, Images 3.3a to 3.5b) the critical focal zone is arrived at somewhere near the point where the imminent client's route crosses the line marked on the floor.

Extract 3 / video part 3.2 Entering the focal zone of proximity

Image 3.3a (34:13:18)   *Image 3.3b*

Over the counter 211

Image 3.4a (34:14:00)

Image 3.4b

Image 3.5a (34:14:18)

Image 3.5b

The marked line on the ground in front of the counter (just crossed by the customer in Image 3.5a) seems to contribute to the definition of the focal zone of proximity. The practical problem of the customer and the officer – the perception of being perceived (Hausendorf 2003) while approaching the counter – is apparently handled by the marking on the ground. This line delimits an area close to the counter. Moreover, the line itself is visible in such a way as to be noticed and respected. One could say that crossing the line actually makes the *imminent* client the *current* client. Given the system of one queue for all counters that is documented in Zurich, the dividing line has lost its prior functionality, but still marks a critical focal zone of proximity – as can be noticed in the last images.

Even though we cannot provide empirical evidence for mutual gaze from eye-tracking data, the available video data documents the precise moment when both participants orient themselves toward each other; that is, they are *able* to perceive being perceived by the other. This is not only manifest in the gaze direction (and presumably in eye contact) but also in the orienting of one's head to the other. The officer turns his head in a finely adjusted way toward the customer's approach and final arrival at the counter. It seems as if the officer is bodily "receiving" the customer. Both participants continue to orient toward each other. The customer continues her approach to the counter, and the officer accurately turns his head in coordination with the approaching customer. In

212 *Heiko Hausendorf*

doing so, he demonstrates that he is taking part in the customer's approach (cf. Hausendorf and Mondada 2017, for a detailed sequence of stills). Note that there has thus far been no verbal exchange between customer and officer, but that in terms of co-orientation and coordination (Schmitt and Deppermann 2007; Hausendorf 2013), interaction has already begun. The use of bodily resources obviously precedes the use of spoken language.

Less than a second later, the officer initiates a greeting ("grüezi" [hello]) even before the customer has arrived and is still approaching the counter. She is not yet "ensconced" at the counter – which would involve actions such as turning, positioning and releasing the trolley, turning her body vis-à-vis the counter, and bending in to lean at the counter. The next images (Extract 3, Video part 3.3) show the variation in the customer's position as a result of such ensconcing activities (see Images 3.6a and b).

Extract 3 / video part 3.3

Arriving has not yet been completed Image 3.6a (34:15:20) 	Image 3.6b  Officer: "**GRÜE**zi: WA:S hetet si gern".[8] [Hello what would you like]
Customer has ensconced herself at the counter Image 3.7a (34:18:03) 	Image 3.7b  Customer: "s **HALBS**, GONtenschwil (.) Retour". [**half**[9] Gontenschwil [=toponym] return]

Ensconcing oneself in front of the counter can be seen as a part of the opening sequence and the responsibility of the customer as the mobile partner who is "coming in". It follows the preceding co-orientation and coordination, and it overlaps with the first words spoken by the officer. In fact, the officer's invitation for a request ("was hetet sie gern?") is finished precisely as the customer takes her final position. As a result of this finely tuned sequence, the customer can formulate her request exactly as she completes her arrival at the counter (Images 3.7a and b) – an impressive example of the micro achievements of co-orientation, coordination, and cooperation. The opening, accordingly, proves to be a *multimodal* achievement that is accurately adapted to the situational circumstances. The social category of being the *current client* is achieved step by step while approaching and arriving at the counter; that is, by making use of the architectural participation cues of the counter. This is the reason why the agent can immediately turn to the client's request ("was hetet sie gern?") so that conversation can proceed most effectively and economically. This, in a nutshell, is how a certain architecture concretely contributes to the configuration of social interaction.

Getting served at the counter: Changing architectures for interaction and changing social practices

Let us now turn to the moment when the client's request is worked on and attended to by the agent. To begin with, we shall continue with the conversation in the case already illustrated in the preceding paragraph. We shall then look at an example from the open service area in order to compare the manner of being served in the two different settings and to illustrate the way conversation over the counter changes along with the transformation of closed- into open-counter settings.

We shall concentrate on the sequence directly following the opening.

Extract 4 / transcription Being served

```
1  SBB:   <<h> GRÜE↓zi:-> [hello]
2         WA:S <<all> hetet si gern.>= [what would
          you like]
3  KUN:   =s HALBS, [half]
4         GONtenschwil rEtour. [toponym return]
5  SBB:   JAwol. [yes]
6         (19.5)
7         CHÖmed si denn- [would you]
8         (0.5)
9         ↑HÜT wider zrugg.[come back today]
10 KUN:   JA- [yes]
11        (5.0)
12 SBB:   und de FA:red sie <<len> Übe:r-> [and you will
          go via]
```

```
13 KUN:  A:r[au.]    [toponym]
14 SBB:     [A:]rau.  [toponym]
15 KUN:  JA,= [yes]
16 SBB:  =JA. [yes]
17       <<p> (s_)halbs REtour,> [half return]
         macht ↑`SIbenezwäntsg=zwÄntsg [bi]tte schö:n.
         [will be twenty-seven please]
18 KUN:                                  [ja-] [yes]
```

The client's request (lines 3–4) is immediately acknowledged by the agent ("jawol", line 5) and successfully worked on afterwards (lines 6–18). Finally, the agent names the price (line 17) so that the payment can be initiated. In between, there have been two requests by the agent (lines 7–9, 12) and there has been silence for some time (line 6, for nearly 20 seconds, 8 and 11). It is the duration within these passages of silence that is most relevant to our argument. The participants start to busy themselves with things other than talking and listening. On the agent's side, it is the work necessary to attend to the client's request. On the client's side, it is mostly waiting and preparation for the next steps, among which is paying. Social interaction is still going on but is dialed down to some extent. It seems that interaction is "on standby", so to speak. We shall go into this interactive mode in some detail since it appears to be a characteristic of talk within the closed-counter setting. We start by looking at the action at the point when the request has nearly been completed.

Extract 5 / video part 1 (ZH_Win_Sch10_Pers2_Gespr14)

Request is nearly completed
Image 5.1a (34:19)

Image 5.1b

Line 4   GONtenschwil r**E**tour.

Both participants are obviously oriented toward and focused on each other by means of gaze, body posture, and speech (Images 5.1a and b). The situation significantly changes less than 2 seconds later, once the client has acknowledged the request (Images 5.2a and b).

Extract 5 / video part 2

After the request (corresponding to line 6) Image 5.2a (34:21)	Image 5.2b

Note that the participants are no longer displaying mutual orientation toward each other. Instead, the agent has started to address himself to the computer keyboard and the client has simultaneously started to busy herself with her handbag. Still vis-à-vis over the counter, the participants seem to be released from focusing on each other, albeit while remaining ready to switch back to focused interaction if necessary. In this sense, social interaction appears to be dialed down to a sort of standby mode. The agent's first request ("chömed sie denn hüt wieder zrugg", lines 7–9) nicely illustrates how focused interaction can immediately be reinitiated if necessary. Compare Images 5.3a and b, which show the moment *before* the request, with Images 5.4a and b, which show the moment when the request is initiated by the agent.

Extract 5 / video part 3

Before the agent's request (agent is still busy at the computer) Image 5.3a (34:34)	Image 5.3b

Start of agent's request (agent and client demonstrating focused interaction)	

Lines 7–9: CHÖmed si denn- (0.5)
↑**HÜT** wider zrugg.

Note that the agent finely adjusts his request to the longer period of standby interaction by hesitating and introducing a small rise in speech intonation. In doing so, he gives the client time to re-attune to focused interaction. As a result, there is ostentatious attention by means of gaze and body posture when it comes to the critical part of the request. We, accordingly, meet a period of interaction on standby, which lasts for as long as the agent is busy at the computer working on the request. Operating the computer temporarily replaces his attendance to the client. Accordingly, social interaction changes from focused to unfocused interaction for some time.

There is some evidence that things change when we turn to the open-counter setting. Of course, there can be no doubt that the same alteration between focused and unfocused interaction can be observed in the open setting as well, but there is something new in addition. It is directly related to the way(s) in which the client's request is treated by the agent. To illustrate our point briefly, we turn to the Zurich open-counter setting and pick out a telling case. We shall skip the process of getting the turn (which is different from the close counter setting and interesting in itself; cf. Hausendorf and Mondada 2017) and ignore the verbal opening (lines 1–4) in order to join the action when the agent has already started to work on the client's request and is commenting on what she is currently doing (lines 45 onwards).

Extract 6 / transcription (ZH_oct_OPEN_sch16_L_pers1_new_gespr6)[10]

```
Getting served in the open-counter setting
1 SBB:      GRÜezi wohl [hello]
2 KUN:      (hallo) [hello]
3           ich hetti gern es billet nach DÜtschland [I'd
            like a ticket to Germany]
4 SBB:      jawohl [yes]
((...))
45 SBB:     ich lueg jetzt GRAD emol= [let me just have
            a look]
46          =vilicht isch ja ersti klass denn so GÜNstig
            [maybe first class is low priced]
```

```
47            dass sie s hi: und retour nämed wänns vilicht
              no en spArpreis git [so you would take a return
              ticket in case there may be a budget price]
48 KUN:       ja ich han ebä im internet scho all[es GLUeget]
              [yes I've already checked the Internet myself]
49 SBB:                                              [händ sie
              GLUe:]get= [you have checked]
50 KUN:       =und han gseh dass die dütsche bahn gar nöd
              GÜNSCHtiger isch= [and have seen that the German
              railway (company) isn't more advantageous at all]
51            =susch isch sie günstiger gsi wiä d ES be be [in
              other cases it has been more advantageous than
              SBB (Swiss railway company)]
52            (äh) das mal ischs jetzt NÖD günstiger je
              nach kurs(vilicht) [this time it isn't more
              advantageous maybe according to the price]
53 SBB:       aso darf ich s ine churz ZEIgä= [so may I show
              it to you]
54 KUN:       =ja [yes]
55 SBB:       (es is zwar ä so bitzli) [it is in fact a bit]
56 KUN:       (ja hm ähähä) [yes]
57 SBB:       ((lacht)) [laughing]
58 SBB:       also das isch (--) sparticket euRO[:pa] [so this
              is budget price Europe]
59 KUN:                                       [ja] gen[au]
                                              [yes exactly]
```

The transcript already hints at the interesting phenomenon: The agent is going to *show* something to the client: "aso darf ichs ine churz zeigä" (line 53). Here we come across a new phenomenon of resources being shared mutually at the counter (see Images 6.1a and b).

Extract 6 / video part 1

Agent is turning the computer monitor	
Image 6.1a	Image 6.1b

54 SBB: aso darf ich s ine churz ZEI**gä**=	

Instead of using the computer as an exclusive technical resource, the agent starts to make the client participate in the working process. In order to do so, she turns the monitor in the client's direction so that both agent and client can

218 *Heiko Hausendorf*

jointly look at it. Note that both participants are oriented to the screen and the manner in which they do this. In what follows, the screen becomes a commonly shared resource. The agent continues to use the screen in order to make clear her point (Images 6.2a–c):

Extract 6 / video part 2

Screen as commonly shared resource
Image 6.2a

Image 6.2b

Image 6.2c

SBB: also **das** isch (—) sparticket euRO[:pa]

What is to some extent impossible at the closed-counter setting, simply because of the window pane and the position of the computer monitor *behind* the pane, is now taking place at the open-counter setting: Both agent and client can easily access the screen. It is positioned on the desk somewhere between client and agent so that the client need only bend forward and turn his/her head to look at the screen. Agents can actively support sharing the screen by turning the mobile computer monitor toward the client. The asymmetry of working resources which is among the social implications of the closed-counter setting is set aside. Accordingly, there is no longer a period of reduced unfocused interaction *on standby* but a mutually shared focus on the visual display of the ticket-sales software. While the closed-counter setting seems to resemble the historical precursor of the ticket machine, the open-counter setting with its shared access to the ticket-sales software obviously bears a striking resemblance to the online booking of tickets at home.

To be sure, we are talking about *tendencies* when comparing the closed- with the open-counter setting. The establishing of shared access to the screen is not assumed to be the normal course of events in the open-counter setting, but it is by no means an isolated case. There is some evidence that we are, in fact, experiencing a maybe far-reaching process of change in ticket-sales interaction, triggered by the new architecture, without having being officially intended and without so far being perfectly implemented. The following images illustrate the remarkable physical effort on both the client's and the agent's side. Accordingly, there are still some material obstacles even in the "open" counter setting which force the participants to some extra exertion (Images 7.1a and b):

Image 7.1a and b Physically achieving shared access to the screen.

These images obviously call our attention to the way in which the strict definition of *inside* vs. *outside* the *counter* is negated in the new, open-counter setting. At the same time, the new setting does not yet seem fully adjusted to what has been postulated before: that agent and client are working together on the request. Perhaps the new setting is even already outdated: Could it be that it allows for the last, transitory emergence of the *agent* as the one being exclusively competent for ticket sales?

Whether this diagnosis proves the case or not remains to be seen. What is already striking is that the new setting obviously invites the participants on both sides to mutualize the technological resources for ticket sales. Along with the monitor positioned halfway toward the client, the agent no longer has exclusive access to the electronic system. There is no need to consider whether s/he is consciously aware of or even pushing the mutualizing of the screen or not. There already seems to be enough evidence that the new, open-counter setting allows the computer to become a sort of third party within the encounter. And, as a matter of course, clients routinely start to attune to the screen as a manifest reference point that is obviously attracting attention. Given the accessibility of the screen in the new setting, it can apparently no longer be ignored as an appealing potential to mutually share the resources that have long been exclusively available to the one *behind the counter*.

Conclusion

It is the phenomena of social interaction at the micro level of discourse that we have in mind when we postulate a transformation of ticket-sales conversations through changing architectures for interaction; the kind illustrated by the participants' jointly attuned speech, visual attention, gestures, and bodily orientation to the material world of designed settings that manifests the configuration and refiguration of discourse through architecture. In the present case, the disappearance of the window pane, and along with it the positioning of the computer screen, initially prove to re(con)figure the way(s) in which the client's request is dealt with in ticket-sales discourse. Empirically observing the sharing of technical resources, we might gain an idea of what has been changing in service talk for some time: the disappearance of traditional dichotomies such as *expert* vs. *layperson* which had been socio-spatially defined by architectures of asymmetry.

Seen through the microscope of video-based interaction analysis, architecture for interaction proves to provide material usability cues which can be taken up by the participants when they start to create their common interactional space of perception, movement, and action. Social selection "lures with the easy and the pleasing", as Niklas Luhmann put it when he accounted for the relationship between society (as the most complex and encompassing social system) and face-to-face interaction episodes (as the simplest and most bounded of social systems) in his sociological system approach.[11] Architecture for interaction, along with its usability cues, help to substantiate our understanding of the way society attracts face-to-face interaction. Note that we are not pleading for any kind of determinism. What we are aiming for is to account for the observation that space as an interactive achievement heavily relies on resources which themselves are dependent not on interaction, but on the preparation and provision of communicative connectivity. This is precisely the nature of architectural navigation, reading, and participation cues. Architecture for interaction not only "plays a role" in the everyday interactive construction of space; it allows one to trace back the interplay of material affordances, bodily resources, and spoken language to concrete forms of social interaction. The general issue of "communicative constructions and the refiguration of spaces" becomes audible and visible at the surface level of discourse.

Notes

1 Work on this chapter was generously supported by the Zurich University Research Priority Program "Language and Space" (see www.spur.uzh.ch/en.html for further details). Many thanks to the members of the related Focused Research Group on "Interactional Spaces" and to Christian Heath, Lorenza Mondada, and Reinhold Schmitt for numerous discussions on ticket-sales conversation at the counter. The concept of "architecture for interaction" has been developed in close co-operation

with R. Schmitt. Many thanks to the editors of the present volume, and to Johanna Jud who gave helpful comments on a first draft of this chapter.
2 This and the following freeze images derive from video recordings collected by Heiko Hausendorf and Lorenza Mondada in 2014 at different Swiss railway stations (cf. Hausendorf and Mondada 2017 and note 7 below).
3 It should not be overlooked that the transition from closed- to open-counter settings goes hand in hand with the emergence of *ticket machines* at railway stations. Ticket machines replace social interactions between humans with human–machine communication, which exclusively depends on the machine's usability and readability cues. This is an issue all in itself that will not be dealt with here, although reflections on this process will be included when we turn to the ways in which the client is served at the open-counter setting.
4 It is easy to see that this concept of communication basically draws on sociological systems theory with its distinction between interaction, organization, and society (Luhmann 2015). As will be sketched out in the following, architecture will be included as part of society by postulating communication through *usability*. Usability is considered a concrete manifestation of reachability. It does not depend on co-presence (see below in this section).
5 The difference between possible, waiting, next, imminent, current, and previous client is introduced in Hausendorf and Mondada (2017).
6 From Adriano Sabini's presentation of his PhD thesis on "Closings at the Counter" at a Zurich workshop on conversation over the counter.
7 The following abbreviated analysis is adopted from Hausendorf and Mondada (2017), in which the study of openings at railway-station counters is presented in more detail. Thanks to Andi Gredig (Deutsches Seminar, University of Zurich) for the layout of figures and images.
8 Capitals in the transcription signal moments that coincide with the stills.
9 Refers to the SBB 50% reduction card (Halbtax).
10 In the following extract, the equals sign (=) suggests a rapid connection between turns. Round brackets suggest that the wording within is an assumed wording, difficult to understand.
11 Cf. Luhmann (1984, Section 10). In the German original it is, "die gesellschaftliche Selektion [lockt] mit dem Leichten und Gefälligen" (588).

References

Barker, Roger G. 1968. *Ecological Psychology: Concepts and Methods for Studying the Environment of Human Behavior*. Stanford, CA: Stanford University Press.
Christmann, Gabriela B., ed. 2016. *Zur kommunikativen Konstruktion von Räumen: Theoretische Konzepte und empirische Analysen* [On the communicative construction of spaces: Theoretical concepts and empirical analyses]. Wiesbaden: Springer VS.
Fischer, Joachim. 2009. "Architektur: 'schweres' Kommunikationsmedium der Gesellschaft" [Architecture: a 'heavy' communication medium of the society]. *Aus Politik und Zeitgeschichte* 25: 6–10.
Fischer, Joachim, and Heike Delitz, eds. 2009. *Die Architektur der Gesellschaft: Theorien für die Architektursoziologie* [The architecture of society: Theories of the sociology of architecture]. Bielefeld: transcript.

Gibson, James J. 1977. "The Theory of Affordances". In *Perceiving, Acting, and Knowing: Toward an Ecological Psychology*, edited by Robert Shaw and John Bransford, 67–82. Hillsdale, NJ: Lawrence Erlbaum Associates.

Goffman, Erving. 1961. *Encounters: Two Studies in the Sociology of Interaction*. Indianapolis, IN: Bobbs-Merrill.

Goffman, Erving. 1967. *Interaction Ritual: Essays on Face-to-Face Behavior*. New York: Anchor.

Gumperz, John J. 1982. *Discourse Strategies*. Cambridge: Cambridge University Press.

Günzel, Stephan. 2017. *Raum: Eine kulturwissenschaftliche Einführung* [Space: A cultural-science-based introduction]. Bielefeld: transcript.

Hausendorf, Heiko. 2003. "Deixis and Speech Situation Revisited: The Mechanism of Perceived Perception". In *Deictic Conceptualisation of Space, Time and Person*, edited by Friedrich Lenz, 249–269. Amsterdam: Benjamins.

Hausendorf, Heiko. 2013. "On the Interactive Achievement of Space – and its Possible Meanings". In *Space in Language and Linguistics. Geographical, Interactional and Cognitive Perspectives*, edited by Peter Auer, Martin Hilpert, Anja Stukenbrock, and Benedikt Szmrezcsanyi, 276–303. Berlin and New York: de Gruyter.

Hausendorf, Heiko. 2015. "Interaktionslinguistik" [Linguistics of interaction]. In *Sprachwissenschaft im Fokus: Positionsbestimmungen und Perspektiven* [Focus on linguistics: Position determinations and perspectives], edited by Ludwig M. Eichinger, 43–69. Berlin, München and Boston: de Gruyter.

Hausendorf, Heiko, and Lorenza Mondada. 2017. *Becoming the Current Client: A Study of Openings at Swiss Railway Station Counters*. Working paper of the UFSP "Sprache und Raum" (SpuR), No. 5. Zürich: Universität Zürich.

Hausendorf, Heiko, Lorenza Mondada, and Reinhold Schmitt, eds. 2012. *Raum als interaktive Ressource* [Space as an interactive resource]. Tübingen: Narr.

Hausendorf, Heiko, and Reinhold Schmitt. 2016. "Interaktionsarchitektur und Sozialtopographie: Basiskonzepte einer interaktionistischen Raumanalyse" [Architecture for interaction and social topography: Basic concepts of an interactionist spatial analysis]. In *Interaktionsarchitektur, Sozialtopographie und Interaktionsraum* [Architecture for interaction, social topography and interactional space], edited by Heiko Hausendorf, Reinhold Schmitt, and Wolfgang Kesselheim, 27–54. Tübingen: Narr.

Hausendorf, Heiko, and Reinhold Schmitt. 2018. "Sprachliche Interaktion im Raum" [Verbal interaction in space]. In *Sprache im kommunikativen, interaktiven und kulturellen Kontext* [Language in a communicative, interactive and cultural context], edited by Arnulf Deppermann and Silke Reineke, 87–118. Berlin and Boston: de Gruyter.

Hausendorf, Heiko, Reinhold Schmitt, and Wolfgang Kesselheim, eds. 2016. *Interaktionsarchitektur, Sozialtopographie und Interaktionsraum* [Architecture for interaction, social topography and interactional space]. Tübingen: Narr.

Hausendorf, Heiko, and Wolfgang Kesselheim. 2016. "Die Lesbarkeit des Textes und die Benutzbarkeit der Architektur: Text- und interaktionslinguistische Überlegungen zur Raumanalyse" [The readability of the text and the usability of architecture: Text and interaction linguistic considerations for spatial analysis]. In *Interaktionsarchitektur, Sozialtopographie und Interaktionsraum* [Architecture for interaction, social topography and interactional space], edited by Heiko Hausendorf, Reinhold Schmitt, and Wolfgang Kesselheim, 55–85. Tübingen: Narr.

Hausendorf, Heiko, Wolfgang Kesselheim, Hiloko Kato, and Martina Breitholz. 2017. *Textkommunikation: Ein textlinguistischer Neuansatz zur Theorie und Empirie der Kommunikation mit und durch Schrift* [Communication: A new text-linguistic approach to the theory and empiricism of communication with and through writing]. Berlin and New York: de Gruyter.

Hindmarsh, Jon, and Christian Heath. 2000. "Embodied Reference: A Study of Deixis in Workplace Interaction". *Journal of Pragmatics* 32 (12): 1855–1878.

Jucker, Andreas H., Heiko Hausendorf, Christa Dürscheid, Karina Frick, Christoph Hottiger, Wolfgang Kesselheim, Angelika Linke, Nathalie Meyer, and Antonia Steger. 2018. "Doing Space in Face-to-Face Interaction and on Interactive Multimodal Platforms". *Journal of Pragmatics* 134: 85–101.

Kluge, Friedrich, and Elmar Seebold. 2011. *Etymologisches Wörterbuch der deutschen Sprache* [Etymological dictionary of the German language]. Berlin: de Gruyter.

Knoblauch, Hubert. 2017. *Die kommunikative Konstruktion der Wirklichkeit* [The communicative construction of reality]. Wiesbaden: Springer VS.

Knoblauch, Hubert, Bernt Schnettler, Jürgen Raab, and Hans-Georg Soeffner, eds. 2006. *Video Analysis: Methodology and Methods: Qualitative Audiovisual Data Analysis in Sociology*. Frankfurt am Main: Lang.

Knoblauch, Hubert, and Martina Löw. 2017. "On the Spatial Re-Figuration of the Social World". *Sociologica* 11 (2): 1–27.

Lawrence, Denise L., and Setha M. Low. 1990. "The Built Environment and Spatial Form". *Annual Review of Anthropology* 19: 453–505.

LeBaron, Curtis D., and Jürgen Streeck. 1997. "Built Space and the Interactional Framing of Experience During a Murder Interrogation". *Human Studies* 20 (1): 1–25.

Löw, Martina. 2001. *Raumsoziologie* [Sociology of space]. Frankfurt am Main: Suhrkamp.

Luhmann, Niklas. 1984. *Soziale Systeme: Grundriss einer allgemeinen Theorie* [Social systems: Outline of a general theory]. Frankfurt am Main: Suhrkamp.

Luhmann, Niklas. 2005. "Einfache Sozialsysteme" [Simple social systems]. In *Soziologische Aufklärung 2: Aufsätze zur Theorie der Gesellschaft* [Sociological enlightenment 2: Essays on the theory of society], edited by Niklas Luhmann, 25–47. Wiesbaden: Springer VS.

Luhmann, Niklas. 2015. "Ebenen der Systembildung – Ebenendifferenzierung (unveröffentlichtes Manuskript 1975)" [Levels of system formation–level differentiation (unpublished manuscript 1975)]. In *Sonderband Interaktion – Organisation – Gesellschaft revisited. Anwendungen, Erweiterungen, Alternativen* [Special Issue Interaction – organization – society revisited. Applications, extensions, alternatives], edited by Bettina Heintz and Hartmann Tyrell. *Zeitschrift für Soziologie* 35 (6): 6–39.

Mondada, Lorenza. 2009. "Emergent Focused Interactions in Public Places: A Systematic Analysis of the Multimodal Achievement of a Common Interactional Space". *Journal of Pragmatics* 41 (10): 1977–1997.

Reber, Elisabeth, and Cornelia Gerhardt, eds. 2019. *Embodied Activities in Face-to-Face and Mediated Settings: Social Encounters in Time and Space*. Cham: Springer International Publishing.

Schmitt, Reinhold. 2013. *Körperlich-räumliche Aspekte der Interaktion* [Physical and spatial aspects of interaction]. Tübingen: Narr.

Schmitt, Reinhold, and Arnulf Deppermann. 2007. "Monitoring und Koordination als Voraussetzungen der multimodalen Konstitution von Interaktionsräumen" [Monitoring and coordination as prerequisites for the multimodal constitution of interaction spaces]. In *Koordination: Analysen zur multimodalen Interaktion* [Coordination: Multimodal interaction analysis], edited by Reinhold Schmitt, 95–128. Tübingen: Narr.

Schroer, Markus. 2007. *Räume, Orte, Grenzen: Auf dem Weg zu einer Soziologie des Raums* [Spaces, places, borders: On the way to a sociology of space]. Frankfurt am Main: Suhrkamp.

Streeck, Jürgen. 1983. *Kommunikation in einer kindlichen Sozialwelt: Eine mikroethnographische Studie* [Communication in a childlike social world: A microethnographic study]. Tübingen: Narr.

Streeck, Jürgen, Charles Goodwin, and Curtis D. LeBaron, eds. 2011. *Embodied Interaction: Language and Body in the Material World*. New York: Cambridge University Press.

12 Innovation and communication

Spatial pioneers and the negotiation of new ideas

Anika Noack and Tobias Schmidt

Introduction

Various academic debates reiterate the major impact of cities as hotspots of creativity (Florida 2002), anchors in a network of global flows (Castells 1996), and centers of economic power (Sassen 1991). The 21st century has thus been labeled the urban age (Amin and Thrift 2002; Soja and Kanai 2010). Nevertheless, cities are also seen as drivers of climate change, creating ecological as well as social challenges (Albino, Berardi, and Dangelico 2015). Some urban quarters are even affected by stigmatized images and deprivation as well as threatened by the erosion of social cohesion. In addition, social exclusion – for example, between locals and migrants, but also of entire neighborhoods – undermine spatial identification processes (Christmann and Jähnke 2011, 220).

In order to face these challenges, innovation is becoming a "message of salvation" (Howaldt and Jacobsen 2010) and "almost an imperative for local actions" (Noack 2017, 118). Processes of social innovation (Howaldt and Schwarz 2010; Moulaert, Swyngedouw et al. 2010; Moulaert, MacCallum et al. 2013; Mumford 2002; Rammert 2013) are receiving particular attention in discussions on urban development and sustainable transformation processes. When social innovation is studied "the social is presented as a core element" (Bock 2012, 59). This moves the question toward local actors as driving forces of those processes (Cooke 2004, 17; Neumeier 2012, 65).

In this regard, the authors consider spatial pioneers as showing particular promise (Christmann and Büttner 2011; Noack 2015),[1] because they have the ability to influence spatial developments – such as in urban quarters – through socially innovative projects. Spatial pioneers are actors who go beyond their own spatial interests and initiate and implement new solutions for local social problems in certain quarters (Noack 2015, 36). Usually, spatial pioneers do not act in isolation, but are embedded in network-structured cooperations and influenced by structural conditions. Thus, on the one hand, as potential innovation agents, spatial pioneers must adapt to the given historical, political, economic, and social framework, but, on the other hand, they are also capable of negotiating, modifying, and reinventing this framework (Schröer 1997, 109). This negotiation process can be fiercely contested, met by resistance, and

DOI: 10.4324/9780367817183-15

accompanied by conflicts that emphasize a continual struggle with innovation (Neuloh 1977). Productively harnessing dissent and conflict moves the question toward communication. In the processes of communication, heterogeneous perspectives and interests meet, and ideas are discussed, exchanged, connected, and resumed in a way that may at times be conflictual. Thus, new ideas can be developed that result in new socio-spatial visions and interpretations of reality, which must again be communicated, transformed, and meaningfully linked in order to be most effective (Christmann and Büttner 2011).

Against this background, this contribution seeks to shed light on the communicative genesis and negotiation of social innovations introduced by spatial pioneers in urban quarters. It starts with an explanation of the term "spatial pioneers" and a brief introduction to current research about social innovations (in the next section). The theoretical perspective chosen by the authors is compatible with the conceptualization of innovations as social and communicative constructs (Christmann 2016; Knoblauch 2013) and, simultaneously, with the methodological approach of researching social innovations in real time through focused ethnography (Knoblauch 2001). The third section presents empirical (ethnographic) data from spatial pioneer Robert Zimmermann and his innovative activities in a formerly remote urban quarter of Berlin-Moabit. In the fourth section, the contribution subsequently illustrates the communicative negotiation of spatial innovation impulses introduced by this spatial pioneer among two very different groups of citizens. Finally, in the fifth section, conclusions are drawn with regard to what influence specific patterns of communication, established role models, processes of power, social conflicts, and the intra-group positions of creative minds have on the introduction, adaptation, and joint development of innovative ideas. This illustrates that heterogeneous knowledge, mutual trust, powerful group positions, and personal innovation ambitions do not per se foster innovation but are situationally interdependent. This calls for a process-accompanying perspective on social innovation with a focus on the communicative genesis of those processes.

Spatial pioneers and the communicative construction of social innovation

In previous studies, spatial pioneers have mainly been associated with representatives of civil society or creative industries that use devalued space as a means of realizing their ideas and creating room for development and freedom (Matthiesen 2005; Lange and Matthiesen 2005). The authors define spatial pioneers as a heuristic concept for actors and groups of actors that go beyond their own spatial interests and initiate, encourage, and socially maintain new solutions for local social problems in certain quarters. This perspective includes both creative freelancers and civil society actors as well as entrepreneurs and representatives of organizations (whether they are public or independent) and political and administrative representatives, assuming that they follow new paths (Christmann and Büttner 2011; Noack 2015).

As network agents, spatial pioneers build up contacts to a wide range of actors, institutions, stakeholders, and decision makers in their district, and they have strategic access to information and distribute it strategically within their network. Spatial pioneers are characterized by a dynamism and an enormous practical knowledge that forms a basis for their imagination and inventiveness. Locally, they enjoy trust and social recognition and have spatial resonance, not least in the form of criticism and detachment, since new impulses also lead to ambivalent, possibly negative consequences for certain groups (Noack 2015, 38).

Hence, we consider spatial pioneers as typical agents in social innovation processes. In order to define social innovation, Zapf (1989, 177) argues that they are "new ways of achieving goals, particularly new ways of organizing, new regulations, new ways of life" with the potential to "alter the direction of social change" (translation by the authors). Apart from a certain degree of novelty, new ideas and practices also have to connect to existing knowledge and practices to gain social acceptance. Thus, social innovations also integrate recombinations of already known things (Schumpeter 1964), rediscoveries, or things that have been adapted to different contexts (Gillwald 2000, 10–11).

When social innovation is studied, it is all the more so that "the social is presented as a core element" (Bock 2012, 59). According to Mulgan and Pulford (2010, 16) "social innovations are innovations that are social both in their ends and in their means". Zapf (1989, 177) also refers to the problem-solving capacity of social innovation processes that are "worthy of being imitated and institutionalized" (translation by the authors). Moulaert et al. (2010) stress that social innovation satisfies unfulfilled social needs, empowers marginalized and excluded groups, and alters network relationships. Thus, social innovation is not only seen as inevitably embedded in community and spatial development processes (Moulaert and Sekia 2003), but also as desirable for spatial transformation.

However, neither Mulgan and Pulford (2010), Zapf (1989), nor Moulaert et al. (2010) reflect on their normative understanding of social innovation as a steady response to diverse societal problems. In contrast, authors like Gillwald (2000, 19), Lindhult (2008, 44), Rammert (2013), and Schwarz, Birke, and Beerheide (2010, 174–175) illustrate that social innovation does not always create new solutions that are helpful for overcoming conflicts and crises, but may also produce new problems or have ambivalent or even negative effects for certain actors.

The theoretical perspective of communicative constructivism (Knoblauch 2013) as well as the concept of spaces as social and communicative constructs (Christmann 2016, 2022; Christmann, Knoblauch, and Löw 2022) correspond with the authors' assumptions. Transferred to social innovation research, this means that innovations are constructs that are externalized, objectified, and internalized by social processes, primarily by communication (Knoblauch 2013). Knoblauch defines communication as "action, which, taking effect on the environment, employs symbols and is orientated toward others: mutual symbolic action" (translation by the authors) (Knoblauch 1995, 53).

Communicative negotiations about new, potentially innovative ideas can be fiercely contested, met with resistance, and accompanied by conflict (Neuloh 1977). On the one hand, such conflict may create opportunities for the emergence of innovation and catalyze processes of social change (Neuloh 1977). On the other hand, conflict diminishes the odds of socially innovative ideas coming to fruition (Neuloh 1977; Noack and Federwisch 2018), especially when they are not grounded in rational arguments (Martens 2010, 374) or negotiated in an atmosphere of mutual trust (Müller 2009). For this reason, trust, tolerance, openness, and acceptance are particularly important in interactions between heterogeneous actors with different perspectives (Ibert 2004). In this sense, heterogeneity stimulates discussion and negotiation, and it creates space for the combination of unusual perspectives and the emergence of unconventional ideas (Bosworth et al. 2016, 457; Noack 2015, 305). But "too much heterogeneity could also act as a barrier to forming sustainable partnerships and lasting social innovation" (Bosworth et al. 2016, 457) and might exacerbate communication problems and even social conflicts.

The role of heterogeneous knowledge and of trust, conflicts, and barriers remains mostly unseen in the ex post reconstruction of "successful" idea careers (Neuloh 1977, 28). By contrast, they become observable in real-time studies on innovation as undertaken by the authors. These enable one to have a look at key resistances, controversies, conflicts, and power struggles as major components of innovation processes (Noack 2015, 185). It is important to stress that a real-time (in vivo) exploration of social innovation does not necessarily imply studying successfully implemented, widely institutionalized, and spatially dispersed social innovation (Gillwald 2000; Noack 2015, 118). This means that not every idea which is deemed innovative develops into a successful social innovation (Noack 2015). Prior to taking a detailed look at the communicative negotiation of potentially innovative ideas, the spatial pioneer Robert Zimmermann[2] will be presented.

Robert Zimmermann: Spatial pioneer in Berlin-Moabit

After moving to Berlin in the early 1980s, 55-year-old Robert Zimmermann became acquainted by chance with the district of Moabit. In a situation characterized by widespread housing shortages in Berlin, he seized the opportunity to rent an apartment in Moabit and soon began to value the benefits of the district. The technically trained, independent energy advisor learned about the scope for spatial design while buying a house and thus gaining access to the local culture of engagement in 2000. Zimmermann expected that regular attendance at meetings of the local council for affected people (*Betroffenenrat*) would bring benefits for the purchase of an abandoned factory building that, at the time, was located in a formally designated redevelopment area. Previously, he had *"never been so politically engaged, but always had a lot to do with technology"* (interview with Robert Zimmermann, henceforth "Interview RZ"; translation in each case by the authors). Step by step, Zimmerman recognized neighborhood commitment as a personal challenge. He transferred his technical experimentation to the field of voluntary work, and about 12 years ago founded a citizens' association with other volunteers from the former *Betroffenenrat*, which he still chairs and to which he dedicates much of his voluntary work.

As a representative of this citizens' association, Zimmermann is also active as an elected member of the Josefspassage residents' committee, the participative body of a federally funded project to enhance the district center in Moabit. Furthermore, the actor is the managing editor of a self-published neighborhood newspaper, published by his citizens' association, and a member of the editorial team of the largest online civic magazine in Moabit.

Spatial visions and motives of commitment: Having a village in the city

As the central motive for his space-related commitment, Mr. Zimmermann names his vision of having a village in the city.

> *The major reason why I actually participate is the desire to live in a village and in Berlin at the same time. ... Not in a village, where the narrow-minded rule, but in a city with a great variety and with a high level of familiarity at the same time.*
>
> (Interview RZ)

The initial motives for commitment with regard to resource generation (information as the capital for a successful house purchase) were gradually replaced by his desire to create structures in the midst of the city of Berlin that link a family village atmosphere with metropolitan diversity. Robert Zimmermann discovers that civic participation has the potential to create a meaningful and identity-establishing community that goes way beyond metropolitan anonymity while still granting him freedom. Thus, his civic participation accommodates both his community-oriented and his space-shaping values.

Ingenious solutions for a better quality of life: Zimmermann's reference to innovation

His diverse career and involvement with the citizens' association demonstrate that Zimmerman frequently follows new paths, both in his professional and his civic activities. Once more, his ambition to innovate becomes apparent when he is looking for "*intelligent ... and ingenious solutions*" for the financial hedging of his civic association. Zimmermann is looking for ideas, "*that are not that trivial, that not everyone can offer*" (Interview RZ). In the generation and implementation of potential innovation, Zimmermann does not operate exclusively strategically, but in a much more undirected and experimental manner. Following the principle of trial and error, he tests new things, pursues successful outcomes, and learns from failures.

With regard to the sustainable financing and maintenance of the citizens' association, Zimmermann says that he

> *has not yet found the philosopher's stone. … It would have been a social innovation, so we asked people from the university … what solutions for financing volunteer structures there are. … I perceive such solutions as innovative that can be realized and finally result in earnings.*
>
> (Interview RZ)

Against the background of a very explicit knowledge of the innovation literature, Zimmermann does not evaluate his own approach as innovative because, to date, they could neither be implemented successfully nor spatially disseminated.

Forms of action: "What I am best at is starting businesses"

Zimmermann's ideas generally do not remain at the hypothetical level of conception, but lead to a claim to "*really do something, to make a difference*" (Interview RZ) in concrete projects and actions (such as neighborhood festivals, corporate partnerships with sponsors, and supporters of his citizens' association). His standard for civil action is always determined by the success of such projects and actions with regard to their implementation and spatial effects. Usually, Zimmermann chooses entrepreneurial practices proven to be particularly advantageous in realizing project ideas pragmatically in the past. "*I have the initiative, I can begin, I am not afraid, and I have firm judgment. And that means I can achieve a lot, simply by the way I behave*" (Interview RZ). As a "man of action", he repeatedly turns his visions into reality and heavily relies on his own effective actions while generating and realizing new ideas. His professional experience as a successful founder of start-up businesses and as a self-employed person illustrate that "*what I am best at is starting businesses*" (Interview RZ). Consequently, Robert Zimmermann decided to transfer his entrepreneurial action approach to the work of the citizens' association and to base its actions on a business plan, which may be considered unusual and innovative in the context of Moabit's citizen involvement.

Motivated by his spatial vision of creating a village in his urban neighborhood, Zimmermann is committed to a higher quality of life. The actor discovers approaches for spatial design and development in socially innovative project ideas. This combination of innovative ideas with an entrepreneurial and pragmatic modus operandi characterizes Robert Zimmermann as a spatial pioneer.

Accordingly, he intentionally designs his cooperations and network relations in a strategic way and as a "*toolkit for innovative solutions*" (Interview RZ). In his view, "*team work and cooperation*" are most important for "*change as well as for dynamic and innovative solutions*" (Interview RZ). Like an entrepreneur, he is mostly in search of win-win situations through strategic cooperation instead of competition with others or involvement in conflicts.

Spatial innovation impulses of a spatial pioneer in group contexts

With the intention of expanding his network contacts and of implementing his innovative approaches and spatial visions, the spatial pioneer Zimmermann accesses a variety of civil society groups in Moabit. The following will refer to the examples of two civic groups in order to illustrate how Zimmermann's innovation impulses are negotiated communicatively.

Social recognition, trust, and central group position: Robert Zimmermann in the Citizens' Association of Moabit

The Citizens' Association of Moabit was founded in 2006 by, among others, the current chair, Robert Zimmermann, and brings together committed neighborhood residents. The citizens' association organizes neighborhood festivals, social services such as playground supervision, tenants' and legal advice, and the publication of the association's own local newspaper. The main idea is to introduce an approach that tries to find entrepreneurial solutions (fundraising, advertising for companies on terms of providing financial assistance, the association's own newspaper as an information *and* advertising platform) for the preservation of the diverse social activities against a background of financial hardship. This socially entrepreneurial approach seems unconventional for civil associations in general, and even innovative for those in Moabit.

Robert Zimmermann holds the chair of the legally responsible association, Mrs. Blum is vice chair, Mr. Falck has a part-time position, and Mrs. Dom is responsible for the association treasury. In addition to these four functionaries, an average of about 10 other participants attend the public meetings held once a month. Overall, the citizens' association has 60 members, but is seeking to increase this number. The citizens' association usually follows an agenda, structuring the sessions and including the transfer of current information from the neighborhood as well as the planning of concrete actions. This agenda is developed by prior arrangement between Mr. Zimmerman, Mrs. Blum, and Mr. Falck, so these three actors go beyond their functional working tasks and thus have personal influence within the group. The inclusion of the agenda item "other matters" offers the other members the opportunity to contribute concerns and issues of their own to the group discussion. The work of the citizens' association is coordinated at the monthly meetings, but also by mail, telephone, and personal contact between the functionaries.

It is, first and foremost, Zimmermann who introduces new spatial ideas and visions to the citizens' association. His ideas typically appeal to the group members and are supported by them, as the following excerpt shows. It also demonstrates his central position within the group[3] in terms of social recognition, influence, and trust – for instance, when Zimmerman is left to evaluate the quality of ideas. Prior to the sequence, Zimmerman informs the citizens' association of the permission given by the Berlin-Mitte district to charitably use a vacant kiosk in the quarter. He plans to open a BMX bike rental shop for children and a workshop to repair the bicycles of local residents on a donation basis.

Meeting of the Citizens' Association, 25 August 2009:

Mr. Zimmermann: *Well, we have considered that we want to organize a day or an afternoon or so, where the required materials are obtained, and then maybe we can share an afternoon with our supporters, the work-instead-of-punishment people, painting this kiosk, taking the gutter into service, and building the solar cells onto it. This will be somewhat prepared. Now of course it would be interesting to find an appointment for that day.*

[The phone rings and Mr. Zimmermann leaves the group for about 2 minutes, during which Mr. Falck and Mrs. Dom discuss a date for the realization of the project.]

Mr. Falck: *The 3 October is German Unification Day. That would be a great occasion to collectively rebuild the kiosk [laughter].*

Mrs. Dom: *Yeah that would suit us well.*

Mr. Meyer: *Tell me, Robert, you have done something with solar cells at a school with a couple of students, haven't you?*

Mr. Zimmermann: *Yes.*

Mr. Meyer: *Don't you think it would be possible to convince them to participate again?*

Mr. Zimmermann: *Oh sure.*

Mr. Meyer: *Well, I mean, you have told us that everyone was very enthusiastic afterwards.*

Mr. Zimmerman: *Yes. The class that constructed the radio, this break radio, the boom box, which is solar powered, are now done and have passed it on to a younger seventh-grade class, who wish to pursue this further and are therefore open to new experiences with solar energy. We can certainly ask them. But that would not be possible until next week, when everyone is back. But that is a good idea.*

In place of the former kiosk waste land, Zimmermann plans a venue that is visually transformed and utilized in a new way; a meeting place where children can borrow bikes and the rest of the neighborhood residents can have their bikes repaired. As part of the transformation, according to Mr. Zimmermann's aims, the kiosk is not only receiving a fresh coat of paint and a new gutter, but will also be equipped with solar panels. The spatial pioneer therefore cares not only about revitalization of the kiosk, "*which has been dead for a long time*" (Interview RZ), but further combines the spatial design of the inhabitants with an innovative and environmentally sustainable impulse by envisaging solar panels as an alternative energy resource for the operation of the kiosk. Thus, this functional redefinition of the kiosk, initiated by Zimmermann and collectively implemented, represents a starting point for spatial development in the urban quarter.

After calling for the transformation of the kiosk, Zimmermann suggests finding a date for its implementation. When his phone rings, he is required to leave for about 2 minutes. In the meantime, Mr. Falck and Mrs. Dom search for a suitable date for this project and land on 3 October. It is only after Zimmermann returns to the room that Mr. Meyer, an association member and former district councilor, contributes a proposal for cooperation. Turning directly to Zimmermann ("*Tell me, Robert*"), Mr. Meyer recalls a solar project organized by the citizens' association with students from the neighboring school and asks whether these students would support the redesign of the kiosk again. The fact that Mr. Meyer does not propose his idea in the absence of Zimmermann to the moderator Mr. Falck, who also has formal power to set the agenda, demonstrates that Mr. Meyer considers Zimmermann to be the idea generator and manager of the solar radio project as well as the bridge to the students and teachers involved in it. Since an explicit referral by Mr. Meyer to Zimmermann is repeatedly observed as a structural principle of communication, it also reveals that Mr. Meyer seeks resonance among those players that have a major social influence in the group, based on decades of experience in district politics. Zimmermann is apparently accredited to be such a person. The fact that Mr. Meyer shares Mr. Zimmermann's evaluation of the project's success without having contact to the school himself ("*Well, I mean, you have told us that everyone was very enthusiastic afterwards*") shows that Mr. Meyer considers the statements of the spatial pioneer to be trustworthy.

At the same time, Robert Zimmermann gives very detailed information to the group – as observed in many meetings – and therefore acts as an "information broker". The actor gathers information through his network of contacts in the district, presents them to the association members, and thus claims his central position in the group. The fact that Zimmerman readily takes up Mr. Meyer's idea and finally honors it as "*good*", illustrates that he is in a group position which allows him not only to introduce his own ideas, but also to pick up others and to judge them. Zimmermann's central position in the group is therefore not based only on his formal role as a chair of the association, but mainly relies on the social recognition of the other participants. They recognize his information advantage, which is part of his strategic network management.

In terms of a self-reinforcing effect, potentially innovative ideas expressed by the spatial pioneer in his prestigious position have a certain emphasis because they encounter fundamental openness and acceptance within the group. One can accordingly anticipate high potential for their implementation.

Mr. Zimmermann is well recognized by the citizens' association members, but also enjoys their trust as their group representative. Among the other regular members of the public association meetings, too, a symmetrical relationship of trust has developed. One reason for the establishment and stabilization of such trust is the regularity and frequency of meetings involving a relatively well-defined group of people. Moreover, the calm and constructive way of talking to each other also supports the establishment of a trusting atmosphere for conversation. The communicative climate in the meetings is collegial and often very humorous. There is much laughter, and conflictual disputes take place quite rarely. Discussions usually proceed objectively and are characterized by mutual exchange of information and multiple negotiations of ideas. Accordingly, all members are equally encouraged to express their opinions and ideas without the fear of negative reactions, such as malice or mockery. This trust-based communicative atmosphere provides the conditions for expressing "*crazy ideas*", as envisaged and repeatedly demanded by Zimmermann.

Such inclusionary attempts at developing an egalitarian process of exchange and a creative dialogue are not always successful. Sometimes, negotiations of new ideas are excluded in favor of a more efficient planning of projects and actions by the decision makers in the group. However, generally, those mechanisms are neither problematized by the group members, nor do they result in conflicts.

The trustful and balanced communicative atmosphere is only disturbed by conflicts, rivalries, and differences between people with competing interests and values. This challenges the balance of power, with its habitualized role allocations and forms of communication, and requires their renewed negotiation. Mrs. Lenz represents such a person who unsettles the communicative atmosphere.

Prior to the sequence given above, Zimmermann had presented the idea (which he had also explicitly framed as such) to found a neighborhood limited company. This idea pursues the goal of involving prison inmates in activities such as renovation work, thus reintegrating them into working and social life. At the same time, the financial profits earned from their work can be reinvested into the association's social projects.

Meeting of the Citizens' Association, 31 March 2009:
Mrs. Lenz: It just occurred to me when you talked about the idea of a neighborhood limited company, whether it might make sense to get in contact with this cooperative in Wedding. Perhaps we should not invent everything from scratch. Perhaps we could [concur] with this cooperative Wedding. This is really something like that. It isn't a private limited company, but a cooperative. Perhaps we could somehow even-
Mr. Zimmermann: What do they do?
Mrs. Lenz: -take part. Yes, they make something like this, they make-
Mr. Zimmermann: What does "something" mean?
Mrs. Lenz: -those who do, regardless of exactly what, renovations, I don't know, all sorts of things where people can work and they offer it in turn to the traders or companies or even individuals or housing associations, who are members of the cooperative. But the goal was just basically the same, to develop something for people, who have somehow worked, in community work or so, and to find something for them that continues that work.

As a result of this presentation, Mrs. Lenz proposes her idea of forming a collaboration with a cooperative in the Berlin district of Wedding, because they would pursue the same concept ("*This is really something like that*"). Mrs. Lenz directly challenges the evaluation of this idea as a reinvention, though she sees it as holding potential for cooperative arrangements and adaptive learning processes. Thus, Mrs. Lenz clearly distinguishes herself from Zimmermann's pronounced orientation toward innovation. The different orientations also become apparent when looking at the types of companies envisaged for the implementation of ideas. Coming from an entrepreneurial perspective, Zimmermann proposes the legal form of a private limited company, whereas Mrs. Lenz sympathizes with the community-oriented form of a cooperative. As a member of the editorial team of the association's local newspaper, Mrs. Lenz is often present at the meetings, but she does not feel herself part of this group. Mrs. Lenz is primarily engaged in an adjoining neighborhood, where she fights for the preservation of the existing quality of life and for social cohesion through the maintenance of residential structures. By contrast, Zimmermann distances himself from Mrs. Lenz's emphasis on the threat of gentrification. He connects quality of life with innovative change and spatial development, whereas Mrs. Lenz engages in the preservation of existing conditions.

Based on these divergent problem perceptions and values, Mr. Zimmermann and Mrs. Lenz compete for the power to interpret within the group. Accordingly, Zimmerman is not satisfied with the information provided about the cooperative and asks in a challenging tone, "*What do they do?*" Zimmermann thus demonstrates his lack of information, and forces Mrs. Lenz to provide more specific information in order to defend the innovative character of an idea of his that had previously been delegitimized by Mrs. Lenz. When Mrs. Lenz continues to talk about the collective's commitment in a very indefinite way ("*Yes, they make something like this*"), Robert Zimmermann impatiently interrupts her and wants to know explicitly what "*something*" means. Mrs. Lenz then adds that services such as renovation are offered within the cooperative in order to supply nonprofit workers with a perspective for future jobs. Following the printed segment, Mr. Meyer intervenes as a third party and tries to relocate the topic of content design of the cooperative to its genesis, thereby mitigating the latent potential for conflict between Mr. Zimmerman and Mrs. Lenz.

Such controversial debates over the meaning, the novelty, and the practicability of innovative ideas – mainly proposed by Zimmermann – are quite rare at the citizens' association. They reveal, on the one hand, that conflicts, rivalries, and differences threaten potentially innovative ideas, especially at an early stage of development. On the other hand, conflicts can facilitate modifications of initial ideas that finally increase their discursive and practical chances of implementation.

That conflicts and frictions can halt innovative ideas is something Mr. Zimmermann experiences in the Josefspassage residents' committee.

Between competition for power and creative competence: Zimmermann's commitment in the Josefspassage residents' committee

Beyond his activities in the citizens' association, Robert Zimmermann is a member of the Josefspassage residents' committee. By regularly participating in such public bodies, he expects to gain strategic networks. In addition to working groups on issues such as transport, parks, and public relations, public plenary sessions, held monthly, are at the core of the work. Through the self-developed procedures of the group, the sessions are highly formalized, such as in the form of a predetermined agenda or regulated speaking times. However, as participant observation reveals, such regulations have not yet been transferred into routine in this relatively young and heterogeneous group. Exchanges between members on controversial views and action approaches in regard to spatial design do not yet proceed in a constructive spirit. The interaction observed in the sessions even shows personalized conflicts between individuals. Thus, for example, Mr. Kranz repeatedly attracts attention by making negative judgmental statements toward other participants. Mr. Kranz attends the meetings both as a local resident and as a representative of the district parliament, being a member of one of the major parties. Together with young politicians from his own party, who are also members of the residents' committee and also have professional skills attained through their work in local politics, Mr. Kranz has formed an informal "faction" that acts as a subgroup. Observed by criteria such as length and frequency of his speeches or the enforcement of thematic priorities in the decision-making processes of the group, Mr. Kranz objectively holds a central interactive position which, however, is based rather more on support provided by the lobby of his informal faction than on personal recognition from other group members.

In this context, Zimmermann tries to participate with his own spatial development ideas. Unlike in the citizens' association, in the residents' committee he is marginalized for his ideas. A sequence presented below is an instructive example. It had previously been discussed in plenary whether it would be reasonable to decide on the provision of street furnishings (and thus use a large part of the money drawn from available funds) within the group or if it might be better to include suggestions from citizens. This discussion, like many others before, was marked by a tense atmosphere. At this stage, the group could not agree on a common attitude and workable compromises, a situation that could also be observed in the negotiation of other issues. Similarly, the group repeatedly addresses their own lack of public perception in the district. Against this background, one of the members assumes at the meeting in May 2010 that a call for participation would hardly reach anyone ("*How can we ever be visible to the outside when we are not even able to agree internally?*"). While the group is not sure how the citizens can be engaged for the topic of "street furnishing", it is Robert Zimmermann who finally introduces an idea.

> Meeting of the Residents' Committee, 17 May 2010:
> *[Mr. Zimmermann is given the floor by the Chair.]*
> Mr. Zimmermann: Yes, that is, yes we could combine both. We replace these boards, you know, the missing ones here and make it a project. [Chuckling] We write on top of the boards: Work with us, design your own neighborhood, so that these benches are placeholders in the future for the call of the citizens to participate-
> *[Mild laughter in the plenary]*
> Person 1:   -that is, uh-
> Chair: -too detailed.
> Mr. Kranz: In which, in what proportion to the fund?
> Mr. Zimmermann: Yes, that is, I think that-

Innovation and communication 237

[*Laughter in the plenary*]
Mr. Kranz [*in a sarcastic tone of voice*]: From the 6,000 euros of Mrs. N.?
[*Laughter by Mr. Kranz, laughter in the plenary*]
Mr. Zimmerman: No, it does not [*laughter in the plenary*], it does not cost much. We will replace some boards and write some-
Person 1 [*in a sarcastic tone of voice*]: Yes, yes. Yes, yes.
Mr. Zimmermann: -somehow-
Person in plenary: Yes, yes. Yes, yes.
Mr. Zimmermann [*with raised voice*]: -a year!
[*Babble of voices in the plenary*]
Mr. Zimmerman: So that [*babble of voices*], I don't think that is so expensive.
Chair: That's too detailed, Mr. Zimmermann, uh-
Mr. Zimmermann: Yes, yes, I know, only-
Chair: -think first-
Mr. Zimmermann: -but this shows me-
Chair: -about the basic rule-
Mr. Zimmermann: -but this shows me that you-
Chair: -with which we proceed here.
Mr. Zimmermann: -that you should collect ideas (raising his voice)-
Chair: -yes-
Person 2 (approvingly): -yes-
Mr. Zimmermann: -perhaps because, as I, I also think that-
Chair: -d'accord-
Mr. Zimmermann: I also think improving the situation is a necessity here, but at the same time you may also connect with a few [*emphasizing the following word*] amazing things when we really want to [*emphasizing the following word*] get the citizens. They sit there and read that they should participate or I do not know what.
Person 3: It [*inaudible*]-
Chair: That is enough for this topic.
Mr. Zimmermann: Good.

Zimmermann's idea proves to be creative, as it clearly distinguishes itself from previous proposals, insofar as citizens would be accessed directly through a visual, project-like approach in public spaces. Involving visual elements within public space, his proposal also responds to the issue of low visibility, which had been perceived by the plenary itself as a major problem. Zimmermann presents his idea with great enthusiasm, but is increasingly hurried under the pressure of the plenum, which gives him no room for unfolding his thoughts (see in particular the frequent interruptions of his speech), but reacts to his proposal with sarcasm. In the context of other groups and events, Zimmermann also tries to convince potential supporters of prospective solutions, rather than focusing on problems, deficits, and resistance (e.g. cash). However, it seems surprising at first, that Zimmermann – as an entrepreneurial socialized actor – does not include the financial feasibility into his considerations. On closer consideration, it becomes clear that he definitely considered the aspect of "financing" ("*It does not cost much*"). But when trying to convince the representatives of his spatial idea, he initially moves this problem into the background. In his role as a socio-spatial visionary, he first refers to the consistency, the practical feasibility, the innovative potential, and the effectiveness of his idea. He tries in this way to raise approval, excitement, and enthusiasm among the others so that his idea can become a participatory project. Zimmermann's efforts are thus mainly aimed at the level of motivation.

With the establishment of politically and parliamentary dominated action and communication routines in the group, which are already based on the formal regulations of communication and are supported and habitualized by political actors such as Mr. Kranz, the integration of free styles of thinking and communication proves to be difficult. As Zimmermann demonstrates in the example given, a newly emerging spatial vision, the creative play of ideas, needs to be defended with objective arguments.

Zimmermann then decides to convince the others with factual arguments on the financial feasibility, but finds himself in a defensive position against Mr. Kranz and the chair. Neither grant him space for these thoughts, as the frequent interruptions demonstrate. At this point, Zimmermann and his idea have already been disqualified ("*That's too detailed*"). Representing similar examples from the group sessions, the sequence presented illustrates the competition for power inside the group with regard to agenda setting between Mr. Kranz and the chair on the one hand ("*think first ... about the basic rule*") and other group members (in the present example, represented by Zimmermann, who is of the opinion "*that you should collect ideas*"). Mr. Kranz and the chair are supported by assenting voices from the plenary, which takes over the role of the referee in this brief dispute and, enabling them to form a powerful alliance through the application of social pressure (Mr. Kranz threatens Zimmermann with mockery and humiliation) and the legitimate agenda-setting power of the chair in his role as moderator, which Zimmermann finally recognizes ("*Good*"). While Mr. Kranz, who is rhetorically well versed, is able to draw support from his own lobby of fellow party members, Zimmerman does not succeed in winning over other group members to his ideas, though he knows many of them from other contexts.

In his own citizens' association, Zimmermann enjoys almost unlimited opportunities for development, because he is socially well recognized and trusted. In the residents' committee, however, he is confronted with many other dedicated and rhetorically competent actors like Mr. Kranz, who have the ability to dominate the communicative scene. The idea expressed by Zimmermann is ridiculed in the plenary, especially by Mr. Kranz. This pattern of devaluation of other people and their communicative contributions in the group interaction more or less provides Mr. Kranz with a subtle influence on the sessions. He quite often succeeds in influencing voting and opinion-forming processes and the determination of thematic priorities. Even against the wishes of many other plenary members (and sometimes at the expense of his personal popularity in the group), he persists in fighting for his own positions. On the one hand, he uses a financial argument; on the other, he relies on degrading others (in this case, Zimmermann) through public ridicule in order to emphasize his own dominant role in the committee. Zimmermann's attempt to introduce new spatial ideas is immediately disqualified by the chair ("*That's too detailed, Mr. Zimmermann*").

In many social contexts, Zimmermann plays the role of an idea generator who is very open-minded with regard to experimentation and, in the course of his professional socialization, has learned to trust the financial feasibility of his own ideas (or, alternatively, who shows his creative potential while searching for new funding models for the citizens' association). In contrast to the homogeneously structured citizens' association, the residents' committee is rather loosely structured and networked. In the manner of a governance arrangement, it consists of heterogeneous actors who follow different role concepts in the handling of public spatial design. As demonstrated in the example, this usually leads to conflict during the necessary communicative processes of negotiation when the habitus of a politician collides with that of an enterprising and pragmatic social entrepreneur. In our case, Mr. Kranz's substantive standards of value and power-oriented communication styles collide with the enthusiasm, creative potential, and practical knowledge of Robert Zimmermann. With his idea of enabling public space to speak for itself by means of street furnishings (in this case, a bench) and inviting people to participate in its design, Zimmermann creates a conceivable approach to collaboratively designing local space, based on the perception that the collective living environment is changeable. However, it is precisely this realistic plasticity, the sense of the small and the environmentally concrete, that the chair criticizes as "*too detailed*". At the same time, Mr. Kranz emphasizes the importance of economic considerations – so to speak on behalf of the plenary – and raises them over Zimmermann's thought experiments, which could in principle lead to shared visions of space.

It is an actor such as Mr. Kranz who introduces routines and patterns of meaning into the group communication that are common to parliament members and political committees. His logical and factual way of reasoning therefore competes with the experimental exploration of creative potential for spatial design (as represented by Zimmermann's idea) and tries to implement economic criteria to serve as a guide for adaptation and evolution of ideas. Using the power resources that he builds up with his faction of fellow party members (for instance, the threat of losing face if ridiculed by the group), Mr. Kranz is able to conduct and establish these (financial) standards for the rest of the group. Since, owing to their power resources, political role-bearers like Mr. Kranz dominate the plenary in the negotiation and decision processes, actors like Zimmermann, who rely on their enthusiasm to wake others' passion for creative spatial design, gain little purchase in realizing their ideas.

An actor like Mr. Kranz risks splitting the group in favor of individual interests. This is in contrast to Zimmermann, who, regarding new impulses for regional development and following principles of inclusion and empowerment of interested others, aims to encourage cooperation rather than confrontation. Zimmermann does not seek to use rhetoric to wield power when he finds himself in rivalry with other power-oriented actors such as Mr. Kranz, who communicates quite aggressively. He develops and promotes creative ideas for collective spatial design, but does not fight about public opinion communicatively.

Conclusion

Ethnographically grounded and theoretically reflective research on the communicative genesis and negotiation of social innovations in spatial development processes is rare. The same is true for spatial pioneers viewed as prospective drivers of those processes. Using the example of spatial pioneer Robert Zimmermann in two very differently structured civil society groups, we can illustrate the complex interplay that specific patterns of communication, established role models, processes of power, conflict negotiation processes, and intra-group positions have on the introduction, adaptation, and joint development of potential social innovations.

With regard to variation and recombination of knowledge, the heterogeneity of actors' groups, with their different knowledge bases and interests, theoretically provides greater opportunities for innovation (Bouwen and Steyaert 1999; Brown and Ashman 1999; Ibert 2004). However, our research proves that this cannot be taken for granted. The Josefspassage residents' committee, a governance-like social setting typical for the context of spatial development, faces severe communication difficulties due to the heterogeneity of the knowledge of its participants. These problems already restrict potential innovation processes at the stage of creatively expressing ideas. There, the creative potential of participatory actors such as the spatial pioneer Robert Zimmermann is threatened by social conflicts and power rivalries.

Some authors understand conflicts as being particularly productive with respect to the stimulation of innovation processes (Dubiel 1999; Martens 2010, 374; Neuloh 1977). Conflicts are considered dynamizing in that they break routines and open space for social change through innovation processes. However, when conflicts are negotiated at a personal rather than an objective level, the potential for innovation is reduced, as the example of the Josefspassage residents' committee clearly illustrates. This group therefore shows potentially innovative characteristics (such as a diversity of perspectives and competencies due to the heterogeneity of actors and fundamental equality of members). Although this relatively young and developing committee is explicitly devoted to innovation, its innovative potential is undermined in connection with group identification, integration, and stabilization processes. In such a case, it seems important to constructively solve controversies (Sperber, Moritz, and Hetze 2007, 87). This means, first, making it possible to express ideas without the threat of losing face and allowing for the communication of ideas, or even constructive debate on spatial development visions. Such is the case in the example of the citizens' association, in which (rarely occurring) arguments about the usefulness and practicability of new ideas are tightly associated with further opportunities for development and implementation.

As this study reveals, it is the development of mutual trust, if nothing else, that is important here. Trust develops more readily and pervasively the greater the similarity between the actors and the sooner they can rely on common reference systems and backgrounds of experience (Müller 2009, 199). In particular, this aspect becomes apparent when groups are still in the process of being constituted and there is thus a struggle for prestigious positions. We assume that a common culture of communication, based on mutual trust, is absolutely necessary in order to integrate those actors who introduce alternative ways of thinking and acting, and who could thus initiate a process of innovation. A trusting communicative environment therefore fosters innovation if it enables equal chances to express new and experimental views on spatial developments. In such a climate, the trust a person enjoys can be transferred to their ideas.

Nevertheless, trust should also be considered in relation to other factors. The innovative potential of a group might also be diminished if the attempt to establish an egalitarian process of exchange and a creative dialogue among all participants does not succeed and the same perspectives dominate in the negotiation of ideas, as the example of the citizens' association illustrates. In such a harmonized milieu, the communicative dynamic, which would potentially be beneficial to the exchange and development of different ideas, often abates (Bender and Hirsch-Kreinsen 2001, 31; González and Vigar 2010, 137).

Regarding the social recognition of an actor, it is also his/her intra-group position that influences whether and how the new ideas that he or she proposes will be further developed. According to Weyer (1997, 135), it is mainly the position of an outsider that promotes thinking beyond established structures and opens up a gateway to new ideas. Our study, by contrast, illustrates the difficulties of peripheral group and network positions as envisaged by Robert Zimmermann in the residents' committee. There, his ideas were marginalized and hardly given attention; this is very different to the citizens' association, where he clearly holds a favored position in the balance of power and where his ideas enjoy particular legitimacy. Such prestigious group positions enable new spatial visions to meet almost unlimited acceptance in the group. Chances for controversial exchange are, however, limited.

As part of process-accompanying research on social innovation, the observation of the communicative negotiation of new, potentially innovative ideas in civil society groups has proven instructive. Heterogeneous knowledge, mutual trust, powerful group positions, and personal innovation ambitions do not per se foster innovation, but are situationally interdependent. This suggests the need for a process-accompanying and real-time perspective on social innovation, with a focus on the communicative genesis of these processes.

Notes

1 The research is based on a project titled "Spatial Pioneers of Urban Quarters: Towards a Communicative (Re-)Construction of Spaces" (2009–2011). This project was carried out at the Leibniz Institute for Research on Society and Space and investigated formerly structurally disadvantaged urban quarters (Berlin-Moabit and Hamburg-Wilhelmsburg) in which actors from the realms of civil society, politics, administration, and/or business had begun pursuing creative solutions to their problems and fostering the development of their community with the help of innovative projects.
2 To preserve anonymity, actual names of actors and places in Berlin-Moabit have been replaced with pseudonyms.
3 The following criteria characterize a central group position: functional competence (e.g. chair, treasurer, workgroup management, etc.), frequent and long communicative contributions, participation in decision-making, and enforcement of personal interests, agenda setting, moderation, and regulation of speech presentations and discussions, social recognition, and broad network contacts.

References

Albino, Vito, Umberto Berardi, and Rosa M. Dangelico. 2015. "Smart Cities: Definitions, Dimensions, Performance, and Initiatives". *Journal of Urban Technology* 22 (1): 3–21.

Amin, Ash, and Nigel J. Thrift. 2002. *Cities: Reimagining the Urban.* Cambridge: Polity Press.

Bender, Gerd, and Hartmut Hirsch-Kreinsen. 2001. "Innovationen in 'transdisziplinären' Technologiefeldern" [Innovations in 'transdisciplinary' technology fields]. In *Kooperationsverbünde und regionale Modernisierung. Theorie und Praxis der Netzwerkarbeit* [Cooperation networks and regional modernization. Theory and practice of networking], edited by Jürgen Howaldt, Ralf Kopp, and Peter Flocken, 29–45. Wiesbaden: Gabler.

Bosworth, Gary, Fulvio Rizzo, Doris Marquardt, Dirk Strijker, Tialda Haartsen, and Annete A. Thuesen. 2016. "Identifying Social Innovations in European Local Rural Development Initiatives". *Innovation: The European Journal of Social Science Research* 29 (4): 442–461.

Bouwen, René, and Chris Steyaert. 1999. "From a Dominant Voice Toward Multivoiced Cooperation: Mediating Metaphors for Global Change". In *Organizational Dimensions of Global Change: No Limits to Cooperation*, edited by David L. Cooperrider and Jane E. Dutton, 291–319. Thousand Oaks, CA: Sage.

Bock, Bettina B. 2012. "Social Innovation and Sustainability: How to Disentangle the Buzzword and its Application in the Field of Agriculture and Rural Development". *Studies in Agricultural Economics* 114 (2): 57–63.

Brown, L. David, and Darcy Ashman. 1999. "Social Capital, Mutual Influence, and Social Learning in Intersectoral Problem Solving in Africa and Asia". In *Organizational Dimensions of Global Change: No Limits to Cooperation*, edited by David L. Cooperrider and Jane E. Dutton, 139–167. Thousand Oaks, CA: Sage.

Castells, Manuel. 1996. *The Rise of the Network Society: The Information Age: Economy, Society and Culture Volume I.* Oxford: Blackwell.

Christmann, Gabriela B., ed. 2016. *Zur kommunikativen Konstruktion von Räumen. Theoretische Konzepte und empirische Analysen* [On the communicative construction of spaces. Theoretical concepts and empirical analyses]. Wiesbaden: Springer VS.

Christmann, Gabriela B. 2022. "The Theoretical Concept of the Communicative (Re) Construction of Spaces". In *Communicative Constructions and the Refiguration of Spaces*, edited by Gabriela Christmann, Hubert Knoblauch, and Martina Löw, 89–112. Abingdon: Routledge.

Christmann, Gabriela B., and Kerstin Büttner. 2011. "Raumpioniere, Raumwissen, Kommunikation. Zum Konzept kommunikativer Raumkonstruktion" [Spatial pioneers, spatial knowledge, communication. On the concept of communicative constructions of space]. *Berichte zur deutschen Länderkunde* 85 (2), 361–378.

Christmann Gabriela B., Hubert Knoblauch, and Martina Löw. 2022. "Introduction. Communicative Constructions and the Refiguration of Spaces". In *Communicative Constructions and the Refiguration of Spaces*, edited by Gabriela Christmann, Hubert Knoblauch, and Martina Löw, 3–15. Abingdon: Routledge.

Christmann, Gabriela B., and Petra Jähnke. 2011. "Soziale Probleme und innovative Ansätze in der Quartiersentwicklung. Beiträge von Social Entrepreneurs und ihren sozialen Netzwerken" [Social problems and innovative approaches in neighborhood development. Contributions from social entrepreneurs and their social networks]. In *Social Entrepreneurship. Perspektiven für die Raumentwicklung* [Social entrepreneurship. Perspectives for spatial development], edited by Petra Jähnke, Gabriela B. Christmann, and Karsten Balgar, 211–234. Wiesbaden: VS Verlag.

Cooke, Philip. 2004. "Introduction: Regional Innovation Systems – an Evolutionary Approach". In *Regional Innovation Systems: The Role of Governance in a Globalized World*, 2nd ed., edited by Philip Cooke, Martin Heidenreich, and Hans-Joachim Braczyk, 1–18. London and New York: Routledge.

Dubiel, Helmut. 1999. "Integration durch Konflikt?" [Integration through conflict?]. *Kölner Zeitschrift für Soziologie und Sozialpsychologie* 39: 132–143.

Florida, Richard. 2002. *The Rise of the Creative Class: And How it's Transforming Work, Leisure, Community and Everyday Life*. New York: Basic Books.

Gillwald, Katrin. 2000. *Konzepte sozialer Innovation* [Concepts of social innovation]. Paper of the Querschnittsgruppe Arbeit und Ökologie, No. P00-519. Berlin: Wissenschaftszentrum Berlin für Sozialforschung.

Gonzaléz, Sara, and Geoff Vigar. 2010. "The Ouseburn Trust in Newcastle: A Struggle to Innovate in the Context of a Weak Local State". In *Can Neighbourhoods Save the City? Community Development and Social Innovation*, edited by Frank Moulaert, Flavia Martinelli, Erik Swyngedouw, and Sara Gonzaléz, 128–140. New York: Routledge.

Howaldt, Jürgen, and Heike Jacobsen. 2010. *Soziale Innovation. Auf dem Weg zu einem post-industriellen Innovationsparadigma* [Social innovation. Toward a post-industrial paradigm for innovation]. Wiesbaden: VS Verlag.

Howaldt, Jürgen, and Michael Schwarz. 2010. *Soziale Innovation im Fokus. Skizze eines gesellschaftstheoretisch inspirierten Forschungskonzepts* [Focus on social innovation. Sketch of a research concept inspired by social theory]. Bielefeld: transcript.

Ibert, Oliver. 2004. "Zu Arbeitsweise und Reichweite innovationsgenerierender Planungsverfahren" [Working methods and scope of innovation-generating planning processes]. *Innovationen und Planung. Reihe Planungsrundschau* 9, 18–43.

Knoblauch, Hubert. 1995. *Kommunikationskultur. Die kommunikative Konstruktion kultureller Kontexte* [Communication culture. The communicative construction of cultural contexts]. Berlin and New York: Walter de Gruyter.

Knoblauch, Hubert. 2001. "Fokussierte Ethnografie. Soziologie, Ethnologie und die neue Welle der Ethnographie" [Focused ethnography. Sociology, ethnology and the new wave of ethnography]. *Sozialer Sinn* 2 (1), 123–141.

Knoblauch, Hubert. 2013. "Grundbegriffe und Aufgaben des kommunikativen Konstruktivismus" [Basic concepts and tasks of communicative constructivism]. In *Kommunikativer Konstruktivismus: Theoretische und empirische Arbeiten zu einem neuen wissenssoziologischen Ansatz* [Communicative constructivism: Theoretical and empirical work on a new sociological approach], edited by Reiner Keller, Hubert Knoblauch, and Jo Reichertz, 25–48. Wiesbaden: Springer VS.

Lange, Bastian, and Ulf Matthiesen. 2005. "Raumpioniere" [Spatial pioneers]. In *Schrumpfende Städte, Band 2: Handlungskonzepte* [Shrinking cities, Volume 2: Concepts of action], edited by Philipp Oswalt, 374–383. Ostfildern-Ruit: Hatje Cantz.

Lindhult, Eric. 2008. "Are Partnerships Innovative?" In *Partnership: As a Strategy for Social Innovation and Sustainable Change*, edited by Lennart Svensson and Barbro Nilsson, 37–54. Stockholm: Satéruns Academic Press.

Martens, Helmut. 2010. "Beteiligung als soziale Innovation" [Participation as social innovation]. In *Scziale Innovation. Auf dem Weg zu einem postindustriellen Innovationsparadigma* [Social innovation. Toward a post-industrial paradigm for innovation], edited by Jürgen Howaldt and Heike Jacobsen, 371–390. Wiesbaden: VS Verlag.

Matthiesen, Ulf. 2005. "Raumpioniere. Ein Gespräch mit dem Stadt- und Regionalforscher Ulf Matthiesen" [Spatial pioneers. A conversation with the urban and regional researcher Ulf Matthiesen]. In *Schrumpfende Städte, Band 2: Handlungskonzepte* [Shrinking cities, Volume 2: Concepts of action], edited by Philipp Oswalt, 378–383. Ostfildern-Ruit: Hatje Cantz.

Moulaert, Frank, and Farikd Sekia. 2003. "Territorial Innovation Models: A Critical Survey". *Regional Studies* 37 (3): 289–302.

Moulaert, Frank, Diana MacCallum, Abid Mehmood, and Abdelillah Hamdouch. 2013. *The International Handbook on Social Innovation: Collective Action, Social Learning and Transdisciplinary Research*. Cheltenham: Edward Elgar.

Moulaert, Frank, Erik Swyngedouw, Flavia Martinelli, and Sara Gonzalez. 2010. *Can Neighbourhoods Save the City? Community Development and Social Innovation*. New York: Routledge.

Mulgan, Geoff, and Louise Pulford. 2010. *Study on Social Innovation*. European Union/ The Young Foundation. http://youngfoundation.org/wp-content/uploads/2012/10/Study-on-Social-Innovation-for-the-Bureau-of-European-PolicyAdvisors-March-2010.pdf

Müller, Jeanette Hedwig. 2009. *Vertrauen und Kreativität. Zur Bedeutung von Vertrauen für diversive AkteurInnen in Innovationsnetzwerken* [Trust and creativity. The importance of trust for diverse actors in innovation networks]. Frankfurt am Main: Peter Lang.

Mumford, Michael D. 2002. "Social Innovation: Ten Cases from Benjamin Franklin". *Creativity Research Journal* 14 (2): 253–266.

Neuloh, Otto. 1977. *Soziale Innovation und sozialer Konflikt*. Göttingen: Vandenhoeck & Ruprecht.

Neumeier, Stefan. 2012. "Why Do Social Innovations in Rural Development Matter and Should they Be Considered More Seriously in Rural Development Research? Proposal for a Stronger Focus on Social Innovations in Rural Development Research". *Sociologia Ruralis* 52 (1): 48–69.

Noack, Anika. 2015. *Soziale Innovationen in Berlin-Moabit. Zur kommunikativen Aushandlung von Neuem durch Raumpioniere im städtischen Kontext* [Social innovations in Berlin-Moabit. On the communicative negotiation of new things by spatial pioneers in an urban context]. Wiesbaden: Springer VS.

Noack, Anika. 2017. "Elderly People in Rural Regions as Promoters of Social Innovations and Changing Knowledge". In *Proceedings of the XXVII Congress. Uneven processes of Rural Change: On Diversity, Knowledge and Justice*, edited by Kristina Svels, 118–119. Kraków, Poland: Institute of Sociology, Jagiellonian University in Krakow.

Noack, Anika, and Tobias Federwisch. 2018. "Social Innovation in Rural Regions: Urban Impulses and Cross-Border Constellations of Actors". *Sociologia Ruralis* 59 (1): 92–112.

Rammert, Werner. 2013. *Vielfalt der Innovation und gesellschaftlicher Zusammenhalt. Von der ökonomischen zur gesellschaftstheoretischen Perspektive* [Diversity of innovation and social cohesion. From the economic to the socio-theoretical perspective]. Technical University Technology Studies Working Paper, WP-1. Berlin: Technische Universität Berlin.

Sassen, Saskia. 1991. *The Global City: New York, London, Tokyo*. Princeton, NJ: Princeton University Press.

Schröer, Norbert. 1997. "Wissenssoziologische Hermeneutik" [A sociology of knowledge approach to hermeneutics]. In *Sozialwissenschaftliche Hermeneutik. Eine Einführung* [Social-science-based hermeneutics. An introduction], edited by Ronald Hitzler and Anne Honer, 109–129. Opladen: Leske + Budrich.

Schumpeter, Joseph A. 1964. *Theorie der wirtschaftlichen Entwicklung* [Theory of economic development]. Berlin: Duncker & Humblot.

Schwarz, Michael, Martin Birke, and Emanuel Beerheide. 2010. "Die Bedeutung sozialer Innovationen für eine nachhaltige Entwicklung" [The importance of social innovations for sustainable development]. In *Soziale Innovation. Auf dem Weg zu einem postindustriellen Innovationsparadigma* [Social innovation. Toward a post-industrial paradigm for innovation], edited by Jürgen Howaldt and Heike Jacobsen, 165–180. Wiesbaden: VS Verlag.

Soja, Edward, and Miguel Kanai. 2010. "The Urbanization of the World". In *The Endless City*, edited by Ricky Burdett and Deyan Sudjic, 54–69. London: Phaidon Press.

Sperber, Michael, Anja Moritz, and Anna-Maria Hetze. 2007. "Bürgerbeteiligung und Innovation. Integrierte Partizipations- und Innovationsansätze in peripheren Räumen" [Citizen participation. Integrative participation and innovation approaches in peripheral areas]. *Berliner Debatte Initial* 18 (2): 85–97.

Weyer, Johannes. 1997. "Vernetzte Innovationen – innovative Netzwerke. Airbus, Personal Computer, Transrapid" [Networked innovations – innovative networks. Airbus, Personal Computer, Transrapid]. In *Technik und Gesellschaft. Jahrbuch 9* [Technology and society. Yearbook 9], edited by Werner Rammert and Gotthard Bechmann, 125–152. Frankfurt am Main and New York: Campus.

Zapf, Wolfgang. 1989. "Über soziale Innovationen" [On social innovations]. *Soziale Welt* 40 (1): 170–183.

13 Talking about hip places
Imaginaries and power among East German reinventions of urban culture

Hans-Joachim Bürkner

Introduction

Not long ago, East German urban development was envisaged as an issue of belated modernization. The urban future seemed to be a matter of predestined pathways of development, political models and planning cultures having been taken over from West Germany after the dismantling of the Berlin Wall in 1990 (Huning et al. 2010, 10). The long-lasting economic crisis of the 1990s and population loss of the early 2000s, though, entailed subdued expectations (Hannemann 2003, 22). Urban shrinkage and the prospect of further decline prompted East German cities to assess their capacities and potential for development anew. The results were novel urban projects which drew on visions of downsizing the built environment while stimulating the city's vitality (e.g. Stadtumbau-Ost; see Bernt 2009; Wiechmann and Pallagst 2012; Radzimski 2016; Haase et al. 2016), a gradual adaptation of global trends of sociocultural urban modernization (such as the Creative City, Lange, Burdack, and Herfert 2006), and a stronger political orientation toward neoliberal "fitness for competition" (Bartholomae, Nam, and Schoenberg 2017).

Pursuing a neighborhood development project named Schiffbauergasse, the city of Potsdam took up the fashionable quest for innovation and creativity in favor of interurban competitiveness at the start of the new millennium. According to the conceptual design, the local culture and economy were to develop new linkages. An inner-city brownfield site, which had been used informally by various civil society actors on a temporary basis, was chosen to provide the physical stage. The project's Internet home page described the underlying philosophy as follows: "Over 25 acres of land located directly at the waterfront, creativity gets pooled: A vivid arts-and-culture scene meets hi-tech firms, thrilling history meets the trendsetting future."[1] The idea was to create an interesting, attractive place near the refurbished historical city center by means of an ingenious planning design. This was a place meant to stimulate the revival of a post-socialist city that locals traditionally regarded as lacking profile when compared to the neighboring capital Berlin (cf. Saupe 2009).

Against the backdrop of the particular challenge of creating a "designer place" from virtual ruins, the planning process had to bring together various

DOI: 10.4324/9780367817183-16

stakeholders who had not previously been associated. Subsumed under the label of "Schiffbauergasse", they had to establish affiliations anew – "anew" because there had been prior occasional land uses established by stakeholders who were already acquainted by sight. These actors required integrating into the new development concept. Back in the 1990s, the area had been appropriated by underground artists and small businesses, who shaped the brownfield site according to their own needs. Having initiated a controversy between top-down political place-making and bottom-up practices of sociocultural appropriation, the new project revealed hidden power differentials among heterogeneous stakeholders. These differentials found their expression in a number of communication dilemmas in the arena of urban development planning.

It was exactly here, situated on a beautiful spot within the urban landscape, that a communicational field of tension developed. It revealed several basic contradictions between the planned definition and the spontaneous social construction of urban places. The concern of this chapter is to explore these contradictions in detail. It will present the ideas and imaginaries as developed by the actors involved, in particular their ideas about the qualities and the appropriate usage of the site. It will also discuss the ways in which these actors launched their ideas and imaginaries into public discourse. The leading question is: Who would assert which kind of imaginary, under which contextual conditions, and by which usage of power resources?

The following stances will encompass repeated changes of perspective, between empirical case description and theoretical reflection, in order to gain substantiated knowledge about the generation, the context dependency, and the staging of the social construction of places. Questions raised by initial descriptions of the local case will be more precisely defined after having discussed research findings drawn from relevant literature. Answers will then be given by interpreting the results of my own qualitative interviews with stakeholders involved in the project. In particular, a critical focus will be laid on the relationship between place-oriented imaginaries and the usage of various power resources.

The Schiffbauergasse development project: Urban governance within a heterogeneous constellation of stakeholders, developed against the backdrop of post-socialist transformation

The industrial brownfield site antedating the Schiffbauergasse project seemed to share its destiny of neglect with many similar post-socialist brownfield zones. Situated between the historical inner city and the history-charged Bridge of Glienicke,[2] the compact area had been unknown to a larger public before 1990. Around 1990, remnants of Prussian hussar garrison buildings with stables and riding halls, a chicory mill[3] dating from the 18th century, a large laundry from German Democratic Republic (GDP) times run in historic industrial buildings, an abandoned gasometer, a coke separator, and a small boat bridge made up the initial physical structure of the location. After German unification, the area was located (literally) in the slipstream of urban development trends. These trends involved the inner city nearby, the historic Sanssouci Park, the University of Potsdam, and the locations of major research institutions (see Viehrig 2002).

The 1990s saw a long period of exclusively subcultural land usage, mainly by "alternative" artists and creative industries that were part of Potsdam's grassroots culture. At first, single vacant buildings were put to use by dance performers, theater artists, and concert organizers. Open-air events performed on mobile stages, mainly pop and rock concerts, contributed to the location's good reputation among subcultural consumer scenes. The informal usage of the brownfield site was initially tolerated, and eventually supported, by the city council. In particular, the city administration provided for the basic technical infrastructure. The formerly provisional facilities were converted to permanent rehearsal and performance venues. By the end of the 1990s, Potsdam city council and the state of Brandenburg drafted a joint development concept that aimed to bring together alternative artists, well-established cultural institutions, and ambitious commercial enterprises. The atmosphere of a location where heterogeneous activities could cross-fertilize, combined with the aesthetic charm of the historic site on the banks of the Havel river, was supposed to symbolically represent the new urbanity of post-socialism. At least part of this locational philosophy was realized by the establishment of external branches of two big global players (a Volkswagen Design Center and an offshoot of the transnational software enterprise Oracle) and the new construction of the municipal Hans Otto theater close to the riverbanks. The city administration, having developed the locational concept in negotiation with local artists and entrepreneurs, introduced a location manager to ensure further coordination of activities on the site. An operating company was founded that was supposed to develop a marketing concept around the brand name "Schiffbauergasse" (meaning "shipbuilders' row"), yet which hardly progressed beyond launching an Internet homepage and advertising individual cultural events.

At first glance, the formula of "attractive mixtures" seemed to be plausible because some locational attributes could be found that fitted the picture. The text of the home page revealed attempts at making extraordinary connections visible – between diverse sociocultures and lifestyles, between the renovated historic structure of the place (the aforementioned hussar barracks and stables designed by the 19th-century neoclassicist architect Otto Schinkel, a laundry house from the late 19th century, etc.) and contrasting modern architecture (the new futuristic theater building resembling Sydney Opera House, the new postmodern Volkswagen Design Center, a multistory car park). The formula of "mixture of culture and commerce" does not render itself immediately intelligible, however. Rather than accentuating existing place attributes, it reveals itself as the product of free imagination for the benefit of maximum advertising appeal. Quite obviously it reflects contemporary political trends that instrumentalize creativity and culture to improve the competitiveness of cities at a global scale (see Florida 2004; Landry 2008). In this specific case, the basic idea had been derived from external urban development concepts envisaged by the local administration and the city council as apt models. According to the location manager (Interview I10P[4]), the economically successful Viennese cultural area dubbed MuseumsQuartier (MQ)[5] provided a number of important inspirations. Important creative ideas were also derived from Anglo-American concepts of urban waterfront redevelopment (Gordon 1997). Single elements of these concepts were taken over in a copy-and-paste manner, supposing that successful models should be implementable in the local home context without further ado. The success of implementation would only be a matter of the skillful introduction of the concept into local public discourse.

Here, however, a number of unexpected obstacles arose. These were created by local political understanding of good practice in urban planning. In Potsdam, prestigious urban projects of the 1990s and 2000s had mainly been guided by traditional, hierarchically organized planning routines – in spite of the fact that there had been an increasing number of controversial discussions about open concepts of communicative planning and about the need to raise the level of participation of local stakeholders (e.g. in the course of regional conferences; see Land Brandenburg 2010). This is all the more astonishing given that other areas of policymaking and planning, such as urban neighborhood management, had already created some public appreciation of collaborative communication and local participation (cf. Feldmann 2002). Like many other local planning projects of that time, the Schiffbauergasse project seemed to be less ambitious in this respect. The local administration installed the planning concept at its own will, and it autonomously supervised the activities of a newly created redevelopment agency. It also controlled the individual construction works.

Despite the top-down pre-conceptualization of the development process, the course of implementation was all but straightforward. Although the location manager intended to create a coherent governance structure, it could hardly be realized. Instead, the administration was confronted by an informal counter concept. The stakeholders from local culture, economy, and planning developed compartmentalized, fragmented relations of communication and reference building. The most intense network building could be observed among long-time resident organizations of the grassroots scene. Early on, these stakeholders developed a high degree of self-organized activity. They established an initial land use pattern and a very particular sociocultural definition of the place. They acted as urban pioneers; that is, as stakeholders who put their imprint on a specific part of urban space while informally appropriating it (cf. Lange and Matthiesen 2005). Through the past 20 years, urban pioneering has been a common phenomenon in the region of Berlin-Brandenburg, encompassing manifold variations of grassroots culture, creative industries, and interim use of urban brownfield areas (Bergmann 2011; Overmeyer and Renker 2005). The Schiffbauergasse stakeholders were able to strongly mold the character and the medial representations of the location by means of regular recitals, festivals, workshops, and exhibitions. From the beginning of the millennium onwards, their relative autonomy has been guaranteed by periodic public funding, private sponsorship, and returns from events and services. They have hence gained an independent status in realizing their projects and activities. A striking indicator of their autonomy is the fact that they have not been considered targets of counseling activities normally offered by state agencies trying to support cultural self-organization at the local level. Two major agencies of this kind (the state committee Socio-Culture Brandenburg[6] and the regional start-up initiative Innopunkt[7]) had settled at the Schiffbauergasse and yet did not declare the local stakeholders relevant to their activities.

While the spontaneous networking activities of creative stakeholders contributed to a local "movement from below", private business did not develop according to the expectations of the initiators of the development concept. Apart from the offshoots of the two multinational corporations at the site, a few small restaurants and service firms were established. Hardly any private enterprise became visible among local network agents. The managers focused on their economic activities and only occasionally developed relationships with other stakeholders in the cultural sector. Their communicative activities were restricted to singular contributions to joint initiatives aimed at improving the external image of the location. All in all, it was nearly impossible to integrate business firms – especially the global players – into already existing local networks.

As a consequence, the location became molded by the first-time creative artists. Galleries and a private museum of modern performance art that were established later did not go beyond adapting to the preexisting constellation of stakeholders. Because of their strong orientation toward national and international audiences, these organizations did not consider it their primary task to assimilate to the local social context. The "alternative" milieu thus represented an undisputed yet heterogeneous local power base. Despite low levels of formal participation in project-related decision taking, they actually were able to informally and sustainably influence the design of the location in their favor. The fact alone that they regularly organized large-scale events, thereby achieving wide public recognition, ensured them an advantage in reputation building and in accumulating interactive negotiation power. By directly interacting with other on-site stakeholders, they were able to temporarily gain opinion leadership and agenda-setting capacities in public discourse.

Given these antecedent developments, the constellation of stakeholders early on had been structurally fragmented and characterized by heterogeneous interests (top-down vs. bottom-up). Views on the concrete location and the expectations for its shaping strongly diverged. The meaning of the place seemed to be defined by each stakeholder or group of agents from a specific personal perspective. As will become apparent, the chance of being able to develop a common understanding of the place was strongly influenced by the individual development interests, the public visibility of these interests, and the individual willingness to negotiate an agreement of interests; those specifically connected with a "strategic" place design and the governance of the place were, however, only seldom discussed openly.

Unsettled conditions: Place-based imaginaries and power

A cursory glance already makes apparent that empirical analysis must pay particular attention to the specific clashes of interest and development ideas as well as to the power relations expressed by them. The task consists in understanding how the definition, the arranging, and the social "handling" of place are part of the establishment of political and everyday projects. These projects generally are informed by the validity claims of competing and contested logics of social change. Particular validity claims can be regarded as being tied to various forms of generating, executing, and protecting power.

The notion of power, as it is used here, follows Bourdieu's concept in stressing the capacity of persons and groups to prompt other agents to act and feel in their favor. This capacity can be generated by direct social interaction, social positioning, and structural stabilization of positions (Bourdieu 1984). Power relations are understood as the outcome of the differential access of individuals and groups to economic, cultural, and social capital, and the social practices based on such access. Differing degrees of access arise from the roles taken by individuals in various economic and political fields of action and from the social positionings associated with them. Once material (economic) capital has been generated, it can be protected either by means of habitus or by means of symbolic power. Symbolic power results from the striving of dominant groups (e.g. educational elites) to legitimize and enforce other forms of power and social meaning (Bourdieu 1990). This aspect of power which is based on the agent's access to power resources will be named "structural power" in the following. Since the positions of agents change according to their utilization of economic, social, and cultural capital, it is not only structurally rooted power which influences their actions. It is also interactive moments of the generation of power that become established because of the interdependence of structure and agency. Power therefore emerges within reflexive connections of social interactions, the building of social positions (via habitualization and institutionalization of action), and the structural consolidation of these positions in the context of differentiated logics of the distribution of capital (Bourdieu 1984).

Variations of power generated by interaction are usually dependent on context; they are hence of a temporary nature. They are acquired by way of direct social communication (e.g. in specific negotiations aiming at balances of interests) or by means of establishing opinion leadership, social assessments, judgements of taste, or postulations for conformity. In contrast to Bourdieu, these variations are here termed "interactional power" in order to achieve a clear distinction from the notion of structural power. Included in its definition is the assumption that within a communication context, habitus (in terms of body language, externalized emotions, and symbolic gestures) generally becomes utilized for the purpose of generating and stabilizing power. Structural power and interactional power are not understood as an opposition, but rather as poles of a continuum containing variable institutionalizations and objectifications of social action.

These definitions, which relate to ongoing social practice as well as to persisting social structures, are compatible with theoretical concepts of political power building. It can be assumed that holders of formal-institutional power (e.g. of the power to decide as guaranteed by the state) are also equipped with larger amounts of accumulated capital and higher social positions.[8] It is likely, moreover, that these agents strongly contribute to the reproduction of structural power. For example, communal quasi-state organizations and their representatives used to be equipped with judicially guaranteed powers of decision-making; frequently they are independent enough to decide how and to whom they delegate this power. Additionally, they have the opportunity to exert definitional power concerning focal concepts, notions, and topics – mainly by way of formally institutionalizing planning procedures and development projects.[9] In many cases, a kind of "localized state-moderated governance" comes about, which strategically, and with regard to the governance of local discourse (agenda setting), becomes streamlined to the needs of local administrations (Fürst, Lahner, and Zimmermann 2005, 233).

Not least for the purpose of reducing uncertainty in the face of the outcomes of open negotiations, politicians and planners attempt to exert direct control of projects and, among other things, preestablish local development concepts. In anticipation of subsequent governance processes, relevant ideas and concepts are rapidly institutionalized and structurally entrenched; for example, in the context of formal measures of urban redevelopment and regeneration, where new stable urban regimes are often established (Franz 2007, 40). Those place-bound aims and procedures which appear most interesting or attractive to these stakeholders – and therefore worthy of funding – might turn out to be overly fixed because of decisions made previously. They might not even be put on the agenda of follow-up negotiation and governance.

In order for analysis to capture the mindscapes related to the recourse of stakeholders on various resources and compositions of power, it is helpful to include the concept of imaginaries. The term "imaginary" was coined during debates in the English-speaking sphere about the theoretical foundations of post-structural political economy (Larner and Le Heron 2002; Le Heron 2006; Jessop and Oosterlynck 2008; Wetzstein and Le Heron 2010). The concept has been much promoted by economic geographers in Australia and New Zealand. The basic idea is that political and economic processes are fundamentally nondeterministic and open-ended; that is, they include high amounts of contingency. They are influenced by institutional context, socioeconomic disparities, and political projects. For their practical elaboration, imaginaries have a particular significance. Imaginaries are understood as context-specific imaginations and ideas which are attached to coherent intellectual projects and strategic concepts (Wetzstein and Le Heron 2010). Within specific contexts and arenas of action, imaginaries of varying origin, key stakeholders, and resources may be combined into political projects (Wetzstein and Le Heron 2010). Economic, political, and spatial imaginaries are often derived from overarching ideologies and worldviews; for example, from neoliberalism, utilitarianism, or pragmatism. They are therefore basically contested or thrown into competition with other imaginaries. By continual processes of interpretation and reconsideration, as they normally occur in a particular discourse, imaginaries undergo changes which in turn have effects on running negotiations, conflicts, governance processes, etc.

In the context of the social construction of places, it can be assumed that such strategically designed arrangements of ideas and imaginaries acquire specific meanings. Definitions of place might represent pointed understandings and biased assessments based on abstractions and general ideas. They might be conceived dependent on contexts, interests, and possibilities to act – according to the logic which has been supplied by the imaginary dominant in that specific context.[10] In the course of defining place, stakeholders prefer to refer to supposedly "hard" realities (e.g. historical developments, traditions), which, however, are part of imaginaries themselves. Therefore imaginaries must be analytically reconstructed with special care, minding their context specificity and strategic significance. The selective references made, their mutual closeness or distance, their interference, and multidimensional impact must be preferred subjects of space-related analysis.

Imaginaries allow for interest-bound ideational arrangements, the implementation of political ideologies, and related configurations of social fields and spaces (Jessop 2012; for the shaping of space according to neoliberal policies, see Boudreau 2007). However, to date their part in urban development and local governance has only roughly been explored; basic empirical studies focus mainly on Asian or Australasian cities (e.g. Wetzstein 2013; see also the overview in Watkins 2015). Urbanist visions and strategic development plans often seem to match the understanding of imaginaries explicated above, but closer inspection reveals a low intensity of open interaction and the prevalence of formal procedures; for example, in the fields of strategic planning (Albrechts 2004) or urban regeneration (see Mah 2012 on "official urban imaginaries" and planned urban futures). Urban scholars therefore have found it difficult to analytically reconstruct the social dynamics connected to policymaking and planning. In-depth ethnographic research is therefore an important point of departure when it comes to detecting the social construction and political/strategic utilization of places, including their ideational origins. A small contribution will be made in the following in connection with an empirical exploration of ideas of development found among the stakeholders of the Schiffbauergasse project. The analysis will focus on the encounter of power-imbued, contradictory, and even antagonistic interests as well as the nature of the imaginaries involved and their context-bound changes.

Place-related imaginaries within a context of antagonistically pre-structured fragments of communication: Empirical findings

Methodology

The empirical materials used for the analysis of place definitions and imaginaries were collected in the summer of 2007 by interviewing local stakeholders of the Schiffbauergasse project. A textual body of 13 transcribed semi-structured qualitative interviews was supplemented by records of participating observations of two stakeholder meetings in the spring of 2010. These meetings had been organized by a private counseling agency which worked at creating a new functional utilization concept for the location.

Interview sampling aimed at representing the most important stakeholder groups at the location. The sample consists of founding members of cultural initiatives and artist groups, managers of private enterprises, and executives of administrative organizations. The individual groups of stakeholders comprise: (i) Creative artists (interviews I01K–I05K), (ii) private enterprises (I06U–I09U), (iii) the city administration (I10P–I11P), and (iv) intermediary organizations (I12I–I13I). The creative artists break down into exponents of the local "alternative" (grassroots) culture that had already acted as urban pioneers back in the 1990s (I01K–I03K) and into exponents of the local "received" culture who appeared at the beginning of the millennium (I04K–I05K). The latter have since engaged on the site in traditional cultural production (theater), in the setup of galleries, and in establishing a museum of modern art. The group of enterprises is represented by interviewees from the two branches of multinational corporations (Oracle and Volkswagen Design Center; I06U–I07U) and small firms or tradesmen (restaurants, boat rental service; I08U–I09U). The intermediaries are leading members of private associations which had been founded in the context of state-funded projects for the promotion of regional socioculture and of regional start-ups.

The analysis of the interviews has been inspired by the epistemological attitude and the methodical recommendations given by exponents of the grounded theory approach (Glaser and Strauss 1967). The technique of open coding has been applied (Strübing 2008), followed by the condensation and generalization of central parts of the text that were indicative of potentially substantial theoretical statements. Although the explication of original statements was in the foreground of analysis, aiming at fully accounting for the variety and shades of meaning, the generalized statements are prioritized here, mainly for reasons of clarity and comprehensibility. The complexity of individual imaginations, attributed meaning, and place definitions is larger than it might appear from the inevitably reductive presentation.

Definitions of place and imaginaries

The definitions of place verbalized during the interviews clearly indicate the similarity of imaginaries which were used by each stakeholder group. Among the members of the individual groups, the ascription of features to the specific place of Schiffbauergasse is generally homogeneous. In contrast, there is tremendous difference between the stakeholder groups as a whole. It appears that imaginaries and professional interests are related to one another. In the following, the definitions of place will be juxtaposed to each other according to their basic orientation. Moreover, based on the assumption that imaginaries and group interests tend to correlate, the definitions of place will be put in

Talking about hip places 255

perspective with regard to the stakeholder interests related to the specific activity on the site.

Group #1 – creative artists

Among the creative artists, the definitions of place are divided according to their professional interests and their biographical connectedness to the Schiffbauergasse. Within this dualism, however, the stakeholders had developed similar orientations.

Both proponents of the **alternative culture** understand themselves as grassroots pioneers during the period of change in the political system in the 1990s. They describe the place by pointing at the visible reminders and symbols of the early post-socialist phase of urban pioneering. The charm of the place which they then appropriated in cultural and social terms consisted of its state of neglect, its free malleability, and its openness to future options. The remote location of the brownfield area had been particularly favorable because it allowed for tranquility and undisrupted work (I01K). The place had retained its distinct atmosphere, with the social and physical "afterglow" of the socialist past still being felt there (I02K). Both speakers point out that the particular character of the place is currently endangered by physical redevelopment and valorization (I01K, I02K). They are afraid that that everything might become "too slick" (I01K) and therefore come to appear lifeless (I02K).

Imaginary: The description of the place reveals that it originated directly from social and professional practice in early post-socialist times. These stakeholders have a collective self-conception which encompasses emphatic feelings toward the East German civil rights movement of those days. They express their pride at having developed autonomous ways of living and working, and at having gathered the necessary material and spatial resources (urban brownfield) without any outside help. This perspective is part of a collective self-understanding which had been developed against the authoritarian societal model of socialism, as well as against the practice of cultural expropriation exerted by the new capitalism "geared by the West".[11]

This imaginary includes relevant forms of sociality and communication. The stakeholders have mostly known each other since the early days of the "appropriation of the place". They have been interconnected by a small, tightly knit network, at times in a very intense manner. Although they express great interest in future open-ended developments, they trenchantly distance themselves from those agents who do not appreciate their pioneer status and their accrued informal claim on the further design of the place. They consider the Schiffbauergasse "their" place, closely tied to their biographies and to the unfolding of the alternative scene of the 1990s. Yet because of more and more stakeholders coming in, and because of recent physical redevelopment, they are afraid of "losing control" of the place (I01K). At the same time they complain about lacking influence on the municipal planning procedures. While the municipality had organized several panels involving all stakeholders, it repeatedly created accomplished facts over their heads; for example, by constructing a large multistory car park in the middle of the area without consulting the neighbors on the site. This obviously contradicted the creative artists' interest in maintaining a convertible, continually redesignable space (I01K).

The perspective later developed by representatives of **high culture** (theater, museums) is structured in a more balanced way, including irony and reserve. The speakers are reluctant to refer to their own biographies, although they have been personally involved in local urban life, at least in one case. Moreover, the communal feeling characteristic of the "alternative" stakeholders is not expressed here. Instead, emphasis is laid on the comment that the Schiffbauergasse is a multifaceted, "beautiful" place (I03K, I04K); moreover, its history would be immediately noticeable. Since it represented a part of "Eastern history", there might however be the risk of it becoming nostalgically transfigured by local stakeholders (including, among others, the "alternative stakeholders") (I04K). Moreover, it would not really turn into a place that appeals to everyone, at least not to the extent that would be generally desirable. Apart from cultural events, there would be hardly any leisure offerings at the location. Except for the target groups for these events, the place would not appear attractive to many.

The interviewees appreciate the Schiffbauergasse as a distinguished place for the presentation of contemporary arts. They clearly consider it a counterweight to the historic city of Potsdam (e.g. the Prussian architectural heritage and Sanssouci) (I03K, I04K, I05K). However, to date it had not been possible to make sparks fly with the diversity of spatial traits and interests present. For example, the connection of diverse architectural elements and cultural mixtures would constitute a high potential for ironic confrontations and discussions about Prussian history. "Rock the Fritz" or "Prussian rectangle mania vs. freaky counterculture" might potentially be implemented as mottos or topics of events, exhibitions, artistic installations, etc. (I03K).

Imaginary: The life-world distance between these stakeholders and the subcultural "pioneers" mirrors the detached assessment of the place. The actors vigorously strive to gain an "objective" stance. From this endeavor, two mutually self-reinforcing tendencies toward socially reconstructing the place arise. On the one hand, the place itself becomes assimilated into a bourgeois scheme of evaluation ("historical value"). Here, it undergoes a procedure of aestheticization. The dominant interpretation involves the assumption that the picturesque contrast between tradition and modernity per se might substantiate public recognition and attractiveness. On the other hand, the element of essential inconsistency is elevated to a general design principle with regard to cultural events, offers made by artists, etc. Parallel to this essentialist understanding – almost as part of an argument by analogy – the place appears to be a suitable projection surface for contradictory aesthetic principles. It is important for these stakeholders to artistically and intellectually make use of this particular opportunity according to the postmodern logic "not only … but also …". The aesthetic contradiction of experiencing high and alternative culture at the same location is highlighted during the interviews several times. The opportunity of visiting the bourgeois

Hans Otto Theater in the evening and subsequently spending the night at a techno party at the "Waschhaus" venue is esteemed a unique and appealing combination of offers.

Regarding diction and verbalized normative claims, the statements resemble the advertisements and sales-oriented descriptions developed by location marketing. In fact, they can be traced at the Internet home page of the Schiffbauergasse e.V., an association founded by the municipal developers of the area. The imaginary addressed by the interviewees follows their neoliberal logic of utilization of urban space.[12] From this perspective, attractiveness emerges from unique combinations of individual offers targeted at specific customer groups on cultural and events markets characterized by severe competition. A direct view of the location based on perceptions and reflections about particular social practices of on-site actors cannot be reconstructed from their statements. Instead, the place is imagined from a general marketing interest, expressed, among other ways, by the objective of creating intellectual and aesthetic pleasure. In this respect, it appears to be vaguely related to a postmodern, hedonistic, middle-class perspective: The perceived elements of space are transformed into suppliers of keywords, into citable samples, and at the same time into projection screens of the production of cultural artefacts. The obvious conformity of this imaginary with a "public" design mission of similar orientation (i.e. the project philosophy aiming to increase attractiveness by means of emphasizing aesthetic paradoxes) was not verbalized by the speakers. Whether they are conscious of this homology remains an open question.

Group #2 – entrepreneurs

When compared to the committed descriptions given by creative artists, the statements made by **private entrepreneurs** seem bland and rarely differentiated. This is particularly true for the representatives of the global players who created touch-down spots at the Schiffbauergasse. The employees of these corporations had not participated in decision-making for the location; those decisions had been taken in headquarters far away. The decision takers preferred the Schiffbauergasse mainly because of its appealing architectural features and the beautiful landscape surrounding it. The ambience was thought remarkable owing to the placement of the company buildings at the charming waterfront; this was expected to guarantee undisturbed creative work. Moreover, employees would appreciate the "symbiosis of rural remoteness and big-city life" in Potsdam (I07K). The large companies did not engage in the several discussion rounds for locational place-making, just as they had not done regarding other local networks – this would not have been consistent with their organizational message. Rather, they sought to make sure that necessary professional tasks could be achieved without external disturbances.

Imaginary: Similar to the definition of the place, its strategic handling is made up in a strictly instrumental way. Both aim to emphasize aesthetic pleasure (the atmosphere at the waterfront of the Havel river, the historical architecture, the view of the urban silhouette, and the surrounding natural landscape), a supportive environment, or decorative elements of economic activities. These are meant to generate added value regarding the motivation and creativity of designers and other employees. The emotional dissociation from the location as well as from social life outside the enterprise is a precondition for this instrumentalization. At the same time, it expresses an attitude of power by which the global players economically furnish their local branches. Part of this attitude is the habit of ignoring those people who are related to the place as social beings, in case their emotions and needs do not serve an economic purpose. From a similar economic standpoint, local municipalities and their representatives are treated as largely irrelevant players. Attention would be paid to them at best in the context of economic decisions (in this case, concrete locational decisions).

The ***resident small-sized enterprises*** produce definitions of place that are less aloof. They nevertheless distinguish themselves through austere pragmatism. From their perspective, the Schiffbauergasse mainly represents a functional site designed for recreation, its features being determined by its very location at the waterside (I08U, I09U). Despite having been declared a place of recreation, it in fact lacked something of the quality of an open-air dwelling. Missing open spaces, walkways, benches, and so forth, would prevent visitors from passing time here except to attend specific events. Moreover, the references to history (e.g. a period of local shipbuilding in the 19th century) and to mainstream culture would be very weak and thus unable to leave an imprint on the place. References would have to be constructed repeatedly in a very artificial manner. The entrepreneurs lament the ragbag of different users and the mostly incompatible types of usage. This would often produce substantial conflict among the actors involved (I09U).

Imaginary: The pragmatism of these stakeholders is part of their economic role as service providers exposed to strong fluctuations of demand. A location which is meant to guarantee sufficient demand on the basis of its attractiveness must display reliable and calculable properties. Against the neoliberal imaginary of globally induced, flexible market conformity, the small entrepreneurs set up the idea of invariable relations between supply and demand. By doing so, they address another imaginary, one that is more related to First Modernity and the stable functional relationships it provided for producers/suppliers and customers. The emerging question of economic survival at a specific location is answered by them in a conservative manner. Because of its seemingly weak facilities and its uncertain potential, the place appears too unpredictable for them. They would prefer a solid, well-presented physical and functional design aiming to guarantee rising numbers of visitors, instead of promoting alternating, colorful sociocultural scenes. This preference is obvious, since the entrepreneurs lack a direct life-world-based link to the evolving milieus and networks (such as in the manner of urban pioneers observable after the German unification). The absence of network relations with this group, but also with other stakeholders at the location, is mirrored by the entrepreneurs' perception that they would not share any interests with other actors.

Group #3 – political planning organizations

The representatives of **political and planning organizations** are not so much concerned about the quality of the place and the meaning attached to it. Instead they adopt the perspective of urban managers, arguing in a normative way and with a focus on actual design options. According to the location manager, it would be most important to do something about the lacking public recognition of the historical significance of the location. Over centuries, the Schiffbauergasse had been a "non-place" located in the slipstream of the city, sometimes even a "landscape of horrors", or up to 1990 also a "prohibited place" within the restricted area of the East–West German border (I10P). Yet repeatedly it had also been a place where historical innovations arose; for example, where the first steamboats in northeast Germany had been produced in the early 19th century by the British entrepreneur John Barnett. Now it would be possible to turn this "non-place" into a social place of experience.

A central officeholder of the local municipality has a perspective on the place that does not primarily involve the issue of history. In her opinion, the more important trait is the contrast between a varied architecture and the natural aesthetic quality of the waterside. She also emphasizes that the Schiffbauergasse had been a gloomy, closed-off place, unable to lend itself an air of familiarity to Potsdam residents. However, its character had already been decisively reshaped by recent uses. As a freshly created "artistic space", it had become outspokenly attractive; in particular, it drew its charm from the encounter of various lifestyles (I11P). An important task of the day would be to establish apt physical conditions and infrastructure. The speaker displays a normatively inspired pragmatism, yet more clearly subordinates the issue of locational design and resulting necessities to the municipal task of urban planning, thereby claiming for the development of sustainable usage concepts.

Imaginary: Neoliberal urban policies and the felt necessity to support urban competition and the generation of attention for cities and its neighborhoods (Mattissek 2008) serve as important framing conditions for the self-positioning of the two last-mentioned stakeholders. They therefore choose a normative language to ascribe meaning to concrete places. The general assumption is that currently visible place qualities might still offer too few incentives to develop sustainable stakeholder activities. Hence the official place concept would constantly run the risk of failure. Their practice of digging for historical treasures and cultural peculiarities in order to transform them into assets of city marketing actually tends to exclude other layers of interpretation, however. This creates a paradox: On the one hand, they implicitly acknowledge the social aspects tied to the "non-place", including the potential of enhanced attractiveness, such as was created by the activities of urban pioneers. They also account for the changeability of uses of and requirements toward the place claimed by various stakeholders. On the other hand, they insist that it is necessary to formulate normative targets and give priority to urban planning procedures and construction projects. Based on this logic, these stakeholders contributed to the very early implementation of the design options preferred by the local administration (e.g. functional buildings), resulting in pre-decisions and obligatory rules for planning practice.

Group #4 – intermediaries

The **intermediaries** purposively display a reserved and reflective attitude toward the location. At the same time, they emphatically acknowledge the opinions and actions of locally rooted stakeholders. They portray these actors as persons who have a "profound feeling for the place" (I13I). The special atmosphere of the site consisted in the fact that the ruins from socialist times could be vaguely perceived while they had been integrated into a place for modern culture (I12I). Because of urban redevelopment and the establishing of venues representing mainstream culture, the Schiffbauergasse meanwhile had developed into a "mainstream location". One interviewee calls the results a "beautiful place" with a particular ambience (I13I), while the other mentions the danger of "redeveloping it to death" (I12I).

Imaginary: Serving as promoters of market-oriented communication, entrepreneurial commitment and emergent marketing-conscious socioculture, the stakeholders draw on the ubiquitous neoliberal imaginary of locational valorization. While developing their own projects according to this orientation, they primarily communicate with their own, mostly translocal clientele. Consequently, they develop a distinctive reserve toward the local stakeholders. When encountering their direct social and economic surroundings at the location, they develop some everyday curiosity, but in their role as professionals they remain detached. The description of place characteristics therefore shows the well-known wording of aestheticization. In the first place, the Schiffbauergasse is declared an "interesting" showpiece of social change. This perspective mirrors the contradiction between the institutional (quasi-state-bound) mission realized by these stakeholders, and their fascination for peculiar, dynamic social practices. Although the intermediaries are subordinate to national power and derived interests, they at the same time tend to act in favor of the autonomy of the grassroots stakeholders. Since this conflictual disposition cannot be resolved, there is only one way out that consists in a reflective distance. This serves to provide professional credibility and commitment to the imaginary once chosen.

Synoptic interpretation: Definitions of place, imaginaries, power, and communication

The exponents of alternative culture are the only stakeholders to display a sense of place that is tied to their specific biographies. For these actors, the identity of the place cannot be negotiated at random because it has been determined by social practice. For almost all other stakeholders, place identity is a matter of more or less variable redefinition. These redefinitions can be observed in two variants: The first displays itself as a postmodern place design adopted from external models by "copy-and-paste" procedures, subsequently altered by local "adoptions" (planning routines, communication procedures, governance processes, business rationales). Because the proponents perceive a universal necessity to position urban places as parts of the entrepreneurial, globally competing city, they also assume that the particular contexts connected to models from elsewhere should basically be similar. The second variant discloses itself as an attribution of meaning based on specific interests and context-dependent preferences. The latter include procedures of aestheticization (aiming at establishing the Schiffbauergasse as a contingent but unified piece of art) and random judgements of taste. Regardless whether references to recent and older histories seem plausible, or whether mixtures and contrasts between different aspects of socioculture, forms of art, and architectural aesthetics make sense, the perspectives on the particular place rarely refer to an essential trait or a dominant, immediately evident structural principle. In most cases, this attitude is a manifestation of down-to-earth pragmatism. It is fully developed among the small entrepreneurs who would go for anything promising economic profit. Place identities appear as arbitrarily "tinkered" here.[13] Sometimes one and the same actor ascribes different features to the same place according to changing frameworks of reference.

Table 13.1 provides a synopsis of the power relations, place definitions, implemented imaginaries, and modes of communication that were empirically detected on site. The stakeholders have been vertically arranged in the fashion of a ranking order, indicating their endowment with structural power. At the same time the strength of their context-specific interactional power is also indicated. This allows for the identification of the positionings of stakeholders within top-down and bottom-up enactments of place-making in more detail. Although the limitations of the text format of this chapter do not allow for thorough interpretation and explication of the correlations between the categories for all groups of stakeholders, at least the most distinctive constellations can be sketched here.

The top-down component is most clearly represented by the stakeholder group "administration". These stakeholders directly refer to market-compliant imaginaries rooted in neoliberal thinking. Their decisionist concept of place design is based on a framework of ideas stressing the importance of increased attractiveness and competitiveness of locations, as well as on thinking in terms of copy-and-paste categories. It aims to produce symbolic and economic profit. The definition of place indirectly mirrors the expectation of profit. It is mediated by the expectation of successfully participating in a global market of performative space-related reputation building ("cool mixtures" of culture and business, places of innovation, and avant-gardism). The features of the place are treated as local ingredients of a globally compatible promise of modernization. This triggers the felt necessity to mobilize local stakeholders.

262 Hans-Joachim Bürkner

Table 13.1 Empowerment, definition of place, imaginary, and communicative orientation of stakeholders at the Schiffbauergasse (own representation)

Stakeholder	Empowerment	Definition of place	Imaginary	Communicative orientation
Administration	*Structurally high*: Decision-making authority, institutionalization *Interactively low*: Failed moderation and hardly mobilized	• Mixture of "culture and commerce" • A meeting of different lifestyles • Abstract design ("a place for experiences") vs. historic location • A place for innovation • A "non-place", a forbidden location in the slipstream • A changing place still being created • A beauty spot, owing to its proximity to the waterfront	• Neoliberal urban policy: market conditions call for design and symbol production • Gain in appeal and attention in the competition of locations • Capitalizes on local history through site design • Import of ideas (copy & paste) • Pragmatic, normative planning activities	• Recourse to top-down routines: detached "proclamations" of location definitions • Forced mobilization: top-down design must be communicatively articulated • Egalitarian rhetoric • Weakly networked with local actors • Insufficient acceptance of the site design
Businesses				
1. Global player	*Structurally high*: Free choice of location, political support *Interactively low*	• Pleasant ambience by the water • Creative site for undisturbed work • Symbiosis of rural seclusion and city life	• Instrumentalist approach to the social and spatial environment • Power-conscious, aestheticizing embellishments of their economic activities	• Do away with communication • Hardly connected to networks at the location • Business as social enclave
2. Small business	*Structurally medium*: Limited resources, but with local political support *Interactively low*	• Local place of recreation • Potentially high (but unrealized) quality of stay • Weak connection to history • No clear image, heterogeneous	• Priority: survival in the marketplace • Pragmatism • Conformity to policy design concepts	• No connection to the ways of life of other actor groups • Hardly connected to networks at the location

Intermediary	*Structurally medium*: Supplier to regional policy, in part with emancipatory aspirations *Interactively low*	• The particular charm of the place: history of the GDR is perceptible, but integrated within modern culture • A pleasant location	• Empathetic view toward the local setting, but professionally distanced engagement in local networking activities
Creative artists: Institutional culture	*Structurally low*: Dependence on state funding, hardly any influence on political decisions *Interactively low*	• Diverse, pleasant location • "History of the east" perceptible • A place for contemporary culture • A counterweight to the historic Potsdam • An exclusive location, not accessible to all	• Reflective distance to what has occurred socially • Aestheticization of locations • Integration of tradition and modernity is important • Danger of "redeveloping to death" • Forward-looking design • Distanced from the ways of life of other actor groups • Participation in cross-locational networking
Alternative culture/spatial pioneers	*Structurally low*: Highly independent from the state, hardly any influence on political decisions *Interactively high*: Intensively networked, leaders of opinion, temporary countervailing power	• A "wild place" • Malleable, forward-looking • History of the GDR is perceptible • Endangered by redevelopment and gentrification	• Reflection, objectivation • Ironic critical distance • Aestheticization of contradictions • Postmodern/hedonistic middle-class perspective • Parallels with top-down designs that conform to the market • Rooted in the alternative movement • Appropriation of place as a component of lifestyle design and forms of work • Counterculture to transformational capitalism • Older, locally entrenched networks of the "pioneers" are the starting point for ad hoc discussions and initiatives "from below" • Little possibility of influence on administration and policy • Initiatives eroded by realities created top-down

Talking about hip places   263

Although these actors claim that they had established a good model and practiced an egalitarian rhetoric to the advantage of everyone, there is no equilibrated communication with the other local agents. A subliminal game of blaming and waiting for excuses creeps in: From the perspective of the local administration, good governance is impeded by the passiveness of consumers and by the divergence of interests displayed by the other stakeholders. In the end, the administration partly ignored the communication dilemma and partly tried to resolve it by falling back on older top-down routines of planning and taking pre-decisions, albeit without much success.

An important driver of top-down mobilization is the underlying imaginary itself. Since survival in the competition of locations is no abstract challenge but a concrete imperative of success-oriented urban policy, there is continual motivation for strategies that aim at rigorously enforcing planning concepts. Structurally guaranteed power (mainly in the form of decisional power) therefore has to compensate for missed opportunities in creating interactional power (e.g. in ongoing governance processes).

The opposite pole consists of formally power-deficient urban pioneers. They preserve an outspoken distance from the state and are generally inclined to create counter-hegemonic cultural projects. Being deeply rooted in local everyday culture, these stakeholders make use of a veritable communicative strength. There is hardly any chance for other stakeholders to act or talk without getting involved with the "Eastern pioneers" and acknowledge their gatekeeping function regarding local discourse. At first sight, the interactional power they generate seems to count little when compared to the structurally anchored decisional power of their counterparts. Yet together with their implementation of imaginaries, they skillfully exploited interactional power to create immediate political pressure. For example, the "alternative" stakeholders skillfully combine their network orientation and communicative competencies with an alternative imaginary contrasting with that of neoliberalism. It is the "right to the city" (Harvey 2003) they claim for – meaning that citizens should have a natural right to make use of, and socially appropriate, their built environment. This idea includes fundamental criticism of capitalist modes of production, of ecological mismanagement, and of the economic exploitation of urban resources by private and institutional stakeholders. This counter concept, positioned against an overpowering market-conform imaginary, serves several purposes at the same time: being able to make strong claims in local public discourse; easily collecting "on-site" social resources; and forcing political opponents into debates about top-down planning habits.

In spite of its empowering function, this counter imaginary seems to be oddly dependent on the hegemonic imaginary of neoliberalism: There is no other way for the counter concept to develop and focus than by constantly referring to hegemonic items. The bottom-up perspective is, therefore, hardly able to produce an autonomous counter power. The enforced subsummation under a hegemonic logic of the system only allows for revisions of planning details and the temporary success of political action. Because of a lack of access to decisions, these stakeholders only have the specific scope of action which has been conceded by more formally powerful actors. In this way, the underlying logic of the "alternative" imaginary establishes the tendency of these stakeholders to retreat into their own self-contained networks, which support them with social and symbolic capital. Under this condition, attempts to address and resist dominant (e.g. public) stakeholders are subject to multiple logical contradictions and ambivalences. While "victories" over formally powerful actors on the basis of temporary interactional power have to be gained again and again, the winners are permanently denied access to decisions. On the other hand, the local administration, which in terms of communication structure seems to be chronically lacking in power, can endure its "defeats" without any difficulty – it has institutionally guaranteed control over decisions and feels safe because their action conforms to "higher" political objectives rooted in neoliberal imaginaries. On this foundation, it can even afford to flirt with its alleged inferiority in public discourse.

The creative artists of the high-cultural sector are one-sidedly equipped with low decisional power and, at the same time, with low interactional power due to lacking networks and weak social capital within the context of the location. As a way out of this double deficit, these actors introduce an imaginary of their own, one of aesthetic dissociation. This imaginary is not independent, however, and needs the counterpart of the hegemonic neoliberal imaginary to gain tangible shape. Dissociation discloses itself by reflexive, critical, and ironic attitudes toward the inconsistencies of everyday life. Contrary to the alternative stakeholders, these actors do not develop a real counter position to the economization of social and urban life. This could have hardly been expected, since these actors are basically dependent on state funding, this fact alone demanding a certain degree of systemic conformity. Rather, they tread the path of satire: The imaginary provides an aestheticization of contradictions that makes criticism socially acceptable.

The "beautiful" venue, uniting contrasts and contradictory elements, seems to be harmless and ambivalent enough to allow for multifaceted connotations and avoid unambiguous political position taking. An intense discourse about definitions of place and place attachments is hardly ever acceptable for these actors, because they play with their "homemade" dissociation and aestheticizing indifference. Harmonies or differences of interest with other actors are perceived, yet hardly provide incentives for them to get involved with the networks existing at the location. Even the fact that they are committed to an imaginary of aestheticizing standoff is rarely reflected on. While effecting aloofness in the course of their own professional activities, they interpret the standoff situation as a necessary response to the experience of vernacular social distance rather than as an outcome of comprehensive idealistic self-positioning. This is probably an easily obtained means of dealing with the ambivalent closeness to the state and the dependency on state funding. When it comes to developing urban spaces with an open-ended perspective, these actors might even be unreliable partners.

Conclusions

To talk about "hip places" is not to talk about a clear-cut phenomenon. In the case of East German urban development, it means talking about different power positions, post-socialist, and post-transformational political culture, overarching spatial and economic imaginaries, and rarely compatible definitions of place. Urban studies faces the challenging task of carefully exploring and empirically reconstructing the ways in which place-based governance, local discourse, and stakeholder communication are related back to dominant and recessive imaginaries. At the same, time the relations found should be discussed with a focus on the question of which future options for citizenship and civil action might arise within specific arenas of urban development. Moreover, it becomes obvious that it is necessary to put a special analytical focus on the embedding of urban development into large trends of economic and political restructuring, such as economic globalization and the worldwide neoliberal economization of the social sphere. New approaches to the forefront of international research might be derived from poststructural political economy and its focus on imaginaries, which has the potential to produce new insight into newly developing, multifaceted connections between everyday life and the multilevel restructuring of societies.

In the case of Potsdam, it can be said that the outcome of the social construction of multiply usable places was, and still is, open-ended. In the period immediately following the empirical study presented in this chapter, the spatial imaginary that had been installed by politics and planning experienced further reinforcement. A follow-up governance process unfolded after the city council declared that the municipal locational management had been a failure, mainly because the stakeholders of the Schiffbauergasse obviously had not sufficiently supported the top-down project and public recognition of the attractiveness of the location had been too weak. In fact, the copy-and-paste strategy had been thwarted by local communication problems and the multitude of individual interests. In order not to be forced to write off the investment in the location, in 2009 the city council engaged a private consulting firm to develop a concept for locational marketing. This concept was meant to enhance the economic attractiveness of the place and prove the marketability of the basic concept of "culture and business". Several workshops were organized to launch a renewed communication process promising low hierarchization in communication. However, though it was moderated by private agents, it was still initiated from above. The city administration obviously had to compensate for its deficit of interactional power. As it soon turned out, the moderators preferred "hard" economic criteria of development over the noncommercial usage interests of independent artists and urban pioneers. The target of generating greater attractiveness for paying customers prevailed over all-competing moments of appeal and usage claims (Hoffmann 2011, 42). This marked the provisional end of the discussion. The governance process concluded in a state of communicative suspense. To this day, it remains an open question whether hegemonic economic imaginaries will ever be able to serve vital social interests and the needs of local artists and small-scale economies. Within the political public of the city, the trendy fusion of "economy and culture" has therefore been tacitly filed under "nice to have" rather than "indispensable".

Notes

1 See www.schiffbauergasse.de.
2 Until 1990, the Bridge of Glienicke served as a border-crossing point between the Federal Republic of Germany and the German Democratic Republic. It was the venue for periodic exchange of political prisoners and secret agents between the two German states.
3 In the 18th and 19th centuries, roasted and ground chicory root served as a cheap substitute for coffee.
4 In the following, I will refer by abbreviations to interview transcripts of my empirical data.
5 Web presence of the MuseumsQuartier Wien, www.mqw.at.
6 The state working group Socio-Culture (LAG SozioKultur) is an association of sociocultural centers and initiatives in the federal state of Brandenburg; see the organization's online presence at www.soziokultur-brandenburg.de/index.php.
7 Former model funding program of the Ministry of Work, Social Affairs, Women and Families of the State of Brandenburg (Ministerium für Arbeit, Soziales, Frauen und Familie des Landes Brandenburg); see www.lasa-brandenburg.de/INNOPUNKT.43.0.html.
8 Theoretical notions such as "decisional power" describe a special variant of possible types of power; that is, the capability of political, economic, and other stakeholders to make binding decisions which are often supported or legitimized by constitutions, laws, and state regulations. Very often, these decisions have a structural effect, setting the framework for action to be taken by less powerful stakeholders. This term has been employed with different connotations, and sometimes unclear references, by regime theory (Stone 1993), elite theories (Klöckner 2007), and organizational theory (Laux and Liermann 2005; Sanders and Kianty 2006, 193). These theoretical schools, however, agree on the connectedness of decisional power to hierarchies: stakeholders who have been attributed decisional power often act at the top levels of economic, political, and administrative organizations. Yet this is not mandatory, since powerful actors can also be found outside the hierarchical structure of formal organizations, such as those which have been endowed with decisional power by the state or other high-ranking organizations.
9 Following Lau and Beck, definitional power is understood here as the "monopolization of offers for definition and interpretation that, by definition, are freely applicable and not predictable by interpreters and interpretations themselves" (Lau and Beck 1989, 20, translation by the author).
10 Being an ideational abstraction, the imaginary always exists prior to any structural hypothesis or devised theoretical concept. Its function is to provide an intellectual embedding of theoretical concepts at the level of different logics and orders of knowledge. This has been impressively shown by Cornelius Castoriadis in his interpretation of Marx's concept of historical materialism (Castoriadis 1987).

11 The term "transformational capitalism" is used here to indicate that the development of East Germany after 1990 has been an integral part of the emergence of variegated pathways of post-socialist transformation (Bürkner 2019). Despite the adoption of West German structural models and political rhetorics, practice at various structural and action levels has developed according to a self-willed logic (*Eigensinn*), often based on informal institutions and unique interpretations of formal regulations. For example, the widespread remoteness of local administrations from "their" local population has to be included within the informal heritage of state-centralist structures and mentalities (Thumfart 2004, 9). It extends even to the implementation of urban regeneration schemes after 2000, which was characterized by outspoken administrative and political paternalism and civil passiveness – despite the fact that regeneration had originally been initialized by the federal government as a participative process based on "integrated" urban development plans and procedures of local governance (Bernt 2009). This phenomenon is mirrored by the generally ambivalent attitudes of the population toward state institutions, ranging between distrust and independent civil commitment (Reißig 1997, 14; Gensicke et al. 2009).

12 The term "neoliberal" here designates a rationale which calls for the primacy of the economy. It is utilized by its proponents to establish unbridled market dynamism in all spheres of life, including related social constructions of space (Peck and Tickell 2002). Accordingly, political action which is in line with market requirements, open competition, and private profit seeking have priority over policies that address social equity and public interest. The implementation of this rationale requires special local governance arrangements (Newman 2014).

13 This notion is utilized in analogy to the sociological term "tinkered identity" (Prisching 2009, 25; see also Hitzler and Honer 1994; Keupp et al. 1999). Tinkered identities are the results of the arbitrary construction of multiple or fragmented identities that individuals perform when dealing with different social contexts. With regard to places, it can be postulated that one and the same individual repeatedly attributes meaning to a specific place depending on different contexts, situations, and interests.

References

Albrechts, Louis. 2004. "Strategic (Spatial) Planning Reexamined". *Environment and Planning B* 31 (5): 743–758.

Bartholomae, Florian, Chang Woon Nam, and Alina Schoenberg. 2017. "Urban Shrinkage and Resurgence in Germany". *Urban Studies* 54 (12): 2701–2718.

Bergmann, Malte. 2011. *Kreative Raumpioniere in Berlin Nord-Neukölln: Raumaneignungen und Repräsentationsformen* [Creative urban pioneers in Berlin North Neukölln: Appropriations of space and types of representation]. Saarbrücken: VDM Verlag Dr. Müller.

Bernt, Matthias. 2009. "Partnerships for Demolition: The Governance of Urban Renewal in East Germany's Shrinking Cities". *International Journal of Urban and Regional Research* 33 (3): 754–769.

Boudreau, Julie-Anne. 2007. "Making New Political Spaces: Mobilizing Spatial Imaginaries, Instrumentalizing Spatial Practices, and Strategically Using Spatial Tools". *Environment and Planning A* 39 (11): 2593–2611.

Bourdieu, Pierre. 1984. *Distinction: A Social Critique of the Judgement of Taste*. Cambridge, MA: Harvard University Press.
Bourdieu, Pierre. 1990. *The Logic of Practice*. Oxford: Polity Press.
Bürkner, Hans-Joachim. 2019. "Regional Disparities". In *Handbook of Political, Social, and Economic Transformation*, edited by Wolfgang Merkel, Raj Kollmorgen, and Hans-Jürgen Wagener, 623–629. Oxford: Oxford University Press.
Castoriadis, Cornelius. 1987. *The Imaginary Institution of Society*. Cambridge: Polity Press.
Feldmann, Kathrin. 2002. "Quartiersmanagement Potsdam 'Stern/Drewitz'" [Neighborhood management Potsdam 'Stern/Drewitz']. In *Vierte Regionalkonferenz der Region Ost – Integrierte sozialräumliche Planung: Für E&C-Akteure und Interessierte der Bundesländer Berlin, Brandenburg, Mecklenburg-Vorpommern, Sachsen, Sachsen-Anhalt und Thüringen. Dokumentation zur Veranstaltung vom 28. November 2002 in Potsdam* [Fourth regional conference of the Eastern Region – Integrated socio-spatial planning: For agents of E&C and interested persons of the states of Berlin, Brandenburg, Mecklenburg-Western Pomerania, Saxony, Saxony-Anhalt, and Thuringia. Documentation of a meeting on 28 November, 2002 in Potsdam], 23–27. Potsdam.
Florida, Richard. 2004. *Cities and the Creative Class*. New York: Routledge.
Franz, Peter. 2007. "Führt die Umsetzung des Programms 'Stadtumbau Ost' zur Herausbildung urbaner Regime in ostdeutschen Städten" [Does the implementation of the program 'Urban Redevelopment East' trigger urban regimes in East German cities]? *Magazin Städte im Umbruch*, 4: 36–41.
Fürst, Dietrich, Marion Lahner, and Karsten Zimmermann. 2005. *Neue Ansätze integrierter Stadtteilentwicklung. Placemaking und Local Governance* [New approaches toward integrated neighborhood development. Placemaking and local governance]. Working Paper: *REGIO transfer 4*. Erkner: Institute for Regional Development and Structural Planning.
Gensicke, Thomas, Hans-Ludger Dienel, Thomas Olk, Daphne Reim, and Jenny Schmithals. 2009. *Entwicklung der Zivilgesellschaft in Ostdeutschland. Quantitative und qualitative Befunde* [Evolution of civil society in East Germany. Quantitative and qualitative findings]. Wiesbaden: VS Verlag.
Glaser, Barney G., and Anselm L. Strauss. 1967. *The Discovery of Grounded Theory: Strategies for Qualitative Research*. Chicago: Aldine.
Gordon, David L.A. 1997. "Managing the Changing Political Environment in Urban Waterfront Redevelopment". *Urban Studies* 34 (1): 61–83.
Haase, Annegret, Matthias Bernt, Katrin Großmann, Vlad Mykhnenko, and Dieter Rink. 2016. "Varieties of Shrinkage in European cities". *European Urban and Regional Studies* 23 (1): 86–102.
Hannemann, Christine. 2003. "Schrumpfende Städte in Ostdeutschland: Ursachen und Folgen einer Stadtentwicklung ohne Wirtschaftswachstum" [Shrinking cities in East Germany: Causes and consequences of urban development without economic growth]. *Aus Politik und Zeitgeschichte. Beilage zur Wochenzeitung "Das Parlament"*, B 28: 16–24.
Harvey, David. 2003. "The Right to the City". *International Journal of Urban and Regional Research* 27 (4): 939–941.
Hitzler, Ronald, and Anne Honer. 1994. "Bastelexistenz" [Tinkered life]. In *Riskante Freiheiten* [Hazardous liberties], edited by Ulrich Beck and Elisabeth Beck-Gernsheim, 307–315. Frankfurt am Main: Suhrkamp.

Hoffmann, Kati. 2011. "Kulturstandortentwicklung: Anspruch und Wirklichkeit. Das Beispiel der Schiffbauergasse in Potsdam" [Development of a cultural location: Aspiration and reality. The case of the Schiffbauergasse in Potsdam]. BA thesis, Berlin.

Huning, Sandra, Thomas Kuder, Henning Nuissl, and Uwe Altrock. 2010. "Zwanzig Jahre Planung seit der deutschen Wiedervereinigung" [Twenty years of planning after German reunion]. *Planungsrundschau*, No. 20: 7–17.

Jessop, Bob. 2012. *Cultural Political Economy, Spatial Imaginaries, Regional Economic Dynamics*. CPERC Working Paper 2012–02. Lancaster: Lancaster University.

Jessop, Bob, and Stijn Oosterlynck. 2008. "Cultural Political Economy. On Making the Cultural Turn without Falling into Soft Economic Sociology". *Geoforum* 39 (3): 1155–1169.

Keupp, Heiner, Thomas Ahbe, Wolfgang Gmür, Renate Höfer, Beate Mitzscherlich, Wolfgang Kraus, and Florian Sraus. 1999. *Identitätskonstruktionen. Das Patchwork der Identitäten in der Spätmoderne* [Identity constructs: The patchwork of identities in late modernity]. Reinbek: Rowohlt.

Klöckner, Marcus B. 2007. *Machteliten und Elitenzirkel. Eine soziologische Auseinandersetzung*. [Power elites and circles of elites. A sociological treatise]. Saarbrücken: VDM Verlag Dr. Müller.

Land Brandenburg, Ministerium für Infrastruktur und Landwirtschaft. 2010. *MitReden – MitMachen – MitRegieren. Dokumentation der Fachtagung zur Bürgermitwirkung am 4. November 2010* [Having a say – taking part – co-governing. Documentation of a symposium on citizen participation on 4 November, 2010]. Potsdam.

Landry, Charles. 2008. *The Creative City: A Toolkit for Urban Innovators*. London: Earthscan.

Lange, Bastian, Joachim Burdack, and Günter Herfert. 2006. *Creative Leipzig? Socio-Economic Indicators, Development Paths and Conditions of Creative Industries in the City Region of Leipzig*. Amsterdam: AMIDsT.

Lange, Bastian, and Ulf Matthiesen. 2005. "Space Pioneers". In *Shrinking Cities, Volume 2: Interventions*, edited by Philipp Oswalt, 374–383. Ostfildern-Ruit: Hatje Cantz.

Larner, Wendy, and Richard Le Heron. 2002. "The Spaces and Subjects of a Globalising Economy: A Situated Exploration of Method". *Environment and Planning D: Society and Space* 20 (6): 753–774.

Lau, Christoph, and Ulrich Beck. 1989. *Definitionsmacht und Grenzen angewandter Sozialwissenschaft: Eine Untersuchung am Beispiel der Bildungs- und Arbeitsmarktforschung* [Power of definition and limits of applied social science: An inquiry using the case of educational and labor market research]. Opladen: Westdeutscher Verlag.

Laux, Helmut, and Felix Liermann. 2005. *Grundlagen der Organisation: Die Steuerung von Entscheidungen als Grundproblem der Betriebswirtschaftslehre* [Foundations of the organization: The governance of decision as a fundamental problem of business management]. Berlin and Heidelberg: Springer.

Le Heron, Richard. 2006. "Towards Reconceptualising Enterprise, Entrepreneurship and Entrepreneurial Processes for Sustainable Futures: Contributions from Economic Geography". In *Enterprising Worlds: A Geographic Perspective on Economics, Environments & Ethics*, edited by Jay Dean Gatrell and Neil Reid, 119–130. Dordrecht: Springer.

Mah, Alice. 2012. "Demolition for Development: A Critical Analysis of Official Urban Imaginaries in Past and Present UK Cities". *Journal of Historical Sociology* 25 (1): 151–176.

Mattissek, Annika. 2008. *Die neoliberale Stadt: Diskursive Repräsentationen im Stadtmarketing deutscher Großstädte* [The neoliberal city: Discursive representations within city marketing of German cities]. Bielefeld: transcript.

Newman, Janet. 2014. "Landscapes of Antagonism: Local Governance, Neoliberalism and Austerity". *Urban Studies* 51 (15): 3290–3305.

Overmeyer, Klaus, and Ursula Renker. 2005. "Raumpioniere in Berlin" [Urban pioneers in Berlin]. *Garten und Landschaft* 1. www.studio-uc.de/downloads/suc_raumpioniere-in-berlin.pdf

Peck, Jamie, and Adam Tickell. 2002. "Neoliberalizing Space". In *Spaces of Neoliberalism: Urban Restructuring in North America and Western Europe*, edited by Neil Brenner and Nikolas Theodore, 33–57. Malden, MA and Oxford: Blackwell.

Prisching, Manfred. 2009. *Das Selbst. Die Maske. Der Bluff. Über die Inszenierung der eigenen Person* [Self, mask, bluff. About the staging of one's own person]. Wien: Molden Verlag.

Radzimski, Adam. 2016. "Changing Policy Responses to Shrinkage: The Case of Dealing with Housing Vacancies in Eastern Germany". *Cities* 50: 197–205.

Reißig, Rolf. 1997. *Transformationsforschung: Gewinne, Desiderate und Perspektiven* [Transformation research: Assets, desiderata and perspectives]. WZB Paper No. P 97-001. Berlin: Wissenschaftszentrum Berlin.

Sanders, Karin, and Andrea Kianty. 2006. Organisationstheorien. Eine Einführung [Organizational theories: An introduction]. Wiesbaden: VS Verlag.

Saupe, Gabriele. 2009. "Das Wechselverhältnis von Berlin und Brandenburg – eine 'Hassliebe' und 'Schicksalsgemeinschaft' seit mehr als 150 Jahren" [The reciprocal relationship between Berlin and Brandenburg: a love-hate relationship and 'community of fate' for more than 150 years]. In *Alles Metropole? Berlin-Brandenburg zwischen Hauptstadt, Hinterland und Europa* [Everything metropolis? Berlin-Brandenburg between capital, hinterland, and Europe], edited by Thomas Weith, Hans-Joachim Kujath, and Annekathrin Rauschenbach, 25–38. Kassel: Verlag Altrock.

Stone, Clarence N. 1993. "Urban Regimes and the Capacity to Govern: A Political Economy Approach". *Journal of Urban Affairs* 15 (1): 1–28.

Strübing, Jörg. 2008. *Grounded Theory. Zur sozialtheoretischen und epistemologischen Fundierung des Verfahrens der empirisch begründeten Theoriebildung (Qualitative Sozialforschung, Band 15)* [Grounded theory: Toward a social theoretical and epistemological foundation of the method of empirically grounded theory construction (qualitative social research, vol. 15)], 2nd ed. Wiesbaden: VS Verlag.

Thumfart, Alexander. 2004. *Bürgerschaftliches Engagement in den Kommunen – Erfahrungen aus Ostdeutschland* [Civic involvement in municipalities – experiences from East Germany]. Working Paper: Betrifft: Bürgergesellschaft 04, Friedrich-Ebert-Stiftung.

Viehrig, Hans. 2002. *Potsdam: Geographische Strukturen im Wandel (mit Exkursionshinweisen)* [Potsdam: Changing geographical structures (with tips for excursions)]. Vol. 22 of *Potsdamer Geographische Forschungen*. Potsdam: University of Potsdam.

Watkins, Josh. 2015. "Spatial Imaginaries Research in Geography: Synergies, Tensions, and New Directions". *Geography Compass* 9 (9): 508–522.

Wetzstein, Steffen. 2013. "Globalising Economic Governance, Political Projects and Spatial Imaginaries – Insights from Four Australasian Cities". *Geographical Research* 51 (1): 71–84.

Wetzstein, Steffen, and Richard Le Heron. 2010. "Regional Economic Policy 'In-the-Making'. Imaginaries, Political Projects and Institutions for Auckland's Economic Transformation". *Environment and Planning A* 42 (8): 1902–1924.

Wiechmann, Thorsten, and Karina M. Pallagst. 2012. "Urban Shrinkage in Germany and the USA: A Comparison of Transformation Patterns and Local Strategies". *International Journal of Urban and Regional Research* 36 (2): 261–280.

14 A systemic model of communication in spatial planning

Ursula Stein

Introduction

Communication has always been an important part of urban and regional planning. In particular, a communicative practice paying close attention to participation and empowerment was developed and subsequently entered the mainstream from the early 1970s onward. The "communicative turn" in planning theory then became a major issue in the 1990s. This paper aims to adapt a model of communication based on systemic and reality-constructive concepts (Schmid 2008)[1] that will help in the understanding and preparation of communication in planning. From such a systemic perspective, communicative planning is part and parcel of the practice of urban and regional planning culture. It requires careful design of planning processes as well as of spatial concepts.

This chapter discusses the role of city and region as place and reason for communication as embedded in a systemic model of communication. It should be mentioned at the outset that this is not a theory, but an attempt to turn an idea into a concept that can serve to shape the attitude and creative competencies of planners and consultants.

Using examples from planning practice, this chapter goes on to illustrate the potential of communicative planning: making better plans and offering opportunities for meaningful communication in a social context. This includes ways of experiencing cities and regions, finding common vocabulary and images, shedding light on conflicts, and combining professional and local expertise.

City and region: Place and reason for communication

This section presents some basic thoughts on communicative spatial planning. In the last decades, participation has gained in political and social significance. In most European countries, citizens are more aware than ever of their concerns and interests. The global process of urbanization has intensified the use of space in cities, and sustainability has become a challenge of ever-growing importance. In their 2030 Agenda for Sustainable Development, the United Nations included the demand that people be involved in the goal to "make cities and human settlements inclusive, safe, resilient, and sustainable" (United Nations

DOI: 10.4324/9780367817183-17

n.d., goal 11.3). Communicative planning thus requires an appropriate model for conceiving and handling communicative situations that deal with the use of space.

Spatial planning is part of social practice

The way we deal with space is a public, common matter. The main reason for this lies in the fact that space is a limited resource needed by everybody. We therefore have to bear sustainability and social justice in mind when using spatial resources.

In modern societies, using public space is not only a part of everyday life – subconsciously experienced and understood as comprising routes to work, school, and shopping, or consciously chosen, for instance, when spending leisure time or working in cafés and public spaces. It can also provide a basic feeling for one's being a part of society. The changing uses of public space are cases in point here; for example, in the boom of open-air cafés, skating, and other sports and in the increasing everyday use of parks and green spaces.

Dealing with space offers unique opportunities to create communication between people from different social strata and life situations who would otherwise generally tend to segregate. Since the ownership and use of space creates conflict, spatial planning must also deal with this. Communicative spatial planning is thus a resource for enhancing creativity in planning as well as for dealing with conflict in a productive way. At the same time, a culture of communicative planning can be a part of a local society's social practice.

Planning needs to be based on communication and participation

The initial statement that "communication has always been a part of planning" points to the fact that communication in planning was not new at the time of the "communicative turn" in planning. It already played an important role when planning was a matter for top-floor offices in which leading planning officials, industry, and commercial representatives and landowners met to draw up the outlines of their city's future development (Selle 2000, 69–70). But in pre- and postwar times, this was the task of the city's chief planning officer. The plan, as a product of expert work, was their focus. In the seventies, however, the demand for a more democratic society had its effects on planning when advocacy planning and public participation in planning procedures were established (Healey 1997; Selle 2000). This "communicative turn" was closely linked to the importance of public deliberation. Later, part of the attention turned back toward the institutional change needed to support the new structures of planning for moving from the authoritative role of the planning expert to an interactive model in which different groups and stakeholders formed part of the planning game (Stein 1995). This can be seen as a necessary part of the change in the predominant notion of the public sector's role in society: moving from the "modern" concept of the "welfare state", which has to secure the well-being

Model of communication in spatial planning 275

of every citizen, to the "postmodern" concept of the "enabling state", which creates or reinforces a framework for interaction and the negotiation between individuals and groups.

Participation in the realm of planning of spatial resources has since become a must for a number of reasons. In general, citizens are today better educated, resulting in a more self-confident claim not to leave decisions about public affairs to politicians and experts. Expert knowledge is seen as a tool that is not neutral.[2] Thus, people want to know about the background of expertise and of planning proposals. Planners and real estate developers increasingly wish to integrate local knowledge in order to find better solutions at early stages of planning and to avoid obstruction at later stages of realization.

Spatial planning needs an appropriate model of communication

Perhaps the best-known basic model of communication is the sender–receiver model, widely known as the Shannon–Weaver model (Shannon and Weaver 1949). In this orthodox model,

> it is to be expected that the reality of the sender A, expressed in his [or her] message when sent through the communication channel, will be received unchanged by the receiver B and appear identical to B's reality [see Figure 14.1]. If not, something has gone wrong and must be repaired. Transferred to human communication, the model suggests that from the viewpoint of the sender, people function in a controllable way. If the receiver's reality doesn't change in the expected way, then someone has a problem.
>
> (Schmid 2006, 2)

Obviously, in accordance with the purposes for which it was created, this model is very technical. Items such as disturbing factors (e.g. noise) and feedback loops were added, but social scientists have since abandoned it for its inability to integrate the social context of communication. The basic model of communication may still be functional for communication based on control-and-command structures, but it takes no account of the chaotic and unpredictable nature of human behavior and the co-creative aspect of giving meaning to sheer information. Bringing in, or tolerating, creative aspects that influence the

Figure 14.1 Sender–receiver: A basic model of communication.
Source: Figure translated from Schmid (2006), based on Shannon and Weaver (1949).

276 Ursula Stein

reception of information but which are not part of its intended focus – such as intuition, hate, hope, or fear – must be regarded as inaccurate in the context of the sender-receiver model.

Systemic thinking provides a supplementary model of communication. It assumes that each communication partner has their own reality and uses any encounter with other partners to promote this reality and its development (see Schmid 2008, 70–71). Part of this model consists of the idea that such realities vary and thus need connecting if something like a shared reality, serving as the basis of communication, should ensue. The creation of shared reality is a necessary effort of communication and a specific competence. This systemic model relinquishes the idea of control because the realities of living organisms are complex, and even they themselves do not know how to control them.

This model of communication as an encounter of stakeholder systems and cultures provides a more realistic and inspiring mindset for communicative planning (see Figure 14.2). Here, little to no understanding of shared reality or interests need be assumed as a starting point. Communicative planning then strives to create opportunities for an encounter that promotes the development of shared perceptions. These may result in shared ideas and realities. If all of these represent only a small part of one stakeholder's perceptions, ideas, and realities, this is not necessarily a problem. It is sufficient that a reasonable number of shared interests emerge and serve as a basis for joint action, such as support for a regional plan or an urban development process.

It should be mentioned that the terms "stakeholder" or "stakeholder system" are used in this chapter to mean a "person, group, or organization that has interests in, or can affect, be affected by, or perceive itself to be affected by, any aspect of the project", as defined by international project management standards (International Organization for Standardization 2012). This is not identical to the use of these words by, for example, systems theoretician Niklas Luhmann. Schmid uses the general description "system or person" for the two elements that are supposed to communicate with one another. Here, the word "stakeholder" has been introduced to the model in adapting it to spatial planning,

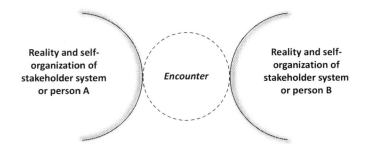

Figure 14.2 The systemic model of communication.
Source: "Encounter of Cultures Model" translated from Schmid (2006).

because communicative planning is about facilitating dialogue between stakeholders in planning processes.

Space in the systemic model of communication

Space is something people – and stakeholder systems – inevitably have to share with each other if they live or work in one area. Neighborhoods, cities, and regions may thus provide very good reasons for communication and encounter. Shared or contested space forms a basis for communication, which necessarily involves the exchange of different perceptions of space and may lead to some form of encounter. At the same time, such an encounter can take place in the same space that is the very object of communication (see Figure 14.3).

Communicative planning arranged according to the systemic model of communication offers a range of opportunities. Some of these are illustrated in the next section, using examples drawn from the author's professional practice.

Communicative spatial planning: Potential of the systemic model of communication

The most natural situations for talking about a neighborhood, development site, city, or region arise when visiting them. Encounters with space can make planning events more meaningful, shared perceptions between stakeholders more probable, and planning networks more stable. An approach to spatial planning which systematically includes space as a key player in the planning process was presented as "experience-based planning" by Henrik Schultz and the author (Stein and Schultz 2008).

Walking and cycling, included as part of site visits, provide slow motion, physical experiences of space. During and after such a physical exercise, mental exercise is of equal importance.[3] Participants share ideas about what they perceive and become aware of the differences in their perceptions. At the same time, common references emerge that can be used in subsequent discussions

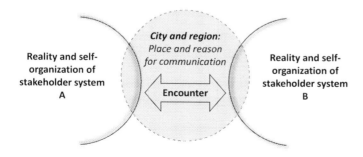

Figure 14.3 City and region in a systemic model of communication.
Source: Own representation.

about the future use and design of space. This does not rely on compulsory, unanimous perceptions! On the contrary, becoming aware of differences is a basic requirement for discovering what can be shared and developed cooperatively. Such awareness is also helpful when it comes to understanding the multitude of perspectives spatial planning has to take into account.

Four examples presented here will hopefully illustrate some of the opportunities that communicative planning provides if it is based on the systemic model of communication:

1. A vision for the development of a medium-sized town makes stakeholders join forces.
2. The design process for a public park helps to resolve conflicts between stakeholders.
3. Local expertise is integrated productively into an international design competition.
4. A metaphor based on images and words intensifies integrative discussions about regional development.

Making stakeholders meet; mobilizing resources and support for urban development

VOERDE 2030, a vision for the city of Voerde in western Germany, aims to identify potential design strategies and set up key projects for the development of the city, numbering about 40,000 inhabitants. A so-called summer program prompted citizens to visit their own city. Three excursions illustrated cross-cutting topics from VOERDE 2030. During an excursion dedicated to "housing", 10 families opened their homes, each from a different era of building in Voerde, to a group of 50 fellow citizens unknown to the hosts. This eventually led to intense discussions about the development of lifestyles and buildings today and in the future. Personal preferences and different points of view became apparent in a relaxed atmosphere. Some weeks later, the excursion on the theme of "constant change" took participants to a school, a farm, a horse-riding club, and a construction firm. Officials from these institutions explained how they adapt to ongoing changes in education, agriculture, leisure, and industry. This resulted in reflections on the tension between conservation and development, an important topic in public debates about spatial development. In a series of public events, planners, politicians, and citizens shaped the key elements of the project's vision as well as a set of priority measures. Ultimately, both politicians and citizens demanded that dialogue between administration, political leaders, and the public should become an important feature in the vision for Voerde.

This example illustrates the triangular setting of the planning process for VOERDE 2030. As different stakeholders meet in the joint experience of spatial situations and in public debate, they exchange views and opinions. Proposals made by professional planners can then go further and use the discussions as points of reference. The relationship between stakeholder groups changes: "The atmosphere in the town has changed. Citizens express more attention paid to the development of their town and greater expectations in political action than before", remarked a leading politician in Voerde.

Shedding light on conflicts; preparing solutions

Communicative spatial planning can use a range of standard methods developed for group facilitation, such as a future search conference (Weisbord and Janoff 2000), an open space (Owen 1997), or a world café (Brown and Isaacs 2005). Mostly, these standard formats need integrating into tailor-made process designs and must be adapted to the specific exigencies of the group and the job. If conflicts prevail, elements of conflict resolution need to be included.

This was the case in the planning of a park at the site of a former slaughterhouse in Wiesbaden. Here, in the late 1990s, young people had occupied one of the halls, preventing it from being pulled down. In the meantime, they developed a nightclub and concert stage that has earned nationwide respect. In 2006, it offered about 50 workplaces and attracted approximately 140,000 visitors. Nevertheless, relationships with the municipality and politicians still suffered from prejudices and negative emotions on both sides. Eventually, the town planning department used some funds to commission a blend of design and mediation processes. The Wiesbaden planning department proposed turning the surrounding derelict area into a much-needed urban park for a young audience. As a first step, the planners commissioned with the project conducted individual interviews with stakeholders casting light on needs, fears, and ideas. The first draft plan for the park then offered an initial opportunity for all stakeholders to come together and look at the common space from the different points of view involved. They shared a creative moment to improve on the design. A second joint workshop finished off this phase of preparation of the new park, which was subsequently realized by the department for public parks (see Figure 14.4).

This example also points to the opportunity of space to act as a common focus of different groups in urban society, a potential that can only be realized, however, in a carefully designed communication process underpinned by reliable action.

Joining professional and local expertise

The systemic model of communication can help to turn the diversity of roles and perspectives from a problem into an asset in planning procedures. In spatial planning, especially in urbanism and architecture, competitions have been the sanctuary of professional genius ever since they were used to bring about high-quality solutions. In recent decades, though, the results of quite a number of competitions have earned public criticism, resulting in a lack of political support and major problems in realization. New ways of integrating

Figure 14.4 Freizeit- und Kulturpark Wiesbaden: The leisure and culture park in use right after completion, 2008.
Source: H. Schultz, Stein+Schultz.

professional expertise and public participation have therefore needed to be conceived.

The city of Cologne put out tenders for a design competition for the east bank of the river Rhine. The river bank is a popular public area with residents of the adjacent, densely built-up neighborhoods, as well as with tourists who enjoy the view of the old city and its famous cathedral across the river. However, intensive use of this recreational asset had partly degraded the space. The city council decided to spend money on a facelift and organized a planning competition for landscape architects from European countries. The competition's two-phase design allowed for the integration of two important communicative features. Before the competition began, owners of adjacent properties were invited to discuss the frame of reference for, and the detailed tasks of, the competition. The workshop design systematically used different points of view in order to shed light on the variety of requirements (design-thinking methodologists call this the "persona" approach). Citizens from the surrounding neighborhoods, the city of Cologne, and the region as a whole were invited to another workshop and the same exercise. Eventually, a two-phase model for the planning competition was implemented. From the designs proposed by the 26 participants in the first phase, a jury picked 6 entries and invited these teams to continue their work in the second phase. Before the start of the second phase, the selected participants presented their proposals in a public forum. Over the course of 6 hours, citizens were invited to look at the plans. The teams were present and explained their ideas in conversation with small groups and individuals. The visitors' comments provided ample local expertise to the teams. Overarching aspects were discussed in two plenary sessions. The teams took home insight and commentary from local experts that helped them to avoid potential errors and to elaborate and sharpen their designs. A few weeks later the jury chose the winner, who then explained his design in a public meeting in which the next steps toward realization were also discussed. Although the project has met a number of technical challenges resulting in a serious increase in costs, it has never lost the support of the city council. Planning officials say that this is due to the multi-stakeholder support created in the communicative work that accompanied the competition (see Figure 14.5).

This communicative work illustrates a respect for different roles and perspectives and integrates these with careful timing into the planning process, in addition to conventional sender–receiver information. The planning process provided the framework for communication between local residents, citizens, inhabitants of the conurbation, landowners, and planners. Shared open space was the focus of communication.

Finding a common language: Words and images

In the Grand Duchy of Luxembourg, a discussion of the spatial qualities of the country's southern region was initiated by the Ministry of the Interior in charge of spatial planning in the early 2000s. Within the framework of a European InterReg project (The SAUL Partnership 2006), close collaboration with planning professionals in the region and with citizens from space-related civil associations such as culture and nature conservation groups was a prerequisite. This aimed to raise awareness of the spatial qualities of the urban landscape of an old mining region, which at that time was about to begin the transformation into a location for modern service business. At the same time, the action was intended to help in preparing a pilot project for a new model of regional planning that included the aesthetic values of space in a rather abstract type of spatial planning. At the very beginning of the project, journeys by bicycle, organized by experts from the regional cyclists' club, allowed people to share their knowledge about different aspects of space. Later, journeys by foot, designed by artist Boris Sieverts, led participants through dense, intensively used areas, as well as unused ones and brownfield areas, in a carefully conceived physical experience. In particular, the journeys with Boris Sieverts produced new perceptual contexts linking old and new elements of the urban landscape. Both old and new perceptions of space were able to serve as individual and common references for those participating in the communicative planning processes that followed (see Stein and Schultz 2008). One of the results was

282 *Ursula Stein*

Figure 14.5 Cologne "Rheinboulevard" planning forum: Visitors and planners discuss propositions.
Source: T. Kemme, Region Köln/Bonn e.V.

a spatial vision (*Raumvision*) which used the metaphor of a "red coast" and its "beaches", "slopes", "harbors", "cliffs", and the surrounding "open sea" (even in Luxembourg). This was one of the many ways to envisage and express spatial situations and to introduce different options for development. This metaphorical approach was based on the geology of the region and on oral history. It was combined with drawings, schematic diagrams, and classical planning language, and it invited a broad range of stakeholders to engage in the discussion of the region's spatial development. "This is the first time I can 'feel' my home region in a planning document", said the Minister for Home Affairs and Planning in one of the workshops (see Figure 14.6).

The Luxembourg project illustrates the necessity of using many different approaches to creating understanding in communicative planning. Physical exposure to space can create common references. Words, images, graphics, and metaphors help stakeholders with dissimilar habits of communication to find common ground.

Model of communication in spatial planning 283

Figure 14.6 Luxembourg South Region journey with Boris Sieverts.
Source: H. Schultz, Stein+Schultz.

Conclusion

Communicative planning needs an appropriate model of communication. A non-hierarchical systemic model of communication meets these needs. It is useful for designing communicative planning processes that contribute to good solutions and broad public support of projects and planning documents. Stakeholders' encounters with one another and with the focal city or region support local and regional communication.

In this context, city and region are both the place and reason for communication. Communicative planning processes provide the framework. As a practitioner, the author advocates the idea that this kind of concept-based communicative planning contributes to creating spatial identity and to supporting space-related cooperative action. The systemic model of communication in spatial planning helps to create living, meaningful, and productive planning processes.

Notes

1 Schmid's thinking is based on, for example, Maturana and Varela (1987) and von Foerster (1999).

2 For many years, the philosopher of science Helga Nowotny has argued that knowledge has transformed from an incontestable institution to a negotiable good (Nowotny and Testa 2009, 150).
3 Separating physical and mental exercise may also be much too simple a model, though. In his research on designing landscapes through walking, Henrik Schultz shows that mental exercises are based, and often depend, on physical exercises and that they are both components in the creation of knowledge.

References

Brown, Juanita, and David Isaacs. 2005. *World Café. Shaping our Futures through Conversations that Matter*. San Francisco: Berrett-Koehler.
Healey, Patsy. 1997. *Collaborative Planning: Shaping Places in Fragmented Societies*. Basingstoke: Palgrave Macmillan.
International Organization for Standardization. 2012. *ISO 21500: Guidance on Project Management*. Geneva: ISO.
Maturana, Humberto, and Francisco Varela. 1987. *Der Baum der Erkenntnis: Die biologischen Wurzeln des menschlichen Erkennens* [The tree of knowledge: The biological roots of human knowledge]. Bern: Scherz.
Nowotny, Helga, and Giuseppe Testa. 2009. *Die gläsernen Gene. Die Erfindung des Individuums im molekularen Zeitalter* [The glass genes. The invention of the individual in the molecular age]. Frankfurt am Main: Suhrkamp.
Owen, Harrison. 1997. *Open Space Technology: A User's Guide*. San Francisco: Berrett-Koehler.
Schmid, Bernd. 2006. *Tuning into Background Levels of Communication: Communication Models at ISB*. Papers of the Institute of Systemic Consultancy (ISB). Wiesloch: Institut für Systemische Beratung.
Schmid, Bernd. 2008. *Systemische Professionalität und Transaktionsanalyse* [Systemic professionalism and transaction analysis]. Bergisch Gladbach: Edition Humanistische Psychologie.
Selle, Klaus. 2000. *Was? Wer? Wie? Warum? Voraussetzungen und Möglichkeiten einer nachhaltigen Kommunikation* [What? Who? How? Why? Requirements and possibilities for sustainable communication]. Dortmund: Dortmunder Vertrieb für Bau- und Planungsliteratur.
Shannon, Claude E., and Warren Weaver. 1949. *The Mathematical Theory of Communication*. Urbana: University of Illinois Press.
Stein, Ursula. 1995. "Raumplanung zwischen Staat, Markt und Gesellschaft: Die wachsende Politik- und Umsetzungsorientierung der Praxis erfordert neue Akzente in der Ausbildung" [Spatial planning between the state, the market and society: The growing policy and allocation orientation in practice requires new emphasis in training]. *Raumforschung und Raumordnung* 5: 393–396.
Stein, Ursula, and Henrik Schultz. 2008. "Experiencing Urban Regions: Visualizing through Experiments". In *The Image and the Region: Making Mega-City-Regions Visible*, edited by Alain Thierstein and Agnes Förster, 141–152. Baden: Lars Müller.
The SAUL Partnership. 2006. *Vital Urban Landscapes: The Vital Role of Sustainable and Accessible Urban Landscapes in Europe's City Regions. The Final Report of the SAUL Partnership*. London: The SAUL Partnership.

United Nations. n.d. "Transforming our World: The 2030 Agenda for Sustainable Development". https://sustainabledevelopment.un.org/content/documents/21252 030%20Agenda%20for%20Sustainable%20Development%20web.pdf

von Foerster, Heinz. 1999. *Sicht und Einsicht. Versuche zu einer operativen Erkenntnistheorie* [Sight and insight. Attempts for an operational epistemology]. Heidelberg: Carl-Auer-Systeme.

Weisbord, Marvin, and Sandra Janoff. 2000. *Future Search: An Action Guide to Finding Common Ground in Organizations and Communities*. San Francisco: Berrett-Koehler.

Index

administration 6, 15, 29, 48, 72, 98, 99, 101, 103, 104, 118, 179, 181–2, 226, 242, 248–9, 252, 254, 260–6, 276
algorithm 11, 65, 68, 73, 154–5, 160, 164–170
anthropologist 8, 43, 78–9, 85
anthropology 9, 34, 38, 56, 120, 192, 223
appropriation 6, 10, 28, 66, 81, 84–5, 97, 127, 174, 176–7, 179, 180, 184, 186, 188–9, 191, 247, 255, 266
architect 28, 36, 132, 145, 148–9, 278
architecture 11–12, 34, 53, 64, 80, 63, 87, 97, 98, 119, 132, 134, 140–1, 151–2, 155, 157–160, 164, 172, **174**, 177, 182, 188, 191, 192–8, 200–1, 203–4, 206–7, 213, 219–222, 248, 256–7, 259, 261, 277
augmented reality, –ies 10, **76–83**, 85–8

Berger, P. 9, 13, 19, 25, 27, 32–4, 37–8, 40–3, 54, 90–2, 99, 109–110, 112, 139, 151
body 6–8, 20, 25–8, 31, 51, 62, 92, 114, 116, 156, 177, 197, 198, 212, 214, 216, 224, 229, 251, 253
Bourdieu, P. 6–8, 13, 20, 33, 58–9, 70–1, 83, 251, 267
building 3, 7, 12, 28, 36–7, 46, 53, 96–7, 103, 115, 123, 128, 132, 140, 142, 150–1, 177–9, 188, 193, 199, 202, 228, 247–8, 257, 260–1, 276

Castells, M. 4, 13, 20, 33, 57, 63, 71, 225, 242
citizen 3, 6, 10, 48, 53–54, 83, 106, 188, 196, 226, 229–239, 241–5, 262, 268, 271, 273, 276–9
city 4, 12–13, 15, 21, 29, 33–4, 36–7, 43, 45–6, 48, 53–4, 56, 60, 82–3, 87–8, 98–9, 106, 110–111, 113, 118, 121, 128, 130, 132, 134, 139–144, 147, 151, 160, 164–173, 180, 188, 191, 227, 229, 243–9, 254, 256–7, 259, 261–2, 264–5, 267–9, 271–2, 275–6, 278–9, 281–2
civil society 98–9, 101, 103–4, 109, 226, 231, 240–2, 246, 267
communication 3–12, 14–15, 29–35, 40, 44, 47–9, 57–9, 61–2, 66, 70–4, 76–7, 79–80, 84–92, 96, 98, 100–7, 109–114, 116, 119–120, 144–5, 150, 152–5, 159–160, 164, 168–170, 172–4, 176, 179, 189–190, 196–7, 198–9, 221–2, **224–8**, 233–4, 238–241, 243, 247, 249, 251, **253**, 255, 260–4, **271–277**, 279–282
communicative action 3–9, 11–12, 19, 24–32, 44, 62, 72, 89–93, 96–9, 103, 105, 107–9, 114–115, 117–120, 129, 139, 159
communicative construction **3–6**, 9, 11, 13–14, 19, **24**, 33, 54, 57, 71, 73, 85–6, 90–1, 93–4, **96**, 107, 110–111, 115, 132–133, 140, 151–2, 171–2, 174–5, 177, 180, 190–2, 197, 220–1, 223, **226**, 242–3
communicative constructivism 5, 9–11, 13–14, 19, 24, 32, 39, 55, 90–4, 111, 159, 171
computer 11, 29–30, 78–81, 85, 88, 140–1, 143–5, 148–150, 155–6, 167, 172–3, 202, 215–220, 245
culture 6–7, 13–15, 33–4, 40, 48, 53, 57, 71–4, 80–1, 87, 99, 110–112, 119, 127–8, 133, 135, 140, 151–3, 178, 192, 198, 228, 241–3, 246, 248–250, 254–6, 260–1, 264–5, 271–2, 274, 278–9

digitalization 4, 10–11, 20, 29, 32, 57, 89, 98, 105, 139, **140–3**, 148–150, 159
discourse 4, 8–14, 19–20, 29, 36–8, **41–53**, 55, 59, 63–5, 69, 83, 90, 92–4, 98, 100,

105–6, 108–111, 120, 124, 135, 159, 172–3, 220, 222, 247, 250, 252–3, 262–4
discourse analysis 8, 10, 14, 37–8, 42–3, 50, 89, 108, 110–111, 135
dispositif 9–11, 37, 43, 45–54, 91, 93, 98, 106, 108, 110
Durkheim, E. 20, 38, 40

economy 4, 13, 15, 33, 63, 71, 98, 99, 103, 242, 246, 249, 252, 264–6, 268–9
Elias, N. 59–61, 82, 104–5, 110
ethnography 49, 151–2, 173, 226, 243

figuration **59–61**, 67, 72–3, 102
Foucault, M. 8, 13–14, 20, 33, 37–8, 41–3, 45, 47, 50, 53–5, 89, 93–4, 110, 189, 192

geographer 8, 120, 252
geography 4, 9, 14, 19–20, 34, 73, 111, 120, 127, 131, 133–4, 135, 191–2, 268–9
Giddens, A. 6–8, 14, 22–4, 27, 33, 45, 47, 55, 61, 70–2, 89, 109–110
globalization 4, 7, 15, 20, 67, 79, 89, 98, 139, 172, 264
governance 3, 13, 73, 91, 99, 101–6, 108–110, 191, 239, 243, **247**, 249–250, 252–3, 261–2, 264, 266–9
government 53, 63–4, 72, 128–9, 191, 266
group 4, 7, 12, 41–2, 51, 61–2, 69, 74, 81, 86, 90–1, 97, 99, 100–2, 104–5, 106, 108–9, 114, 117, 119, 124, 128–131, 143–4, 171, 187, 220, 226–7, 231–241, 250–1, 254–9, 261, 265, 272–4, 276–7, 279

Habermas, J. 29, 37, 44, 59, 72
hardware 31, 80, 177, 194
Hepp, A. 4, 9–10, 14, 57–62, 64–6, 68–70, 72–4, 105, 110–111, 139, 152, 173
history 5, 29, 41, 72, 75, 86, 88, 94, 97, 99, 133–5, 139, 246–7, 256, 258–9, 280

imaginary 32, 36, 53, 83, 88, 117–118, 247, 252–3, 255–260, 262–5
information and communication technologies 66, 74, 150, 154, 159
infrastructure 6, 11, 30–1, 43, 6, 48, 51, 53–4, 57–9, 65, 67, 69, 76, 78, 82–5, 87, 145, 147, 151, 154–7, 164–5, 169, 172, 179, 186, 193, 248, 259
institutionalization 39, 68, 92, 94, 97, 109, 251
interaction 7, 9, 12, 21, 26–7, 30, 37–9, 41, 44, 59–60, 74, 78, 84–5, 88, 96, 113, 117, 124, 132, 134, 152, 154, 156, 159, 164, 168–9, 172–3, 175, 177, 190, 194–200, 206–7, 209–210, 212–6, 218, 219–224, 228, 236, 238, 251, 253, 262–3, 273
Internet 20, 48, 57, 73–4, 78–9, 82–3, 85, 88, 217, 246, 248, 257
interview 11, 53, 70, 73, 108, 113–116, 119–122, 124, 129–130, 142, 145–153, 157, 165, 175, 181–2, 184–5, 188, 191, 228–230, 232, 247, 249, 254, 256, 265, 277

Keller, R. 9, 10, 13–14, 36–9, 42, 49, 50, 53–5, 90, 92–3, 111, 171, 244
Knoblauch, H. 4, 9–10, 12–14, 19–20, 22, 24–5, 31–3, 39, 41, 54–5, 70–1, 73, 76, 85–7, 89–90, 92–5, 97, 99, 105, 110–112, 114–115, 119, 132–3, 139, 142, 147, 152, 156, 159, 168, 171–2, 174, 177, 192, 195–6, 223, 226–7, 243–4
Knorr-Cetina, K. 30, 31–4, 69–70, 73–4, 159, 170, 172–3
knowledge 4–6, 8–11, 13–14, 20, 27–9, 31–3, 36–47, 49–51, 53–5, 62, 83, 89–94, 97–8, 100–1, 103, 105–111, 113–114, 116–118, 121–2, 128–130, 133–4, 140, 142, 144, 149, 153, 159, 164, 172, 174, 176–7, 179, 185, 198, 226–8, 230, 239–241, 243, 245, 247, 265, 273, 279, 282
Krotz, F. 29, 34, 57, 59, 72–4, 139, 153, 173

language 6–8, 10, 12, 20, 22, 24, 28–9, 31–3, 38, 41–2, 44, 51, 55, 77, 91–2, 95–7, 114, 117–119, 127–8, 133–4, 174–6, 187, 190–1, 197–8, 212, 220, 222–4, 251, 259, 279–280
Lefebvre, H. 6, 8, 14, 20, 34, 37, 54–5, 84, 87, 89, 111
Löw, M. 3, 4, 6, 7–9, 11, 13–15, 19–27, 31, 33–4, 41, 47, 54–5, 70–1, 73, 76, 83, 85–90, 95–7, 99, 101, 105, 110–116, 132–4, 139, 147, 152, 158–19, 168, 171–4, 177, 192, 195–6, 223, 227, 243
Luckmann, T. 9, 13, 19, 25, 27–8, 32–4, 38, 40–3, 54, 59, 73, 90–2, 99, 109–110, 112, 139, 151
Luhmann, N. 8–9, 15, 58–9, 73, 89, 197–8, 220, 221, 223, 274

map 6, 28, 31–2, 79, 82, 117, 119–121, 127–8, 132–5, 140–1, 143, 145–8, 150, 152–3, 160–1, 164–5

288   Index

mapping 11, 29, 82, 108, 114, 119–121, 124, **127–135**, 141, 147, 152, 164, 175, 181
Massey, D. 6–8, 15, 20, 34
materiality 8–9, 12, 15, 23, 25, 34, 37, 39, 45, 50, 83, 90, 92–3, 111, 120, 129, 131, 134, 149, 174
media 4, 6, 10, 14–15, 29–30, 34, 47, **57–9**, 61–2, 64–74, **76–80**, 82–8, 90, 92–3, 95, 98–9, 100, 103, 105, 106–7, 110, 112, 118, 124, 135, 139, 140, 155, 159, 172–3, 197
mediation 28–31, 49, 73, 117, 277
mediatization 4, 10–11, 14, 20, 27, 29, 30–2, 34, 57–9, 61–2, 64–73, 78, 89, 98, 105, 111, 139, 152–4, 158–9, 164, 168–171, 173
methodology 41–2, 49, 55, 71–2, 181, 198, 223, 253
methods 41, 50, 82, 86, 108–9, 114, 119, 120, 124, 127–8, 130–5, 141–2, 147, 151–3, 165, 171, 174, 177, 181, 221, 223, 243, 277
mobility 28, 48, 99, 112, 121
modernity 14, 29, 32, 55, 73–4, 111, 152, 172, 192, 256, 258, 268

negotiation 11, 44, 82, 91–3, 102–4, 106, 108, 127–8, 174–6, **179–181**, 189, 225–6, 228, 233–4, 236, 239–241, 244, 248, 250–3, 273
neighborhood 12, 36, 43, 51, 54, 62, 69, 75, 109, 146, 171, 180, 193, 225, 228–232, 234–6, 243, 246, 249, 259, 267, 275, 278
network 3–4, 8, 13–14, 31–3, 37, 39, 49, 57, 61, 63–4, 67–8, 71–2, 76–8, 85, 87, 91–2, 99, 101–6, 108–110, 127, 132, 135, 143, 147, 155, 157, 158–9, 193, 225, 227, 230–1, 233, 235, 239, 241–5, 249–250, 255, 257–8, 262–3, 275

objectivation 10, 19–20, 25–8, 32, 91–2, 95–7, 115, 120, 124, 159
operation of synthesis 23, 26, 31

Park, R. 5, 6, 8, 15, 21, 34, 36, 81
participation 3, 46, 48, 53, 85, 103, 106, 189, 198–200, 206, 213, 220, 229, 236, 242, 244–5, 249–250, 268, 271–3, 278
place 4, 7–9, 12–15, 23, 26, 30, 33–4, 37–8, 44, 48, 51, 53–4, 57, 72, 80, 82–3, 88–90, 101, 105, 107, 113–115, 117–118, 120–1, 127, 130, 134, 145, 147, 150, 156, 158,
170, 176–9, 181, 185, 188–9, 191, 193–4, 196, 202–4, 223, 232, 242, **246–251**, 253, **261**–3, 264, 266–7, **271**, 275, 281–2
planning 3–4, 6, 9, 11–12, 80, 84, 87–8, 103, 109–110, 119, 134, 139, 140–1, **143–154**, 156, 165, 174–5, 178–9, 182, 188, 192, 231, 234, 243, 246–7, 249, 252–3, 255, 259–262, 264, 266–8, 270, **272–6, 278–282**
planner 9, 11–12, 36, **139**, 140–150, 252, 271, 273, 276–277, 279–280
politics 10, 15, 34, 40, 42–3, 45–6, 48, 53–4, 55, 71, 74, 98–9, 103, 112, 152, 192, 233, 236, 242, 263
policy 15, 72, 112, 151, 179, 244, 249, 253, 262, 269–270, 282
power 5–6, 8, 11, 13, 19, 28–9, 31, 34, 38, 41, 43, 48, 50, 53, 55, 60, 63, 65, 67, 71, 73–4, 79, 92–4, 98, 100, 103–4, 106, 110, 116, 128, 133, 135, 146, 155, 157, 171, 175–6, 177–9, 187, 189–191, 225–6, 228, **233**–5, 238–241, **246–7**, 250–3, 258, **260–5**, 268
practices 6–9, 11–13, 22, 24, 26–7, 33, 37, 41–8, 50, 52–5, 59–63, 65, 67–8, 70–4, 76–7, 82–3, 84, 92, 95, 97–8, 115–119, 121, 124, 128, 133, 135, 139–141, **143–151**, 153, 156, 158–9, 164, 167–9, 174–181, 184, 188–190, 192–3, 198–9, **213**, 227, 230, 242, 247, 249, 251–2, 255, 257, 259–261, 266–7, 271–2, 275, 282
process 3–4, 5, 7–12, 19–21, 23–4, 27–9, 32, 38–40, 42–5, 48–51, 54, 57–60, 62, 65, 67, 69–70, 73, 76–7, 79, 83, 89, 90–4, 96, **98–107**, 109–110, 114, 120–1, 124, 127–9, 131, 139, **140–5**, 147–150, 153–6, 158–160, 165, 167, 169–170, 174–6, 179–180, 189, 191, 195–6, 216–7, 219, 221, 225–8, 234, 236, 238–241, 243, 245–6, 249, 252–3, 261–2, 264, 268, 271, 274–7, 279, 281

reconstruction, (re)construction 4, 10, 11–13, 29, 33, 42, 45, 50, 52, 54, 71, 80, 85, **89**, 90–1, 93–7, **99–101**, **103–8**, 131, 109–111, 120, 132, 143, 151, 171, 174, 191, 228, 243
refiguration 3–5, 9–10, 11–14, 20, 31–3, 54, **57–8**, 65–8, 70–1, 76–7, 80, 85–6, 89, 98, 105, 108–111, 132–3, 139–141, 144, 150–2, 158–9, 165, 170–2, 191–2, 194–6, 206, 220, 243

Sassen, S. 20, 34, 225, 245
Schutz, A. 25–6, 28, 32, 34, 38, 59, 74
Simmel, G. 5, 15, 20, 34, 36
social actor 4, 42–9, 105, 109
social construction 3, 5–6, 8–9, 12–14, 28–9, 32–3, 38–9, 42–3, 54–5, 77, 89–92, 94, 110, 130, 151, 160, 247, 253, 264, 266
social constructivism 5, 9, 10–14, 19, 24, 32, 37, **38–9**, 41, 55, 90–4, 111, 159, 171, 227, 244
social media 68, 106, 155
social reality 3, 19, 24, 34, 41, 43, 69, 74, 77–8, 92, 94
social relation 24, 27, 42–3, 60, 101
society, –ies 6, 9–10, 13–14, 20, 22, 28–9, 31–4, 38, 40, 53, 55, 57–63, 65, 68–75, 78, 86–90, 92–3, 97–9, 101, 103, 104, 109–110, 117, 119, 131–4, 139, 151, 153, 172, 189, 195, 220–1, 223, 226, 231, 240–2, 245–6, 267–8, 272, 277, 282
sociology of knowledge 5, 13, 33, 37–8, 41–3, 50, 54–5, 90, 110–111
sociology of knowledge approach to discourse 14, **36**, 37, **42**, 55, 90, 111
sociologist 7, 20, 36
sociology 4–5, 9, 13–15, **19–22**, 33–4, 36–8, 40–3, 48, 50, 54–5, 72, 74, 88, 90, 110–112, 119, 124, 132, 134, 173, 192–3, 196, 221–3, 243, 245, 268
software 31, 73, 80, 145, 147–9, 158, 160, 194, 218, 248
Soja, E. 19, 20, 34, 225, 245
spacing 7, 10, 11, 23, 26, 28, 47, 54, 83, 96, 115, 117–118, 158–159, 168, 171
spatial order 21, 23, 31, 36, 39, 146, 158, 169, 175, 180
stakeholder 3, 9, 12, 144–5, 150, 227, 247, 249–250, 252–6, 258–265, 272, 274–7, 279–281
state 32, 56, 59–60, 63–4, 66, 133, 151, 179, 190, 193, 243, 248, 250, 252, 254, 260, 262–7, 272–3, 282

Strauss, A. 36–7, 53, 56, 59, 74, 142, 153, 181, 192, 254, 267
subject 6–11, 19, 23–8, 30, 43, 46–9, 51–3, 55, 64, 81, 83, 89–93, 96, 98–9, 108–9, 112, 114–115, 117, 119–124, 128–130, 160, 174, 189, 197–8, 200, 253, 263, 268
subjectivation 19, 20, 27–8
Suchman, L. 32, 35, 142, 153, 156, 173
symbol 10, 28, 34, 42, 49, 62, 98, 133, 227, 255
synthetic situation 20, **29**, 30–1, 159–160, 167, 170
systems theory, –ies 8, 15, 58, 109, 112, 197, 221

technology, –ies 4, 10, 12, 20, 29, 30–1, 46, 48, 51, 61, 65–6, 69, 71–4, 76–85, 87–8, 105, 139–140, 142, 144–5, 149, 154, 156–7, 159, 165–6, 168–170, 172–3, 193, 228, 242, 245, 282
temporality 28–9, 127
territory, –ies 21, 23, 81, 87, 124, 126–8, 133, 135
theory, –ies 3, 5, 7–9, 11–15, 19, 20–5, 32–4, 37–9, 42, 49, 54–5, 58, 68, 71–4, 77, 82–4, 86, 88–92, 99, 104, 109–110, 112, 118, 133–5, 139–140, 142, 151, 153, 159, 176–7, 181, 192–3, 197, 221–3, 242–5, 254, 265, 267, 269, 271, 282
transformation 3, 4, 9, 11, 20, 29, 30–2, 45–6, 51, 57–9, **65–71**, 89, 91, 93, 98–105, 108–110, 135, 153, 159, 177, 191, 195–6, 213, 220, 225, 227, 232, 247, 264, 266–270, 279
translocality 4, 30, 105

urban design 3, 132, 141, 152

virtual reality, –ies 78–9, 81, 87, 151